Creative Thinking, Problem Solving
and
Decision Making

Thomas L. Saaty

Library of Congress Cataloging-in-Publication Data
Saaty, Thomas L.

Creative Thinking, Problem Solving and Decision Making
ISBN 9 digits: 1-888603-03-8
ISBN 13 digits: 978-1-888603-03-3

1. Creativity 2. Inspiration 3. Problem Solving 4. Decision Making 5. Mental Blocks
6. Lateral Thinking 7. Imagination 8. Innovation 9. Estimation 11. Morphological Analysis
12. Hierarchy 13. Evolution 14. Genius 15. Humor 16. Brainstorming 17. Synectics
18. Networks 19. Priorities 20. Positive Thinking 21. Playfulness 22. Eureka 23. Puzzles
24. Art 25. Science

Thomas L. Saaty
University of Pittsburgh
322 Mervis Hall
Pittsburgh, PA 15260
Phone: 412-648-1539
Email: saaty@katz.pitt.edu

Published by RWS Publications
4922 Ellsworth Avenue
Pittsburgh, PA 15213
Phone: 412-414-5984; 412-621-6546
Fax: 412-681-4510
www.rwspublications.com
sales@rwspublications.com

This book is also available in Farsi and Arabic. For information on how to obtain the translated books contact: rozann@rwspublications.com

Printed and Bound in the United States of America

To download free Powerpoint slides rich in content and color to accompany this book go to: www.superdecisions.com/~saaty/creativity

This book makes an original and very basic contribution to creative thinking with its discussion of order and priority that are an integral part of the subject. It is safe to say that this idea has never been discussed and developed in detail by any other author in a book on creativity. To do any creative thinking and act on it, one needs to eventually create order among things. There are always many factors involved and different ways to proceed and these must be prioritized and synthesized and a choice made in a systematic way rather than by largly hazardous trial and error as is usually done, for example, with inventions of complex systems.

World famous versatile mathematician Janos Aczél writes:

Dear Tom, Thank you for your book Creative Thinking...I admire (really, am flabbergasted by) all the information, wit and knowledge you had put into it! .. My admiration is global and great for the whole book...

J. Aczél
University of Waterloo

To John the Great

Table of Contents

Table of Contents

Preface

The fundamental premise of this book is that creativity can be taught – and learned – quite effectively. This might come as a surprise.

It may also come as a surprise that intelligence (or the lack of it) does not restrict creativity. This has been validated in practice. That is the second premise of this book. In fact, creativity only requires enough intelligence to enable one to think a little and to collect one's ideas in a purposeful manner. One may not be very intelligent, yet one can be a creative genius. For example, Beethoven was a genius at music but a sad case at arithmetic.

The third and last premise of this book is that a high degree of intelligence as measured by the I.Q. need not be correlated with a high degree of creativity.

We have used the words *intelligence* and *creativity* without defining them. In general parlance, intelligence is the mental ability to learn and understand. Creativity is the ability to exhibit imagination and originality as well as routine skills in problem-solving. The purpose of teaching creativity is to stimulate imagination and encourage originality.

To learn to be creative, one must apply oneself constantly. We echo President John.F. Kennedy's exhortation: "So, my fellow Americans, ask not what your country can do for you, but ask what you can do for your country," with: "So, my caring readers, ask not what this book can do to make you creative, but ask what you can do to exercise imagination and originality to become more creative."

The ideas of this book owe their origins to four phases of my life. The first was during my early childhood, when I learned, through children's books and stories my father told me, about the lives of creative artists, scientists and funny people. I had unbounded and irrepressible awe of, and enthusiasm for, the subtle and subdued, the funny, the exuberant and fantastic, for the sacred and for the profane. I liked to be surprised. My early life was surrealistic, with many pleasant surprises at times and extremely painful ones at other times. I was also very disciplined in my education, particularly at the Quaker school I attended. And I learned early in life that if you want it done, you had better get up and do it.

The second phase was in my twenties, when my interest in the phenomenon of creativity led me to include an essay on the subject in a book I wrote. Because it was the first of its kind in the field, it was translated into Japanese and into Russian. I discovered that others were also interested in investigating the creative process itself.

The third and most important phase involved (and still does) my own creative contributions. Over a period of many years I have done research in various areas of mathematics (the Four Color Problem), operations research (the art of giving bad answers to problems to which otherwise worse answers are given), and management science. During the Kennedy and Johnson years I worked at the Arms Control and Disarmament Agency in the Department of State in Washington, D.C. We used to go to Geneva to negotiate arms control agreements with the Russians.

Subsequently, but still in the third phase, as professor at the Wharton School, University of Pennsylvania, I developed my theory for decision making, the Analytic Hierarchy Process (AHP); its generalization to feedback, the Analytic Network Process (ANP). Later I generalized it further to the brain and neural firing, the Neural Network Process (NNP). The first two theories for which I won the gold medal award from the International Society for Multicriteria Decision Making, are represented in Chapter 7 on decision making. The development and expansion of these theories was a great challenge to my knowledge and creativity. I learned much about creativity and how to bring it forth in the process.

The fourth phase was teaching and writing in a course on general problem solving that created the attitude and environment that led my university to ask me to teach a course on creativity. As I understand it from my student's evaluations of the course, they loved it and told their friends and colleagues to take it. So I have a sizeable crowd in my classes. The philanthropist, the late Arthur Brosius, on hearing me speak to the board of trustees on creativity, donated a chunk of money whose proceeds are used to award a prize in his name every term to the most creative students. I am fortunate to be chairman of a committee to decide on the best contributions that earn the awards. All this, along with teaching the course, required expanding my material into a manual that has evolved into this book. As a hobby over the years, I have collected, edited, and made up jokes that I published in 19 different joke books. From them I have extracted and included a few at the end of Chapter 2 some of which the reader will enjoy.

This book is intended to be both challenging and entertaining. It is designed to help readers feel more comfortable with the topic, and more confident of their own creative abilities. I hope to inspire readers to try the exercises in creativity presented here, and invite them to laugh, to scowl and disagree, and most of all, to explore what may, at first seem like unfamiliar territory. Each of us possesses immense resources, and this book provides an opening to allow them to come forth. I have attached a disk at the back of the book containing numerous Power Point color slides that I use in giving short talks on creativity. The slides are essentially a summary of some of the material in the book. I have used them to introduce the subject and even to teach classes among others, in such diverse places as the University of Tianjin, China; Comenius University, Bratislava, Slovakia; and the University of Shiraz, Iran. The material I teach is useful to people, no matter what their nation, culture or native language.

I am grateful to several people who helped produce this final version of the book. They are, my good and beloved friend Larry Boone who was also my coauthor of the book *Embracing the Future* from which I borrowed material for Chapter 4, my wife Rozann Saaty, my daughter Linda Kolker, Dr. Kirti Peniwati, Dr. Ozden Bayazit, Emily Tipping, my creative and artistic student Susana Nahmias, and my former secretary Sarah Lombardo.

Creativity, an Essay

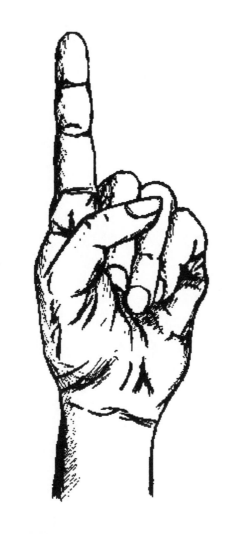

Chapter One

Credo

"Necessity is the mother of invention," the adage goes. One needs a new idea, a tool to bring it about, and mastery of both. Creative people are driven by a feeling that something new and different needs to be done, and are passionate about transforming inner vision into external reality. The fresh eye perceives what more experienced people often miss.

A Context for Considering Creativity

There is an awe-inspiring transformation taking place in our universe. It is changing the physical dimension of matter and energy to a new spiritual dimension of thought, creativity and consciousness. It is taking place in us and through us. We can see it with our own eyes and feel it in our own lives. We all have an opportunity to refine, focus and accelerate this transformation by drawing on our genetic potential and using the opportunities we have to contribute creatively to the collective mind.

The meaning in our lives is found in the hope and aspiration we attach to this collective mind and the compelling need for diversity and breadth that we must bring into it. None of us can provide the universal variety that all of us working together can. It is little wonder then that creation, processing and sharing of information are the major themes of creativity and progress in our time. That is why computers and telecommunication, powerful mechanisms for developing and expressing the collective mind, have become the most popular tools of our time.

It is remarkable that in a list of the top 100 largest public companies in the world, the leading company is in computer software and the exchange of information, with an estimated worth of nearly a half a trillion dollars.

The next stage in the revolution in human progress will make use of the information and communication giants of today to create industries and activities that explicitly capitalize on creative thinking and decision making as intense and accelerated undertakings in all areas of human endeavor. Decision-making goes hand-in-hand with setting priorities and allocating valuable and scarce resources. Group decision-making and conflict resolution are critical for our survival and for the quality of the lives we lead.

What ideas are the bases for this transformation in the business world? This book offers the reader ideas, theories and exercises, researched by a growing body of scholars and practitioners, about how to develop and make greater use of the many potentials that we all have. Exposure and practice are what we need. Decision-making with the Analytic Hierarchy Process is a novel and widespread approach today that is explained here alongside creativity and problem solving. To our knowledge, no other book covers these areas with the tools we describe here for decision-making.

Anyone who has owned a domestic pet such as a dog recognizes that animals are intelligent. They learn to make associations that help them perform some tasks routinely. With some tutoring, they improvise new things on their own. They are intelligent but not creative like us. Creativity needs learning with diligence and reflection to solve problems.

Why should we bother with creativity? Does it matter? Yes, because our life matters to us, and our survival matters to nature. The survival of our species is the sum of the survival of individuals. Anything we do to help ourselves matters.

By learning about creativity and practicing it on different problems, we improve our understanding of the process and are more inclined to do it again and again. We also increase our discipline, alertness and willingness to apply our talents whenever the opportunity arises. Success breeds courage and courage spawns enterprise. Our attitude changes. Little by little we become more original, as we learn to listen to the inner voice of instinct and intuition. Inspiration takes over and the process becomes spontaneous and natural. Learning about creativity is not unlike learning how to swim. One must practice at it to learn to do it. There is no other way.

History records the creativity of our species in the way we have approached problem solving. Some of the great religions began with the setting down of laws concerning what people should *not* do. In modern society, however, considerable thought is devoted to probing for cause before judgment is passed. This more tolerant approach has evolved through the compilation and analysis of cumulative experience. Although there are still "thou shalt nots," there are an increasing number of "thou mayests." And, in the "thou mayests" we find the opportunity to be daring, to be enterprising, to be – in a word – creative.

Historically, there have been those who held that the educated person was the one who was well-versed in Latin and in Greek literature. Those proficient in other branches of knowledge were popularly regarded, in the words of Thomas Huxley, as "more or less educated specialists". Strong disagreement exists among those who attempt to judge which branch of knowledge is superior. Does philosophy reign supreme over science? Is the spirit of the problem solver inferior to that of the poet? This is a futile argument. The creative thinkers in any field provide the energy for achievement in that field. Without them, little progress can be made anywhere.

> **The imagination imitates. It is the critical spirit that creates.**
> Oscar Wilde
>
> **The reasonable man adapts himself to the world; the unreasonable one persists in trying to adapt the world to himself. Therefore, all progress depends on the unreasonable man.**
> George Bernard Shaw

The creative power that gives life its values is basic and necessary. Whether that creative power takes the form of a religious expression, an artistic creation, or a scientific discovery, it is, for modern society and modern man, the element by which we can expect history to judge our success. To be civilized or "educated" is no longer adequate: the creative spirit must also be present. We cannot afford to regard "creativity" as a luxury for our leisure moments. It is an integral part of our ability to survive.

In the broad sense, all of mankind's creative activities can be seen as attempts at solving problems. Creativity provides direction. It supplies ideas that are "autocatalytic" by creating the atmosphere for the generation and expansion of other ideas. Creative ideas are "pregnant" ideas.

The ability to create exists in each of us – admittedly, to varying degrees and according to our individual inclinations – but within each of us nonetheless. With some effort, we can discover and use these inclinations and innate talents to attack the problems for which they are best adapted.

The Realm of Creativity

One could argue that any human endeavor is open to the expression of creativity.

At the very least, the domains where worthwhile creative effort may be exerted are sufficiently varied to offer each of us an opportunity to exhibit originality. Each time we experiment with the creative process, we strengthen and enhance our mental potential and thus broaden our individual abilities to make original contributions. These potentials are imperfectly demonstrated in history in the form of a civilization's challenge, growth, and decay (decay being the last stage that results when individuals in a society are unable to develop the necessary creative expressions to meet their new challenges). If we can come to agreement on what constitutes "progress," then we can construct a platform for evaluating creativity in terms of its contribution to the progress of society.

Goals and objectives are often a necessary impetus for creativity. Even when such goals are not immediately apparent, they are often intrinsically present. At the same time, severe regimentation stifles creative talent.

In fact, new fields of knowledge are frequently opened and explored as a result of the revolt of creative individuals against regimentation. Even in fields of practical endeavor, a compromise between regimentation

and spontaneity is required to provide an atmosphere sympathetic to both applied and basic research. Today, both government and industry have become acutely aware of such a need and have set out to create an atmosphere conducive to the generation of ideas. Our ability to compete successfully in the world of ideas will be enhanced.

The Limits to Creativity

In an abstract sense, there may be no limits to creativity. From a practical perspective, however, we encounter pressures that limit creativity every day. We face the need to keep certain tentative objectives in mind and evolve new ones as required. This is necessary if only because our creative potential is delimited by time. Although some of our creative potential is available for unfettered explorations in the "spirit of the creative mind," a considerable portion of our potential is required to achieve objectives essential to the completion of any given effort.

An analogy with individual survival illustrates this point. Most of us usually turn to leisurely creativity only after we have ensured, by means of creativity or otherwise, that our basic needs are satisfied. On the other hand, we also recognize that a life devoted only to the satisfaction of immediate needs is likely to be a dull one. Single-minded devotion to basic needs alone would kill the urge toward creativity, and, in the end, the practical goals would suffer as well.

Fostering Creativity

An essential element in education is the stimulation of creativity, imagination and even fantasy. This is a delicate task that requires teachers to pay special attention to the scholarly presentation of ideas. Lectures on methods can help students tap into their inherent creativity. However, successful stimulation typically also requires adequate

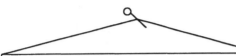

The purpose of education is to help us survive and to pack more excitement into our lives.

motivation, such as the encouragement of curiosity for its own sake, that we find in modern European and American cultures. The acknowledgement and prestige that accompanies successful scholarship and re-

Knowledge is already known, and to teach it to people is just getting that knowledge repeated in many memories and does not add to our human potential. What we want for sure is to use knowledge in ways that make people creative because creativity adds to our potential. Knowledge is a means, creativity is an end because it keeps the mind busy with new challenges to solve problems and expand the dimensions of consciousness.

search demonstrates the value we place on creativity and original thinking. Without such motivation we would have little inclination to explore, to discover, to develop.

Individuals must ultimately be able to achieve a modicum of success in resolving a problem within a given technical discipline. Otherwise, stimulation merely pushes us towards frustration, not the satisfaction of our goals. To arrive at such successful outcomes (that is, at "correct" responses), the method(s) used to stimulate creativity are most effective

when they are developed independently for each subject.

For example, by guiding a child to discover the abstractions that relate to the many concrete instances with which he or she is already familiar, we can assist that youngster in developing mathematical concepts. But the final degree of abstraction, together with the intermediate stages, should be carried out independently by the youth. The results need not coincide with the conceptions of the teacher, whose role is to provide guidance for continued explorations and abstractions, not merely rote responses. When complete explanations are given to a learner, in any field of endeavor (not just mathematics), some of the personal thrill of discovery is lost. At the same time, students who successfully develop the habits of independent thinking through individual exploration still benefit from the ongoing encouragement as well as the exposition of facts and methods from their teachers. Encouraging children in the habits of patient, independent thinking needs to begin early. Experience indicates that it is more difficult to cultivate creativity in the later stages of education, when our mental habits and expectations are already set.

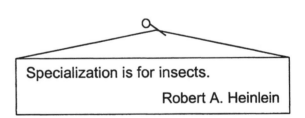

Specialization is for insects.
                          Robert A. Heinlein

Without the ability to think independently, the mind focuses on the acquisition of facts and details and is limited to established avenues of expression.

What we regard as the varied manifestations of creativity, whether they are ingenious and revolutionary ideas or artistic masterpieces, are neither spontaneous nor isolated. By studying the training, methods, and accomplishments of great men and women, we may find suggestions for stimulating creativity. Consider the popular notion that Newton, on being struck by a falling apple, spontaneously discovered the law of gravitation. This is patently false. Newton had accumulated a vast store of knowledge in one of the finest institutions of learning of his time, Cambridge University, where he had received profound and detailed scientific training. His discoveries were a consequence of much thought and experimentation; his knowledge of Kepler's results provided a basis for the discovery of the law of gravitation. Simply stated, a creative individual is also most likely to be a trained individual. Training provides us with the exposure not just to creative ideas but also to the facts and discipline that permit concrete results to emerge from creative activity.

We need not limit ourselves, however, to our individual specialties in order to tackle problems creatively. The inclination toward independent thought can easily be stunted by overspecialization. When our talents are too thoroughly absorbed in technique, little opportunity remains for our broader creative abilities to assert themselves.

A creative colleague of mine once remarked that "a specialist who works all his life in one field may produce a great succession of papers. But too often it happens that a sameness of thought sets in and every result looks like every other: the morning light is lost. A little of the spirit of the amateur may give much of the spirit of adventure and is ... closer to the freshness in the air of discovery."

Several studies assessed the opportunities for productivity at different ages. Wide agreement exists that the productivity of an individual's more advanced years is usually based on the expansion and development of ideas conceived in his or her earlier years of research and discovery. We sometimes assume that people are most creative in their younger and more formative years (between the ages of 16 and 40), but that is not always the case and there are numerous individuals who have made significant contributions later in life, whether in art, in science, or in business. Furthermore, an ensuing series of successes frequently lead an individual to undertake responsibilities of a different sort, as when a person shifts from being "hands-on" with a given body of work to being the manager of a team of professionals performing the work.

For example, in most scientific fields and in mathematics, the heightened creativity that results in significant contributions to the field usually occurs roughly between the ages of 30 to 36. This appears to be true, except perhaps in astronomy, where a long period is required to collect data before publication. In that field, research indicates that the age range in which practitioners produced their most significant results is between 40 and 44. These findings indicate that there are periods of maximum productivity in various fields.

Generally, rising pay rewards scientists for increased output until the top brackets carry them to administrative jobs. Often such individuals are assigned responsibilities that deprive them of the opportunity to be prolific in their specialty. They may, nevertheless, find numerous other challenges that open opportunities to exhibit a high degree of creativity as managers and administrators - a role in which creativity is far more difficult to measure.

7

Some Historical Examples of Creativity

Let us turn our attention briefly to some historical examples of creativity - some not immediately discernible as such, others instantly obvious in their ingenuity. Machiavelli's rules for success serve as an excellent example of creativity at work in a difficult field. Granted, Machiavelli is considered by some to be unethical – and, in truth, he had little success in putting his principles into practice for himself. However, having derived the rules, he was highly successful in imparting them to his prince. Through the ages, some men more than others have been able to bend with circumstances and capitalize on changes in plan to good advantage. Machiavelli's "The Prince" is concerned with discovering from history and from contemporary events how principalities are won, how they are held, and how they are lost. The book has an empirical foundation, drawing on examples from fifteenth-century Italy.

The lessons we can learn from Machiavelli are revealed in his approach to statesmanship (seen by some as devious), but which are actually, in part, built on clever gamesmanship. Machiavelli rightly points out that it is futile to pursue a purpose, political or otherwise, by methods that are bound to fail. If we hold a particular end to be good, then we must find adequate moral means for its achievement. Machiavelli suggests that the science of success – which he defines as attaining one's purpose – can be better studied by observing the way of the wicked (of whom there are many more) than of the saints since the former have no qualms about utilizing methods not approved by the latter. Machiavelli's theme has been propounded and extended in modern works.

In a light-hearted vein, England's Stephen Potter has taught and written extensively about the need for versatility in handling difficult situations. In his books "Gamesmanship," or the art of winning games without actually cheating, and "Lifemanship," or the art of "getting away with it" without being an absolute "plonk," Potter points out that it is not always necessary to be an expert to arrive at a workable solution. Thus, it may be possible to win a chess game not by finesse, but rather by employing tactics which frustrate one's opponent: taking a long time to make a move, humming, filling the room with smoke, reading a newspaper, and assuming an air of nonchalance. When one's opponent has relaxed his efforts as a consequence of this gamesmanship, one may be able to move in for the kill.

Some people believe that such methods are based on evil intent. We could debate that point endlessly, of course. Few people, however, would deny the importance of knowing how others plan their strategies. If we tolerate liberal expressions of the mind, then perhaps we can also tolerate varied expressions of personality. It is naive to assume that the entire world consists of honest and disciplined people bent on utilizing their talents. We must admit the usefulness of a flexible personality that adapts to different circumstances. Business practice today has expanded to include a wide-ranging set of strategies. Sometimes, these go far beyond, and do not conform to, the principles of ethics and religion we learned in our youth.

Examples of thinking which lead to successful action abound in everyday human activities where individuals are driven to invent solutions using limited resources. The following are a few elementary examples. A persistent Neapolitan, whose new watch had been stolen, stopped people at random for three years, asked the time, and carefully examined the watches they consulted. He finally located his watch. His method was one of exhaustion. Living in an age when timing devices were not readily available, Galileo used his pulse beat to measure the period of a swinging lamp of a cathedral in Pisa. Alexander the Great, passing by in his conquering sweep across Asia Minor, tried unsuccessfully to untie the Gordian knot. Having little time to waste, impatiently he drew his sword and slashed the knot in two.

Here we discern, perhaps more than anything else, the element of enterprise and the human desire to accept a challenge. Enterprise need not always consist of tasks as Herculean as cleaning out the Augean stables. The thoughts and plans a dexterous craftsman applies to the making of a single piece of beautiful jewelry are not unlike those of an industrialist planning an undertaking from its initial concept to its completion.

To achieve most goals we must have concrete conviction; otherwise, we fall to the mercy of chance and circumstance. The Neapolitan could hardly have found his watch - which he apparently wanted very badly - if he had not proceeded with a plan and a conviction. All too often, distraught hesitation is fatal to enterprise. Courage is the essence of it. Any action is sometimes preferable to hesitation or to the deferment of action until the "perfect" solution, the "perfect" moment, is found. Still, there is greater risk in activity.

"Genius is 1 per cent inspiration and 99 per cent perspiration"

—Thomas Edison

Motivation and Creativity

Individual motivations influence and affect expressions of creativity. For example, creative expression may arise out of a traumatic experience, as was the case with Beethoven. Realizing that he was growing deaf, he reacted not by quitting, but by dynamically and persistently communicating his feelings through even greater compositions, such as the Ninth Symphony, the Great Fugue, or the Hammerklavier Sonata. His later works exhibit an increased complexity, originality and depth of expression.

The need for a mortally urgent solution may result in creativity. Consider the medical corpsman who, faced with a critically wounded soldier, cut a hole in the man's trachea, broke off the top of his fountain pen, and inserted it within the man's throat so that he might breathe. What more graphic demonstration might there be of the great presence of mind that a creative person can muster during a moment of pressure?

A state of excitement may often give rise to a creative surge. Vincent Van Gogh, who painted more often than not in a state of frenzy, admitted that his emotions were sometimes so strong that he worked without being aware of working but that, even so, the strokes of his brush came with a sequence and coherence, like words in a book. A burning desire to communicate may drive a painter to expression through the use of shapes and figures and colors; a writer through the symbolic, experiential or analytical deployment of words.

Whatever the incentive – challenge, excitement, competition, the desire for improvement, or a simple impulse to create for self-expression – no person is motivated solely by a single stimulus but rather by a combination. For many of us, there is no one great moment of sudden discovery, but only the patient, grinding analysis and, finally, the teleological conclusions derived from our findings. That is why "Genius is 1 per cent inspiration and 99 per cent perspiration" is such an oft-quoted maxim. Persistence and perseverance are the handmaidens of creativity. Michaelangelo's Sistine Chapel is a monumental creative work unmatched in the variety of religious themes captured there and the expression and emotion depicted in them.

Marie Curie, for instance, in her search for bodies possessing the power of radiation, undertook to examine all known chemical bodies, not only the single compounds, salts, and oxides, but also samples of minerals from the collection at the School of Physics. Under her husband's direction, almost anything she could lay her hands on was subjected to analysis. Her continuous questioning, testing, exhausting of possibilities, and relating of results finally brought her what she had been seeking: proof of the presence of a new element.

Methods and Manifestations of Creativity

Clearly, we need to understand the various methods we can employ to creatively attack a problem.

❧ Trial and Error

One way, of course, is through trial and error. "We must try other experiments," said Louis Pasteur when, in his search for a cause and cure of rabies, experiment after experiment failed. Thomas Edison tried thousands of versions of his lightbulb. Out of many possible contingencies, one ingenious solution

may emerge. I do not mean to imply that we must try all possible contingencies, but rather that those aspects or experiments that seem to have direct bearing on a hypothesis ought to be identified and verified. Should our initial efforts fail, then it is up to us to face the challenges of determining what other related experiments might be undertaken. Frequently, we might need to reshape the hypothesis in order to have the approximate answer fit the statement of the hypothesis. In other words, to verify a given hypothesis, we may need to be recursive in our efforts, successively adapting and approximating until we achieve a successful final result. Leonardo Da Vinci suggested the following: "When you wish to produce a result by means of an instrument, do not allow yourself to complicate it by introducing many subsidiary parts but follow the briefest way possible, and do not act as those do, who, when they do not know how to express a thing in its own proper vocabulary, proceed by a method of circumlocution and with great prolixity and confusion." The passage cited is from "The Notebooks of Leonardo Da Vinci," p. 65, edited by E. MacCurdy, published by George Braziller, Inc., New York, 1956.

It may require hundreds of works to achieve one that is superior and imaginative. Sometimes we discover that a particular style is common to a group of productions that have been received with considerable appreciation. This is apparent in the work of Johann Sebastian Bach. In his frenzy to produce the required Sunday quota of cantatas for the church for which he was *Kappelmeister,* Bach

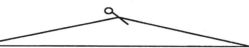

Expert after expert missed the revolutionary significance of what Darwin had collected. Darwin, who knew less, somehow understood more.

composed more than 200 church cantatas, oratorios, masses, preludes, and hymns. Of these, some were more powerful, more evocative than others. These survive today and are still performed in churches and concert halls. Bach was not merely productive, he was daring as well. The church authorities of his day often reprimanded him for the daring improvisations he created, for Bach had little compunction about moving a section from a secular cantata into a sacred one if it suited his purposes. Untiring experimentation, the attempt at new effects, and the indulgence of his own ideas of fun – all are characteristic of his compositions.

✌ Incubation and Illumination

Eureka, Eureka – within all creative people, as was the case with Archimedes in the picture above, who discovered specific gravity in his bath tub and rushed naked to tell everybody, a period of incubation precedes the point of illumination or discovery.

Henri Poincaré, describing his own discoveries, explains how after – and only after – a long period of previously subconscious work, flashes of sudden illumination appeared to him with striking and fruitful effect. Gauss described how he arrived at a proof of a theorem which had baffled him for two years – not through painful effort, but like a sudden streak of lightning. He could not say what was the connecting thread between his previous knowledge and sudden success.

✌ Recreation and Representation

Often, we can achieve creative results through the re-creation and representation of already familiar things and ideas. Cubist art provides us with a metaphor for this mode of achieving creativity: it presents a familiar object from several points of view at once by cutting the whole into pieces and putting those pieces back together again in an unconventional way.

Immanuel Kant, working from and subsequently rejecting the previous Cartesian and Lockean theories, developed a new philosophy--that logic alone cannot reach the ultimate truth--in his "Critique of Pure Reason." His pupil, Johann Gottlieb Fichte, went one step further and constructed a philosophy of pure idealism. Here we find a sequence of philosophical ideas, each one based upon the previous one, then pushing beyond it to a new conception. The fugal form in music also illustrates this type of creative reconstruction by stating and restating the principal theme using variations in form and harmony.

✌ Mastery of expression

Any work, whether created with words, paint, music, metal, or clay, is more forceful when presented with a mastery of expression. Vincent Van Gogh, employing individual brush strokes used by no artist before him, communicated his own excitement. To him, form and color were only the means to express his emotions; to him, green and red were expressive of men's passions.

✎ Talent for Organization

A talent for organization is another way in which we see creativity made manifest. Some of the world's greatest religious leaders have been organizers. Moses, in the wilderness, organized thousands of fleeing, often disgruntled, slaves into a coherent community and then maintained the community, demonstrating tremendously creative organizational skills.

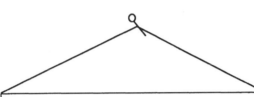

Creative genius seems to be a mixture of skepticism and naivete; skepticism regarding the dogmas implied in traditional modes of thought, combined with the willingness of a wide-open mind to consider far-fetched theories

Charles Darwin used considerable initiative to present, in a masterly and orderly way, the vast array of scientific facts upon which he based his theory of evolution. It was Darwin who gave the advice: "If I had my life to live over again, I would have made a rule to read some poetry and listen to some music at least once a week; for perhaps the parts of my brain now atrophied would thus have been kept active through use. The loss of these tastes is a loss of happiness, and may possibly be injurious to the intellect, and more probably to the moral character, by enfeebling the emotional part of our nature."

John D. Rockefeller's capacity for organization and leadership enabled him to build a great oil trust and to expand his influence and direct control to many other industries. Bill Gates changed the world of computer-users by standardizing computer operating systems and conventions, so that computer programmers and users could speak the same language and not have to re-learn or re-invent everything for every new program they created or used.

In philosophical thought, as well as in daily conversation, ideas often occur that are remote from the original subject. One idea leads to the next, and an entirely new chain of ideas is formed. Called "serendipity," this gift for finding valuable or agreeable things we have not sought for is a highly useful tool in creative thinking. The word was coined by Walpole, an Englishman, in an allusion to the princes in the Persian tale, 'The Three Princes of Serendip,' who in their travels were always discovering, by chance or by sagacity, things they did not seek. While considering a subject under study, our minds frequently wander to ideas which are rather removed from the problem at hand, but which turn out to have bearing on other problems. Thus, while considering one problem, we may discover that we have found a solution to another. Often, however, we encounter problems for which no well-defined method for solution is known. Sometimes it is difficult even to form a coherent framework for the problem. In such circumstances, we must frequently violate the syllogisms we have learned and make independent assumptions, formulating the problem differently and finding our own unique solutions.

Creativity and originality are enhanced by other mental tools and operations, for example by comprehension, memory, judgment and imagery, but are not the same as these other functions.

❧ Creativity and Comprehension

Comprehension is a necessary tool in the development of creativity. However, developing comprehension alone is not sufficient. It may spawn habits of rigidity and constrain us to think only in strictly defined channels, inhibiting creativity. We should also note that the inability to apply learned techniques to problems bearing a resemblance to the example being studied is not sufficient proof of a lack of creativity.

Although comprehension enables an individual to pass certain scholastic tests and meet social standards, it may also produce complacency. This is often the result of the delusion that meeting these tests and standards is sufficient and that we have no need to exert ourselves towards higher standards which may be more subtle or unclearly defined. Maturity, together with the added responsibilities of adulthood, often brings us into an active role, rather than the passive role inherent in learning to comprehend.

❧ Creativity and Memory

Memory is the conscious recall of past events and the recognition and retention of knowledge or skills. Memory provides us with a storehouse of information from which patterns of thinking are formed. It is our mind's power to revive past experiences. Imagination brings together pieces of our memories, building up combinations of images and ideas.

Experiments have shown that our impressions, are, in fact, much more accurate and intense than experience usually reveals. It

has been estimated that an individual retains about 10 billion "snapshots" during a lifetime. Each of these individual memories is broken into bits and stored in the impressionable molecules of hundreds of cells. Dissection of the parts continues to the finest units. Objects and scenes are observed to have a multitude of properties such as shape, size, color, texture, smell, etc.; ideas have subtle properties. We have not yet learned how storage or reconstruction of these memories takes place. In the pursuit of creativity, we generally tap memory that involves logical understanding, rather than accessing our less analytical verbal, i.e., rote, memory. Our memories are imperfect and, as a result of memory errors, we may exaggerate certain impressions and cause others to fade--remembering the desire instead of the fact. Logical events sometimes become increased in rigor as a function of memory. To improve memory and its contribution to creative thinking, mnemonics experts recommend a number of techniques, among them:

a) The close involvement of oneself, one's senses, emotions, and aesthetics in the situation one wishes to retain.

b) Learning things as a whole, rather than in parts, unless they are too long and complex. In this manner, better use is made of the relationship between the parts, and wasteful repetition is eliminated.

❧ Creativity and Judgment

Judgment, i.e., interpretation aided by previously acquired ideas or concepts, can help guide us in our creative processes. Complex thinking synthesizes many judgments and the process of reasoning entails formulating new judgments built on the success or failure of previous judgments. Discrimination, the process of arranging things into groups or classes, is one of the simpler forms of judgment. It is important to cultivate good judg-

> The secret of creativity is that while we must be courageous, determined and intelligent to survive on the path of our own lives, we also need to be cautious, flexible and adaptive for the survival of our race into the "eternal" future. This means that our lives should depend more on compromising and to a lesser extent on our own fixed strategies. Compromising needs creativity to find ways other than those we are fixed on. It also needs flexibility to live in a world that is forever presenting us with new challenges and new opportunities for which we are unprepared with our previous knowledge and inclination.

ment, because it is indispensable in evaluating alternative hypotheses and selecting optimum conclusions.

✺ Creativity and Imagery

Imagery also plays an important role in the way people think. Although evidence indicates that we can think without imagery (image-less thoughts), the use of images as models for thinking has been shown to be a valuable mental tool. Individual differences in imagery are so great that any statement about them would surely be controversial. However, all our senses are associated with some form of imagery – mostly visual and auditory. Many people, for instance, hear sounds in their "mind's ear" or recall pictures of past events "in their mind's eye." Since imagery is unstable and fleeting, it is an unreliable guide for rigorous thinking. However, in the hypothesis-forming stage, recalled

images can suggest patterns that may prove useful to creativity.

The variety of perspectives which we acquire through independent habits of thought and expression provide us with extended awareness and enable us to perceive a wide range of contingencies. The value of this is not that we can always pluck a successful solution from the broad array of perspectives we bring to bear on a problem. Instead, we can, when working over a wide range of phenomena, occasionally present an "ingenious" solution or idea which others have missed. This is closely related to our ability to make assumptions when attempting to solve a problem. The capacity to select the important assumption from the many is one key to arriving at a successful solution. However, there is always the risk that we may become attached to a less-expected idea and assign too much importance to it. We need good judgment, therefore, to discern the probability of occurrence and usefulness of a remote contingency from a workable one and to be able to give it the proper credit.

The inability to select the best mode of action (i.e., the failure to exercise good judgment) can be seen in this story of one highly imaginative individual who mailed a check to his bank for deposit and did not receive a receipt. He concluded that either the check was not received by the bank or that the bank had been robbed. After worrying about the problem for a few days, he felt that some action was necessary to relieve his worry, so he proceeded to the police to inform them that the bank had been robbed!

✺ Creativity and Expression

Expression is the way in which we manifest talent; satisfactory expression requires enterprise and understanding. To gain access to human minds conditioned by past experiences, a new message usually requires continuous repetition in various forms. Thus, we need a flexible method of reciprocal communication to obtain our desired responses. Effective communication is a complex matter. Ideas are best presented in a variety of ways, to make it easier for others to understand them. Inadequate communication invariably leads to misunderstanding.

In as much as the world of experience contains people as well as ideas and objects, it is essential that each of us expand not only our communicative capacities, but also our set of values. The first helps to ensure that we can effectively convey our ideas and induce action; the second enables us to know when to resist mediocrity and when to place personal relations above ideas. Success in action depends partially on one's ability to control a situation without sacrificing people.

Conventional methods for originating ideas have been found by some companies to be unnecessarily restrictive both in scope and in usefulness. Rigidity of established patterns of thinking may too often lead to failure to utilize (or even consider) as many of the possible solutions of a problem as are conceivable. The main objective of a committee working on the solution of a problem may finally become that of determining reasons why suggested ideas will not work rather than how they should be modified to aid in the solution.

Traditional conference discussions tend to break down into debates over the pros and cons of a single course of action. Realizing that such is often the case, an increasing number of enterprises have begun to adopt methods of group creative thinking to facilitate the origination of ideas and concepts oriented toward the solution of problems.

Usually questions of logic and rigor do not enter into the initial work; several possible answers for solving a problem are amassed by the group. In general, such a group can see more facets of a problem than are typically seen by an individual working alone.

Someone once wrote, "The creative scientist lives in the wilderness of logic, where reason is the handmaiden and not the master. I shun all movements that are coldly legible. I prefer the world where the images turn their faces in every direction, like the masques of Picasso." From this perspective, we see that our first act of imagination must sometimes violate reason and only subsequently be subjected to rational analysis in order to make the products of our imagination useful so they can be integrated into the logical framework of the mind.

In addition to the knowledge available to us from others, we are each at liberty to satisfy our own curiosity, to seek our own answers. This situation is better described by Immanuel Kant, who shrewdly observed that, rather than drawing its laws from nature, human intellect imposes its laws on nature, where "laws" presumably means "models." Thurber's rooster put this idea in homelier language when he boasted that if it were not for his crowing the new day would never dawn.

Logical thinking is not without its limitations. First, it generally assumes that there is a single right answer (in the group problem-solving approach mentioned above, a large number of possible answers are amassed, rather than looking for the one "right" answer). Second, logical thinking often stifles the use of valuable intuitive insights. When a process like group interaction is employed to generate initial ideas and approaches, the rigor associated with logic is postponed to the analytical phase of the creative process.

The Group Creative Process

Let us take a quick look at three different group processes which are frequently used to generate creative thinking and problem solving.

The first is brainstorming. To encourage idea generation, this procedure emphasizes that the participants think in terms of the quantity of ideas that it can generate, rather than assessing their quality. Evaluation comes later. The main advantage of this "free-wheeling" method is that it points out the many avenues available to solve a problem. Critics of this method contend that it tends to produce superficial answers that then require considerable time for evaluation and selection. Brainstorming does not present a particularly good opportunity for studying the creative process. Participants realize that few very original ideas are presented in a session and there is no way of discerning to what extent an idea may have been taken from previous suggestions.

An individual attempting to use the brainstorming method on his own may start out by jotting down and accumulating ideas in the hope of obtaining his own suggestions for possible methods of solution. The simple questions, "How would I do it?" and "How many alternative solutions are there?" when remembered and applied, often contribute to the origination of constructive ideas.

A second method centers around defining the problem, rather than a possible solution, in many different ways. Possible solutions are sought and evaluated for a best approach toward an answer. Finally, the solution is obtained by producing the structure that yields an answer to the problem. This procedure is generally effective and leads to a better understanding of the problem, together with the technical principles involved. It also avoids superficial answers. However, the method is time-consuming and costly and does not allow a full use of creative imagination in finding inspired answers.

The third technique examines the concepts which underlie the problem, rather than focusing on the problem itself. This approach postpones early solutions and enables the use of old techniques. It, too, is time-consuming and requires broad knowledge as well as a great deal of rapport among the participants.

When conducting a brainstorming session (preferably with about 15 participants), the facilitator must be positive and supportive.

The result of such a group session is to encourage individuals and stimulate their enthusiasm for submitting useful ideas. When applied to industrial problems, in addition to giving the employee the advantage of closer identification with the organization and its goals, such methods improve interdepartmental communications and enhance the receptiveness of supervisors to new ideas.

Polya wrote in his book *How to Solve it* that if you keep trying a method to solve a problem and it fails to do the job, abandon it and try another method. Don't stutter forever on one approach like the monkey whose hand stuck as he grabbed a banana inside a tree trunk and he could never let go, even to save his hand and life. The monkey had no capacity for imagination applied to problem solving and called lateral thinking, which is sideways and out of the rut thinking. General imagination is a form of ordered or directed

16

chaos. Studies have examined interactions among individuals in group meeting settings.

On an average, about 56 per cent of the acts during a group session are problem-solving attempts. The remaining 44 per cent are distributed among positive and negative reactions and, in a ratio of 2: 1, asking questions. A speaker's first remark is likely to be a reaction; the second, a problem-solving attempt. After a negative reaction, the members of the group seem to feel that they must make another problem-solving attempt which meets with a positive reaction. The participation of each individual declines gradually rather than suddenly. The program is successful when unopposed acceptance of a problem-solving attempt is finally reached; in other words, a hypothetical steady state has been achieved in the feedback process that alternates between the problem-solving attempts of one person and the social-emotional reaction of another.

The individual who succeeds in the problem-solving process does more of it and acquires a rank order by task ability. In a group without consensus, there is some confusion initially on who is the best idea man, and it frequently requires time to build consensus, a task that is easier in a group with similar backgrounds. In some groups, the members reach a high degree of consensus in their ranking of "who had the best ideas." In one set of experiments, the top idea man had about an even chance of also being best liked at the end of the first meeting, but by the end of the fourth meeting his chances were about one in ten. The best-liked man is usually second or third in the participation hierarchy. The task leader "locks onto" and addresses the most responsive person. The best-liked man talks to and agrees more with the top-ranking idea specialist than with any other member. They form a supporting pair. The

original rank order of task ability is finally restored after some oscillation.

Creativity Favors the Prepared Mind

Creative thinking is most important in the early phase of discovery where daring hypotheses and their testing are required. Hence, each of us must resist our mind's tendency to think only along the prescribed channels in which it has been trained and strive to engage our imagination freely.

A broad outlook and extensive experience add to one's versatility in problem handling. It is not a waste of time for an individual to present his own ideas on the solution of a problem before plunging into someone else's. Because of time limitations, we cannot always afford to exhaust the literature or, frequently even, commence what might be a fruitful search for the solution. The trained mind should have some useful suggestions of its own - as the example, given earlier in this chapter, of the corpsman who ingeniously used a part from a pen to enable a wounded soldier to breathe attests.

> "Chance only favors invention for minds which are prepared for discoveries by patient study and persevering efforts."
>
> **Louis Pasteur**

We can cultivate our ability to discriminate among results by applying ourselves to a problem, regardless of its complexity. Through the success of this effort, we can begin to develop general principles for handling a wide variety of problems. Thus, we may conclude that the best way to learn how to solve problems is by being exposed to them and making our efforts at solutions–sophisticated or not.

While this is a recommended and valuable procedure in the abstract, we should also recognize the practical pressures to properly channel and harness individual talents and energy. Children must be taught how to cope with the problems of everyday life as they encounter them. Their natural curiosity inevitably leads to questions of all sorts and to both possible and impossible problems for their parents. With maturity and a certain amount of training, the individual will retain awareness of the existence of problems everywhere, and an interest in their creation and solution.

The study of any science consists in the acquisition of useful reflexes and independent habits of thought. We need constantly to distinguish between what we assume and what has been proved, endeavoring to assume as little as possible at every stage. The acquisition of useful reflexes should not, however, be separated from the perception of their usefulness. For example, the usefulness of problem solving is two-fold: to train individuals to apply some important method and to develop their originality by guiding them along some new path. A certain degree of self-confidence is also helpful in announcing one's ideas without feeling embarrassed or uncertain.

> "Saturate yourself through and through with your subject and wait."
>
> **Lloyd Morgan**

Assessing the Constraints on Creativity

Originality is one test of creative thinking; convention, however, is a great discourager of originality. Among the social constraints fed into every human mind are the moral ones. Occasionally these may hinder our ability to achieve an optimal solution to a problem. We have all been confronted with occasions when truth, which is demanded by our moral structure, would cause suffering, which is unacceptable within that same moral structure. The better we understand these dilemmas, the more direct and careful will be our efforts in solving the problems we face.

One useful method we can employ for determining and understanding constraints is to examine the extremes and then gradually introduce limitations, noting their effect. If the constraints are flexible, then greater freedom in the use of imagination and fantasy becomes possible. Often, we may be more interested in a rational justification for a course of action, rather than in precise numbers. In such cases, we are able to use both technical and non-technical methods to derive a solution that gives us the desired order of magnitude to which we aspire.

Free use of the imagination is certainly helpful. However, imaginative creations, in order to materialize, need to satisfy certain physical or material restrictions, i.e., they must be traceable to real life or be an abstraction ultimately derived from it. Let us consider a few examples. For instance, there are reasons why a man conceived as being 20 feet tall may be doomed to crawl. A cross section of his leg would show that it does not increase in the required proportion to his height and weight; his greater size would cause his leg to break if he tried to ambulate upright.

18

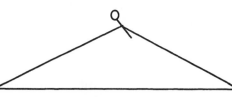

GIVE YOURSELF A WHACK ON THE SIDE OF THE HEAD

The more often you do something the same way, the more difficult it is to think about doing it any other way. Break out of this 'prison of familiarity' by disrupting your habitual patterns. Do something *DIFFERENT*.

Roger von Oech.

Stories of giant mutant ants developing as a result of atomic explosions constitute splendid fiction. When considered geometrically, however, we realize that the surface area of the ant must grow as a square and the volume as a cube. Such ants, therefore, would not have sufficient apparatus for the diffusion of oxygen to their tissues and possibly could not survive. Finally, think about the speed of light as a limiting speed that is one of the corollaries of the theory of relativity. Thus far, we have no evidence of a motion faster than the speed of light. Consequently, useful speculations cannot violate this assumption without pitfalls. Still, it does not hurt to try and interpret movement in the universe at faster than light, warp speeds. It is exhilarating and very optimistic. It lets loose the imagination. Einstein, the person who assumed the speed of light as the limiting speed in his theory of relativity, also observed, "Imagination is more important than knowledge."

Teaching Creativity

There are courses in which the creative talent in individuals is brought out by presenting bizarre situations and asking for solutions of problems for which the student can see solutions in his own environment but not in the special environment for which he is required to find a solution. Such a course sets up a model. It demands the abandonment of conventional thinking in order to solve problems within new, unfamiliar limits established in the model. Think of all possible ways of putting a man on top of Mount Everest, no holds barred.

Yet even here, no definition of creativity is given. The approach used requires creative engineering without ever saying what creativity is. Thus, in the preceding pages, I've offered examples of creativity and the conditions from which creative results may flow. You, as a reader striving to develop your own creativity, must react to those examples that have the greatest meaning to you. Then you must try to understand why others had no meaning. When you can comprehend the latter yet see how these examples contribute to creativity, you will have performed a creative act.

Creativity is essentially the act of an individual. It can come solely from within or it can be generated by a team working together in such a way that a team consciousness arises to which the individual members contribute. Creativity thus becomes the result of "team individuality." I have tried to suggest materials and models to help you understand creativity. If, however, by making your own analyses to reach this understanding you find you must contribute of yourself, you will then be practicing creativity, a far more important phenomenon than understanding it.

There is an analogy between what a teacher can do to help students be more creative and how open systems interact to enrich each other. While it is true that a person's inner feelings and individuality are essential for bringing out one's creative talents, one needs to learn from experience, particularly from other people, in order to excel at making creative contributions.

All purposeful systems are open, adaptive and learning, influenced by other systems and influencing them at the same time. The characteristics of an open system are determined by its inner structure and by the outside environment with which it interacts. Balance in such a system derives from the appropriate mixing of inner with outer characteristics that makes it possible for that system to function by fulfilling its potentials with few problems.

There are sufficiently distinct differences between any two systems that neither system has in it the potential and knowledge to enable the other system to meet its own potential needs. The second system must find out for itself what works well for it in its particular environment. Therefore, the best that the first system can do for the second is neither to provide it with all that works well for the first system itself (which may not work well for the second), nor with what is thought to be best for the second, but can only be imperfect and incomplete and not attained by the second system's efforts. The upshot is that a balance must be provided so that the second system is neither too cold to serve itself, nor too hot from being forced and pressured with what cannot work naturally for it. It must be given just enough to make it simmer, to look after itself.

Elementary Analytical Problems and Projects

Why do we think that a variety of problems presented as puzzles are helpful in imaginative thinking? Creativity is a relative thing. Constructive actions of individuals in survival problems are creative expressions. If someone had at his disposal a collection of puzzles, which contained all the niceties of thinking, one would consider education in those puzzles as enriching and valuable in solving other problems. A real-life problem may be considered as a chain of puzzles for which the solution of one puzzle is an assumption of the next. By studying the different subtleties developed through cumulative experience, one essentially acquires a greater capacity for inventiveness. Whether a person lacking in imagination can be enriched by solving such problems can only be answered individually. There must be incentive and interest.

Some problems posed here are aimed at encouraging fluency in imaginative expression of ideas. Logical thinking alone would not be sufficient for solving problems whose complete statement cannot be given until some investigation has been made. Imagination is the only tool that provides the link with broader perspectives. It depends on the technological state of mankind. Its value is frequently judged by both its artistic and non-artistic contributions that expand experience.

It is difficult to teach people through formal devices to use imaginative thinking. The "problem" approach is a possible alternative. These arguments, though inconclusive, are further supported by classroom experiments with which several people have had success.

The problems selected are meant only to serve as a challenge and a guide to the reader in stimulating his interests. It is hoped that he will develop his own techniques in expanding and analyzing each problem separately, pointing out differences in the method of thinking and in the perspective gained from each. In addition to these problems, projects are suggested. Despite a division of the problems into classes, some overlapping cannot be avoided. The classification is by no means rigid.

Poem by Rudyard Kipling following the story "Elephant's Child" in "Just So Stories"

I keep six honest serving-men
(They taught me all I knew);

Their names are What and Why and When
And How and Where and Who.
I send them over land and sea,
I send them east and west;
But after they have worked for me,
I give them all a rest.
As well as breakfast, lunch, and tea,
For they are hungry men.
I let them rest from nine till five,
For I am busy then,
But different folk have different views;
I know a person small
She keeps ten million serving-men,
Who get no rest at all!
She sends 'em abroad on her own affairs,
From the second she opens her eyes
One million Hows, Two million Wheres,
And seven million Whys!

Exercises

❧ In practicing creativity we need to:

Be big in heart, generous in spirit, and both imaginative and logical in mind. Be loving, compassionate, giving and forgiving, and decisive. Be a good sport and a pleasant and willing participant in life. None of us is perfect, but there is no harm in trying.

❧ Also be:

1. A collector of something or of many things and treasure them to show that you are a caring person. What sort of things can you collect right now? Go get them.
2. A cleaner, repairer and storer of things.
3. A list maker of things to be done.
4. A map drawer and a direction giver.
5. A story narrator, recounter and fabricator to suit the mind of the listener and a passionate joke teller.
6. A brainstormer, never running out of ideas.
7. Able to do many things with your hands, arms and legs.
8. Able to do things for others voluntarily and graciously, without waiting to be thanked.
9. Able to draw or paint a picture, paint a wall, do a dance, play an instrument, ride a horse, train an animal, darn a sock, sew a torn dress or make a garment, repair a leaking faucet, glue a crack, make or assemble and finish furniture, repair a car, mow a lawn, make and install a curtain, put out the garbage, pick up and properly dispose of unpleasant objects anywhere and on and on.
10. Able to express your feelings and opinions effectively and successfully to get good results.
11. Able to work with computers.
12. Able to decorate a room, or an object, or even yourself when needed.
13. Make jewelry.

14. Able to add ten more items to this list. Do it now.

⮞ Here is a list of things to try that can loosen you up to be more creative:

1. Go home by a different route today and do it again tomorrow.
2. Cook a meal.
3. Smell and reflect on a new odor, pleasant or unpleasant.
4. Eat something different and create the mood to enjoy it, or hate it. Don't be neutral.
5. Draw a picture using colors you intensely dislike.
6. Eat a food you hate and try to like it with appropriate and helpful interpretation.
7. Greet people openly and warmly to give them a good sense of self-identity. Shake hands firmly and pleasantly and look people in the eye.
8. Engage a stranger on the street or in an elevator in a conversation without making him or her feel intruded upon and uncomfortable.
9. Pick up a piece of rotten wood and look in it, or turn over a stone and pry loose the dirt under it to find the worms and slugs.
10. Give a dollar to a needy person and say "you are welcome" if and when thanked. Give ten dollars when asked for just one.
11. Hum a melody of your own concoction and keep coming back to it until it is polished and is worth remembering for occasions.
12. Ask someone to tell you a joke or you tell them one. When someone tells you a joke, laugh heartily, it is a gift.
13. Add ten more items to this list. Do all these things on and off to keep your nature unfrozen and make you more alert and adaptive.

⮞ A Grand Exercise in Imagination

The best testimonials to creativity are the studios of the masters who trained the young by assigning them simple tasks to improve their carefulness conscientiousness and their third eye or ear in the mind to judge and guide the hand or the mouth with delicacy and finesse. Training sensitizes the controlling parts of the brain and the spirit that moves people to create. Describe in very careful words how you imagine one-by-one the apprenticeship of a painter, sculptor, mathematician, musician, writer, scientist, engineer, and philosopher in childhood that inducts him or her into the discipline and eventually makes him or her leader in that field. Mention things that you think had to happen such as: getting up early in the morning and staying late at night, missing sleep and meals, repetition, praise, punishment and insults, small tasks to be performed, gradually building up to bigger and bigger ones, happy and sad days with disappointments, emotional ups and downs that all go into the making of a creative genius. Let developing this exercise be a source of inspiration for you to emulate the discipline and training needed on the way to stardom.

⮞ Projection

Now say in a few words how you would go about inspiring and training another person in your own area of creativity. How would you validate any claim of the success of your method short of waiting a very long time to find out? How would you train a child or a young person to be creative in an area in which you yourself are not creative?

❧ The Creation of a Universal Consciousness

Consider the proposition that all forms of existence contribute to the creation of a higher order purposeful entity whose strengths are reflected in the moment to moment repetitions of acts or states of all these forms, animate or inanimate. Assuming that there is much more power in purposeful life forms than in physical matter, outline those aspects of human nature that can be developed and highlighted with energy and determination that would overwhelm the static nature of the solid and gaseous matter of the universe to create the most diverse, creative, intelligent, abstract and universal, compassionate and thoughtful entity. What would you personally want to contribute in this act of creation that is close to your own nature? How would you apply your own will to make this contribution?

❧ Nine Challenging Exercises

Here are nine tantalizing and challenging exercises that will test your analytical thinking and lateral creativity. The answers are given at the end of the chapter.

♣ Exercise 1.
Connect the following dots, using four straight lines. Do not lift your pencil from the page.

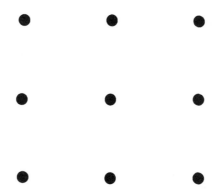

This exercise is a classic example of creativity and is often considered unsolvable because people restrict themselves to drawing lines within the perceived "box". To complete the puzzle, however, one must extend the lines "laterally" outside the perceptually imposed boundaries.

♣ Exercise 2.
In the following coded quotation consisting of 21 words, not counting the author's name, each letter stands for a corresponding letter in the original quotation. Decipher it.

ABCADB   EFGHDI   BJBG   KFLB   MNB   CO   PEB
PEOPLE   HARDLY   EVER   MAKE   USE   OF   THE

A→P B→E C→O D→L
E→H F→I G→J K→K L→L
M→M N→N O→O P→P Q→Q R→R
S→S T→T U→U V→V W→W X→X
Y→Y Z→Z

OGBBHCK PEBI EFJB, OGBBHCK CO PECMWEP.
FREEDOM THEY HAVE FREEDOM OF THOUGHT

STNPBFH PEBI HBKFTH OGBBHCK CO NABBUE FN UCKABTNFPSCT.
INSTEAD THEY DEMAND FREEDOM OF SPEECH AS COMPENSATION

– LSBGLBWFFGH
KIERKEGAARD

♣ Exercise 3.
Join A to A, B to B, C to C and D to D, each with a continuous path along the grid without any two paths touching. There are two ways to do this. Find them. This exercise is taken from an old issue of Eureka, the Journal of the Archimedean society, Cambridge University, England.

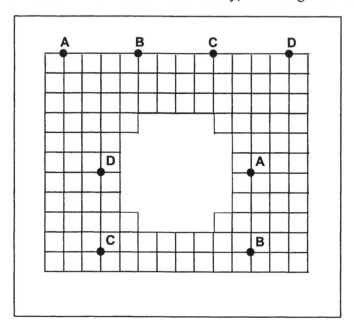

♣ Exercise 4.
There are five beautiful girls, two of them have black eyes, and the other three, blue eyes. The ones with black eyes always give a truthful answer to any question, whereas the three with blue eyes were born liars and never answer with the truth. You must discover which of them have black eyes and which blue eyes. You are not allowed to see them, but you may question three girls, one question to each one. From the three answers you must solve the problem and explain the reasoning that led you to your answer.

♣ Exercise 5.
Move only two matches so that both numbers are the same (you have to use all the matches in the figure). There is more than one solution to this problem.

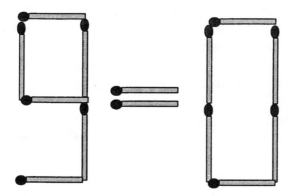

♣ **Exercise 6.**

Four matches are arranged as in the following figure, with a piece of paper in the middle of the cup shape. Move two matches to obtain the same figure leaving the paper outside the cup shape.

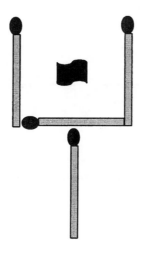

♣ **Exercise 7.**

By making a single cut, divide the figure below into two congruent parts.

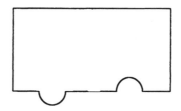

♣ **Exercise 8.**

A psychopathic killer starts at the room in the bottom left corner, which has two doors as shown in the diagram. Each intermediate room has a prisoner in it that he kills. The exit room has the warden in it that he also kills and escapes. How does he do it if he never returns to a room with a dead man in it? Because he immediately faints on seeing a dead body. How does he escape? Every room has a door to every adjoining room. He kills everybody.

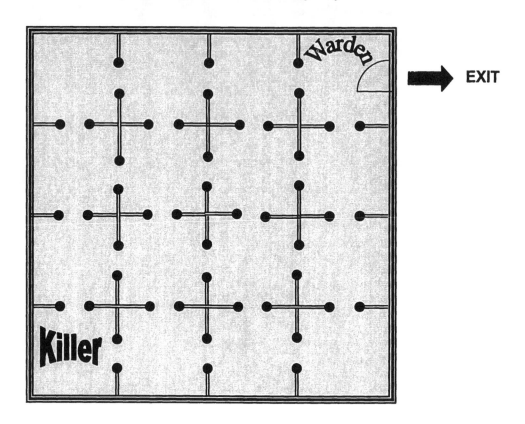

♣ **Exercise 9. Get up and do it now as fast and efficiently as you can**

A regular polyhedron in three dimensions is bounded by congruent regular polygons in such a way that any side of each polygon lies on two and only two polygons, its solid angles are equal, and it has no holes. There can be at most five regular polyhedra in three dimensions. To see that, we know intuitively that a solid angle is contained by plane angles less than 360 degrees. The sum of the angles of five identical equilateral triangles that meet at a vertex of a polyhedron is 300 degrees and make one possible polyhedron if every other vertex also has five such triangles. Similarly, four and three triangles can contain a solid angle as their sums are 240 and 180 degrees respectively. Thus with triangles we can have at most three regular polyhedra. In fact we do, they are the icosahedron, the octahedron and the tetrahedron. One other regular polyhedron can be constructed with three squares meeting at a vertex, the cube, and one other from pentagons, the

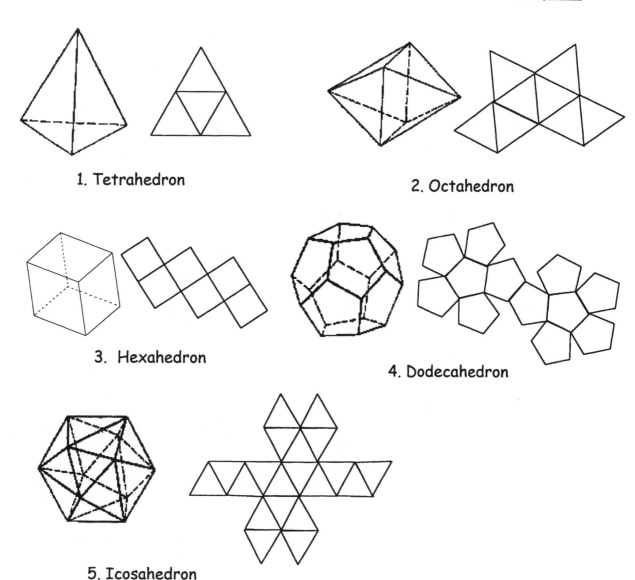

1. Tetrahedron

2. Octahedron

3. Hexahedron

4. Dodecahedron

5. Icosahedron

dodecahedron. The angle of a pentagon is 108 degrees obtained by partitioning it from its center with equilateral triangles and noting that the angle of each triangle at the center is 360/5 = 72 degrees. One cannot use a hexagon because the sum of the angles of three hexagons is 360 degrees, and similarly higher-sided polygons cannot be used. Thus there can be at most five regular polyhedra in three dimensions. Time yourself to construct these figures from material around you in the shortest time possible. One student did it in 12 minutes.

Creativity Exercises

ৡ **Informal problems taken from several sources (see, for example, Osborn's book, "Applied Imagination")**

1. Your refrigerator seems to be heating up for no apparent reason and you suspect that when you close the door the light bulb does not go off. How would you validate your concern?

2. Now consider a more complex situation: You are outside a room with no windows and only one door. On the wall are three light switches, which can only be turned on or off. Each switch is connected to one and only one light bulb inside the room. You may manipulate the switches in any way. Then you may enter the room only once to observe the light bulbs. When you exit, you must be able to correctly assign each switch to its light.

3. You are a doctor out in a summerhouse in the mountains. You only have one fountain pen and a sheet of paper but no other means of writing. Your fountain pen runs out of ink. You receive an urgent call and must drive to the city. You must leave a message for your son who is out playing somewhere. What do you do?

4. Early each afternoon, Miss Waldron put the cash receipts of the firm where she worked into an envelope and took them to the bank a few blocks away. One day, soon after leaving the office, she noticed that two men were following her. Clutching the envelope tighter, she quickened her pace.

A minute later one of the men behind her called, "Slow down, sister! I have a gun here! We want that money!"

There was no one else in sight at the time, and no place she could dodge into for safety. Yet Miss Waldron not only saved the money without a struggle but also left the two men with nothing to do but walk off. Can you guess how?

5. How did refrigerator designers expand the capacity of refrigerators without changing the size of the body?

6. How did paper towel manufacturers make the towel useful in more ways?

7. A family needs a change from just plain vegetables for dinner; what to serve?

8. A couple in a one-room apartment needs a desk and a serving table, yet hasn't room for both; how do they fill their need?

9. Many homes with metal cabinets installed needed more hooks on interior shelves on which to hang cups. Yet hooks couldn't be screwed into the metal as into wood; how to fill the need?

10. People complained that their work gloves became dirty and messy too fast when used in the kitchen, garden and elsewhere involving contact with dirt and grease; how to fill their need for something better and less costly?

11. Many people asked for something better than the old-fashioned vegetable grater, because peelings scattered over the dish or bowl onto the table surface; how to fill their need?

28

12. A woman wanted to read all the latest books, and liked owning books. Yet she felt she couldn't afford to buy all of them, and didn't like waiting her turn for weeks and months at the local library; how did she fill her need?

13. Leading manufacturers of macaroni products realized the need to make them more attractive to children so women with large families would serve macaroni more often; how did they add special appeal to children?

14. Producers of vitamins realized that, beyond making people know the benefits of vitamin capsules for the family, it was necessary to remind people to use them daily at one or more meals; how did they solve this need?

15. A creative manufacturer developed a mending tape with a remarkable adhesive on the back. Applied to many different types of fabrics, the tape would mend a crack, hole or tear instantly. But the big problem became: how to present so commonplace an item as mending tape so it would catch special attention and attract many purchasers?

16. Women wanted lipsticks in many shades. But an alert manufacturer challenged himself this way: "How can I make sure women will buy my lipsticks in all the shades?"

17. You have a big, heavy dog and a scale. How would you weigh the dog?

18. You are sitting in an airplane waiting for takeoff and next to you sits a child holding a fully blown balloon hanging over the aisle. Which direction will the balloon move as the plane takes off?

Solutions to Creativity Exercises

1. Open the door and touch the bulb.

2. Don't turn on one switch. Turn another switch on for another few seconds. Turn the third switch on permanently. Then go in and feel the two unlit bulbs to find which is hotter. This gives you the correspondence between switches and bulbs.

3. Put a couple of drops of water in the pen.

4. She stopped suddenly at the intersection and put the package into the mailbox.

5. They put shelves in the doors.

6. They put designs on them.

7. Stuffed vegetables with rice, mixed vegetable dishes and Chinese vegetable dishes.

8. Use a secretary type desk with an extra flat board slightly sticking out on which the slamming board rests when open and covers paper mess when closed.

9. Make loops in string and put it all around length of shelf before installing shelf-hang cups.

10. Use cheaper, disposable plastic gloves on top for grease. Alternatively, make left and right gloves indistinguishable.

11. They now have a large bowl with a grater on the lid, which has sides that extend a few inches from the rim of the bowl and keeps the peelings from scattering on the floor. Also, they could use a food processor.

12. She can become a reviewer for a local paper that would then present her with books. She can work at the library and buy those she specially likes. She could start a book club with each member buying one book every six weeks and swapping them weekly.

13. Made them in the form of alphabet letters.

14. They put them in a food usually taken everyday in a meal, for example, bread, milk and cereal.

15. Advertise football player's jerseys torn in games and mended on the spot. Castaway on an island mending his rubber boat. Astronaut on moon mending his punctured suit.

16. Package them all in one long segmented tube, each bottom serving as the lid for the lipstick below.

17. Put him/her in a bag or a blanket if you can't lift him/her yourself.

18. The balloon will move forward because the air will be compressed towards the back of the plane, causing the balloon to float on the current.

Mechanical Invention

1. Suggest superior equipment or methods to permit a blind individual to carry on normal human activity such as walking without a cane, reading a normal printed page, seeing a movie. Do not worry about engineering technicalities. Use any method that makes some sense to you.

2. Everyone who has eaten a soft-boiled egg has, on occasion, been plagued by bits of shell which, because of human error, fell into the dish. What effective method or instrument can you suggest for shelling an egg or for minimizing this unappetizing hazard?

3. Describe a robot whose abilities are basically the same as those of a human being and are achieved by known mechanical devices. List some of the uses to which such a robot could be put. Extend your thinking to a community of these robots.

Uninhibited Imagination

1. C.K.'s wife had left the car windows completely open, and it began to rain. C. K. was in his pajamas. He put on his raincoat, walked to the car, and found all the doors and the trunk closed. He succeeded, without opening any door of his new sedan, in closing the windows and locking the doors. He did not remove any part of the car to do this. How was the task accomplished?

2. Show that six straight line segments are needed to connect sixteen points arranged in a square array by a continuous path? (Reduce to the nine point problem).

3. Jules Verne wrote to his father, "Everything one man is capable of imagining, other men will be capable of realizing." Indicate the extent to which this statement is true. Give some counter examples.

4. Find extended future use of television.

5. It is desirable and useful, in the course of examining an object, to consider it as an entity, unrelated to any surroundings, and to determine its various properties:

mathematical, physical, chemical, bio-logical, psychological, aesthetic, etc., (wherever applicable); then relate it to its surroundings; and try to imagine its utility in every conceivable manner. Do this exercise with an ordinary melon.

6. See if you can mention 20 different ways to produce light?

7. What is the object whose silhouettes from three perpendicular directions are a circle, a square, and a triangle, respectively?

8. Assuming it is possible to find a rational framework that can be used to relate any two ideas (or objects) in a feasible manner (not always scientific), select two ideas, or objects, with no apparent connection and try to find such a framework. Also, select one such idea and ask someone else to provide an idea he thinks is unrelated to it, then show him how they can be related. Distinguish between scientific ad pseudoscientific explanations. This is the first step in creating theories. Carry out this exercise with people of different backgrounds and note the variety of approaches.

Flexibility of Thinking Problems

Each problem is an equation that can be solved by substituting the appropriate words for the letters. Have fun with them! (See reference to Von Oech).

Example: 4L.C. = G.L. (4 Leaf Clover = Good Luck)

1. 3 P. = 6

2. 4J. + 4Q. + 4K. = All the F.C.

3. S. & M. & T. & W. & T. & F. & S. are D. of W.

4. E. – 8 = Z.

5. C. + 6D. = N.Y.E.

6. A. & E. were in the G. of E.

7. 1 + 6Z. = 1M.

8. A.L. & J.G. & W.M. & J.K. were all A.

9. S. + H. of R. = U.S.C.

10. L.D. painted the M.L.

Answers for the First Eight Challenging Exercises

♣ **Exercise 1.**

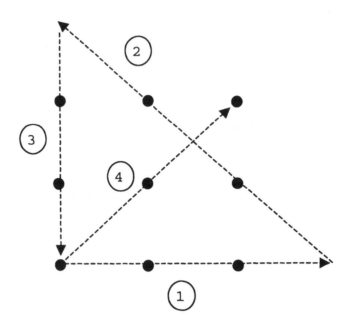

♣ **Exercise 2.**

PEOPLE HARDLY EVER MAKE USE OF THE
FREEDOM THEY HAVE, FREEDOM OF THOUGHT.
INSTEAD THEY DEMAND FREEDOM OF SPEECH AS COMPENSATION.

-   KIERKEGAARD.

♣ **Exercise 3.**

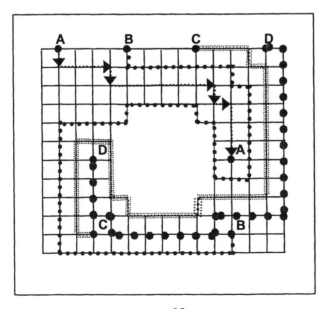

♣ Exercise 4.

Ask the first girl the color of her eyes. It does not matter what she says because she would say "black". Ask the second girl what the first said. She says that the first said she had blue eyes (a liar). Ask the third what the first two girls said. She says the first said she had black eyes and the second blue eyes (true). Thus the first and the third have black eyes and the second, fourth and fifth girls blue.

♣ Exercise 5.

In addition to the solution shown here one can make two zeros and two 9's with the equal sign remaining in the figure in both cases.

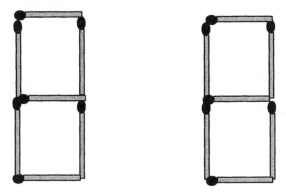

♣ Exercise 6.

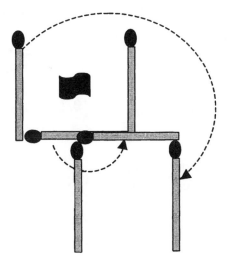

♣ Exercise 7.

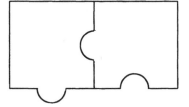

♣ **Exercise 8.**

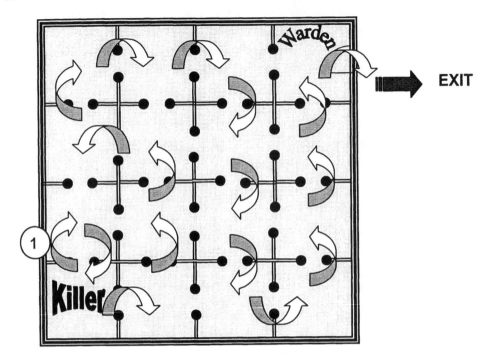

Answers for the Flexibility of Thinking Problems.

1. 3 Pairs = 6

2. 4 Jacks + 4 Queens + 4 Kings = All the Face Cards.

3. Sunday & Monday & Tuesday & Wednesday & Thursday & Friday & Saturday are Days of the Week.

4. Eight – 8 = Zero

5. Christmas + 6 Days = New Year's Eve.

6. Adam & Eve were in the Garden of Eden

7. 1 + 6 Zeros = 1 Million

8. Abraham Lincoln, James Garfield, William McKinley, & John Kennedy were all assassinated.

9. Senate + House of representatives = United States Congress.

10. Leonardo Da Vinci painted the Mona Lisa.

Creativity Revisited

Chapter Two

Introduction

It is better to sleep on things beforehand than lie awake about them afterwards.
–Baltasar Gracian

In this chapter, we will consider creativity from both conceptual and methodological standpoints, with the hope that this material not only informs but also inspires. Creativity is much more than raw natural talent. Creativity requires imagination, the ability to reason, intelligence, memory, strong interpersonal skills, and sometimes a love for others and their own creativity.

Intelligence, wisdom and creativity are three kinds of mental ability. If creativity is the talent to make contact with the life force within and outside us, then intelligence is the ability to bring that force to the conscious mind and process it for diverse uses. Wisdom arises from the balancing of the variety we take in through social and personal learning, reflection and experience, and what we give out through practice. Wisdom (_what_ to do) increases over the years while some aspects of intelligence (_how_ to do) decrease.

R.J. Sternberg has arrived at some interesting conclusions about these three abilities from his theories and from empirical work. There is .94 correlation between intelligence and wisdom (they are the closest), .69 between intelligence and creativity and .62 between wisdom and creativity (they are the farthest apart).

Intelligence has been studied through the _psychometric_ I.Q. approach (verbal comprehension and verbal fluency, number, spatial visualization, inductive reasoning, memory, perceptual speed and deductive reasoning),

the _information processing_ approach (cognitive-correlates such as how fast lexical information is retrieved and cognitive-components such as success in using analogical reasoning), the _diversified-ability_ approach, the _multiple intelligences_ approach of Gardner – linguistic, musical, logico-mathematical, spatial, bodily-kinesthetic, interpersonal, intrapersonal – and the _triarchic_ approach of Sternberg – the internal world, the external world, and the experience of the individual.

Wisdom has been studied through the _multidimensional scaling_ approach (experience, intuition, pragmatism, understanding, gentleness, empathy, intelligence, peacefulness, knowledge, reflection, sense of humor, observation ability and age), and the _neofunctionalist_ approach (expertise in some areas of knowledge, richness in the definition and solution of problems, pragmatism in life, uncertainty in problem definition, and relativism in judgment and in recommendations for action).

For creativity, Sternberg mentions some different methods of study:
- Psychometrics – testing for word fluency, associational fluency (the ability to produce many synonyms for a given word in a given amount of time, and ideational fluency (producing many ideas in a short amount of time).
- Personality-correlates – creative individuals prefer complexity, are more psychodynamically complex, more independent in their judgments, more self-assertive and dominant, have high aspiration levels, value independence and autonomy, are productive in orientation and are concerned with personal adequacy.
- Biography – study of eminent scientists and of geniuses.
- Historiometrics – examines sociohistorical factors that influence creativity,

such as being first-born, losing parents through death in childhood, coming from a famous family, and being influenced by past creative thinkers.

- Social psychology – reviews effects of variables such as educational, work and cultural environments. Creativity is found to be undermined – by extrinsic as opposed to intrinsic motivation, by evaluation and its attendant anxiety, and peer pressure. Creativity is enhanced by teachers who value autonomy, by encouraging responsibility to initiate new activities, and by freedom from administrative interference.
- Cognitive psychology – the nature of creative insight and what it is.

The three mental abilities have also been examined in terms of non-metric dimensions and their positive and negative polarity. They are given in respective pairs as follows:

For intelligence, the positive and negative polarities of the different dimensions are: 1) practical problem solving ability that attains goals; verbal ability that enables one to converse on any topic, 2) intellectual balance and integration that helps one recognize similarities and differences; goal orientation and attainment, 3) contextual intelligence involving learning from past mistakes or successes and knowing what is going on in the world; fluid thought characterized by fast thinking, grasping mathematics, spatial ability and high I.Q.

For wisdom the dimensions and their polarities are: 1) reasoning ability; sagacity, 2) learning from ideas and environment; judgment, 3) expeditious use of information; perspicacity in offering solutions on the side of truth and right, and reading between the lines.

For creativity the dimensions and their polarities are: 1) non-entrenchment; integration and intellectuality, 2) aesthetic taste and imagination; decisional skill and flexibility with gut feeling in making decisions after weighing the pros and cons, 3) perspicacity in questioning societal norms, truisms and assumptions together with the willing to take a stand; drive for accomplishment and recognition, 4) inquisitiveness; intuition that represent the weakest of the dimensions.

The lessons learned from the foregoing and drawn by Sternberg are summarized as follows:

The layperson thinks that an intelligent individual solves problems well, reasons clearly, thinks logically, uses a good vocabulary, draws upon a large store of information, and aims for achievement of goals. The specialist thinks that knowledge and the ability to use it to weigh possibilities are requirements for intelligence.

The layperson thinks that a wise individual is intelligent but also seeks as much information as possible and reads between the lines. The artist adds insight and balancing insight and logic to transform creativity into concepts, and sensitivity. The business executive emphasizes maturity and understanding limitations of one's actions, having long term perspective, the ability to distinguish substance from style and appreciating the ideologies of others. The philosopher requires balanced judgment and non-automatic acceptance of the prevailing wisdom. The physicist thinks that a wise person knows the factors contributing to a situation, knows previous work on the problem, knows the important problems in the field and the necessary techniques, the human and political elements involved, and whether the solution produces important results.

The layperson thinks that the creative person has a freedom of spirit and both thinks and acts in unconventional ways far beyond personal and environmental limitations. In art there is the requirement for imagination and originality with an abundance of ideas, and for risk taking. In business the requirement is for new ideas, and escaping conventional thinking. In philosophy the creative person toys with ideas imaginatively, classifies and systematizes knowledge and never accepts the "accepted". The physicist is concerned with inventiveness, the ability to find order in chaos, and the questioning of principles; the ability to give approximate solutions, find shortcuts, and go beyond standard methods in problem solving; and with making discoveries by finding reasons why things happen the way they do.

Systematic approaches to creativity begin with the creative person's creative traits and inner conditions involving attitudes, humor, personal habits, persistence, physiology, temperament, and values. Then they move to the creative problem identified: beauty and aesthetics, efficiency, expression. Creativity is then used to solve the problem or transform it with the aid of imagination, learning, motivation, perception and thinking. This leads to a creative outcome such as dance, music, painting, poetry, invention and theory. All this comes about through a creative environment and cultural influences.

G.F. Kneller, in his book The Art and Science of Creativity (Holt, Rinehart and Winston, Inc., 1967), presents the subject in chapters on: *meanings* of creativity by defining it, searching for the novelty arising from it, its relation to intelligence and to problem solving; *theories* of creativity identified as philosophical and psychological; the *act* of creativity involving phases and conditions; the *person* and her/his creative traits, habits

as a student, and growth in childhood and adolescence; *education* emphasizing originality, appreciation of the new, inventiveness, curiosity, inquiry, self-direction, and sense-perception; and a final chapter called the *seed* talks about self-realization and actualization, openness, learning as appropriating the ideas into ones attitude and thinking.

The theories of creativity vary.
- Philosophical theories look at creativity as: divine inspiration, madness, intuitive genius, a force of life, or a cosmic force.
- Psychological theories involve: associationism, Gestalt theory about the reconstruction of structurally deficient gestalt or patterns.
- Psychoanalytic theories look at creativity as the product of conflict in the unconscious mind.
- Neo-psychoanalytic theories regard creativity as a product of the preconscious rather than the unconscious, essentially being open to recall when ego is relaxed.
- Theories stimulated by Freud include those that regard creativity as an expression of inner drive, or as openness and receptivity to experience, or as convergent-divergent thinking, or finally as bisociation.
- Finally, there are physiological theories concerned with the effect of the endocrine glands, along with talent and training, on creativity.

A. H. Koestler, in his book The Act of Creation (A Laurel Edition, 1964), developed a comprehensive theory of creativity that is all-inclusive and encompasses the variety of theories and speculation in the literature. Bisociation, a term coined by Koestler, is the connecting of previously unrelated levels of experience or frames of reference. Bisociation occurs not only in scientific and artistic creation, but also at every level of the organic hierarchy. A male bird will often take over the female's task of feeding the young, if she dies, although this is contrary to his habit. To do so, he must bisociate two activities that are normally unrelated for him, finding food and looking after the young. A pattern of thought or behavior (called a matrix) is governed by his set of rules (or code), either learned or innate. At the same time, he possesses a certain flexibility, so that he can react selectively to a range of circumstances.

"Habits are the indispensable core of stability and ordered behavior; they also have a tendency to become mechanized and to reduce man to the status of a conditioned automaton. The creative act, by connecting previously unrelated dimensions of experience, enables one to attain to a higher level of mental evolution. It is an act of liberation-the defeat of habit by originality. "When two independent matrices of perception or reasoning interact with each other, the result is either a collision ending in laughter, or their fusion in a new intellectual synthesis, or their confrontation in an esthetic experience." Koestler distinguishes between association and bisociation as follows:

person who has done work that is of value or of significance to society and has applied unusual skill to produce it. It is not a matter of luck. Outstanding ability, high value of work and recognition are critical in defining genius.

In The Key to Genius, (Prometheus Books, 1988), D. J. Hershman and J. Lieb, explore in great depth the critical effects of mania-depression on genius. Mania and depression were thought to be a disturbance in catecholamine metabolism. Now it is thought that additionally, prostaglandins, cyclic nucleotides and calcium are also involved. E. Kretschmer wrote: "The spirit of genius ... is no free floating, absolute power, but is strictly bound to the laws of blood chemistry and the-endocrine glands."

Tradition says that the creative person must suffer beyond what ordinary mortals endure on the assumption that suffering is essential to creativity. Aristotle said, "All extraordinary men distinguished in philosophy, politics, poetry and the arts are evidently melancholic." Thomas Carlyle insisted that the genius experiences both extremes of

HABIT	ORIGINALITY
Association within the confines of a given matrix.	Bisociation of independent matrices.
Guidance by pre-conscious or extra-conscious processes.	Guidance by restrained sub-conscious processes.
Dynamic equilibrium.	Activation of regenerative potentials.
Rigid to flexible variations on a theme.	Super-flexibility.
Repetitiveness.	Novelty.
Conservative.	Destructive-constructive.

One can become temporarily known as a genius for reasons that do not have much to do with the quality of one's work. For example one may lead a colorful life, obtain timely publicity, and have a personality that fits the stereotype of genius, even when people are unable to see that there is no talent to support the image. A genius is more likely to be a

recognized mania and depression: "A great soul...alternates between the highest height and the lowest depth." The degree of talent, quality of training, and type of manic-depression are all decisive to the outcome of being recognized as a genius. But it is possible that some people have such extraordinary talents that they can be as geniuses without assistance from the manic-depression syndrome.

According to Robert S. Albert, editor of the anthology *Genius and Eminence*, genius is: "(1) the rare but radical *disruption* of preceding manners, attitudes, customs, or cognitive habits; and (2) the performance of complex tasks in manners and styles rarely observed."

Genius has a better chance with the first statement below that is almost true.

Talent + Training + Persistence + Passion ⇔ Creativity

I added passion above. By passion we mean the obsessive striving to attain a higher awareness of the world. Creativity is an important component of this effort. I would like to offer the reader two more formulas.

Talent + Training + Persistence + Passion + Manic-Depression ⇔ Genius

---

According to Hershman and Lieb, there are three levels of mania in decreasing order of severity: mania, hypomania, and mild mania. Mania, thought to contribute to periods of creativity, is noted for quick changes of mood. In the blink of an eye, the manic with psychotic delusions or hallucinations may become tearful or angry. From euphoria there is most commonly a change to irritability, dissatisfaction, intolerance, fault-finding, and rage if pressured or even mildly criticized. Sometimes a person who is manic destroys objects and physically attacks loved ones, with later regrets. In the extreme, the manic may threaten and even commit suicide.

Depression can make one a perfectionist. In deep depression, intellectual processes are impaired and slow. The depressive feels unmotivated, lethargic, tires quickly, and needs more rest and sleep. There is loss of will to work and a reluctance to do anything. What suffers are memory, the ability to think, the capacity to create ideas and solve problems, comprehension, and even the ability to form complete sentences. Unless the state of depression is extreme, the depressive can still perform routine and mechanical tasks, but with poor creative quality. The capacity for enjoyment and interest in work are lost. The individual becomes pessimistic and desperate about ever having had talent, and is critical of his work which he may abandons or even destroy. Depression can lead to periods of creative sterility in anyone, regardless of occupation or profession.

Philosophers, mathematicians, scientists, and others in scholarly professions receive from mania a general heightening of the intellectual process, many insights and original ideas,

---

It is our duty as men and women to proceed as though limits to our abilities do not exist...
We are collaborators in creation.

Teilhard de Chardin

---

improvement in memory, increased speed, easy and effortless comprehension, abnormal energy with the creative urge to "get up and do it" and the capacity to build and work with complex structures of thought. The writer and poet acquire through mania greater access to vocabularies, similes and metaphors, becoming more eloquent and imaginative. Artists become more sensitive to the visual qualities of the outer world and of their own work. Here are five great geniuses with whom mania-depression have not been clearly associated: Moses, Jesus, Marx, Freud and Einstein. The great mathematician Leonhard Euler (1707-1783) had three qualities that helped him to be supremely creative and productive: a unique gift of memory, a rare ability to concentrate, and steady quiet work. No mention of depression is made in his case. One wonders whether there are genetic influences that are more likely to dispose some people to manic-depression than others.

We use words and reason to describe creativity, but have difficulty saying exactly what it is and how it is manifested. Creativity is like poetry and art. It is best understood by seeing it, hearing it, or even better by doing it.

For centuries, scholars have tried to define creativity. This in itself is not an easy task. For example, creativity is not merely problem solving. Creativity involves conceptualizing by reaching into the unknown and giving meaning to something. The definitions below illustrate just how complex the concept of creativity really is.

Creativity is discovering or inventing something imaginative, often useful and above all, original.

How many things does one have to create to be considered creative? When does creativity become recognized? Is it enough to say, "Ten years ago I created a unique recipe?" Probably not. Creativity is a perpetual attitude, not just one or two or a handful of accomplishments over a lifetime.

♣ Creative thinking is the process of sensing difficulties, problems, gaps in information, missing elements, something askew;

making guesses and formulating hypotheses about these deficiencies; evaluating and testing these guesses and hypotheses; possibly revising and retesting them; and finally communicating the results.

> **"Creativity is not the direct result of intelligence, talent or skills,"** says Denise Shekerjian in her book <u>Uncommon Genius: How Great Ideas Are Born</u>. "Instead it comes from having an open, 'beginner's mind'; from curiosity, close observation, divergent thinking, biassociation (seeing relationships between apparently unrelated factors), and intuition; from an absence of negative judgment, where 'failure' is learning; and from a tolerance for the 'long-dance of uncertainty' that precedes most breakthroughs."

♣ Creativity, in art or in science, consists of the ability to present information in a light which had not appeared before, but which nevertheless adds to a coherent pattern already publicly available.

♣ Originality often consists of finding connections or analogies between two or more objects or ideas not previously shown to have any bearing on each other.

♣ Creativity is a process that involves the association and radical combination, organization, and integration of two consistent, but habitually incompatible, frames of reference.

♣ Creativity involves the relating of things or ideas that were previously unrelated. The essence of creativity in problem solving is the ability to break through constraints imposed by habit and tradition to find "new" solutions to problems.

From these various perspectives, several revealing themes do indeed emerge. Creativity usually involves the processing of information, the recognition of patterns, and the ability to relate ideas that are often understood to be distinct.

Creativity is difficult to define for several reasons. First, it can only be identified in its finished state. A person cannot just sit down and be creative like sitting to read a book. Second, one's creativity is determined by the end product. This product cannot be judged to be creative until it is analyzed in its proper, relevant, problem-solving context. Third, one cannot judge the merits of creativity until its usefulness and meaning are applied to the situation. For example, a person stranded on an island, who burns the island to get the attention of any over passing aircraft would probably not be considered "creative", as the result may be a destroyed island and no rescue.

One definition generally seems safe: creativity demands that one give something of oneself. It is an act of contributing something unique to a field or endeavor. We are the source of creativity. Creative thinking and problem solving is a participative activity, not a spectator sport. To find what we are seeking, we need to look inward. If the solution is not in us, it is certainly not in the stars. That is why we are not going to sit in a comfortable chair, look at the problems of the world, and complain that life could be better. It is not likely that "they" will solve the problem for us and conveniently pass the answer along.

Intelligent people tend to hold the line as conformists. They learn from school and

from home not to be too creative to please their teachers. Creativity involves risks and appeals to the rebels in society who are greater risk takers. We need to create an environment in organizations to encourage creativity and to prevent fear of personal loss for taking creative risks.

> **Scientific genius is the capacity to be surprised.**
> **Poincaré**

Creativity is sensitive to factors both internal and external to the individual. Mental exercises are one technique for developing one's creativity. Each of these topics will be covered in turn, in this chapter.

Framework for the Creative Process

It has been proposed that the level of creativity of a product or response varies as a function of the levels of each of several components or stages. Each component is necessary, and not one of them is sufficient for creativity in and of itself. Thus, although this framework cannot be considered to be a detailed mathematical model of the creative process, it is, in a general sense, a multiplicative model. No component may be absent if some recognizable level of creativity is to be produced, and the level of each component for a given individual's attempt at a given task determines that individual's overall level of creativity therein.

1. Presentation of Problem

The initial step in the proposed sequence is the presentation of the task to be engaged in or the problem to be solved. Task motivation has an important influence at this stage; if the individual has a high level of intrinsic interest in the task, that interest will be sufficient to engage the process. Under these circumstances the individual, in essence, poses the problem to her or himself. In other situations, however, another individual presents the problem. It is possible, of course, for someone else to pose a problem that the individual finds particularly interesting; however, it is likely that in many cases an externally posed problem is not intrinsically interesting to the individual.

2. Generation of Solutions

The second stage may be considered preparatory to the actual generation of responses or solutions. At this point, the individual builds up or reactivates a store of information relevant to the problem or task, including a knowledge of response algorithms for working problems in the domain in question. In the case in which domain-relevant skills are rather impoverished at the outset, this stage may be quite a long one during which a great deal of learning takes place. On the other hand, if the domain-relevant skills are already sufficiently rich to afford an ample set of possible pathways to explore during task engagement, the reactivation of this already-stored set of information and algorithms may be almost instantaneous, occupying very little real time.

3. Novelty of Response

It is in the third stage that the level of novelty of the product or response is determined. Here, the individual generates response possibilities by searching through the available pathways and exploring features of the envi-

ronment that are relevant to the task at hand. During each "run" through the sequence, the individual follows a particular cognitive pathway to a solution or response. The flexibility with which cognitive pathways are explored and the attention given to particular aspects of the task are determined by both creativity-relevant and by the extent to which a particular pathway is followed in pursuit of a solution. In addition, creativity- relevant skills can influence the sub-goals of the response-generation stage by determining whether a large number of response possibilities will be generated through a temporary suspension of critical judgment or a decision to keep response options open. Task motivation, if it is intrinsic rather than extrinsic, can add to the existing repertoire of skills a willingness to take risks with this particular task and to attend to aspects of the environment that might not be obviously relevant to attain a solution. When a task is heuristic, necessitating a search of possible pathways, what determines which pathways are explored? It has been suggested that possibilities are produced more or less by a blind or random process. Certainly, the search can be narrowed down by various methods. However, some amount of blind search is always required with tasks of this nature. The more possibilities there are to be explored and the

UNDERSTANDING DECISION MAKING

If you are competing with another person or group or even with nature and both groups' decisions are uncertain, the winner will be the one who deals with uncertainty best.

better the strategies for exploring them rapidly, the greater the likelihood of producing a novel yet appropriate response. Some degree of luck, however, is always an element.

4. Validation of Responses

Domain-relevant skills again figure prominently in the fourth stage - the validation of the response possibility that has been chosen on a particular trial. Using domain-relevant techniques of analysis, the response possibility is tested for correctness or appropriateness against the knowledge and the relevant criteria included within domain-relevant skills. Thus, it is this stage that determines whether the product or response will be appropriate, useful, correct, or valuable - the second response characteristic that, together with novelty, is essential for the product to be considered creative according to the conceptual definition proposed earlier.

5. Decision Making

The fifth stage represents the decision making that must be carried out on the basis of the test performed in Stage 4. If the test has been passed perfectly – if there is complete attainment of the original goal – the process terminates. If there is complete failure – if no reasonable response possibility has been generated – the process will also terminate. If there is some progress toward the goal – if at least a reasonable response possibility has been generated or if, in Simon's (1978) terms, there is some evidence of "getting warmer" – the process then returns to the first stage, where the problem is once again posed.

Conditions for Creativity

"It is well known that the right conditions must prevail in order for creativity to flourish."

A very simple example of a seeming aberration that inhibits creativity is that of a musician with perfect pitch who had a hair land in his eardrum after a haircut, depriving him of his musical talent until the problem was diagnosed and the hair removed.

Are people simply born with a creative streak? Are there conditions that foster creativity? Creativity starts from within the individual. However, we must also recognize the influences that the external world exerts. To be creative we need to remember that much of what we currently accept as "truth" is what we have been conditioned to believe. Conditioning is both the social and the psychological disposition to interpret things in certain ways to suit our needs. But truth changes, and this change depends on creative imagination. It also depends on a capacity to see things differently and to adapt personal thinking and behavior to new points of view. Adapting to the future rests with our ability to construct changing versions of reality as we continue to experience life in different ways. Awareness of our prior conditioning is the first step toward any new, creative activity.

Washington as Usual

Two Washington bureaucrats went fishing in the mountains outside of the city. They kept hauling in fish after fish. The boss told his assistant, "Mark this spot on the lake so we can come back and catch more fish tomorrow." As they approached the shore, the boss asked, "Did you mark the place?" "Yes," said the assistant, "See, I marked it right here on the edge of the boat." "You idiot!" said the boss, "They may not give us the same boat tomorrow."

Creativity is up to the individual. One can learn how to be more creative by developing the following traits that promote creativity. As important as external factors may be, they are only of secondary importance when compared to internal factors. Creativity starts from within the individual. Many of the dysfunctional aspects of our external environments can be overcome with an open mind and a positive attitude.

Arthur B. VanGundy, in his book Creative Problem Solving, classifies the factors affecting creativity into two kinds: internal and external. Here they are, together with our modified version of his explanations of these factors.

In no particular order, major factors involved in positive, internal creative climates are:

1. Internal Factors of Creativity

1.1 *Receptiveness to new ideas.*

To utilize our creativity to its fullest potential, receptiveness to new ideas is important. Even if we initially disagree with a new idea, it may still be worth our attention. Considering an idea can lead to new ideas, so it is important to encourage individuals to take into account the positive aspects of any new idea before dismissing it. Being closed-minded when solving problems is like riding a bicycle with only one good wheel – it is difficult to reach the goal.

1.2 *Curiosity.*

It may have killed the cat, but we need to be curious about our environment to deal with its problems. Solving problems creatively and effectively requires asking a variety of questions. Albert Einstein was a master of this; he questioned the obvious when no one else would, extending the range of his problem solving ability as a result of curiosity and of looking for explanations and solutions.

1.3 *Independence.*

Thinking independently generates new perspectives in problem solving. The most creative individuals are not overly influenced by the opinions of others, and are not afraid to maturely express their viewpoints, even if others disagree strongly.

1.4 *Perseverance.*

Individuals like Thomas Edison achieved greatness through perseverance. It is important to keep working on an idea, even if others resist.

1.5 *Risk Taking.*

Unless one takes risks, one will never produce anything creative. The Pet Rock was a risky product concept. But it made marketing history by selling what basically was just a stone, packaged in a way that motivated people to pay money for a commodity available for free in their own front yards.

1.6 *Discipline.*

Even though free-thinking is essential to the creative process, it must be done in a structured manner. Discipline is needed to attack a problem within each stage of the model.

1.7 *Playfulness.*

Just as many toys for toddlers teach youngsters vital problem-solving skills, adults should not be afraid to "toy" with their ideas. If you take a look at many creative departments in the top advertising agencies, you will find toys, "fun rooms", and other seemingly frivolous examples of what may appear to be silliness. This kind of atmosphere keeps the creative juices flowing as advertising whizzes come up with new and innovative ways of solving even the greatest marketing challenge. These people look at problems from every possible perspective.

1.8 *Impulsiveness.*

Don't hold back. If it pops into your mind, write it down. Even though we are taught it is not good to jump to conclusions, do not repress new ideas or thoughts, but do generate all the data first, then judge the outcome later.

The creative person has a desire to grow, the capacity to be puzzled, awareness, spontaneity, spontaneous flexibility, adaptive flexibility, originality, divergent thinking, openness to new experiences, no boundaries, perme-

ability of boundaries, yielding, readiness to yield, abandoning, letting go, being born every day, discarding the irrelevant, ability to toy with elements, change of activity, persistence, hard work, composition, decomposition, recomposition, differentiation, integration, being at peace with the world, harmony, honesty, humility, enthusiasm, integrity, inner maturity, self-actualization, skepticism, boldness, faith, courage, willingness to be alone, I see, I feel, I think, gusto for temporary chaos, security in uncertainty, tolerance of ambiguity.

FLOWERS ARE RED
Harry Chapin 1978

The little boy went first day of school
He got some crayons and started to draw
He put colors all over the paper
For colors was what he saw
And the teacher said...What you doin' young man
I'm paintin' flowers he said
She said...It's not the time for art young man
And a way it should be done
You've got to show concern for everyone else
For you're not the only one
And sh...
Fi... man
...n
...flowers any other way
...s have been seen

...n the rainbow
...n' sun
S... ...nd I see every one
We... ...You're sassy there's ways
that ...uld be
And you'll paint flowers the way they are
So repeat after me...
And she said...
Flowers are red young man
Green leaves are green
There's no need to see flowers any other way
Than the way they always have been seen...

But the little boy said...
There are so many colors in the rainbow
So many colors in the mornin' sun
So many colors in a flower and I see every one
The teacher put him in a corner
She said...it's for your own good
And you won't come out 'til you get it right
And all responding like you should
Well, finally he got lonely
Frightened thoughts filled his head
And he went up to the teacher
And this is what he said and he said
Flowers are red, green leaves are green
There's no need to see flowers any other way than
the way they always have been seen
Time went by like it always does
And they moved to another town
and the little boy went to another school
And this is what he found
The teacher there was smilin'
She said...Painting should be fun
And there are so many colors in a flower
So let's use every one
But the little boy painted flowers in neat rows of
green and red
And when the teacher asked him why,
This is what he said...and he said
Flowers are red, green leaves are green
There's no need to see flowers any other way than
the way they always have been seen.

2. External Factors of Creativity

Besides individual traits, the environment also plays a major role in the promotion of creativity. The environment can dramatically affect the way a person acts and reacts to any given situation. As Chapin's lyric suggests, even the most creative person's creative ability can be inhibited by an intimidating or uncomfortable environment. The following are some key external factors that can lead to creative thinking.

The environment in an organization is likely to be conductive to creative thinking if it has certain desired attributes. The first listing contains external factors involving task-related elements in the environment; the second listing is concerned with people-related environmental elements.

The list of external factors that follows is concerned primarily with people-related elements that should be present in an organization. In general, the climate of the organization will be characterized as positive in this area if it:

2.1 Encourages open expression of ideas.

Too often, employees are made to believe their ideas do not matter, and may even be career threatening. Upper management should take a clear position on the commitment to creative idea production, let it be known, and, perhaps most importantly, demonstrate this commitment.

2.2 Accepts "off the wall" ideas.

An organization should tolerate what may be perceived as unconventional ideas. Because of individual differences, not everyone will present similar ideas. Different approaches should be respected as a variety of perspectives on a problem increases the odds of developing a solution that will please everyone.

2.3 Provides assistance in developing ideas.

There is an old Pennsylvania Dutch saying that even the best apple still can use polishing, and the same can be said of ideas. In organizations, even the best employee idea should go through revision. And, sometimes even the seemingly non-idea can be made into a workable one through a few modifications. This is not to say no idea should be rejected, but ideas should be given a fair hearing and allowed to develop.

2.4   *Encourages risk taking.*

Again, it should be stressed that taking a creative risk does not mean taking a career risk. It means that the atmosphere should encourage calculated risk taking (but not anything goes, irresponsible risk taking). This could range from encouraging an employee with a new idea to setting up a system to judge ideas on a formal basis.

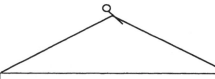

1. **Provide freedom to do things differently.**
2. **Maintain an optimal amount of work pressure.**
3. **Provide realistic work goals.**
4. **Use a low level of supervision.**
5. **Delegate responsibilities.**
6. **Encourage participation.**
7. **Provide immediate and timely feedback.**
8. **Provide necessary resources and support.**

2.5   *Provides time for individual efforts.*

Employees need personal time to help them reach goals and solve problems with their own personal creativity. This time can help an employee consider all possibilities and feel more involved with the problem-solving process. Employees also need to feel that they will be rewarded for their efforts in these individual projects, as long as it is in the best interest of the company.

2.6   *Recognizes the value of ideas.*

Mark Twain once said "I could live for two weeks on a compliment." External rein-

forcement can give employees the motivation needed to climb the mountain of problems they face everyday. A satisfied employee is a motivated, productive employee capable of solving problems because he feels his efforts are worth something to the company.

2.7   *Rewards effort*

Creativity is motivated by several kinds of circumstances. Curiosity is the most intrinsic and obvious, but there are others. Einstein, to some extent, was motivated by fame. He had a barber wax his hair and was photographed to show that the inner power of his mind was electric and could make his hair stand up. Edison sought riches with his more than one thousand patents.

Edison probably did more practical good for humanity than Einstein, and he got his reward with money. Einstein was rewarded with fame – in our time people mention his name more often as a creative person than Edison's. The Nobel Prize is another powerful reward.

Exercising Your Creativity

"The creative process involves two kinds of thinking: divergent and convergent."

To stimulate creativity in **divergent thinking**, an exercise employing a cantaloupe is used! Imagine twenty widely disparate uses for the melon, from the smallest part, the seeds, to the whole object. Accept no limits on your imagination, no matter how seemingly crazy or off-color the suggestions may be. Ready for another challenge? Imagine how a dog could use the melon. Finally, imagine five uses that a bacterium could make of the melon.

The contributions people made over the years about the uses of a melon cover a wide range, from the very useful variety of eating or drinking it: cold or hot, fried or boiled, from melon ice cream to melon juice and liqueur. Some would use it as a bowl, a ball, or a projectile in a cannon. Its meat can be used for paste, or for coloring purposes. Its skin can be used to make sandals. One person went so far as to buy several melons and weave their skins into a strong rope intended for use in a bridge across a chasm. The seeds of a melon have chromosomes and genes in which some of our original heritage may lie. The exercise is then extended to using the melon for all our needs. With only melons in this world and nothing else, we must satisfy all our needs. Our houses are entirely made of melons, and so are our beds, our utensils and other instruments, hardened when necessary. Incidentally, how would one make a knife, a fork or a spoon from a melon? A melon, like a pumpkin, can be carved with candles placed inside for Halloween. The number of possibilities is unlimited and can go on for hours, with new insights generated serendipitously.

Such divergent thinking expands and broadens the thought process. It is similar to a prism spreading a beam of white light into an array of colors. Divergent thinking begins with a specific problem or idea and generates alternatives or different perspectives. The object is to entertain possibilities and avoid closure.

Another type of exercise encourages creativity in **convergent thinking**. Connect any two widely disparate objects or ideas by a stream of logical relationships, for example, the North Star and a pencil on your desk, or this book and an alligator. Convergent thinking is a process of narrowing and reducing and is similar to a magnifying glass that converts light into a narrow but powerful beam. When one thinks convergently, one begins with a broad perspective and narrows the focus to fine detail. The objective is to reach a solution and obtain closure.

By making many associations of ideas with which one is familiar, the subconscious goes to work on the subject, independent of thinking and rational consciousness, and is able to create new possibilities and solve difficult problems. The mathematician, Henri Poincaré, recounts the story of mathematical explorations he made by drinking strong coffee and brooding over his subject for hours, without success. The answers came to him in a flash, at completely unexpected times several days later, at very strange places, without being engaged in thinking about the matter at that time.

In 1879, Luis Pasteur, remembering Edward Jenner's proof a century before, that people who had had cow-pox were immune to smallpox, realized that vaccinating people with a weakened microbe built their resistance to more virulent forms of it.

Creativity can be viewed as a process, a systematic series of steps that results in a unique contribution. One theory of the creative process first formulated by Wallace in his 1926 book identifies four distinct steps: preparation, incubation, illumination, and verification. During the preparation stage, the individual observes, searches, collects data, and thinks freely. In the second stage, incubation, the individual internalizes and subconsciously orders the gathered information. A significant struggle may occur, a subconscious conflict between what is currently accepted as reality and what may be possible, a future reality. Successful incubation can lead to the harvesting of fresh ideas and new ways of thinking. The individual realizes the solution during the illumination stage, much like Archimedes': Eureka! Eureka! And finally, during the verification stage, the creator seeks corroboration and verification of the solution.

Creative thinking is a skill, not just a natural talent. Like tennis, bridge playing, and other skillful activities, creative thinking must be practiced if it is to be developed and maintained.

Creativity can be enhanced by directing one's interest. Hone in on an idea, live with it, massage it, embrace it, reshape it. Reforming one's perceptual filters will facilitate creativity. Encourage strangeness in thought, try new thinking patterns to improve the accuracy, scope, and flexibility of personal filters. Increasing the breadth of knowledge and observation will enlarge the memory base. Practicing new associations and trying new relationships between ideas may be fruitful. The chess grandmaster keeps the brain muscle exercised not only through practice but by extensive consideration of problematic situations and different alternative solutions.

In Becoming a Writer, Dorothea Brande proposed the following regimen for writing creatively, but it is also applicable to other creative forms.

1. *Hold Your Mind Still.*
Close your eyes and think of nothing. Shut down your restless, fluttering, and busy mind. Entertain no thoughts. It is not as easy as you may think.

2. *Practice Mind Control.*
Choose a simple object like a rubber ball. Hold it in your hand and look at it. Concentrate on it alone. Now close your eyes and continue seeing the ball. Think of nothing else. After a few moments, let the idea of the

ball slip out of your mind. Call it back. Let it go again.

3. *The Idea as the Object.*
Try holding an idea in your mind much like the ball. Focus on the idea, keeping all else still. After a while, the idea will take on a form and color. Pay attention. What other ideas may be appearing on the periphery of the central idea?

4. *The Magic in Operation.*
Focus on your idea. Now see its solution. What does the finished product look like? Pay no attention to everything in between, just see the idea and its outcome.

Now take these pictures out for a walk. Forget about them and walk until you are mildly tired. Turn around and walk back to your starting point at a smooth and easy pace. Do not hurry. Call the pictures back into your mind. Look at the whole picture. Don't be concerned with details.

5. *Inducing the "Artistic Coma".*
Now bathe, still thinking in a global way. Then go into a dim room, lie down or sit in a low, comfortable chair. Do not move again. Make your body quiet. Then quiet your mind. Be still, not quite asleep and not quite awake.

After awhile (it may be twenty minutes or two hours) you will feel an impulse to rise. It will be a surge of energy. Obey at once; you will be in a slightly somnambulistic state indifferent to everything but your idea. Go to your paper or typewriter and create. You are in the artist's state.

6. *Valedictory.*
The quality of your creation depends on you and your life, your sensitivity and experience, and how well you have developed your skills. Feel free to alter the steps of this process. Find what works for you and practice creating.

What if you formed still-wet potato chips into a shape that allowed you to stack them neatly? You could get an entire bagful into a slender, protective canister. That, as legend has it, was the beginning of Pringles. Whether consumers liked eating them was another matter. But the packaging problem had a new solution.

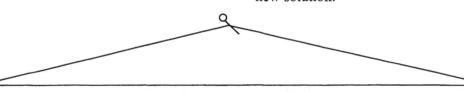

THE CASE OF ELIAS HOWE.

For years the inventor Howe had tried, without success, to perfect the sewing machine. One night, he dreamed. He saw himself captured by savages who dragged him before their king. The king issued an ultimatum: if within twenty-four hours Howe did not produce a machine that sewed, he would die by the spear. Howe searched for a solution, but nothing came. The deadline passed and the savages were approaching. Clutching their spears menacingly, they stood over him. Slowly they raised their spears; Howe saw the points coming toward him. Suddenly, as he stared at the tips of their spears, he forgot his fear. Howe realized that each spear had eye-shaped holes. He immediately awakened, realizing that for his sewing machine to work, the eye of the needle must be near the point. Getting hastily out of bed, he ran to his laboratory, filed a needle to the proper size, drilled a hole near the tip, inserted it into the sewing machine, and sewed.

Training for Creativity

Making associations with nature is a commonly encouraged method for stimulating innovative thinking. For example, if you are addressing the problem of packaging potato chips, try to relate them to nature. What is similar to potato chips? Leaves! Have you ever taken a walk on a pleasant autumn day? Dry leaves crumble under your feet like potato chips.

That's the problem. But wet leaves don't crumble, they compress nicely.

Earlier we posited the difficult question, What is life? and claimed that no one has a complete and descriptive answer. One can approach this question in a creative way by using analogy.

Here are a few examples offered by Roger Von Oech (<u>A Whack on the Side of the Head: How to Unlock Your Mind for Innovation,</u> 1983.)

> Life is like a poker game. Sometimes you deal and sometimes you are dealt to. Both skill and luck are important elements. You can bet, check, bluff, and raise. Sometimes

you win with a pair, sometimes you lose with a full house. But whatever happens, it is best to just keep shuffling along.

Life is like a jigsaw puzzle. But you don't get the picture on the front of the box to show you what you're trying to assemble. Often, you're not even sure you have all the pieces.

Life is like eating a grapefruit. First you have to cut through a tough skin. Then it takes a couple of bites to get used to the taste. And just when you start to like it, you get squirted in the eye.

Life is like a bagel. It is delicious when it is fresh and warm. Often, however, it is just hard. The whole in the middle is its great mystery; what it is and why is it there? Yet it wouldn't be a bagel without it.

Interestingly, creativity can be approached by imagining the mind as an instrument that best solves problems involving personal survival. That is, if we are not pressed with some urgency to avoid a serious threat or to obtain an important reward, the subconscious mind does not work intensively to produce a solution. Some people may simply not be creative on a casual basis. To stimulate creativity, identify a problem and concentrate as if your survival depended on its solution. Learn and think all you can about it. It will get solved somehow. It must!

Creativity may be augmented by adopting a checklist of approaches. Take each idea and put it to other uses, adapt it, modify it, magnify it, minify it, substitute in it, rearrange it, reverse it, or combine it with another idea. Kenneth Mac Crimmon has developed a

---

Mac Crimmon's Checklist
1. **Modify current alternatives to the problem.**
2. **Adapt solutions from others.**
3. **Hurdle obstacles to solutions.**
4. **Relate problem components between actual and desired states.**
5. **Associate remote entities.**
6. **Change perspectives, for example, by sitting in a different chai in your office or imagining how Albert Einstein or John Wayne would handle this problem.**
7. **Use free thinking (incubate the problem).**
8. **Fantasize.**

checklist of activities useful for identifying alternative solutions to problems. His checklist ranges from the well structured to the more loosely suggestive.

Creative Techniques and Exercises

The following four techniques can be used in a variety of problem solving situations to stimulate creative thinking.

They are:
Brainstorming,
Synectics,
Morphological Analysis
Lateral Thinking

The nine points problem discussed in Chapter One satisfies the four steps of creativity. The points and their number are chosen through brainstorming and are then connected

53

THE IMPULSE PRINCIPLE
If you have to solve a difficult problem, you must apply an impulse or a jerk to it like pulling a rusty nail out of a wall-it does not come out by pulling gently.

(synectics) in different ways using straight lines. Synthesis is obtained through morphological analysis by arranging them in three rows of three points each and connecting them with straight lines. The solution requires lateral thinking to extend the lines out of the constraints of the points as corners so that only four lines are needed.

How do brainstorming, synectics, morphological analysis and lateral thinking apply in music, painting, and sports?

You have to think of notes and small phrases and connect them to make melodies and combine them morphologically to make a piece with introduction development and recapitulation. You must ensure it is broad and lateral in variety. In painting it is the same as in music layout. In sports one must go through movements as part of bigger sub-games of an entire game.

The exercises given below are examples of how each of the methods can be applied to a classroom situation.

1. Brainstorming

The aim of brainstorming is to produce checklists of ideas, relevant to solving a problem. Unconventional ideas are sought.

Evaluation and criticism are delayed to the end to encourage freedom in generating concepts.

⮚ Brainstorming Exercises

Define a Word - Take a common word like "list" or "right" and write down all the possible meanings for that word. Repeat.

Sniglet - Make up a word and write it on the board. Have the students make up a definition for the word. Or write a very obscure word down and have the students suggest meanings for it. (Similar to "Haberdash")

The Reason Why - The Professor should come into class with his arm in a sling or lie down in class or do something abnormal and ask the class to suggest as many reasons as possible to explain or rationalize that act.

2. Synectics

This is the joining together of different and apparently irrelevant elements to solve a problem. It involves the use of analogical thinking, to discover similarities between things that may first appear to be dissimilar. One deliberately seeks metaphors to test assumptions about possible solutions. Diverse talents far removed from the problem under investigation may be invited to participate.

⮚ Synectics Exercises

The Story of Two Unrelated Things - Each student is asked to write any two subjects on two separate pieces of paper. Each will be folded and put into a hat. Then the papers will be shuffled, and each student will select two pieces of paper out of the hat. The student would then write a story that relates the two topics.

Around the Room in 26 Letters - Each student takes turn in naming an object beginning with the letter "A" proceeding around the room until the alphabet has been completed. The object's relationship must be obvious or if it is not, then the student must formulate a rationale for the relationship. For example, A-apple, B-banana, C-cocoa (grown in the region), D-dark (dark chocolate), etc. This forces students to think spontaneously without time to prepare a response.

Finding Relationships - Split the class into two groups consisting of pairs. Give them ten minutes to come up with a story on how they could be related to one another. The students' stories must be based on true factual information in their own lives. This increases the intensity of interaction between each group. The time constraint is important for this game to generate quick, creative thinking.

3. Morphological Analysis

This is a tool for ensuring that all information potentially relevant to the solution of a problem is systematically examined. All the information available is grouped into "attributes" of concepts, since they may suggest feasible alternatives. The exhaustive nature of the process reduces the risk of novel combinations (i.e. solutions) being overlooked. The systematic and objective synthesis of possible solutions avoids the constraints of preconceived ideas.

Ideas, imagination, and creativity make us aware of things and are necessary pieces of the jigsaw puzzle of understanding. We need organization and precise synthesis to put

things together and arrive at the exact levels for making tradeoffs. Often the options we have identified are all close, but to choose the best one among them can make a huge difference. To be enlightened with reason is not enough. In business we need a technology of thought to implement reason.

Similarly, to get rid of a belief or to do something new, one must do something radical, more than just small, incremental changes in old habits. Something more like "Damn the torpedoes, full speed ahead," by shocking oneself out of a rut, with ideas out of the blue, with improvisation, intelligence, energy and action, like the mouse that roars at the lion to annoy and scare it. Opening the Gordian Knot with a sword is an example of this principle.

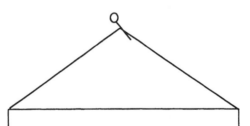

Analytic Hierarchy Process

The AHP is a process for structuring and prioritizing decision problems by relating alternatives to criteria and to objectives and then to an overall goal. It is the method for performing morphological analysis. The AHP can be utilized to help students categorize attributes. Emphasize all the combinations to generate all possible alternatives and use judgment to relate them according to priority.

❧ **Morphological Exercise**

Case Study - Have the class read a case study on a topic which interests them like the soft drink industry, a beer company, a publishing company, or any topic of interest and prepare a problem which may occur in that activity.

The students can then generate all possible plans of actions and all combinations of actions for its solution and discuss and determine which course of action would be best. This term, devised by de Bono, describes a number of techniques for restructuring conceptual patterns and creating new ones, essentially looking at familiar data in new ways using breadth rather than depth. This may involve using incorrect information as a step towards a correct solution. It may deliberately seek out irrelevant information and attempts to interpret it in a favorable way for solving a problem. It involves attempts to randomly look up such an irrelevant data or story and imaginatively bend it for practical use.

4. Lateral Thinking

Lateral Thinking is an attitude and a way for expanding thought and imagination. The attitude is to look at things in different ways.

A teacher can also be regarded as a potential friend, a father or mother figure, a sounding board for ideas, policeman or a judge. In thinking, we need judgment to stay in boundaries when we want and movement to switch channels when we also want. Provocative and shocking ideas are helpful.

The methods to encourage switching channels in lateral thinking are:

1. Stepping Stone (Suspend judgment and move out of conventional thinking).
Use good and bad ideas to move to a new channel. For example how can a teacher not wear a tie but even be more presentable?

2. Escape (Choose provocative, anti ideas e.g. planes land upside down. The advantage is pilots see better. Thus the cockpit should be lower.)

Identify the main track of thinking and deliberate escape from it by asking if every detail has to be that way? Is conformity only shown by a tie? A doctor is allowed to show up in a white lab coat.

3. Random Stimulation

Random Stimulation means to choose a totally different idea to move out and find a way back to the subject.) Select a random word and associate it with the central subject. For example the word tadpole with teacher means tail which means assistants which means multiplying the teacher by taking on assistants who would tail him around and become teachers who take more assistants.

The following four scenarios are amusing examples of lateral thinking. Notice how, in each case, the dilemma was approached from an unconventional and very unexpected perspective.

The Missing Spoon.

At a dinner party a man noticed that a guest pocketed a sterling spoon. Not to embarrass him, he said I am a magician. I can pocket objects and let them appear in someone else's pocket. He put a spoon in his pocket and asked the man to take it out of his own pocket.

A Tale of Two Stones

A man had borrowed a bit of money from another man and could not pay him back. The other threatened to put him in jail unless he let him marry his beautiful daughter and forgive him the debt. The man and his daughter were horrified. The lender proposed to mitigate the situation by proposing to put a white and a black stone in a bag and the girl drawing one. If she gets the black stone she would marry him. Standing over a path made of stone, he slyly put two black stones in the bag which the girl noticed. When she took out a stone she dropped it among the other stones, thus losing it. She then suggested that the other stone in the bag be examined to see what the color of the lost stone should be.

Columbus' Egg Trick.

Sometime during 1493, 4 to 6 weeks after his return from his first voyage, Columbus was at a party. One member of the group said to him: "If you had not undertaken the expedition someone else from Spain would have". Columbus made no reply but took a hard boiled egg and said: "Gentlemen, you make it stand here without support. The egg was passed around the table, each person attempting to make it stand without support. No one succeeded. When the egg came to Columbus' hands, he crushed the egg down on one end. They said anyone could have done this. He said: "Why didn't you do it?"

King John and The Abbot

King John,. Richard the Lion Hearted's brother was a despot. He ruled while Richard was away fighting the crusade. One day he heard that an abbot was living too well in the Abbey, serving the best of wines, enjoying good food and sometimes a few luxuries not available to the king himself. The king was jealous and determined to put an end to it by doing away with the abbot. He told him that he knew of his style of life and would not tolerate it. In fact, the king said, "You are going to die unless you come back in three days with answers for three questions: How do I go around the world in 24 hours? When will I die? What am I thinking?"

The abbot left the king's presence very depressed and discouraged. He could not see how even a single one of these questions had a reasonable answer. He set out to inquire from people. He went to the great university of his day, Oxford, and asked the great scholars what to do. The three days were practically gone; he returned to his abbey despondent. He was certain that his end was at hand. Walking through the meadow that evening he encountered his witty shepherd. The latter asked how he fared, upon which the abbot told him the entire story and that the next day the king aimed to end his life.

The shepherd thought for a minute then said, "Don't people say we look alike? Let me go in your place. Just lend me your cloak and tell me where to go." After some objection, he let him go. The next day, the shepherd appeared before the king in the abbot's clothing. "So you are back to answer my questions," said the king. "I am going to try, your majesty. They are very subtle and difficult," said the shepherd.

"How do I go around the world in 24 hours?" asked the king. "Wake up before sunrise and as the sun's disk appears in the horizon, run to it, catch it and hang on until it is back in 24 hours. Then you get off." The king was amused by this imaginative answer but thought that he would get him on the next one.

"When will I die?" asked the king. "My Lord will die when his last breath has expired," said the man. The king now laughed openly. He had not expected such correct and choice replies.

Now the impossible question. "What am I thinking?" asked the king. The shepherd rose and threw off the abbot's cloak and took off the beard and said, "You think I am the abbot, but I am his shepherd."

The king was very pleasantly surprised by the answer and fell over backward with laughter. He liked the shepherd and rewarded him with gifts and forgave the abbot for high living.

Seven Characteristics of Creative People (*John Adair*)
1. **Intelligence**
2. **High self-motivation**
3. **Ability to hold contradictory thoughts**
4. **Curiosity**
5. **Independent mind**
6. **Not too introverted, not too extroverted**
7. **Wide interests**

❧ Lateral Thinking Exercise

Current Events - The students may choose a current event that they wish to discuss. They generate all related topics and sub-topics under that event. One then selects the most irrelevant of those sub-topics and asks the students to create a scenario where that sub-topic would be of major importance in the event.

For example, if the current event topic is political change in Russia and the sub-topics are Russian, US/Russian relations, Russian people's unhappiness, Vodka consumption in Russia, increased Vodka marketing efforts in the US, etc. The scenario could be created about how increased Vodka sales in the US may affect political change Russia. This exercise demonstrates how seemingly irrelevant or insignificant information can have an impact on the bigger subjects.

A Few More Problems Put Your Creativity to Work!

1. Why couldn't the Loch Ness monster fantasy be real? There would have to be a family of such monsters to have offsprings. They would have to come up to the surface for air every few minutes and all would have to have been there after the ice age 10,000 years ago when Loch Ness was frozen solid like an ice cube. What lessons do we learn from this explanation to deal with similar hoaxes. In 1994 a survivor of the 1934 publicized fantasy of Loch Ness confessed that it was a long neck like object floated on a toy submarine later photographed from a distance by an innocent person and given publicity.

2. You are the manager of a ski area. Your customers complain they are spending too much time waiting in line to ride the one chair-lift. State-law requires that there must be a period of fifteen seconds between chairs. Since there is not time to install a new chair-lift this season, how should you modify your chair-lift operating policy to satisfy the customers' complaints?

3. The postmaster in a small town found a letter in his mailbox with only three words in the front, as follows:

> WOOD
> JOHN
> MASS

As he was examining the envelope, which was properly stamped but had no return address, he noticed that the police chief had entered the post office. He told the chief that he didn't know where to deliver the letter. Sure enough, the letter reached its correct destination. What were the right name, city and state?

4. A man usually takes the 5:30 P.M. train, arriving at his station at 6:00, when his wife picks him up and drives him home. One day he took the 5:00 P.M. train, arriving at 5:30 P.M. at the station. He began walking home.

His wife, starting out from home to meet him at the usual time, met him on the way and brought him home 10 minutes before the usual time. How long did the man walk?

The first feeling about this problem is that there is not ample information to solve it. Nothing is said about how fast the man walked, or how fast the wife drove, or when she left home every day to meet him at the station. However, it is assumed that there is no ambiguity in the information so that an answer is possible.

5. Draw six points on a paper and connect each of them to every other one, using a straight line or a curve that does not cross itself. What is the minimum number of crossings you can do it with? Notice that four points can be connected without any crossings by drawing one diagonal inside the figure and one outside. Do the same for five points and do it again for seven points and eight points each time with a minimum number of crossings. That number for n points is given by

$$n(n-2)^2 (n-4)/64 \quad \text{n even}$$
$$(n-1)^2 (n-3)^2/64 \quad \text{n odd}$$

How would one prove that this is always true? Can you do it?

A Creative Attitude

The secret to being creative is not discovered in the reading of this chapter but in the application of its ideas. What is an important problem to solve? How can you solve it? What must you do to solve it? Creative people possess positive attitudes towards life's problems. They do not see problems at all but opportunities for developing creative solutions. On rare occasions and with a few people this attitude is expressed through a crescendo, through a burst of creativity that peaks and dies off, leaving a noticeable mark. But for most people, creativity is synonymous with the enjoyment of everyday life. It is part of their positive attitude to entertain the idea of change. They are flexible enough to embrace rather than resist the future. They know they have what it takes to survive the conundrum.

Positive Thinking

The difficult we do immediately, the impossible takes a little longer.

Negative Thinking

Things we say to ourselves that close down our creativity department.

I am not a mind reader.

I can't do the impossible.

I have never seen a thing like this before.

This is not the kind of thing I like to think about, let someone else do it.

This is not for me, I am a special person, a simple person, a complicated person, a nice person.

Thoughts on Creativity and Humor

"Humor is the only domain of creative activity where a highly complex stimulus produces a massive and specific physiological reflex – laughter".

–Arthur Koestler

It is a "luxury reflex" in that it appears to serve no biological purpose. Laughter does not help us to withdraw our hand from a dangerous flame or turn our head to avoid a blow. If anything, a strong response of laughter weakens us physiologically, leaving us gasping for air or doubled over defenselessly. From an evolutionary viewpoint frivolity seems a mistake, for it fails to complement basic fight or flight responses.

Yet humor is not a folly of nature. It is the trademark of a sophisticated mental development so characteristic of our species that man has been called the laughing animal. Laughter is the safety valve for an overflow of emotional energy.

At first, in the series of events leading to a laugh, there is a superficial meaning that arouses an emotion appropriate to a serious situation. But then arrives the realization of a latent meaning to the stimulus contradicting the first and demonstrating an incongruity in our thinking. We are fooled and we know it. The outlet of laughter provides immediate relief to the resulting superfluous emotional excitement. It is also a release for emotions arising during conflict situations and can provide resolution for troublesome predicaments. Laughter, like most forms of creativity, is a unique possession of humankind.

Humor is that cognitive ability to accept and appreciate life's incongruities, and it is closely related to other cognitive pursuits such as scientific discovery and the creation and enjoyment of art.

Three types of creativity are represented in the figure: scientific discovery, artistic originality, and comic inspiration. Arthur Koestler points out that the logic pattern is the same for all three forms. The key is the discovery of hidden similarities. In scientific discovery, the reshuffling of ideas produces new knowledge concerning nature and our relation to it. In art, we see objects or ideas in a new form through an expression or interpretation we can understand but had not generated on our own. In humor, the discovery of hidden similarities produces a harmless realization of incongruity, which results in laughter. Medical researchers see the laser beam as a surgeon's knife; the poet envisions a tree as a prayer to the Creator; and the caricaturist demonstrates the similarity between Bob Hope's nose and a ski jump. The playful pun is similar to the poet's rhyme and to word puzzles that require skills similar to those that scientists used to decipher the Rosetta Stone.

Emotional patterns, however, are different for each creative form. Humor is characterized by a touch of aggressiveness, whereas scientific reasoning is emotionally detached. Still, in humor as in scientific or mathematical problem solving, there is a problem statement or premise, some form of development, and finally the punch line, conclusion, or problem solution. On the other hand, the poetic image is sympathetic and admiring, inspired by positive emotions.

For much of history, humor was viewed with disdain because of its aggressive nature. Socrates thought that by laughing at what is ridiculous in our friends, we mix pleasure with malice. Aristotle viewed laughter as intimately related to ugliness and debasement; Cicero believed the province of the ridiculous lay in a certain degradation and deformity; and Descartes held that laughter was a manifestation of joy mixed with surprise or hatred. Thomas Hobbes wrote in Leviathan: "The passion of laughter is nothing else but sudden glory arising from a sudden conception of some eminency in ourselves by comparison with the infirmity of others, or with our own formerly."

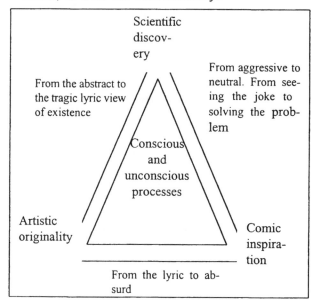

Only recently, and we believe importantly, scientific discovery, artistic inspiration, and comic inventiveness have been recognized as similar domains of creative activity that require remarkably similar cognitive approaches.

A sense of humor will help us escape from inevitable frustration when dealing with large-scale human problems such as conflict, hunger, and oppression. The future will doubtless be a somewhat troubling, even threatening, experience, because we will be required to accommodate many changes in our personal lives and in society as a whole. The faster and more often things change, the more mistakes will be made. Incongruities, inconsistencies, and instabilities will be in-

evitable, and our capacities for dealing with such situations are limited. We can get angry, curse those who upset the secure order, and withdraw from potential trouble, defending our psychological comfort by shutting out the imperfect world and its errors. Or we can learn to laugh at life, appropriately and gracefully, secure in the belief that some trouble and pain must be tolerated if progress is to be achieved.

While there are those who incorrectly believe that life is no more than a cruel joke, the real fool is the one who at all times takes it seriously. We cannot help but believe that those who learn to smile at themselves and the world will possess that extra degree of flexibility that will prepare them for future success.

A Final Exercise on Creativity

Objective:

A. To learn how creativity is involved in a real-life and day to day problem solving process.
B. To learn how working in a group improves creativity and makes a difference in the problem solving process and the quality of its outcome.
C. To learn how humor fits in the process.
D. To learn what factors enhance and limit creativity in group problem solving.

Creativity involves the following processes:

A. *Preparation:* Research and understand the problem.
Incubation: Mull over the problem, reflect on it.
Illumination: Insight.
Verification: Check that it is solved.

B. *Brainstorming* (*Alex F. Osborn*)*:* Imagination

Synectics (*William J. J. Gordon*)*:* Logic.

Morphological Analysis (*Fritz Zwicky*)*:* Organization.

Lateral Thinking (*Edward deBono*)*: (as opposed to vertical thinking*) Embed the problem in a bigger setting (Completeness).

Class Project

❧ **In Class**

a. Groups of two students are formed.
b. Each group agrees on a common problem to be solved. A problem is defined as unacceptable local condition that can be altered. Solving a problem is defined as finding the most appropriate action/change to alter the condition. Select a problem in which working in a group and doing research can make a difference in the outcome.
c. The group members work on their own to list all the elements of the problem (for example: objectives, stakeholders, criteria, alternatives, etc.). Obtain spontaneous (without incubation or research) individual solutions using one's present knowledge.
d. The group members exchange their lists.
e. Each individual, working on his/her partner's list, organizes the elements in such a way as to facilitate the process of finding the solution and to justify the solution (for example, by indicating cause-effect relationships or flow of influence). Obtain spontaneous individual solutions using information from one's partner without having a group discussion.
f. The group members work together to obtain a spontaneous group solution.

❧ **Outside Class: individual preparation and incubation.**

a. Each individual obtains more information about the problem.
b. Each individual identifies changes or revisions needed in both the approach to the problem (more elements, different relationships) and the solution itself.

❧ **In Class: group agreement.**

Align and agree on the updated approach and/or solution.

❧ **At Home: individual finalization and evaluation.**

a. Finalize solution to the problem.
b. Prepare a report (individual) with respect to the learning objectives listed above.

Describe in detail the creative process experienced in the problem solving exercise, with respect to the various processes discussed above.

❧ **In Class**

Discussion and input from participants (Final presentation before class).

Some tips and points for discussion:

1. Keep record of each step and take notes on what happens along the way to be used for reference in the report. It is more a report on the process of solving a problem than on the content of the problem.
2. What do you learn from the similarities and differences between your list and your partner's list?
3. How does information sharing improve the quality of the outcome?

4. How would more research (preparation) and more time to think (incubation) improve the spontaneous problem solving process and the quality of its resulting solution?

5. Does the process involve humor? If it does, does it add anything to the problem solving process and the quality of its outcome? Explain why, when and how it happens. If not, also explain why and what needs to be done to make humor work.

6. What are the factors that enhance or diminish creativity?

7. How does this process improve your understanding about creativity and your perception about yourself as to whether or not you are a creative person? Provide your own description of creativity.

Jokes' Appendix

Laughter is the essence of mankind.
                                    –Francois Rabelais

If you wish to glimpse inside a human soul and get to know a man, don't bother analyzing his ways of being silent, of talking, of weeping, or seeing how much he is moved by noble ideas; you'll get better results if you just watch him laugh. If he laughs well, he's a good man.

                                    –Fyodor Dostoyevsky

A terrible liar is one who not even the opposite of what he says is true.

Laughter isn't a reaction to the degree of humor at all. It is more of an intuitive response to an irreconcilable set up, a reflex reaction to a situation that doesn't immediately jive with the brain.

Madness frequently discovers itself merely by unnecessary deviation from the usual modes of the world.

Sterility is hereditary

Nothing in the world can take the place of persistence. Talent will not: nothing is more common than unsuccessful men with talent. Genius will not: unrewarded genius is almost a proverb. Education will not: the world is full of educated derelicts. Persistence and determination alone are omnipotent.

I couldn't wait for success . . . so I went ahead without it.
                                    –Jonathan Winters

The guy who invented the wheel was asked by a young upstart, "Sir, what are you planning to work on next?"

Even if there is nothing to laugh about, laugh on credit.

☺ Laugh to Last

Can the sick laugh away physical ailments? Doctors studying humor say they can. The very act of laughing is actually good exercise. In an average laugh, the diaphragm, thorax, abdomen, heart, lungs and possibly even the liver get a brief workout. Laughing can clear foreign matter from the respiratory system and speed up circulation and heart rate. If the laugh is especially vigorous, a fall-on-the-floor special, it flexes muscles in the face, arm and legs. Humor also relieves boredom, tension, guilt, depression, headaches and backaches. A recently developed hypothesis is that laughter stimulates the brain to produce hormones called catecholamines, such as epinephrine, norepinephrine and dopamine.

These hormones may *then* trigger the release of endorphin and enkephaline which work as natural opiates that can reduce pain or discomfort from arthritis, for example, or chronic allergy. They can also block physical pain and possibly also psychological stress.

He had the face of a man born to lead a lost cause, with the additional sorrow that it would ostensibly triumph.

If your life bores you, risk it.

You have no idea how the likes of us feel when we hear the tread of the giant behind us. Brahms of Beethoven

☺ Don't be too Smart

A man went into a drugstore and asked for a stamp. The druggest said, "You didn't see a sign that said 'Post Office' did you?" The man said, "No I didn't see a sign that says 'Barn' either but I see they have a jackass in here."

Never put off until tomorrow what you can avoid altogether.

☺ Dangers of Debate

A man stood on the edge of a bridge ready to jump and end it all. A passer by persuaded him to go first for a walk with him and talk things over. Surely, things couldn't be so bad. If after the walk and talk he still wanted to jump, the promise was that he would not be prevented from doing so. After an hour of walking and talking, the two men came back to the bridge and both jumped.

Plagiarism saves time.

☺ Misunderstood Question

A major problem with exams is that the person taking one may misunderstand the question. In my town, when I was a little boy, one Sunday the preacher asked that everyone in the congregation who wanted to go to heaven should stand up. Everyone stood up, except one man. "You sir," the preacher demanded, "Do you mean to say that you don't want to go to heaven when you die? "

"Oh," said the man. "When I die, yes. I thought you were getting up a load for right now."

Eagles may soar, but weasels don't get sucked into jet engines.

☺ Wrong Medicine

A man with a bad cough consulted his doctor for a remedy. The doctor prescribed some medicine, but by mistake wrote the prescription for laxative. The man took the medicine and called back complaining that the cough was no better. So the doctor said that he would ask the pharmacist to double the dosage. The man was back on the phone complaining that his cold was still very bad. So again, the doctor increased the dosage. Finally, seeing no improvement, the doctor asked the man to go into the office. "How are you doing?" asked the doctor. "I am not doing well, doctor," said the man. "Are you still coughing?" asked the doctor. "I wouldn't dare," replied the man.

The beatings will continue until morale improves.

In theory, there is no difference between theory and practice, but in practice, there is.

A perfectionist is one who takes great pains and gives them to other people.

☺ The Bare Facts

A nude man on the street was picked up by the New York Police. They said, "How come you are in this condition?" He replied, "I was at this party on Long Island and we all got to drinking. Then someone suggested that we all take off our clothes. We did that and then suddenly the lights went out and I heard someone say, "O.K. everybody, let's go to town -- and I guess I am the first one to arrive."

Never underestimate the power of very stupid people in large groups.

What is the Age of Pericles?
I reckon he was about forty.

☺ Forward or Aft?

An elephant wandered away from a circus one night and the next morning being hungry, decided to have a quick snack from a backyard vegetable garden. The woman who owned the garden was horrified by the situation and called the police. "Officer," she implored, "Come quickly. There's a great gray beast in my garden, pulling up my cabbages with its tail." The desk sergeant, suspecting a hoax, snarled, "Yeah, lady, and then what's it doin' with 'em"? "W-well," stammered the woman, "If I told you, you wouldn't believe me."

Artificial Intelligence is no match for Natural Stupidity.

☺ The Philosopher

A man from a country with deep-rooted religious culture had a fiancée picked for him without seeing her. The day came when he was to visit her family and be with her. He was shy and scared and asked his father what to say. His father said that there were three subjects he could discuss: Food, the family of the two and philosophy. He said, "Food you can talk about easily because you would have eaten before you go into the parlor and so you will have no problem. As for the families, you can talk about the number of each and their individual members. For philosophy, you have the whole day to talk about it."

So when he went visiting, they ate spaghetti and after dinner the couple went into the parlor while the man continued to mumble to himself, "food, family, philosophy; food, family, philosophy."

Starting conversation, he said, "Do you like spaghetti?" Abruptly and with disdain she said, "No!" So much for food he thought. Now to family. "Do you have a brother?" he said. With equal vehemence she said, "No!" "That is that," he said to himself. Finally, to philosophy; he asked, "If you had a brother, do you think he would like spaghetti?"

Jane:
If you think the house needs cleaning, let's move to another tree.
Tarzan

A man brought a grandfather clock into the shop of a watchmaker. "Vat zeems to be ze trouble?" the watchmaker asked. "The clock only says tick-tick-tick," the man said. "It used to say tick-tock-tick-tock."

"Ah, yez," the watchmaker said. "Ve'll fix zat. Ve have vays to make it tock."

TEAMWORK ... means never having to take all the blame yourself.

He is a zero with the rim knocked off.

What is the chief cause of divorce?
Marriage.

☺ Sign Language?

A Swiss guy, looking for directions, pulls up at a bus stop where two Englishmen are waiting.

"Enschuldigung, koennen Sie Deutsch sprechen?" he says. The two Englishmen just stare at him,

"Excusez-moi, parlez vous Francais?" The two continue to stare.

"Palate Italiano?" No response.

"Hablan ustedes Espanol?" Still nothing.

The Swiss guy drives off, extremely disgusted.

The first Englishman turns to the second and says, "Y'know, maybe we should learn a foreign language."

"Why?" says the other, "That bloke knew four languages, and it didn't do him any good."

No one should be allowed to play the violin until he has mastered it.
–Jim Fiebig

☺ Advice

While attempting to change a flat tire in front of an insane asylum, a man put the lug nuts in the hubcap that rested on the road. Another car went by and spattered the screws into the woods so the man could not find them. A man standing behind the fence of the asylum motioned him to come near. He then told him to take a screw from each of the other wheels and use it to hold the tire replacing the flat. The man said to his advisor, "How come a knowledgeable man like you is in such a place?" The man behind the fence said "I may be crazy but I am not stupid!"

☺ Disarming Truth

The defense attorney was vigorously cross-examining the coroner, "and before you signed the death certificate, had you taken the man's pulse?" "No," responded the coroner. "Well, did you listen for a heartbeat?" the attorney asked. "No, sir." "Did you check for breathing?" "No." "So when you signed the death certificate, you had not taken any steps to make sure the man was really dead, had you?" persisted the lawyer. The coroner, by now very tired of the browbeating, turned to the jury and said, "Well, sir, let me put it this way: the man's brain was sitting in a jar on my desk, but for all I know he could have been out there practicing law somewhere."

Rome did not create a great empire by having meetings, they did it by killing all those who opposed them.

☺ How It Really Was

Where was the Declaration of Independence signed?
At the bottom.

Where were the kings of England crowned?
On their heads

What is the difference between the constitution of the year three and the constitution of the year eight?
Five years.

The Queen of England has little political power. In fact she is just the blockhead of the government.

☺ The Helpful Companion

A man sees flashing red and blue lights in his rear view mirror, and is pulled over by a police officer.

The man says: "What's the problem officer?"

Officer: "You were going 75 miles an hour in a 55 mile an hour zone."

Man: "No sir, I was going 65."

Wife: "Oh, Harry. You were going 80." [Man gives wife a dirty look.]

Officer: "I'm also going to give you a ticket for that broken taillight."

Man: "Broken taillight? I didn't know about a broken taillight!"

Wife: "Oh, Harry, you've known about that taillight for weeks."
[Man gives his wife another dirty look.]

Officer: "I'm also going to give you a citation for not wearing your seatbelt."

Man: "Oh, I just took it off when you were walking up to the car."

Wife: "Oh, Harry, you never wear your seat belt!"

Man turns to his wife and yells: "Shut your damn mouth!"

Officer turns to the woman and asks, "Ma'am, does your husband always talk this way to you?"

Wife says: "No, only when he's drunk."

Sign in a Zurich hotel:
    "Because of the impropriety of entertaining guests of the opposite sex in the bedroom, it is suggested that the lobby be used for this purpose."

Algebra was the wife of Euclid.

Jones' Motto:
Friends come and go, but enemies accumulate.

☺ Of Age and Experience

There is the story of a young bull and an old bull grazing on a hill overlooking a herd of cows grazing below. The young bull turns to the old bull and says "Let's run down and take care of some of them." The old bull said, "No hurry young bull, let us walk down and take care of all of them."

The complex conjugate of a complex number is very complex.

The different kinds of senses are common sense and nonsense.

☺ Slow to Catch On

"What is your name?" the man asked. "Brown without a 't'," said the boy. "What was that you said?" "Brown without a 't'." "But Brown doesn't have a 't'," said the man. "Yes, I said so twice," said the boy.

☺ Job Application

Dear Sirs:

Am a knitting technician capable of supervising department, train men, write orders, set up machines. Complete responsibility of knitting departments. Machines: Al 10 - TJ 1 - LHDS - LH Ta Tal. Your ad asks for a ROF man. I set up Supreme Machines 20 years ago with wheels. Have been told that is it.

Am 55 years of age, seeking $30,000 per year. Can arrange your position if you pay my weekly expense of room and board plus salary. Can commute home on weekends. Five day week.

Yours truly,

John J. Doe

Boss's Reply

Dear Mr. Doe:
In answer to your letter addressed to the Knitting Times' for a Knitter-Mechanic, this is to inform you that you do not have anywhere near the experience required for the job in question.

In regard to your letter, I would be curious to know if you would also like your employer to pay your withholding tax and cover you up at night, so that you don't catch cold.

When you find a position like the one you described in your letter, please let me know, as I would also be interested in something like that. I would even give up my own business for it.

Yours truly,

XXX

Wyatt:
OK - I'll meet you at the O.K. Corral at 3:00.
Doc

Why is psychoanalysis a lot quicker for men than for women?
When it's time to go back to his childhood, he's already there.

☺ Watch It

A proper Boston lady heard two telephone repairmen working near her house use what she considered improper language. She wrote the telephone company about it and the manager asked the foreman to make a report.

The foreman wrote "Me and Spike Williams were on this job. I was up the pole and accidentally let the hot lead fall on Spike and it went down his neck. Then Spike looked up at me and said, 'Really, Harry, you must be more careful. '"

The nobles had the privilege of extinction from taxation.

A merry heart doeth good like medicine.
Proverbs 17:22

☺ Soap Box Logic

A soap box speaker at Hyde Park Corner in London was always in the habit of telling his audience that when the revolution comes, "We will all have strawberries mit cream." He emphasized that as a right and a consequence of the coming revolution. One day the speaker felt a tugging at his pants which

he at first ignored. But it went on, interrupting his speech. He finally looked down and there was a little kid pulling at his pants. He said to the boy, "Go away young boy, don't you see I am busy talking?"

But the boy continued the tugging. Finally, the man said, "What is it you want little boy?"

The boy said, shaking his head from side to side, "But ... but ... I don't like strawberries with cream!"

The speaker, pointing a finger at him, said sternly, to make his point, "Little boy, when the revolution comes, you will like strawberries mit cream."

Go the extra mile. It makes your boss look like an incompetent slacker.

☺ A Joint Venture

While wandering near the fence of a farm not very far from its coop, a hen came upon a very bored looking pig lying in its mud bath. The hen started up a conversation. "Hey, Piggy," she said, "why don't we go into a business venture together?"

The pig, sallowing deeper in his mud said, "What would we do, Henny?"

Henny said, "We could sell ham and eggs."

"My dear," said the pig, "For you it is only a daily effort, but for me it is a total commitment."

We waste time, so you don't have to.

☺ Pythagoras Revisited

Three Indian squaws were admitted to a Phoenix maternity ward at the same time. Chief Wampum, head obstetrician, assigned one to a buffalo hide, the second to an elk hide and the third to a hippopotamus hide. At any rate, the squaws on the elk and buffalo hides each produced a six-pound son. But the squaw on the hippopotamus hide mothered healthy six-pound twins. All of which proves, of course, that the sons of the squaw of the hippopotamus equal the sons of the squaws of the other two hides.

Abraham:
Boy! Have I got a surprise for you!
Sarah

☺ The Donkey's Choice

A man speaking about the advantages of prohibition came to the high point of his lecture where he asked the audience, "Now, suppose you had a pail of water and a pail of beer and offered them to a donkey. Which would he take? "

They replied in unison, "the water."

"Why does he take the water," asked the lecturer.

"Because he is an ass," came a voice from the gallery.

Doing a job RIGHT the first time gets the job done. Doing the job WRONG fourteen times gives you job security.

Two robbers were robbing a hotel. The first one said, "I hear sirens. Jump!" The 2nd one said, "But we're on the 13th floor!" The first one screamed back, "This is no time to be superstitious."

All you need in this life is ignorance and confidence, and then success is sure.
–Mark Twain

Succeed in spite of management.

☺ A Dentist's Epitaph

This dentist is filling his last cavity.

When you breathe you inspire. When you do not breathe you expire.

Why did God create man before woman? Because you're always supposed to have a rough draft before creating a masterpiece.

INDECISION is the key to FLEXIBILITY.

☺ George's Memory

A man, on meeting another in the street, "Hey George, what have you done to your hair? You have dyed your hair. And look at that, you are also wearing glasses. What has happened to you with all these changes?"

The man replied, "I am not George."

"What? And you have changed your name too?"

A census taker is a man who goes from house to house increasing the population.

A zoo visitor who was pleased at seeing a lamb and a lion sharing a pen praised the zookeeper for fulfilling the biblical prophecy that these natural enemies would one day live peacefully side by side. "But sir," replied the attendant, "We put in a new lamb every day."

☺ **Chinese in Action**

A professor once told his class that the Chinese multiplied so fast that if they marched over a cliff in a column of four abreast at two rows per second, the line would never be emptied. A student objected, "But how can they multiply while they march, sir?"

A snooze button is a poor substitute for no alarm clock at all.

☺ **Philosophy or Common Sense?**

Sherlock Holmes and Dr Watson went on a camping trip. After a good meal and a bottle of wine they lay down for the night, and went to sleep.

Some hours later, Holmes awoke and nudged his faithful friend. "Watson, look up at the sky and tell me what you see."

Watson replied, "I see millions and millions of stars."

"What does that tell you?"

Watson pondered for a minute. "Astronomically, it tells me that there are millions of galaxies and potentially billions of planets. Astrologically, I observe that Saturn is in Leo. Horologically, I deduce that the time is approximately a quarter past three. Theologically, I can see that God is all-powerful and that we are small and insignificant. Meteorologically, I suspect that we will have a beautiful day tomorrow."

"What does it tell you?"

Holmes was silent for a minute, then spoke. "Watson, you bonehead. Someone has stolen our tent."

☺ **Why God Never Received Tenure at the University**

1. Because He had only one major publication;

2. It was in Hebrew;

3. It had no references;

4. It wasn't published in a refereed journal;

5. Some even doubt He wrote it Himself;

6. It may be true that He created the world, but what has He Published or done since?

7. His cooperative efforts have been quite limited;

8. The scientific community has had a very rough time trying to repeat His results;

9. He has not been showing up to teach His classes;

10. His students are not doing well using His text;

11. His work has too many cliches;

12. Surely something as old as that must be out of date.

If you can stay calm, while all around you is chaos…then you probably haven't completely understood the seriousness of the situation.

You can't can can if your shoes are too loose

☺ **Umbalo-gong**
Two anthropologists fly to the South Sea Islands to study the natives. They go to two adjacent islands and set to work. A few months later one of them takes a canoe over to the other island to see how his colleague is doing. When he gets there, he finds the other anthropologist standing among a group of natives. "Greetings! How is it going?" says the visiting anthropologist. "Wonderful" says the other, "I have discovered an important fact about the local language! Watch!". He points at a palm tree and says "what is that?". The natives, in unison, say "Umbalo-gong". He then points at a rock and says "and that?". The natives again intone "Umbalo-gong!". "You see!" says the beaming anthropologist." They use the SAME word for 'rock' and for 'palm tree'!" "That is truly amazing!" says the astonished visiting anthropologist, "On the other island, the same word means 'index finger'!"

Hang in there, retirement is only thirty years away!

At a communist party meeting after much heated debate and objections one asked the speaker, "Do you have an opinion of your own?"

The speaker said, "Yes, but I don't agree with it."

Aim Low, Reach Your Goals, Avoid Disappointment.

☺ **Manãna**
A Spanish speaking student of the Russian language went to her professor and asked him, "Professor, do you have in Russian any equivalent of our Spanish word manãna?" After a brief reflection, the professor said to her, "Why yes, in Russian we have 27 equivalents for manãna, but none of them conveys the same sense of urgency!"

Living is a fatal disease.
        –Richard Chadwick

A woman tells her husband, "You are so stupid that even if there were competitions of the world's most stupid people, you are so stupid that you could not win the first place but only second."

Life is the worst sexually transmitted disease. It is always terminal.

☺ **An Act of Courtesy**

The other day I saw an old man walk up to a boy standing by a street corner and ask him: "Y..y..young m..man, c..c..could y..you t..t..t..tell m..me where t..to catch the bus?" The young man did not reply. So the old man with a red face asked again: "S..s..say y..y..young man, I a..am in a h..hurry. p..p.. please t..t..tell me."

The young man still did not answer and the old man walked away looking mad. So I walked up to the young man and said, "Why didn't you tell him? You could see he needed to know."

He said: "D..d..d..do y..y..you th..think I wa..wa..want him t..t.. to hit m..me?"

When the going gets tough, the tough take a coffee break.

What is the difference between a bald man, a man with no son, and an orphaned monkey? The bald man has no apparent hair, the man with no son has no heir apparent and the orphaned monkey has no hairy parent.

☺ Heed Your Wife, Save Your Life

The mayor of a town in China was afraid of his wife. Someone said to him, "Mayor, how can you, a powerful man, be afraid of your wife?" The mayor replied, "Everybody is afraid of their wife and I'll prove it to you." So he gathered all the married men young and old in a large meeting hall. He said, "Those of you who are afraid of their wife go stand by the wall." They all did except for one fellow who remained seated. The mayor went to him and congratulated him and said, "Why didn't you go stand with the others. I always suspected there was one brave man who is not afraid of his wife." The man said, "My wife told me not to stand where there is a crowd!"

A certain preacher had a habit of constantly using the rhetorical question, "Why are we here?" in his sermons. Another preacher advised him to stop using it since his congregation had grown very tired of it. The preacher agreed, until one day he was called to conduct a service at the state hospital. Since these people had never heard his sermons, he decided to return to his old standby.

When they gathered in the chapel at the state hospital, he paced up and down the aisles asking, "Why are we here? Why ARE we here?" Suddenly, a little lady stands up and says, "I know, I know, we are here because we are not there!"

To a lay person: 1 is a prime, 2 is a prime, 3 is a prime, ... all numbers are prime.

To an engineer, 1 is a prime, 3 is a prime, 5 is a prime, 7 is a prime ... all odd numbers are prime.

To a physicist, 1 is a prime, 3 is a prime, 5 is a prime, 7 is a prime, 9 is not a prime (it must be an experimental error), 11 is a prime, 13 is a prime.

Leif:
Check out the countryside first to see how close you are to the edge before you make ANY deals.
Erik

An axiom is a thing that is so visible it is not necessary to see it.

☺ The Substitute

A famous physicist was chauffeured around to give talks. After a few tens of times his chauffeur said, "I can give this talk as good as you." So he let him. When the question period came, the chauffeur was asked a question to which he answered, "That is a silly question. Even my chauffeur can answer that."

Eccentricity is a symptom of genius.

☺ Power of Repetition

The English teacher was trying to encourage her pupils to increase their vocabularies. "If you will repeat a word 18 times, it will become yours forever," she said.

Immediately, a pretty girl in the back row began to say!, "George, George, George,....."

If you lose say nothing. If you win say less.

Charlie Smith, the former slave who died at the reported age of 138, once had been asked his secret. "I smoked, I drank, I chased women," he confessed. "If I'd known I was going to live so long, I'd have taken better care of myself."

A person who smiles in the face of adversity ... probably has a scapegoat.

In Germany, when a new baby is born, the custom it to kiss it on the forehead for a great thinker, kiss the eyes for a great sea captain, and kiss the lips for a great speaker. At a recent dinner, the speaker, after having been introduced by the toastmaster, turned to him and told the above story after which he added, "I don't know where they kissed you, but you certainly make a good chairman."

A father sent $10 in a letter to his son in college and wrote, "Enclosed is $10 as you requested in your letter. Incidentally, ten dollars is written with one zero, not two."

Secretary of State:
Buy it! Napoleon needs the cash and will sell cheap. And think of the killing we can make on riverfront lots.
Jefferson

~~Catherine Anne Jane Anne Catherine~~
Katharine:
At last–my one true love, my darling wife.
Forever Yours,
Henry

By all means marry. If you get a good wife, you'll be happy. If you get a bad one, you'll become a philosopher ... and that is a good thing for any man.
–*Socrates*

To see if a limb is broken, wiggle it gently back and forth.

☺ Hard Decisions

A man with a toothache sees a dentist's sign:
Tooth Extractions
With Pain ………………………………….$10
Painless …………………………………..$5

He's in great pain, so he goes in to check if the sign is correct. "Yes, yes," says the dentist. So the ailing man sits down. The dentist prepared the instruments, and got a grip on the tooth. As he started to pull, the man reminded him, "Remember–painless." "Okay," said the dentist as he began to really pull on the tooth. The man began to whimper, "Ouch, Ouch!" "Watch it," said the dentist, "if you start screaming it will cost you $10!"

A 12 year old taking the famous eleven Plus examination in Britain answered the question, "When you take 8 from 93 as many times as possible, what do you get?" I get 85 every time".

Prometheus:
Could we talk about getting an endorsement from you.
Bic Lighters

☺ **Brace Yourself for This One**

Recently a guy in Paris nearly got away with stealing several paintings from the Louvre. However, after planning the crime, getting in and out past security, he was captured only 2 blocks away when his van ran out of gas. When asked how he could mastermind such a crime and then make such an *obvious* error, he replied, I had no Monet to *buy* Degas to make the Van Gogh."

Orville:
I checked. They don't make elastic bands that big.
Wilbur

☺ **The World According to Student Bloopers**

One of the fringe benefits of being an English or History teacher is receiving the occasional jewel of a student blooper in an essay. I have pasted together the following "history" of the world from certifiably genuine student bloopers collected by teachers throughout the United States, from eighth grade through college level. Read carefully, and you will learn a lot.

The inhabitants of Egypt were called mummies. They lived in the Sarah Dessert and traveled by Camelot. The climate of the Sarah is such that the inhabitants have to live elsewhere, so certain areas of the dessert are cultivated by irritation. The Egyptians built the Pyramids in the shape of a huge triangular cube. The Pyramids are a range of mountains between France and Spain.

The Bible is full of interesting caricatures. In the first book of the Bible, Guinesses, Adam and Eve were created from an apple tree. One of their children, Cain, asked: "Am I my brother's son?" God asked Abraham to sacrifice Isaac on Mount Montezuma. Jacob, son of Isaac, stole his brother's birthmark. Jacob was a patriarch who brought up his twelve sons to be patriarchs, but they did not take to it. One of Jacob's sons, Joseph, gave refuse to the Israelites.

Abraham Lincoln became America's greatest Precedent. Lincoln's mother died in infancy, and he was born in a log cabin, which he built with his own hands. When Lincoln was President, he wore only a tall silk hat. He said, "in onion there is strength." Abraham Lincoln wrote the Gettysburg address while traveling from Washington to Gettysburg on the back of an envelope. He also signed the Emasculation Proclamation, and the Fourteenth Amendment, which gave the Ex-Negroes citizenship. But the Clue Clux Clan would torture and lynch the ex-Negroes and other innocent victims. On the night of April 4, 1865, Lincoln went to the theater and got shot in his seat by one of the actors in a moving picture show. The believed assassin was John Wilkes Booth, a supposedly insane actor. This ruined Booth's career.

Bach was the most famous composer in the world, and so was Handel. Handel was half-German, half-Italian, and half-English. He was very large. Back died from 1750 to the present. Beethoven wrote music even though he was deaf. He was deaf so he wrote loud music. He took long walks in the forest even when everyone was calling for him. Beethoven expired in 1827 and later died for this. France was in a very serious state. The French Revolution was accomplished before it happened. The Marseillaise was the theme song of the French Revolution, and it catapulted into Napoleon. During the Napoleonic Wars, the crowned heads of Europe were trembling in their shoes. Then the Spanish gorillas came down from the hills and nipped at Napoleon's flanks. Napoleon became ill with bladder problems and was very tense and unrestrained. He wanted an heir to inherit his power, but since Josephine was a baroness, she couldn't bear him any children.

The sun never sets on the British Empire because the British Empire is in the East and the sun sets in the West. Queen Victoria was the longest queen. She sat on a thorn for 63 years. The reclining years and finally the end of her life were exemplary of a great personality. Her death was the final event that ended her reign.

–Richard Lederer
St. Paul's School

The greatest thrill to a musician is to handle the handle that Handle handled.

☺ **The Magician and the Parrot**

A magician was working on a cruise ship in the Caribbean. The audience would be different each week, so the magician allowed himself to do the same tricks over and over again. There was only one problem: The captain's parrot saw the shows each week and began to understand how the magician did every trick. Once he understood he started shouting in the middle of the show:

"Look, it's not the same hat."

"Look, he is hiding the flowers under the table"

"Hey, why are all the cards the Ace of Spades?"

The magician was furious but couldn't do anything; it was, after all, the captain's parrot. One day the ship had an accident and sank. The magician found himself on a piece of wood in the middle of the ocean with the parrot, of course. They stared at each other with hate, but did not utter a word. This went on for one day then another and another. After a week the parrot said: "OK, I give up. Where's the boat?"

If it is a man you want, you've got to get a man like a man gets got.

The secret of success in politics is sincerity. Once you have been able to fake it, the rest is easy.

Why are most Italian males called Tony? Because when they shipped them to New York, they wrote TO N.Y. on their foreheads.

Humile = Humble + Servile

"Our wines leave you nothing to hope for."
–Menu of a Swiss restaurant

☺ **Airline Advertisement**

Fly with us and you will never walk again.

We eat what we can and we can what we can't.

One cliché is worth a thousand dissertations.

☺ **Runaway Situation**

An oil company was struck with a disaster as one of its largest oil wells caught fire. They quickly consulted one fire extinguishing company, but it turned out they wanted eight million dollars to put out the fire, and that was too much. In looking around, they came by the name of a certain Mr. Guilini who asked for a million dollars and he was given the job. The next morning a truck was seen to be running towards the fire at very high speed and with great noise it plunged into the fire. Twenty men jumped out coughing, jerking their heads, and stomping out of the heat and the fire was gone.

Mr. Guilini was given a check for a million dollars. Someone asked him what he was going to spend it on. He said, "I don't know, but first I have to fix the brakes on the damn truck."

☺ **Disaster Strikes Again**

A fellow without a job knocks on a door looking to do odds and ends. The owner said, "Yes we have something for you to do. We have a porch in the back yard that needs painting, but it might take you a while because it is rather large." The man went to work on it

In a half-hour he was back saying he was finished. "Finished already," the owner said. "That is impossible. "

"Yes I am finished; I even gave it a second coat. But one thing, it wasn't a Porsche, it was a Ferrari."

In her school essay on "Parents," a girl wrote: "We get our parents at so late an age that it is impossible to change their habits."

☺ **Which One Are You?**

There are three categories of people in this world, those who know how to count and those who don't.

☺ **Great Scientific Discovery**

Not all chemicals are bad. Without hydrogen and oxygen, for example, there would be no way to make water, a vital ingredient in beer.

☺ **Ha**

If it were necessary to tolerate in other people everything one permits in oneself, life would be unbearable.

☺ **Short Quiz**
The following short quiz consists of 4 questions and tells whether you are truly a "professional".

1. How do you put a giraffe into a refrigerator?

The correct answer: Open the refrigerator, put in the giraffe and close the door. This question tests whether you tend to do simple things in an overly complicated way.

2. How do you put an elephant into a refrigerator?

Wrong Answer: Open the refrigerator, put in the elephant and close the refrigerator. Correct Answer: Open the refrigerator, take out the giraffe, put in the elephant and close the door. This tests your ability to think through the repercussions of your actions.

3. The Lion King is hosting an animal conference, all the animals attend except one. Which animal does not attend?

Correct Answer: The Elephant. The Elephant is in the refrigerator. This tests your memory.

OK, even if you did not answer the first three questions, correctly, you still have one more chance to show your abilities.

4. There is a river you must cross, but it is inhabited by crocodiles. How do you manage?

Correct Answer: You swim across. All the Crocodiles are attending the Animal Meeting! This tests whether you learn quickly from your mistakes.

According to Andersen Consulting Worldwide, around 90% of the professionals they tested got all questions wrong. But many preschoolers got several correct answers. Anderson Consulting says this conclusively disproves the theory that most professionals have the brains of a four-year old.

☺ **Unlimited Imagination**

Sir Ernest Rutherford, President of the Royal Academy, and recipient of the Nobel Prize in Physics, related the following story:

Some time ago I received a call from a colleague. He was about to give a student a zero for his answer to a physics question, while the student claimed a perfect score. The instructor and the student agreed to an impartial arbiter, and I was selected. I read the examination question: "Show how it is possible to determine the height of a tall building with the aid of a barometer." The student had answered: "Take the barometer to the top of the building, attach a long rope to it, lower it to the street, and then bring it up, measuring the length of the rope. The length of the rope is the height of the building."

The student really had a strong case for full credit since he had really answered the question completely and correctly! On the other hand, if full credit were given, it could well contribute to a high grade in his physics course and certify competence in physics, but the answer did not confirm this.

I suggested that the student have another try. I gave the student six minutes to answer the question with the warning that the answer should show some knowledge of physics. At the end of five minutes, he hadn't written anything. I asked if he wished to give up, but he said he had many answers to this problem; he was just thinking of the best one. I excused myself for interrupting him and asked him to please go on. In the next minute, he dashed off his answer, which read: "Take the barometer to the top of the building and lean over the edge of the roof. Drop the barometer, timing its fall with a stopwatch. Then, using the formula $x=0.5at^2$, calculate the height of the building." At this point, I asked my colleague if he would give up. He conceded, and gave the student full credit.

While leaving my colleague's office, I recalled that the student had said that he had other answers to the problem, so I asked him what they were. "Well," said the student, "there are many ways of getting the height of a tall building with the aid of a barometer. For example, you could take the barometer out on a sunny day and measure the height of the barometer, the length of its shadow, and the length of the shadow of the building, and by the use of simple proportion, determine the height of the building." "Fine," I said, "and others?"

"Yes," said the student, "there is a very basic measurement method you will like. In this method, you take the barometer and begin to walk up the stairs. As you climb the stairs, you mark off the length of the barometer along the wall. You then count the number of marks, and this will give you the height of the building in barometer units. A very direct method."

"Of course. If you want a more sophisticated method, you can tie the barometer to the end of a string, swing it as a pendulum, and determine the value of g [gravity] at the street level and at the top of the building. From the difference between the two values of g, the height of the building, in principle, can be calculated."

"On this same tack, you could take the barometer to the top of the building, attach a long rope to it, lower it to just above the street, and then swing it as a pendulum. You could then calculate the height of the building by the period of the precession".

"Finally," he concluded, "there are many other ways of solving the problem. Probably the best," he said, "is to take the barometer to the basement and knock on the superintendent's door. When the superintendent answers, you speak to him as follows: 'Mr. Superintendent, here is a fine barometer. If you will tell me the height of the building, I will give you this barometer.'"

At this point, I asked the student if he really did not know the conventional answer to this question. He admitted that he did, but said that he was fed up with high school and college instructors trying to teach him how to think.

The name of the student was Niels Bohr." (1885-1962), Danish Physicist; Nobel Prize 1922; best known for proposing the first 'model' of the atom with protons & neutrons, and various energy state of the surrounding electrons – the familiar icon of the small nucleus encircled by three elliptical orbits – but more significantly, he was an innovator in Quantum theory.

"We take your bags and send them in all directions."
    –Copenhagen airline ticket office sign

☺ **After all, it is all Relative**

Einstein was riding on a train to Kiev. An old man sitting next to him asked him where he was going. Einstein replied that he was going to Kiev to lecture on his theory of relativity. The old man asked, "What is that?" Einstein, trying to come up with a simple explanation said, "Well, for example, two hairs on a head are too few; two hairs in the soup are too many. That is relativity." The old man looked at him, underwhelmed, and said, "and with THAT you're going on a lecture?"

I would propose the following statements as descriptive of creative artists, and perhaps also of creative scientists:

Creative people are especially observant, and they value accurate observation (telling themselves the truth) more than other people do.

They often express part-truths, but this they do vividly; the part they express is the generally unrecognized; by displacement of accent and apparent disproportion in statement they seek to point to the usually unobserved.

They see things as others do, but also as others do not.

They are thus independent in their cognition, and they also value clearer cognition. They will suffer great personal pain to testify correctly.

They are motivated to this value and to the exercise of this talent (independent, sharp observation) both for reasons of self-preservation and in the interest of human culture and its future.

They are born with greater brain capacity; they have more ability to hold many ideas at once, and to compare more ideas with one another-hence to make a richer synthesis.

In addition to unusual endowment in terms of cognitive ability, they are by constitution more vigorous and have available to them an exceptional fund of psychic and physical energy.

Their universe is thus more complex, and in addition usually lead more complex lives, seeking tension in the interest of the pleasure they obtain upon its discharge.

They have more contact than most people do with the life of the unconscious, with fantasy, reverie, the world of imagination.

They have exceptionally broad and flexible awareness of themselves. The self is strongest when it can regress (adding primitive fantasies, naive ideas, tabooed impulses into consciousness and behavior), and yet return to a high degree of rationality and self-criticism. The creative person is both more primitive and more cultured, more destructive and more constructive, crazier and saner, than the average person.

Frank Barron, Scientific American, Sept. 1958

Examples of Creativity and Creative People

Chapter Three

Introduction

An invention is a purposeful, new, largely original or novel way of making or doing something trivial or serious. The outcome itself may or may not be new. Some inventions are quick solutions to problems whereas others may evolve over a long period of time. Some inventions are a direct response to a problem that needs a solution, frequently discovered through accidental thinking and experience --such as learning to fasten clothes with pins, then with tied strings, then with buttons, hooks, eyes, and finally with zippers. Other inventions are a byproduct of discovery and extensive research, such as all the electric devices and appliances ranging from motors to dynamos, x-ray machines, radio, television and so on, that were developed after the discovery of electricity and electric fields.

In contrast with invention, which is mostly technological, discovery is concerned with the growth of knowledge, and usually has no clear purpose. It is concerned with exploring things and determining how to view them in light of new knowledge and understanding. The outcome of discovery is not as predictable as that of an invention. Discovery doesn't necessarily lead to invention, nor should it. If an invention occurs, it may be a long time after a discovery was made. Invention can occur without discovery, as happened in all the years before our age of science. In our time the two are frequently simultaneous because of organized research to understand and solve problems. In the 20th century, both invention and discovery were less of an individual act and became a concern of governments and industrial organizations with their directed research.

In his book, The History of Invention, (Facts on File, 1987), Trevor Williams postulates that the day of the versatile, individual inventor -- the Leonardo DaVinci, James Watt, Benjamin Franklin, Eli Whitney, or Thomas Edison -- is largely over. "The future lies mainly with men not only highly trained but perceptive of the needs of the day, working within teams in large organizations, whether private or national," he writes, adding that therein lies a paradox. Does the existence of an invention lead to uses being found for it, or is an invention created in response to a need?

George de Mestral, the inventor of Velcro, was quoted as saying that an inventor "is simply a madman who has a transcendent idea – a spark of light."

Usually an inventor's passion and patient effort, with frequently failed experiments over an extended period, drive him to the solution he is after. The solution frequently appears as a sudden inspiration but is more likely to be a recollection of something similar already in the memory of the hard working, very knowledgeable and dedicated inventor.

Motivations of inventors are diverse. People who invent things are driven by money or curiosity or by the desire to have something to make their everyday lives easier. The following lists of inventive people and their inventions, past and present, demonstrates how and why people are inspired to experiment with and create new things and ideas.

Inventions

Ballpoint Pen

Brothers Ladislo and Greg Biro (Ladislo was a journalist fed up with refilling fountain pens and correcting splotches) developed the ballpoint pen in 1938. Although they called the pen a ballpoint, some countries still refer to it as a Biro.

Band-Aids

Earle Dickson, an employee of Johnson & Johnson, came up with the Band-Aid for his wife. She frequently suffered cuts and burns in the kitchen, and he made her a supply of gauze squares stuck to tape, covering the tape carefully with crinoline to stop the glue from drying out.

Dog Biscuit

Bakery owner F.H. Bennett made this novelty item from meat products, milk, and minerals in 1908. When the National Biscuit Company bought Bennett out in 1931, the soon-to-be-named "Milk Bone" was the only bakery creation it kept making.

Electric Guitar

Although there is some dispute over who invented the electric guitar first, Leo Fender gets credit for developing the first solid-body electric guitar to be mass-produced. An electronics enthusiast, Fender experimented with ways to make guitars louder, and became interested in guitar design after fixing customers' external pickups. He developed a solid body guitar with a block of wood and magnetic pick-ups connected to an amplifier. The Fender Broadcaster was produced in 1948.

Frisbee

College students in New England figured out that empty pie tins from the Frisbie Baking Co. of Bridgeport, Connecticut, could be flung and caught. In 1948, a Los Angeles building inspector William Morrison and partner Warren Franscione took the idea a step further and created a plastic version of the pie plate that would

sail farther. The pair split up, but Morrison pursued the idea and produced the plastic toy, giving it a patented, sloping edge. Owners of the Wham-O toy company bought rights to the design and named it the Frisbee in honor of the bakery.

Heart Surgery – Bypasses and Transplants

As early as 1893, African-American surgeon Daniel Hale Williams sewed up a stabbing victim's pericardium. Research by John H. Gibbon Jr. led to a 1953 operation on a heart failure patient using a machine to shunt the blood. Michael DeBakey performed the first coronary bypass operation in 1964, using transplanted leg veins to bypass clogged arteries to the heart. In 1967, Christiaan Barnard and a team of 20 surgeons completed the first heart transplant into a human, South African grocer Louis Washansky. Washansky was given immune suppressants to stop rejection of the donor organ, but he died of pneumonia 18 days later.

Insulin

For decades, medical science had searched for a treatment for diabetes – at the time a death sentence in many cases. In 1921, a team of researchers at the University of Toronto isolated insulin, a hormone in the pancreas that lets the human body digest carbohydrates, and changed the lives of many patients. Frederick Banting, Charles H. Best, J.J.R. Macleod and J.B. Collip are credited with the discovery and subsequent clinical trials. It wasn't until the 1980s that scientists discovered a method of producing human insulin, instead of using animal insulin in treatments.

The Internet

In the 1960s, the U.S. Department of Defense created the Advanced Research Projects Agency Network (ARPANET) as a means of safeguarding sensitive communications. One of ARPANET's most popular features was electronic mail. As use of ARPANET broadened, the military formed its own network, as did other federal agencies. This network of networks, or internetwork, came together in the 1980s when a common language was created for all computers. In 1991, Swiss-based CERN developed the World Wide Web.

Liquid Paper

In the early 1950s, Bette Nesmith, a single mother, encountered the electronic typewriter on a new secretarial job. To cover up her numerous mistakes, she filled an empty nail polish bottle with water-based white paint. Coworkers began asking for their own bottles, and a friend suggested she sell the product locally. Using her kitchen and garage as a laboratory and warehouse, she improved the formula and began filling hundreds of orders in her off-work hours after the substance -- which she first called "Mistake-Out" and later changed to "Liquid Paper" -- received a mention in a trade magazine. She eventually quit her day job and built on the cottage industry. Gillette paid $48 million for her company in 1979.

Nuclear Fission

In the 1930's, chemist Otto Hahn and radiochemist Fritz Strassmann focused on physicist Enrico Fermi's work with uranium. Hahn and Strassmann bombarded a piece of uranium with neutrons and then tried to figure out what happened as an outcome. They didn't know they had created the first artificial nuclear fission reaction, splitting a uranium nucleus into loose neutrons that started a chain reaction in other nuclei. A year after their experiments, in 1939, Austrian scientists Lise Meitner and Otto Frisch were able to show that the Hahn-Strassmann reaction had produced more

energy than it consumed. The scientific community then began to realize the overwhelming potential and destructiveness held by nuclear fission.

Trampoline

As a youth, George Nissen became fascinated with high-wire acts at the circus and the fun they had bouncing around on their safety nets. As a high school student in 1926, Nissen scoured the town dump for springs, rubber inner tubes and scraps of iron. He got his hands on an industrial sewing machine and turned his family's garage into a workshop. More than a dozen years later, he began traveling around the country, promoting his perfected trampoline.

Vaseline

New York chemist Robert Chesebrough began toying with a way to recycle the black gunk cleaned off of oil rigs after a visit to Titusville, Pa., in 1859. He managed to reduce it to a white jelly that he termed "Vaseline" after the German word for water (wasser) and the Greek word for olive oil (elaion). Persistent marketing and demonstrations led to its becoming a burn salve and all-purpose ointment in practically every household.

Velcro

Swiss engineer George de Mestral would never forget a two-week hunting trip he took in 1941. Picking cockleburs off his pants and off his dog, de Mestral began to wonder if the cocklebur's clinging ability could be reproduced as a fastener for fabric. He spent eight years trying, quitting his job and obtaining large loans in the process. Finally, after numerous setbacks, Velcro debuted in the early 1960s. He encouraged his company's executives to allow employees to take two-week hunting holidays.

Viagra

Viagra, the first pill to treat impotence in men, took the world by storm when the U.S. Food and Drug Administration approved it in 1998. Researchers at Pfizer Inc. had been looking for a heart disease drug that would prevent blood clots and enhance blood flow. Tests showed that their prototype had quite a different effect – penile erections. The drug, sildenafil citrate, was developed from Nobel Prize-winning research by Robert F. Furchgott, Louis J. Ignarro and Ferid Murad that showed nitric oxide – known more as an air pollutant – acts as a signaling molecule in the cardiovascular system. Nitric oxide also is released during sexual stimulation, increasing blood flow to the penis.

Virtual Reality

In the 1950s, scientists first toyed with the concept of displaying digital images on computers. Pilots began training on computerized flight simulators in the 1960s. Ivan Sutherland is credited with building the first fully functional, head-mounted 3-D display in 1970 at the Massachussets Institute of Technology. In the 1980s, NASA and the Pentagon developed computer-generated training systems. Simnet, as it is called, lets military personnel rehearse for combat in real time.

Inventors

Mary Anderson

Touring New York City on a streetcar in 1903, Alabama native Mary Anderson found inspiration watching the driver repeatedly get out of the vehicle to wipe off the windshield by hand. People teased her about the drawing she made for a swinging arm with a rubber strip that would wipe a windshield by pushing an inside lever. But a year later, she earned a patent for the windshield wiper. The device was a standard feature on automobiles by 1916.

Edwin H. Armstrong

As a teenager, Edwin Armstrong read about Guglielmo Marconi's landmark wireless transmission across the Atlantic and decided to become an inventor. He took over his family's attic, building a web of wireless apparatus. In college, he developed the feedback circuit that remains at the center of all radio and television broadcasting technology. Although he lost a court challenge over the patent, the scientific community stuck by him as its true creator. Armstrong went on to develop, fund and build the first FM (frequency modulation) radio station, which offered greater clarity by varying the frequency of radio waves over a wide band of frequencies. The industry resisted FM technology because of cost, and in 1954, faced with ill health, another patent lawsuit and financial hardship from personal investment in FM, Armstrong committed suicide.

Benjamin Banneker

Born in 1731 to a slave and his free wife, Benjamin Banneker came to be known as a mechanical genius. After seeing his first watch, Banneker spent two years handcarving a working wooden clock with a wooden mechanism. He compiled an almanac of his own research data on tides, medicines, mathematical formulas and astronomical events, and sent a copy to Thomas Jefferson. George Washington appointed him to a six-member team planning what is now Washington, D.C.

Beethoven

Ludwig van Beethoven was a composer of heroic music, whose early career was shaped by his drunken father coming home late at night and awakening the boy to play

Creative Thinking, Problem Solving and Decision Making

How to be Creative

An introduction....

How to be Creative

1. It is not having many ideas but pursuing one of the many possible ideas with persistence and imagination that is a high mark of creativity; not to be complacent and easily satisfied, but to put forth the effort and stick with it. When you get a solution, push it hard vertically, and look for other solutions laterally, until you are satisfied there are no more.

2. Get outside of the box by being willing to be childlike. It is OK to blunder. Do not be afraid to make mistakes. Use humor. Learn to have courage to risk thoughts and pursue a line of thinking that does not initially make sense.

3. Suspend judgment. Be positive, flexible, open-minded and imaginative. Later you can bring to bear your analytical talents to judge, but not in the beginning.

4. Create a SAFE environment for creativity. Reward innovation and perseverance, and not just good performance.

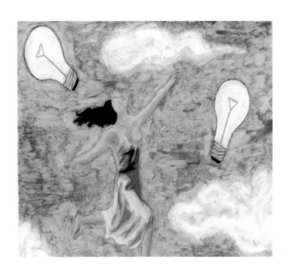

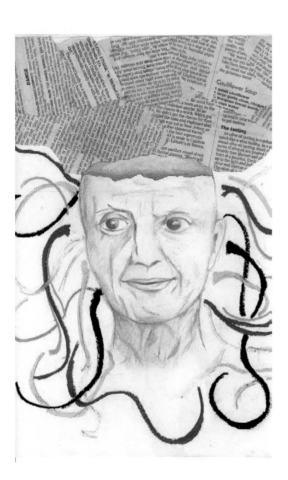

5. Get up and do it. Activate yourself to do it on the spot. Go look up a reference that might help you, or a person, or go to see and learn: NOW, not later; today, not tomorrow. Learn to trigger your leg muscles to move on demand, do not procrastinate, obey the call to explore at all costs. Einstein said that the legs are the wheels of creativity. Try to make it exciting, imaginative, inspiring and rewarding. Let your attitude and creativity be a light to brighten the world around you and even farther away.

6. Be practical, try to interpret your theme in many ways, particularly ones about the value of the idea, whether material or spiritual.

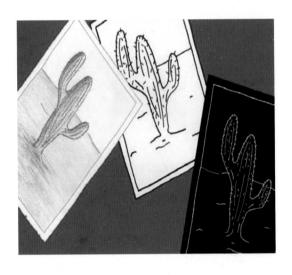

7.   After thinking, try to explain what you are after to someone else. Listen to their suggestions; they may be just what you need. Get your hands and all your physical self involved as partners in the quest for creativity.

8. Do not alienate your body from cooperating with your thoughts. Train it, reward, and humor it.

9. If at first you don't succeed, try and try again. Never give up. Creativity is 99% perspiration and 1% inspiration.

10. What is creativity for? You have to live with yourself for the rest of your life. Try to make it exciting, imaginative, inspiring and rewarding.

Try your Creativity

1. Formulate the foregoing ten suggestions in the form of the ten commandments.

2. Do the same in the form of ten exhortations.

3. Do them as ten funny jokes.

4. Do them in very precise, laconic, and terse phrases.

5. Recompose them as poetry.

6. Reshape them as sports activities.

7. Make drawings to illustrate them.

8. Write an impassioned speech to inspire people to follow them.

9. Write each of them in an opposite contradictory negative form.

10. Abbreviate them using acronyms that can still be understood.

11. Make a crossword puzzle that contains the essential ideas in them.

12. Rewrite them as a set of deductions from axioms about creativity.

13. Write a prayer that is built around them.

14. Make swear words using the ideas and language contained in them.

15. Write an epitaph for someone using some or all of them.

16. Suggest practices and ways to enhance the development and use of each of them.

17. Rewrite them so children can understand them.

18. Rewrite them in another language(s).

19. Use them in a speech to people in jail to turn their minds to creative acts.

20. Compose a musical piece with several short parts to emphasize the ideas in each.

21. Tell a Martian about them using some very basic way of communication.

22. Introduce mathematical symbols to represent and quantify them and use algebra or set theory to restate them in more precise terms.

This book differs from all other books on creativity barring none. Why? Because all books including this one advocate the creation of many new ideas, but to the best of our knowledge no other book but this one provides a rigorous and justifiable way to help one to prioritize and choose the best from all those ideas to serve a given goal or purpose. This book shows the reader by using a quantitative mathematical theory developed by this author over a 35-year period how to prioritize and choose the best ideas in a mathematically justifiable way. It also shows how to structure hierarchies with a goal and prioritize the criteria according to their importance to the goal and then the alternatives to attain the goal in terms of each of the criteria. The final step is to synthesize the different priority outcomes of the alternatives with respect to the criteria by using the priorities of the criteria to obtain the best overall alternative. This approach is being widely used in industries and governments throughout the world particularly to allocate scarce resources according to priority.

the piano for him emulating the prodigy Mozart who played the violin before princes at the age of seven. Beethoven was the first composer to include metronomic markings in his scores. He is known for using his mastery of music to methodically improve on his own ideas. Over a period of months or longer, he would repeatedly play the pieces he had put down on paper, refining them until he was completely satisfied.

George Washington Carver

A frugal bachelor all his life, George Washington Carver was born a slave in Maryland in 1864. He went to school at age 10, and later earned a bachelor's degree in agriculture and a master's degree in science in Iowa. In 1896, he took a teaching position at Tuskegee Normal and Industrial Institute in Alabama, where he developed more than 300 uses for the peanut and 100 uses for the sweet potato. Carver educated poor rural families about growing and living off those crops. He refused to patent or capitalize on most of his work: His epitaph reads, "He could have added fortune to fame, but caring for neither, he found happiness and honor in being helpful to the world."

Marion Donovan

One could argue that Marion Donovan had inventing in her blood; her father and uncle invented an industrial lathe used to make guns. Donovan's own big creation came out of her frustration with her baby daughters' leaky cloth diapers. She took a shower curtain and fashioned it into a diaper cover that snapped into place and wasn't as binding as the rubber pants most parents used. In 1947, she developed and patented an improved version of the "Boater" made of parachute cloth with an absorbent lining. Sales took off, but Donovan had to make the Boaters herself because she could not interest a manufacturer. Within a few years, though, she sold her idea for disposable diapers for $1 million. In an interview at the time, Donovan was quoted as saying she never thought of herself as an inventor, but that her "invention happened by gradual steps with necessity nudging me." Donovan's other inventions include a folding clothes hanger and the "Zippity-Do," an elasticized zipper pull that made it easy for women to zip and unzip the back of a dress.

Thomas Edison

No one has broken Thomas Edison's record of more than 1,000 patents. Not bad for someone faced with hearing loss and plenty of financial setbacks. An aggressive marketer, Edison's strong will saw him through the inventing process. It is said he tried 10,000 ways to develop the incandescent light bulb, and failed at every one. What he needed was material for an element that would have enough electric resistance to heat up and glow, yet not burn. During a nap, he remembered learning how charcoal was made – by starving burning wood of oxygen. He immediately went to the lab, placed an element between two electrodes, covered the setup with a glass jar and used a vacuum pump to extract the air from the jar. Edison continued to modify his invention.

Albert Einstein

Albert Einstein had to write an essay in secondary school to be accepted into a technical college in Switzerland. He wrote that he saw himself studying math and physics because of his "disposition for abstract and mathematical thought, and my lack of imagination and practical ability." Most would dispute Einstein's opinion of himself, in light of his discovery of the special and general theory of relativity, and a formula showing that mass and energy are equivalent.

Philo Taylor Farnsworth

Utah native Philo Taylor Farnsworth showed a keen interest in science while still in high school in the 1920s, exploring everything from the molecular theory of matter to car engines. He had to leave college early when his father died, but he landed a job at Crocker Research Laboratories in San Francisco. There, he began the experiments that led to his holding more than 300 patents. Most were television related: focusing and contrast controls and scanning. He also developed the first, basic electron microscope, black light for night vision, and two methods of using nuclear fusion for energy.

Henry Ford

Known as a tinkerer, Henry Ford didn't invent mass production techniques or the car. But he was innovative enough to adapt assembly methods of manufacturing to the automobile industry. Before his creative approach, it took 12 and half hours to make one Model T car. Afterwards, it took less than two hours.

Benjamin Franklin

A prolific inventor, Benjamin Franklin is credited with developing the Franklin Stove, the rocking chair, Daylight Savings Time, the first public library, and bifocals, which he made for himself at age 83.

Sigmund Freud

Sigmund Freud revolutionized the way people viewed their desires, motivations, and relationships with others. Born in Moravia in 1856, Freud graduated from medical school and studied in Paris under the renowned neurologist Jean-Martin Charcot, who worked with patients suffering from what was then called "hysteria." Charcot showed Freud that condition was rooted in emotional, not physical in problems. Freud began his own studies on hysteria in Vienna, laying groundwork for what would become known as "psychoanalysis." He became internationally recognized – and criticized – in 1900 when he published "The Interpretation of Dreams." The work postulates that dreams represent an individual's deepest desire. He later came up with other theories about the role of sexuality in an individual's development, and his ideas gave rise to other psychoanalytic schools of thought.

Frances Gabe

Oregon mother and businesswoman, Frances Gabe hated housework more than most. Her intense dislike of household chores prompted her to spend 40 years inventing equipment to make her home self-cleaning. By pressing a button in each room, Gabe could activate a Cleaning/Drying/Heating/Cooling unit mounted at the ceiling that would wash and dry the entire room similar to a car wash. Sloping floors carried away water, and valuables were protected under glass. Gabe also created self-dusting bookshelves, a clothes closet that also served as a washer/dryer, and self-cleaning sinks and toilets.

Charles Goodyear

Charles Goodyear spent five years experimenting with ways to make India rubber a more useful product. A Philadelphia hardware salesman, Goodyear's business had gone bankrupt and he had turned to inventing – developing an improved valve for rubber life preservers. The manufacturer told him that rubber, with its inability to stand up to extreme heat and cold, was what really needed to be improved. Goodyear had little money and limited knowledge of chemistry, but he plugged away at treatments to strengthen rubber. His breakthrough was an accident – he spilled a rubber-sulphur mixture on a hot stove. Although he patented the process, known as vulcanization, in 1844, Goodyear failed to make money from his discovery and died in debt.

Werner Heisenberg

German physicist Werner Heisenberg had been working on the Bohr-Rutherford model of the atom. A hayfever sufferer, he took a break in the spring of 1925 to the pollen-free island of Heligoland in the North Sea. After a few days, a new idea came to him and he began to feverishly work on it. He applied a mathematical system to atomic physics so he could work out problems with experimental data instead of visual models. His end result was a further development of matrix algebra and the well-known uncertainty principle in physics for which he won the Nobel Prize.

Mary Phelps Jacob

Mary Phelps Jacob had bought a sheer gown for one of her New York society soirees, and she didn't like the way the whalebones in her corset poked out past the plunging neckline and appeared through the fabric. So she tied two silk handkerchiefs together with a ribbon. Friends clamored for their own piece of lingerie, and Jacob obtained a patent in 1914 for her "backless brassiere." She sold the patent to Warner Brothers Corset Company.

Thomas Jefferson

The nation's first patent officer and third president, Thomas Jefferson earned the title "Godfather of American Invention" for his variety of ideas. He is credited with inventing the lazy Susan, dumbwaiter, folding campstool and revolving writing table, all in the interest of conserving motion. He also refined the plow, and began using it at Monticello, his Virginia estate, in 1794.

Steve Jobs and Steve Wozniak

Steve Jobs and Steve Wozniak collaborated in Jobs' garage to develop the first widely popular desktop computer, the Apple, in the 1970s. Wozniak was a college dropout who designed his first computer at age 13. The friends' first project was building illegal "blue boxes" to make free long-distance phone calls. Apple Computers quickly grew into a multimillion-dollar company, offering creative new products that took user input into account.

John F. Kennedy

"...Let the word go forth from this time and place, to friend and foe alike, that the torch has been passed to a new generation of Americans born in this century..."

In his 1961 inaugural speech, John F. Kennedy demonstrated creative leadership when he asked America's Baby-Boomers to believe in themselves and follow his example. After Russia sent the first man into orbit around the Earth, Kennedy told America the country would send a man to the moon and bring him back before the end of that decade. It happened in 1969, after Kennedy boosted NASA funding and infrastructure to achieve the goal. His success was so great, that Kennedy's vision of a moonwalk remained and was made to happen several years after he was assassinated.

Dr. Martin Luther King

Dr. Martin Luther King turned frustration and stalemate into creative opportunity when he went to jail in 1963. As president of the Southern Christian Leadership Conference, King and others were demonstrating for civil rights in Birmingham, Alabama. Police were instructed to arrest all of the demonstrators in a nonviolent way. King decided to join his troops and go to jail, a move that legitimized nonviolent protest and outraged the nation. His "letters from Birmingham jail" mark a turning point in the civil rights movement.

Margaret Knight

A tomboy who made her own kites as a child growing up in Maine, Margaret Knight began inventing early in life. She visited her brothers in a clothing factory and worried that someone would be injured in the equipment. She invented a stop-motion device to prevent accidents. While working for a paper bag manufacturer, she invented a machine that would make flat-bottom bags that could stand on end. She also developed many domestic contraptions, such as a barbecue spit and a machine that would cut off and sew hoes.

Jiddu Krishnamurti

Jiddu Krishnamurti espoused a kind of self-analytical, non-dogmatic, logical spirituality that blends the internal and external, the personal and social without making unfounded cosmic assumptions. He was a revolutionary spiritual philosopher in that he insisted on having no followers or organization of believers.

Stephanie Louise Kwolek

A native of New Kensington, Pa., Stephanie Louise Kwolek graduated from Carnegie Institute of Technology in 1946 with a chemistry degree. She intended to work and save money for medical school, but ended up enjoying her job at DuPont creating hundreds of new polymers. One of Kwolek's pioneering material creations led to Kevlar, a polymer fiber five times stronger than the same weight of steel that is used in bullet-proof vests and fiber optic cable.

Stephen LaBerge

Stephen LaBerge has been the pioneering scientist in the field of "lucid dreaming," a state of conscious dreaming during which an individual can make a dream "productive" by affecting its content and consequences. LaBerge also created a method for lucid dreamers to communicate with researchers under laboratory conditions.

Hedy Lamarr

Better known for her Hollywood film career, Hedy Lamarr learned about military technology as the wife of an arms dealer in her native Austria. She became interested in how one could send radio signals while protecting them from enemy interference, and revisited the problem in Hollywood with film score composer George Antheil. Antheil brainstormed ideas based on his knowledge of player piano technology. He and Lamarr received a patent in 1941 for a device they invented, which divided signals into parts and sent them separately across different frequencies. The military first used the technology in 1962, after the patent had expired.

Georges Lemaître

A mathematician and catholic priest, born in Charlroi, Belgium (1894-1966), and studied mathematics and science at Cambridge University. He calculated after examining the general theory of relativity that, unlike the eternal universe of Newton and Maxwell and the stable and unchanging universe of Einstein, the real universe of astronomy is expanding, and that in the beginning the world happened a little before the start of space and time. "This is the most beautiful and satisfactory explanation of creation to which I ever listened," said Einstein. It was sarcastically called the "Big Bang" by Fred Hoyle, the Cambridge astronomer. Doubts persisted until the winter of 1998, when two separate teams of astronomers at Berkeley found by observing supernovae that the expansion was increasing rather than decreasing through gravitational pull, as they had expected.

Charles Lindbergh

Flying was Charles Lindbergh's passion; he left college to become a stunt pilot, and later completed Army flight school to deliver mail. A group of Missouri businessmen gave Lindbergh the financial backing he needed to design a plane, the Spirit of St. Louis, for an attempted solo flight from New York to Paris in 1927. Eight years earlier, a New York hotel owner had put up a $25,000 prize for the first person to make the trip. After Lindbergh's successful flight, which took nearly 34 hours, he returned home to a hero's welcome, and the stage was set for the development of commercial aviation.

Guglielmo Marconi

Using existing knowledge about invisible electromagnetic radiation, coherers and antenna circuits, Guglielmo Marconi was able to send wireless Morse code signals more than one and a half miles. He followed that experiment with a transatlantic transmission; in 1901, he sent a signal from the southwest tip of England to St. John's, Newfoundland. Marconi received the Nobel Prize in Physics in 1909, and started successful businesses in England and the United States.

Paul McCartney

Beatles frontman Paul McCartney claimed to have written the most covered and one of the most popular songs in rock and roll history –"Yesterday" – during the middle of the night. Here is his account from a 1984 "Playboy" magazine interview:

"I fell out of bed. I had a piano by my bedside and I…must have dreamed it, because I tumbled out of bed and put my hands on the piano keys and I had the tune in my head. It (the music) was all there, a complete thing. I couldn't believe it. It came too easy. In fact, I didn't believe I had written it. I thought maybe I'd heard it before, it was some other tune, and I went around for weeks playing the chords of the song for people asking them, 'Is this like something? I think I've written it.' And people would say, 'No, it's not like anything else, but it's good.' "

Elijah McCoy

One can credit Mrs. Elijah McCoy for the inventor's work. She nagged her husband about not having a place to iron clothes and about him watering the garden – so he invented the ironing board and sprinkler. The son of fugitive slaves, McCoy is best known for inventing a way to automatically lubricate the brakes on locomotives while the engine was running. His development was often asked for as "The Real McCoy. "

Michelangelo

Michelangelo was reluctant to take on Pope Julius II's commission to paint 12 apostles and other decoration on the ceiling of the Sistine Chapel. When he was given the freedom to paint whatever he wanted, Michelangelo set to work with a small crew of other painters. He became unhappy with how things were progressing, however, fired the workers and removed the paintings. He started over on his own, and finished the giant creations of Biblical stories four years later. His depictions of human anatomy and form are said to have changed subsequent artistic work in the Western world.

Samuel F.B. Morse

Samuel F.B. Morse gave up a successful portrait-painting career to pursue science after a discussion with scientists about electromagnetism experiments. He needed some help on the finer points of electricity, but determined that pulses of electrical current could convey information over wires. Morse, who graduated from Yale University in 1810, patented different kinds of pumps with his brother, Sidney Edwards Morse. Samuel Morse worked out the elements of a telegraph relay system in 1835, and was able to demonstrate the system two years later. Morse applied for a patent in 1840 for "Morse code," an electronic alphabet used to deliver messages. The first message, "What hath God wrought," was sent between Baltimore and Washington in 1844.

Mozart

Both Wolfgang Amadeus Mozart and his sister were considered musical prodigies, thanks in part to the tutelage of their father. Mozart began composing as early as age 6. He is known for receiving inspiration in dreams and during his waking state, and for his ability to conceive of an entire concerto at one time and hurry to write it down before it disappeared from his mind. A sickly child and adult, he died a poor man at age 35, but not before composing more than 600 pieces of music.

Louis Pasteur

French chemist Louis Pasteur enjoyed a distinguished career in academics. He began to study fermentation at the request of an industrialist who noticed undesirable byproducts appearing during fermentation of sugar into alcohol by yeast. Pasteur theorized that microscopic organisms called germs were entering the process. He also suggested that different kinds of germs caused different types of fermentations, and that the same could be said for disease. Pasteur applied his theories about preventing spoilage of perishable foods to beverages, showing that heating the liquid at a low temperature for a certain amount of time, pasteurization killed the microbes.

Robert Plant

Led Zeppelin lead man Robert Plant is said to have improvised most of the lyrics to "Stairway to Heaven," one of rock and roll's most enduring songs. Plant is said to have been staring into a roaring fire during a rehearsal at a remote cabin when the lyrics started coming to him.

Charles Richter

A physicist by training, Charles Richter began working in a seismological laboratory in Pasadena in 1927. He developed a scale originally used to measure California earthquakes that was soon in use around the world. Other such scales were already in existence, but Richter's was believed to be more accurate.

Frank Scoblete

Frank Scoblete invented a system for throwing dice that can limit the chance of rolling a seven. A well-known gambler and craps player, Scoblete has published books in an effort to help people improve their chances at casinos. The rolling technique is based on the premise that when two dice are matched up, with their respective number three sides aligned in a "V," no combination anywhere on the die amounts to seven. With practice, Scoblete believes people can gain an advantage in a craps game.

Steven Spielberg

For someone who couldn't get into film school, Steven Spielberg proved that following your creative vision can lead to groundbreaking work. Considered the creator of the "summer blockbuster" film genre with "Jaws", Spielberg was 13 when he won his first prize for movie making. He made $100 off of a movie, "Firelight," he made at age 16 and screened at a theater near his Arizona home. Despite being rejected by film schools, Spielberg took individual film classes, and through a class project won a contract with Universal-MCA. Spielberg's use of rich color, memorable music and special effects changed Hollywood filmmaking.

Igor Stravinsky

Igor Stravinsky had many musical influences, and was known for drawing on them to create his own fiery compositions. A riot broke out over the first, guttural performance of Stravinsky's "The Rite of Spring," which many agree to be one of the most influential pieces of 20th century music.

Sir Joseph Wilson Swan

Originally a pharmacist's apprentice in England, Sir Joseph Wilson Swan discovered a dry plate method of making photographs. He was working to develop an electric light bulb the same time as Edison. With the help of generators and more efficient vacuum pumps, he created a practical incandescent filament lamp, and was promptly sued by Edison. The two inventors ended up settling their grievances and joining forces. In his search for a workable filament, Swan ended up discovering a substance that became the basis for rayon fabric.

Leo Szilard

Hungarian scientist Leo Szilard conceived the idea of a nuclear chain reaction, theorizing that if an element could emit two neutrons when one was absorbed within its nucleus, a chain reaction could be sustained. At the time, he had no idea what that element would be. When developments in nuclear fission emerged later on, he convinced his colleagues not to publish their results lest they fall into the wrong hands. Szilard, a lifelong pacifist, helped build the nuclear bomb, but argued against its use in overpopulated areas.

Edward O. Thorp

Gaming expert Edward O. Thorp developed a system of counting cards in blackjack. Casinos have had to take many precautionary measures to keep card counters from gaining the upper hand, thanks to Thorp's observations and research. His book, "Beat the Dealer," offered the landmark revelation that a casino could be beaten at its own game.

Leonardo da Vinci

Leonardo da Vinci taught himself Latin so he could read scientific literature. His strong desire to understand how and why things work led to many discoveries that were well beyond his day. He discovered the principal of sound waves after hearing a church bell, did numerous dissections and chronicled the human anatomy, and drew up engineering plans for a helicopter, armored tank and submarine.

Alessandro Volta

Alessandro Volta is credited with inventing the modern electric battery in 1801. Born in Italy, Volta didn't speak until he was 4 years old; at 14, he decided to become a physicist. He developed the forerunner of the modern capacitor, and stored and electric charge by filling bowls with a saline solution and connecting the liquid with strips of different metals. The force that moves electric current, the volt, is named for him.

Ruth Wakefield

The proprietor of the Toll House Inn in Massachusetts, Ruth Wakefield, found herself rushing to make Butter Drop Do cookies one day in 1933. She ended up breaking the chocolate into chunks instead of melting it, hoping it would melt while baking, and invented one of America's favorite cookies – chocolate chip. The recipe took off after it was published in a Boston newspaper.

George Westinghouse

George Westinghouse learned about gears and pistons while working in his father's shop. After serving in the Civil War, Westinghouse briefly attended college and then returned to work at his father's, where he earned the first of 400 patents, this one for a small rotary steam engine. He also developed a device for replacing derailed rail cars, and worked to improve railroad brakes to improve what he considered appalling safety conditions on the tracks. Instead of relying on individual brakemen to stop each train car, Westinghouse came up with a system of air brakes that could be centrally controlled by the engineer. He earned the first of many air brake patents in 1869, and in his early 20s, Westinghouse organized a company to produce the invention. He went on to found the Westinghouse Electric Company in 1886, acting on his belief that alternating current held more promise than direct current, which was limited in its transmission to a few miles. With the help of other inventors, the company developed equipment to transmit high-tension electric current and gave birth to large-scale electrical generation.

Eli Whitney

The son of a Connecticut farmer, Eli Whitney paid his way through Yale University fixing machines for people. He moved to Georgia to teach and go to law school, but the job didn't work out. Whitney befriended Yale alumnus and plantation manager Phineas Miller, who complained of the labor-intensive method of cleaning green seed cotton. Although there is great debate over who really invented the cotton gin, Eli Whitney is credited with successfully building and patenting such a machine in 1794. He made little to no profit over the revolutionary machine, but later put his stamp on the firearms industry, creating machines to make standardized musket parts and implementing assembly line-like production techniques.

Woodrow Wilson

President Woodrow Wilson pushed his progressive views after the U.S. entered World War I in 1917. He offered up a Peace Programme with his own Fourteen Points, and insisted that the plan should be the basis for Armistice. With his Fourteen Points, Wilson attempted to guarantee national independence for all peoples involved in the war by breaking the Central Powers' will to fight.

Stories and Creative Solutions to Problems

Microsoft & Creativity

Bill Gates, co-founder and CEO of Microsoft, has often freely proclaimed that he is not an innovator and does not like to be a leader in software development, a high-risk business with an unpredictable future. He prefers other companies to come up with the innovative ideas and test their marketability. If successful, Microsoft would either try to acquire their technology, or develop products for similar applications.

Bill Gates claims that as a result of this kind of thinking, his company began from extremely modest and basement style beginnings, and has grown to become the dominant software developer in the world, while making him the richest man in the world.

Bill Gates is a very creative person who knows how to apply his creativity to various techniques of market development. His famous contract with IBM to develop MS DOS was what took Microsoft from an ordinary small-scale software company to become a major player. In that contract, he was sufficiently creative to devise a way to serve IBM, while maintaining the licensing rights of his operating system.

In hindsight, many analysts claim that it was the shortsightedness of IBM to have allowed Bill Gates to get away with such contract. Perhaps shortsightedness was a contributing factor. But if we project back to the early 1980's, very few people would have had the vision to recognize the importance of software, and even fewer its potential growth.

Bill Gates was creative enough to propose such a contract to IBM, and IBM was shortsighted enough to accept it. Bill Gates is a very creative marketer.

Code Breaking WWII

During WWII, the British intelligence agency was perplexed by the torpedoing of merchant ships off the coast of England and Ireland. They were intercepting unintelligible messages from the Germans to their U-boat commanders. To speed the deciphering and the effectiveness of intercepting messages, the agency invented what was called the Turret machine that was an extension of a code breaking process formally done by hand. It was so successful that the allies were sinking German submarines at the rate of one a day. The Turret machine was used until 1944 when the Germans caught on the code breaking through double agents

and in turn increased the possible correct answers exponentially with a new machine. The British then in turn created what is not commonly known, the first programmable computer to break the new German code. The "computer" was ordered to be destroyed by the British Government after D-Day to protect their intelligence operations and the first computer title in turn went to the "eniac" one year later.

Shaka Zulu - The Monkey Trap

In the late 19th century, a group of monkeys ate and destroyed the plants in the freshly planted fields and terrorized the people of a small Zulu village in Africa. The monkeys eluded the traps that the villagers set for them and continued their depredation. Perplexed the villagers took their problem to their great king, Shaka Zulu. The king proposed that 'The only way to catch a monkey is to put something shiny in the trap'. For that he offered the villagers his gold necklace as bait for the trap. A bamboo cage was built with the necklace placed slightly deep enough in it not to be reachable by a monkey. The monkey would then have to enter the cage to get it and the door would be closed on it by the villagers, thus trapping it. They got rid of the monkeys.

Creativity & DNA

James Watson, an American geneticist, and Francis Crick, an English physicist, collaborated for some time at the University of Cambridge in England, to discover the structure of the DNA.

Other researchers had tried many approaches, but none of them could come up with a satisfactory description for the structure of the DNA.

The story goes that one night in 1953, one of these two scientists had a dream. He dreamt that two snakes were intertwined with each other and were dancing. He woke up startled from the dream. It was then that their intensive detective work came to its culmination in the form of the two strands of the DNA being held together in the now famous double helix form.

Corning Glass Creative Salesman

In the first year of marketing its recently invented shatterproof glass, Corning Glass had a super-star salesman who out-sold all others. At their annual meeting to honor salesmen, he recounted his successful strategy as follows: "It is very simple. When I go to a potential client, I simply take one of the samples out of my briefcase, put it on their desk. Then I take out a hammer, and go Bang!!! The glass breaks without shattering and they are amazed to see this dramatic demonstration. From there on, I simply have to fill out the order forms." The sales went up dramatically the following year because all the other salesmen were doing what the super-salesman told them he did. But he remained the star. At the annual meeting he told them how he changed his strategy to maintain his lead in sales. He said: "Last year when I told you about my sales technique, I knew that every one of you would to do the same thing. So I had to get creative and come up with something new. This year, much as last year, when I visited a client, I would sit down, take a sample out of my briefcase, and put it on their desk. Then I'd take out my hammer, but this time, instead of me breaking the glass, I would simply hand the hammer over to the client and ask them to break it."

Creative Shortsightedness of Xerox

In 1970, Xerox Palo Alto Research Center (PARC) opened in Palo Alto, California. Xerox set up this special laboratory, with a number of inter-disciplinary teams of researchers and brainstormers. Their objective was to re-define the future of Xerox, so when the paperless office takes over, Xerox, the document company, would still be in business.

The team had come up with numerous ideas and prototypes of hardware and software to facilitate such development. It created the prototype of the personal computer (Alto), the first Local Area Network for linking office computers (Ethernet) and the first commercial laser printer. There were also innovations such as icon-based computing - - the system of on-screen symbols and a "mouse" pointer to issue commands - and windows-based computing itself also came into being at PARC to name a few.

Xerox management was ingenious in recognizing that the paperless office is inevitable. Instead of fighting it, they decided to become creative pioneers in that field. But their shortsightedness was that they were unable to see the future as their hand picked team saw it.

Steven Jobs of Apple computers, and Bill Gates of Microsoft both admit that they made full use of some of the pioneering work of the Xerox laboratory approaches and prototypes. Yet Xerox management failed to recognize the creativity of its own team, while the computer and software industry became many times greater than the photocopying technology.

Creativity at Apple Computers

Apple Computers is a good example of the ups and downs of the creative process. Apple had great ideas and people loved their computers that were simple and easy to use. Their "desktop" way of organizing material on the computer – with its trash can for cleanup – appealed to the non-techies. But Apple had problems. Its technical ideas were far ahead of the time, but its managerial and marketing approach was tight-fisted, more suited to last century thinking. They did not make their operating system widely available so that others could write programs that would run on their computers, thus increasing the applicability and demand for their computers. On and off Apple had a surge of creativity that brought it back, but then it would again lapse into red ink.

Through competition, Apple was forced to go back to the drawing board and create something new and better, and then the Macintosh series came out and gave Apple the much-needed revival that it was looking for. But again, mainly through a battle of the egos, creativity was stifled in Apple, and it lost its market share. Red ink was flowing freely. With its creator, Steven Jobs, returning, the company seems again to be poised for a comeback.

The Concept and Symbol for Zero

In the real number system, zero is the only number that is neither negative nor positive, it represents the boundary between the negative and positive numbers.

The Babylonians used the written symbols for numbers thousands of years before the symbol for zero was invented. Zero was introduced initially, not as a number to be used in computation, but as a position marker to distinguish between such numbers as 123, 1203, and 1023.

The Mayans, about the 1st century AD, used a small oval containing an inner arc to denote zero. About 5 centuries later the Hindus began to use a circle or a dot as a symbol for zero; the dot later fell into disuse. These Indian mathematicians wrote numbers in columns, and they used the zero to represent a blank column. The Hindu word for zero was sunya, meaning empty or void. This word translated and transliterated by the Arabs as sifr, is the root of the English words cipher and zero.

Give Unto Caesar that which is Caesar's...

The Pharisees plotted how to entrap Jesus in his speech. They sent their disciples to him, with the Herodians, saying, "Teacher, we know that you are a truthful man and that you teach the way of God in accordance with the truth. And you are not concerned with anyone's opinion, for you do not regard a person's status. Tell us then what is your opinion: Is it lawful to pay the census tax to Caesar or not?" "Knowing their malice," Jesus said, "Why are you testing me, you hypocrites? Show me the coin that is used to pay the tax." They handed him the Roman coin. He said to them, "Whose image is this and whose inscription?" They replied, "Caesar's." At that he said to them, "Then give unto Caesar that which is Caesar's and unto God that which is God's."

Contrast in Quantity

Bonzai Chobe, a samurai in ancient Japan was well liked by the common people and greatly disliked by the nobility. One day he forced an innkeeper to let him take an afternoon nap in a room that was prepared for a nobleman. He was awakened by the innkeeper when the nobleman arrived and asked the nobleman what he might do to make amends. To humiliate him, the nobleman simply asked him for a bowl of noodles, a common dish that every poor person ate. Unintimidated, Chobe turned the tables on the nobleman by sending out to buy all the noodles in town which were piled in front of the inn for all to see. "There is your bowl of noodles," he told the nobleman.

Marketing Fame

An ancient Chinese lord asked his physician, a member of a family of healers, which of them was the most skilled in the art. The physician, whose name was synonymous with medical science in China replied, "My eldest brother sees the spirit of sickness and removes it before it takes shape, so his name does not get out of the house. My elder brother cures sickness when it is extremely minute, so his name does not get out of the neighborhood. As for me, I puncture veins, prescribe potions and massage skin, so from time to time my name gets out among the lords."

V-1 Buzz Bomb

Anthony Nerad was able to deduce the essential design & mechanisms of the V-1 Buzz bomb by listening to actual bombings on the radio. Nerad found corresponding notes that matched the sound on the piano. He had studied the design of pipe organs & knew that creating a desired tone required a definite volume of airspace. To make the kind of sound the bomb made as it descended through the air, it had to be of a specific size and shape. From this information he was able to draw schematics. He presented the drawings to the war department to crack the mystery of the design of the bomb. This shows that to solve some problems, it is important to work

backwards from the effects to imagine the possible causes.

Pirates of the Caribbean

Using all the senses was important to Disney the creative genius behind Disneyland. Disney would inquire: does it look right, sound right, smell right, and feel right? He went through this exercise when creating Pirates of the Caribbean. But there was something he felt was just not authentic. He questioned himself and others. He ended up taking a suggestion from a janitor who grew up in New Orleans, which is where the Pirates of the Caribbean were intended to mimic. The janitor told him that on summer nights there would always be fireflies in New Orleans. Instantly, Disney shipped in fireflies to complete the experience until the fireflies could be later replicated mechanically.

Deaf Beethoven

When Beethoven was turning more and more deaf, he sawed off the legs of his grand piano. That way, when he played the piano he lay on the floor, and could "feel" what he was playing and could continue writing great music without actually hearing it.

Problem Solving

Chapter Four

"Thinking is the talking of the soul with itself."

-Plato-

"All truly wise thoughts have been thought already thousands of times; but to make them truly ours, we must think them over again honestly, till they take root in our personal experience."

-Goethe-

There are three kinds of people: those who make things happen, those who watch things happen, and those who never know what hit them. At any given time, each of us is any one of these three kinds of people. To keep ahead, we should carefully set our priorities to bring about the goals we want and to alert ourselves to events beyond our control. A well-informed and prioritized pursuit of carefully considered alternatives is the best application of our considerable problem solving skills and the only effective means of forging the future we desire.

While the simplest organisms exhibit the rudimentary problem solving ability to search for food to sustain themselves for the moment, human beings are capable of considering the future and creating elaborate systems (agricultural, economic, political, and so on) that diminish uncertainty and ensure long-term survival. In this manner, we solve problems that have not yet occurred. Beyond preventing meaningful problems that threaten our survival or comfort, we solve problems that are not even real; we create problems because solving them is a valued form of entertainment. Common examples include the problems we create for ourselves in activities like chess, poker, and crossword puzzles, and even in the tools and gadgets we proliferate to deal with minor daily tasks.

The philosopher Edmund Husserl writes, "Awareness... is consciousness through and through, the source of all reason and unreason, of all justice and injustice, of all reality and fiction, of all that is worthy and unworthy, of all deeds and misdeeds." He affirms that we must be aware of the important events

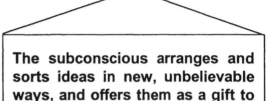

The subconscious arranges and sorts ideas in new, unbelievable ways, and offers them as a gift to us.

that surround us to gain control over our problems; there is no other way.

Awareness leads us to see that our goals may not be fulfilled unless we solve problems by removing barriers standing in the way. Problem solving is intrinsic in nature. It is not unique to human beings. To perpetuate itself, a functioning system must solve the problem of assuring the availability of inputs and of using outputs with a degree of organization, if for no other reason than to secure the flow of more inputs. A seemingly simple colony of ants exhibits a high degree of organization to find food, to protect themselves, and to produce more ants to ensure their continuation.

Julian Huxley, in *Man in the Modern World*, observes that something like the human mind might exist even in lifeless matter. To draw a parallel for this curious proposal, he notes that before its harnessing two hundred years ago, the only known forms of electricity were found in lightning and in a few fish. Electrical activity appeared to be a rare phenomenon that was of no particular importance in nature; but following man's comprehension and systematic study of electrical activity, it was discovered to be central to all nerve function, from conscious thought to the fertilization of an egg. Huxley suggests that all natural occurrences involve mental activity, although the mental happenings are at such a low level of intensity that they cannot be detected. In higher animals, mental activity is reinforced through an organized system like the brain to reach a high level of intensity; therefore we become aware of it. According to Huxley, all nature has a degree of awareness and solves problems.

Jung's concept of the "collective unconscious," which like a body connects the lives of all creatures (the amoebas, worms, and man alike) suggests there are no isolated psychic processes, just as there are no isolated life processes. One is in all, and all in one. He imagines the collective subconscious as a kaleidoscope of instincts, each holding delicately in place all the others and each shifting and changing with every "twist" of

> **The unconsciousness of man is the consciousness of God.**
>
> **Henry Thoreau**

consciousness. Some have interpreted this proposed connection among all living things as a source of inspiration to be tapped for solving problems. Without being specific, we might propose its link to the creative subconscious.

But we are neither a colony of ants nor a pack of wolves working together to preserve our species. We aspire to understand and control nature, not to carry out its pre-programmed edicts; to better our condition and to improve life for future generations. Human beings are distinguished from other animals in three

ways: biologically, psychologically, and socially. The biological distinction relates to our mental processes, which have far greater unity than the rigid compartmentalization found in the mind and behavior of animals. The psychological distinction is our capacity for abstract thought. We have the ability to generalize from observation of simple cause-effect occurrences to laws that govern a wide class of phenomena. The social distinction relates to our affiliation with various groups or units such as churches, professional societies, political parties, and nations; each based on some organized tradition and culture. Making the future better for succeeding generations by using these unique tools is as strong an instinct for us as the drive for species preservation that leads the meekest maternal animal to fight a hopeless battle against an overwhelming predator to protect her helpless young.

The drive for betterment necessitates change, and change creates problems. Decisions made and actions taken to solve current problems do not always produce anticipated effects, resulting in new or unforeseen dilemmas. Also, conditions under which old solutions worked may change, and new solutions to old problems must be found. Fortunately, we need not begin as helpless novices to develop vital problem solving skills. Useful lessons concerning how to recognize and formulate problems, develop solutions, and evaluate their impact can be learned from experienced and wise problem solvers.

Recognizing Problems

Problems are unacceptable local conditions that can be altered. A sick child presents a parent with a problem. Mass produced, easily accessible medicines are well-recognized solutions for many such problems. If local conditions cannot be altered (for example, if no known cure for the illness exists), then the broader system in which the problem arises may have to be redesigned. If children are transmitting the illness to each other at school, practices and procedures for interactions at school need to be changed. If the system cannot be effectively altered, the condition may have to be accepted. (Parents and children must learn to live with the potential for contracting an illness that can be neither cured nor prevented.) Many of our predecessors had to deal with problems in exactly this way.

It is not easy to detect and define problems. Narrow vision prevents recognition of broad, significant problems, and some problems are so subtle that they may escape detection until they expand to threatening proportions. Recognizing problems calls for some important personal qualities: imagination, alertness, caring, experience, and even a desire for fun and excitement. Facing a problem and sticking with its solution also calls for character, patience, courage, and discipline.

It is not always easy to recognize a problem. Something that is a problem to one person may not be noticed by another. A condition judged as perfectly acceptable by one individual can be unbearable to another. To learn to identify problems, we need training and sensitization. Some problems are detected because they make us uneasy, because they disturb our physical or mental equilibrium. Others are recognized because they stimulate our curious, problem solving nature or because we strive to improve the quality of our existence. Sometimes the intellectual process of solving challenging problems produces contentment and satisfaction. At other times only the implementation of a workable solution brings the bubbling mind to rest.

It is intriguing to consider which problems are real and which are invented or are merely the portion we see of larger problems we do not know about. The first step in problem solving is to recognize the <u>real</u> problem. We must resist the temptation to narrow our focus too quickly, before all the elements of the problem have been considered from a broad perspective. For example, the illegal shipment of silicon chips to unfriendly nations may appear to be a real problem. Yet we know that if our relations with these nations were to improve, as they did with China, the problem would not be regarded as an acute or real one. Lack of friendly relationships with other governments is the real problem, which, if solved, would eliminate the narrower concern.

Broad consequences of solutions should also be considered during problem solving efforts. What could happen to other systems if proposed solutions are adopted? Will new and difficult problems be created? Will actions be counterproductive? Familiarity and involvement with a diversity of situations and problems aid in the development of a broad, meaningful value system that can be useful for considering tradeoffs between the solution to one problem and the possible creation of others.

Attitudes Toward Problems: the Mysterious Riddle Solver and the Pragmatist

The modern scholar and philosopher Earl MacCormac, in <u>A Cognitive Theory of Metaphor</u>, refers to the writing of the great economist John Maynard Keynes, who described Isaac Newton's attempts to reconcile mathematical physics with his intuitions about the world as follows:

"Newton was not the first of the age of reason. He was the last of the magicians, the last of the Babylonians and Sumerians, the last great mind which looked out on the visible intellectual world with the same eyes as those who began to build our intellectual inheritance rather less than 10,000 years ago.

Why do I call him a magician? Because he looked out on the whole universe and all that is in it as a riddle, as a secret which could be read by applying pure thought to a certain evidence, certain mystic clues which God has laid out to allow a sort of philosopher's treasure here to the esoteric brotherhood. He believed that these clues were to be found partly in the evidence of the heavens and in the constitution of the elements (and that is what gives the false suggestion of his being an experimental philosopher), but also partly in certain papers and traditions handed down by the brethren in an unbroken chain back to the original cryptic revolution in Babylonia. He regarded the universe as a cryptogram set by the Almighty..."

The lingering riddle-solving mentality of our time may be a hangover from the rebellion of the scientific age against the dogmatic and stifling hold of the medieval church. This too-easily accepted science-based approach is shrouded in the mysteries of language, style, and history, which cast a sacred aura, much like the practice of the medicine man in a tribe of aborigines. The prevailing, hidden attitude is that the mind can take in and manipulate data according to certain canons to concoct enchanting answers to the most complex of problems. Sometimes we forget that the problems themselves are defined in the language and mentality of the very magicians who benefit from the perpetuation of this attitude.

The attitude of mesmerizing, abracadabra riddle solving can obfuscate and delay an open, multifaceted attack on problems. Still, in the case of some individuals like Newton, it provides an incentive and a sense of importance to unraveling the mysterious. Usually a more humble attitude is more effective in trying new combinations. It is helpful to realize that our minds are limited in their ability to comprehend the vast unknown, but that they can help us deal effectively with problems if we have access to basic knowledge and learn to be flexible in our definition of problems and in how we develop solutions. Riddle solving is entertaining and can generate new activities, but it also can mislead us to believe that solutions are all in the mind and not in the facts that change our understanding of what is the real problem.

To a wishful person, the simplest way to solve a problem is to avoid it; he or she imagines that no problem exists. Many insignificant dilemmas are best handled in this way. But if this approach becomes a habit, one will surely find oneself in serious trouble. A good indicator of whether a problem is worthy of our attention is to evaluate the potential gain were the problem to be solved and the loss were it not solved (the cost of solving it and the cost of avoiding it).

Sometimes we must immerse ourselves in a problem to get a better understanding of it. For example, many people have found that to appreciate the problems of the poor it is best to live with them rather than to spend a long time analyzing and trying to comprehend their situation in the abstract. Even when a problem is understood, potential solutions may not be obvious. And even when answers are known, it takes a long time to implement a workable solution. Good problem solvers have the courage to involve themselves in problems and the patience to derive and implement answers that work.

Understanding is not always gained by dissecting a problem into its most basic parts. Developing gestalt through vigorous involvement can produce an unspoken understanding and a "feeling" for a dilemma that is considerably more valuable than volumes of "hard" data. After the feeling for a problem has been internalized, it may be left alone to percolate within the subconscious, until one day something will trigger an idea and a solution will emerge.

The creative subconscious is known to be constantly at work. To derive the greatest benefit from the churning of the subconscious, it is helpful to keep an open mind, explore new ideas, and avoid negative attitudes. Negativity stultifies vision and understanding. It suppresses our natural ability to connect what is already known with the new problem. In simple terms, negativity leads to the oversimplification of complex, new situations because it prevents the problem solver from looking beyond the same tried-and-true ways that have led to solutions in the past. The negative thinker is too likely to believe that if old solutions do not work, nothing will work.

A useful role also exists for the conscious mind in problem solving. It is the ability to look for and find more information about a situation, to formulate and test possible solutions, and to analyze their effects without waiting for events actually to happen. The conscious mind expedites understanding and pulls together any and all available pieces to formulate solutions. Because some problems produce disastrous consequences, it is not expedient to wait for them to happen before studying them. Such problems can be modeled and examined as if they have occurred,

and their hypothesized consequences can be analyzed to understand the importance of solving them. For example, numerous problem solvers are studying the effects of a nuclear winter, the after effects of a full-scale nuclear war. In doing this, people, particularly leaders, are becoming frightened enough to work on the reduction of arms. Studying the potential outcomes helps today's problem solvers view situations in a more active and positive perspective.

There is a caveat in problem solving. One can develop the idea that opportunities for solutions are abundant and that determination and willpower will eventually produce desired results. This is not always true. Effective problem solvers appreciate the value of the timing of their solutions. One metaphor says that if corrective measures are postponed too long, a patient who might otherwise have been saved with minor attention will expire. Expedient, practical solutions are much more desirable than elegant answers that cannot be delivered on time.

There are also limitations on our ability, scope, and energy to solve problems. As exciting as it might be to welcome challenging problems with an open mind, there are also times when an abundance of problems can overwhelm and cripple us. It is wise to give some thought in choosing the appropriate challenge. Scaling Mount Everest is a magnificent accomplishment, but many ambitious climbers did not fully realize that the risk was much greater than the reward, and gave up their valuable lives in the attempt. Intelligence should be exercised, too, in budgeting our problem solving efforts. Freedom to solve many different problems creates satisfying opportunities, but taking on too many problems can itself be a problem. A good problem solver needs to ask, "Is this a significant problem? Does it need to be solved? Does it make sense for me to try to solve it? Is it worth the effort? " The following guidelines may be useful in identifying important, solvable problems:

❧ Guidelines for Recognizing Problems

1. Are you sure this is the problem you want to solve? Why do you want to solve it?
2. Are there other related problems, perhaps easier ones, which should be solved first? List them.
3. Does anyone need a solution? Are you sure you need a solution? Why?
4. What is a solution needed for?
5. What effect should a solution have?
6. How much will it cost to solve the problem? What resources are available?
7. How much benefit will be realized from a solution?
8. If the problem is ignored, will it go away over time?
9. Remove yourself from the problem and look at it. Is it significant? What is your vantage point for this judgment?
10. Can a change in existing law or administrative policies eliminate the problem?
11. Can this be viewed as someone else's problem? Perhaps you can get that person to solve it or help solve it.
12. Who is the best person to describe the problem? Why?

Formulating Problems

When a problem finally takes shape, it may be clear and well structured. In that case, its solution is likely to follow well-defined steps. To replace a broken pane of glass, most people know what the problem is and what needs to be done to solve it. But many important real-life problems are ambiguous, unstructured, and involve intangible factors. For-

mulating such problems takes courage, imagination, and a willingness to transcend the limitations of common problem solving methods and sometimes even social mores. We may be called upon to think the unthinkable.

Problems are of different kinds. A **remedial** problem has origins in accidental or unanticipated occurrences. For example, an airplane crashes and an investigative team searches for clues, identifies a cause, and proposes actions to prevent the crash of other airplanes. An **optimization** problem entails accomplishing a task in the most efficient manner possible. An **allocation** problem involves the best distribution of a limited resource; **sequencing** and **scheduling** problems, the best method of organizing a series of tasks. A **network-routing** problem looks for the identification of the best route between different points so that one may move from one point to another in the shortest time or distance and at minimal cost. **Competitive** problems deal with choice in interactive situations in which the result of one person's choice depends on the choices made by others. Competitive problems are commonly encountered in situations such as war, marketing, and bidding for contracts. **Search** problems seek best ways to get the information needed to make a decision. Issues of cost, time, and accuracy are frequently faced by problem solvers who must look for more information or act on the data currently in hand. As new advances, inventions, and improvements are developed, the problem of **transference** is encountered. How can we remain abreast of the numerous ideas and tools that are constantly being developed? **Prediction** of future events, the ups and downs of the stock market, of the means of transport in the year 2050, of life expectancy in thirty years, is another problem category. **Conflict** resolution is yet another area of problem solving. Each of these problem types has stimulated the development of various approaches to obtain solutions.

Problems can be studied in their real-world environment (in situ) or by constructing hypothetical scenarios or thought experiments that afford the problem solver the flexibility to vary problem parameters artificially and to test alternative ways of viewing the situation. Possessing an ability to formulate a problem in a useful and appropriate way, therefore, is an important step in the solution process, one that depends on the individual's knowledge, experience, and creative ability to impose a structure on an unstructured situation. Imagination plays a useful role in identifying the components of this structure. The following guidelines are useful in formulating a problem:

➣ Guidelines for Formulating Problems

1. Define the problem in a short statement.
2. Describe the history of the problem, concentrating on its causes.
3. State your objectives and the constraints on possible solutions.
4. What is the current solution?
5. What is wrong with the current solution?
6. What is the ideal? What would you really like?
7. Could you implement the ideal solution?
8. What are the minimum requirements for a satisfactory solution?
9. View the problem from the perspectives of others. How would an economist look at the problem? A lawyer? A clergyman?
10. List all the solutions you can imagine.

Solving Problems

There are indeed many different kinds of problems, but there are also many different kinds of minds and attitudes to deal with them. Some people look for problems and genuinely enjoy solving them. Philosophers and grand thinkers like to contemplate the most global, elusive, and transcendental problems of existence (many of these "thinkers," however, have difficulty assembling their child's new bicycle on Christmas Eve).

Practical minds keep municipal and household problems under control. Creative engineers, research scientists, and even thinkers enrich society with ideas and devices for solving old and new problems. Puzzle solvers have a capacity for dealing cleverly with well- structured, intricate, intellectual problems, but may or may not have a practical turn of mind. Mathematicians work on esoteric problems that they can communicate only to fellow mathematicians - art for art's sake.

No rule-of-thumb exists for becoming an expert problem solver. The best way to develop good universal problem solving skills is to engage oneself in the practice of problem solving and learn to enjoy it with enthusiasm (see the exercises in this chapter for some samples). To spare the novice many headaches, some useful hints can be found consistently in the works of great scholars: incubation inspiration, and revelation. If a problem is important enough, it is absorbed by the subconscious (incubation), and somehow we become agents of internal forces that provide a constant flow of ideas and possibilities (inspiration), until the conscious becomes aware of a solution (revelation), and the burning flame is quieted. More than knowledge is at work here. There is art in the creative dialogue between the workings of the subconscious and the naive hankerings of the conscious mind for clear and definite answers.

It would be unrealistic to think that when we apply **logic** and **reason** to our problems, we are somehow pure, objective, and unconditioned by outside influences. Actually our feelings and subconscious thoughts are produced from constant cultural and environmental conditioning. By tightening the way we use logic, we invite the domination of personal conditioning and preferences. There is no master style of problem solving that should be institutionalized as deeply as, say, the methods used to learn reading, writing, and arithmetic. Rules of scientific reasoning or logic, for example, are not universally applicable to life's complexities. When encountering the astounding diversity of this world's puzzles, flexible approaches for identifying solutions are mandatory.

Wayne Wickelgran's goal-directed view of problems and solutions involves three types of information: givens, operations, and goals. **Givens** represent what is accepted as true about the world of the problem at the onset of the work. **Operations** are actions that transform givens and solve the problem. **Goals** are the desired terminal states within the world of the problem. When goals are achieved, the problem solver knows the operations have been effective.

Applying this terminology to the problem of auto theft, for example, the givens include the current design of auto doors, windows, and ignition systems; the state of poverty and drug usage in society that leads to criminal acts; the propensity of car owners to commit insurance fraud; the existence of markets for stolen cars and car parts; and the current state of law enforcement by police and criminal justice systems. Examples of possible operations include changing auto designs to make cars theft proof, reducing the effects of social problems that lead to crime (e.g., by creating more jobs), altering theft insurance coverage, eliminating markets for stolen vehicles, increasing police surveillance, or stiffening penalties for convicted offenders. The goal in this instance may be a 25 percent reduction in the automobile theft rate.

Each of the operations mentioned will produce effects that influence several aspects of our lives, not just those dealing with stolen cars. The price of cars or of car insurance might be driven upward by adopting some of the alternatives, police coverage at banks and jewelry stores might be reduced, or taxes might be raised to build more prisons. It takes a creative, knowledgeable, and experienced problem solver to understand the present situation, imagine alternative solutions, and project their consequences in relation to the goal.

Effective problem solving also requires considerable training. One of the most powerful ways to prepare to be a successful problem solver is to become familiar with both conceptual and formalized tools. Conceptual tools include practical, everyday living knowledge gained from a familiarity with hardware stores, lumber yards, sewing and craft shops, and the like. More formalized tools and strategies obtained from books and learned practitioners include scientific and mathematical knowledge and ideas and practices from engineering, political and military endeavors, social and economic sciences, and art and music. Less formalized, sometimes outrageous approaches include astrology, tarot cards, and voodoo. Anything that is of interest to any sector of humanity can be a stimulus and a source of excitement to the curiosity of a good problem solver.

George Polya provides a comprehensive and practical four-step procedure for solving a problem. The first is to **understand the problem** by determining what is known and unknown, what the data may be, and what the conditions of the problem are. One may attempt to answer the questions: Is it possible to satisfy the conditions? Are the conditions sufficient to determine the unknown? To facilitate understanding, draw a picture of the problem - any type of figure, graph, diagram, or the like. Separate the problem into parts, if appropriate. *Write something down.*

The second step is to **devise a plan of attack**. Consider whether you have seen this problem before in a similar guise. Do you or your friends know of a related problem that has been solved? Can you use it or a piece of it? Restate the problem using different terms. Look at it in more general or more specific terms. It is important in this step to develop different perspectives on the problem. Try different ways. *If one way does not generate results, forget it. Try another. Don't get bogged down. Don't solve problems in the sticky mud.*

The third step is to **carry out the plan**. Check each step carefully. Does each step follow from the previous one and lead into the next? Try to show that the solution works.

The fourth step is **to examine the solution**. Look back at it to check the result. Can you arrive at the same answer with a different method? Can you explain it to someone else and have them see it at a glance? Can you use the result you have obtained or your method you used to solve it to solve some other problem?

John Bransford and Barry Stein propose a similar strategy for problem solving they call the IDEAL process:

I = Identify the problem.
D = Define and represent the problem.
E = Explore possible strategies.
A = Act on the strategies.
L = Look back and evaluate the effects of your activities.

They believe good problem solving is a skill that can be developed like many others if a general approach is learned and consistently practiced. There is no magic to solving problems. Unfortunately, however, it is a skill many do not pick up because it is not part of most formal education programs.

A problem solver's approach to any dilemma can be limited or misdirected by assumptions held about the problem, assumptions that may be unnecessary or incorrect. Below are some useful strategies for exposing implicit assumptions that may impede good problem solving:

1. *Searching for inconsistencies.* After generating an idea, search for alternatives that are reasonable but inconsistent. For example, when your car won't start, you may assume its battery is dead. Perhaps this happened before and a new battery was required. But if you find the headlights shine brightly and the radio blares, inconsistencies have been discovered that rule out your idea.

2. *Worst-case analysis.* While considering a potential solution, imagine the worst that could happen at each step, then imagine how likely such an occurrence may be. If a serious "worst case" can be supported by reasonable assumptions, you may rule out adoption of the alternative you are considering. Suppose, while looking for a new job, you decide southern California is a desirable location. What is the worst that could happen? Well, you could be involved in a massive earthquake and slide into the sea. If you believe this scenario is based on reasonable assumptions, rule out this option and look for a more stable choice.

3. *Making predictions.* The correctness of fundamental assumptions can be probed by making predictions based on the assumptions. Scientists frequently test their theoretical assumptions by performing "thought experiments" that involve prediction. Albert Einstein imagined a person riding a streetcar that was headed away from a large clock. He tried to predict how the clock would appear to the person if the vehicle were traveling at the speed of light. He forecast that the light being reflected by the clock would keep up with the rider; therefore he would always see the same image of the clock, thinking it was always the same time. Such unreasonable predictions helped Einstein comprehend the inadequacy of the implicit assumption that time is absolute and led him to other formulations based on relativistic concepts of time.

4. *Seeking criticism.* A final strategy for testing assumptions is to ask others for criticism. Many problem solvers shun this approach because it exposes them to potentially harsh, even embarrassing, feedback. The good problem solver needs to develop an insensitivity to criticism and to accept it for the truth it may uncover. Developing and using a group of trusted colleagues who have sympathetic, helpful attitudes is most useful. The latter point is important to remember when one is asked to act as a critic for another thinker.

Operations research (OR) is a developing field that attempts to provide objective and quantitative bases for solving managerial and administrative problems. OR is an applied science that combines principles of logic, mathematics, statistics, and behavior with theories of communication, decision-making,

organization, and general systems. It focuses on the performance of entire systems rather than on parts of systems operating separately.

The Aristocrat

The true aristocrat is one who operates as if he or she is above it all, and has the outlook that some problems are not worth solving. He thinks that problem solving is a middle class working bee kind of activity. He reasons that the number and variety of problems is unlimited and that one cannot tangle with all of them. If one spends all his life on problem solving and establishes a reputation as a good problem solver, he gets more and more problems dumped on him. Between the natural pride he feels in solving a new problem and the fact that he has more problems to solve, soon he has no time left for anything else. It takes talent to know when not to solve a problem. The aristocratic or successful leader does not solve every problem. He ignores many and for others he gets help. This leaves him lots of time for speculating about the true meaning of life and whether or not he is enjoying it.

An OR approach to problem solving has three essential parts. First, OR uses a systems orientation that recognizes that the behavior of any part of a system has an effect on the behavior of the whole system. OR attempts to consider interdependencies and to search for problem causes throughout the system, not in the local area where the problem is experienced. Second, interdisciplinary teams of experts are used to gain diverse perspectives on complex problems and to bring to bear a large arsenal of research techniques and solution tools. Third, scientific methods of research are adapted for use in the field where the operation of large systems can be observed directly. The close control of the laboratory environment is abandoned in favor of personal observation and data collection in the system's real-world setting.

Some useful guidelines for solving problems follow:

✌ Guidelines for Solving Problems

1. Does the problem have a solution? How do you know?
2. List all possible alternative solutions. Is the list exhaustive? How do you know?
3. List all your assumptions about the problem. Are there inconsistencies?
4. Ask others to criticize your assumptions. Are some unnecessarily limiting?
5. Think of the optimal or near-optimal solution.
6. Think of an average solution.
7. Think of an approximate solution.
8. Start at both ends (from the raw data and the hypothesized answer) and move toward the middle to develop justification.
9. Start in the middle and move toward the ends.
10. Embed the problem in a larger context and solve it.
11. Abstract the problem to a simpler formulation.
12. Can you derive a solution from a related problem?
13. Simulate the problem in search of a solution.
14. Construct a working hypothesis.
15. Develop and test the hypothesis.

16. Define the utilities and payoffs in the problem under study. How do you measure them?
17. How sensitive is the solution to changes in the problem definition or data?
18. Analyze the faulty solutions to get a better understanding of the preferred ones.

Accepting the Limitations of Solutions: Compromise

Even the seemingly most perfect of answers must be applied in an imperfect, highly interrelated world. An improvement made in one area may detract from other areas. For example, the elimination of nuclear arms in the European theater (a presumably positive step for a safer and saner world) may well cause involved governments to spend much more money on conventional military forces. The newly created situation may increase the chances of touching off a conventional war among previously peaceful countries, and at the same time drain the financial resources that otherwise could have contributed to improved living conditions for the citizens of the countries.

How can the inevitable tradeoffs of decisions and actions be judged? This is the challenge for being effective in the future: not to depend on pulling a magic, final answer out of our technological/scientific hats, but learning how to view problems with a broad perspective; creatively developing alternatives; judging the value of these alternatives and their consequences; making a good choice; implementing it; and being satisfied with it.

To deal with these matters, science must be combined with individual and social values to develop a decision process based on many goals and criteria that are important to numerous constituents. Fortunately, in recent years progress has been made in this area. One extremely useful methodology is the Analytic Hierarchy Process (AHP).

When traditional techniques are employed to model complex problems, the problems are often simplified to accommodate the model builder's need to express its parts in measurable terms (dollars, tons, numbers of accidents, days until completion, and so on). When such simplified models do not work, we blame the result on intangibles such as politics or capricious human behavior. But these are precisely the controlling factors that must be dealt with and measured to derive realistic answers. Problem solvers need to stop making simplifying assumptions to accommodate known quantitative techniques and deal with complex situations as they are. To be realistic, models have to include and measure all important quantitative and qualitative factors. This is the function of the AHP. It is a methodology for modeling unstructured problems in the economic, social, and management sciences through pairwise comparisons, allowing for conflicts and tradeoffs. As an example, a problem solver is given the flexibility to trade decreased satisfaction with the design of a new car for increased gas mileage and passenger safety, or to compare a decrease in a country's gross national product with the number of lives that may be saved by adopting a new government policy. A computer software package, Expert Choice, adapts the Analytic Hierarchy Process for use on personal computers.

Below are a few guidelines problem solvers can use to analyze the effects of their potential solutions:

⌘ Guidelines for Analyzing the Impact of the Solution

1. How can you communicate the problem and its solution to others?
2. What is the most effective way to convince different people your solution is good?
3. What is the impact of your solution on people, things, expenses, and so on?
4. Which people should be involved in implementing the solution?
5. What personnel commitments, organizational structure, and equipment are needed to implement your solution? Can you attain them?
6. What happens to the existing organization after the solution has been implemented and the problem solved? Whose interests have been served? Who is likely to resist?
7. Can the organization solve other problems?
8. How can people be motivated to solve this and other problems?
9. What are the sanctions on, or threats to, the individuals and organizations involved?
10. What is the moral impact of the problem and its solution on people?
11. Will there be a chain reaction, either creating new problems or solving other problems, as a result of the solution?
12. Are there residual problems that must now be solved?
13. Can you use what you have learned to solve other problems?
14. Have your horizons been broadened?

Problem solving is as natural to human beings as gathering nectar is to a honeybee. It makes us feel as though we are reaching our potential by utilizing to the fullest extent and for the greatest good those natural assets that are uniquely ours. By honing our memory, sense of humor, creativity, and desire for betterment that make us good problem solvers, we can confidently and effectively handle the challenges with which fast changing events bombard us. As skillful problem solvers, we can face the future bravely with head erect and eyes open. We are capable of planning desired changes that will improve existence for our successors, never fearing change or failure, but always anticipating so that a quick step can be taken to avert greater problems and to reestablish ourselves on another route to our goal.

Examples

Before moving into problem solving methodologies, consider the following examples. (See reference to Frauenthal and Saaty at the end of the book).

❧ Symmetry - Analytic Versus Synthetic Thinking: The Cup of Coffee and the Cup of Milk

Imagine you are given a cup of coffee and a cup of milk, with equal amounts of liquid in the two cups. A spoonful of milk is transferred from the milk cup to the coffee cup, the coffee is stirred, and then a spoonful of the mixture is returned to the milk cup so that

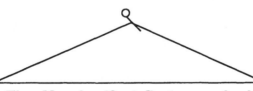

The Moral - if at first you don't succeed then:

1.   **Copy Someone Else**
2.   **Try and Try Again**
3.   **Stop and Think**

at the end the amount of liquid in the cups is still the same. Is there more milk in the coffee cup or more coffee in the milk cup or what? Most people say there is more milk in the coffee cup, a few say the reverse and still fewer say they are equal. The feeling about this problem is that the first transfer of milk to the coffee cup so dilutes the spoonful in coffee that the best transfer of the mixture cannot take back much of it, hence leaving more milk in the coffee cup than coffee in the milk cup. Of course, not being able to take back much of it should make it possible to take a lot more coffee in the spoonful. But people don't think of it that way.

Insight: Notice that whatever amount of milk is missing from the milk cup is replaced by an equal amount of coffee (and vise versa), because at the end each cup has the same amount of liquid with which it started.

Solution: It is therefore obvious that there are equal amounts of coffee in the milk and milk in the coffee.

One can verify this with algebra, but with more effort. However, the algebra assumes homogeneity of the mixture in the coffee cup after stirring. This assumption is artificial but unfortunately is needed to carry out the algebraic argument that the second spoonful has the same ratio of coffee to milk as there is in the entire coffee cup.

❧ Continuity - But Not Circular - Reasoning: The Ski Area Problem

You are the manager of a ski area. Your customers complain that they are spending too much time waiting in line to ride the one chair lift. State law requires that there must be a period of fifteen seconds between chairs.

Since there is not enough time to install a new chair lift this season, how should you modify your chair lift operating policy to satisfy the customers' complaints?

Most people suggest that the solution is to run the chair lift more quickly. This is, however, the wrong thing to do. The state-mandated warning time would then require that the chairs be moved further apart, with the result that no more skiers would be carried up the hill. In fact, the number of skiers transported up the hill is absolutely limited by the waiting time.

Insight: The proper way to view this problem is as a closed cycle for any given skier. Each individual does one of three things: ski, ride the lift, or wait in line to ride the lift.

Solution: Making the reasonable assumption that the time to ski from the top of the hill to the bottom is unaffected by the speed at which the lift is operated, it is clear that the time not spent skiing is divided between sitting on the lift and standing, waiting for the lift. Clearly, by running the lift more slowly, with the chairs more closely spaced, individuals spend longer riding the lift and hence less time waiting in line. While this solution may appear unsatisfactory, it does respond to the customers' complaints.

❧ The Weakness of Imparity: The National Football League Problem.

Not long ago the NFL consisted of two conferences of 13 teams each. The rules of the league specified that during the 14-week season, each team would play 11 games against teams in its own conference and 3 games against teams in the opposite conference. Prove that this is impossible.

The initial method for solution that comes to one's mind is to represent each team by a point (vertex) and then to show games by lines between pairs of points. Such a model is called a finite graph. While essentially a correct beginning, trying to prove the impossibility of the above schedule by enumeration is very lengthy.

Insight: Think about the games within and across conferences separately. In fact we can solve the problem by looking only at the games within a conference. Clearly, the lines representing games within one conference must connect two different points (teams) within the conference. Thus there must be an even number of ends-of-lines since each line has two ends.

Solution: The schedule demands that, within each conference, 13 teams each play a game against 11 other teams in the conference. This makes for $(13)(11) = 143$ ends-of-lines. Since this is an odd number, the schedule is impossible.

Note that, as one would expect, the NFL never succeeded in satisfying its own scheduling rule. What is the minimum number of teams that would have to violate the scheduling rule in order to make a feasible schedule?

❧ Standing Back to See the Answer: The Tennis Tournament.

A tennis tournament director wishes to organize an elimination-type of tennis tournament. The names of all the people who enter are put into a hat and then drawn out in pairs. The two people in each pair play against each other, with the loser retiring from the tournament. The names of all the winners are put back in the hat, pairs are drawn out again, and the play-off takes place. If at any time there are an odd number of names in the hat, the name left over after the drawing of the pairs remains in the hat until the next round (i.e., that person gets a "bye" in that round). The director wishes to know how many matches will have to be played if N people enter his tournament. How many will there be?

Let us, for example, consider the following cases:

N = 31, 32, 33, 34.

The analytic solution for the problem may be obtained as follows:
N = 31
15+8+4+2+1 = 30
N = 32
16+8+4+2+1 = 31
N = 33
16+8+4+2+1+1 = 32
N = 34
17+8+4+2+1+1 = 33

Insight: We may argue as follows: Everyone but the winner loses exactly 1 match and is then out of the tournament.

Solution: Therefore N-1 matches must be played.

☙ Conditional Thinking: Prospecting for Gold

Given a chest with three drawers: the first contains two gold coins; the second, a gold and silver coin; and the third, two silver coins. A drawer is selected at random and a coin is taken out. The coin is a gold one. What is the probability that the second coin in that drawer is a gold one?

Many people argue as follows. Since a gold coin was found in the selected drawer, it must be either the drawer with two gold coins or the drawer with one gold and one silver coin. Thus there is a 50:50 chance that the remaining coin is gold. This is wrong!

Insight: List all of the possible ways of drawing two coins, denoted by G_i, and S_i, (i = 1,2,3), out of a drawer.

Drawer 1	Drawer 2	Drawer 3
G_1G_2	G_3S_1	S_2S_3
G_2G_1	S_1G_3	S_3S_2

Solution: Of the 6 possible realizations, only 3 have a gold coin drawn first (underlined). Of these 3, two have a gold drawn second. Thus Prob. (second coin in drawer is gold / first coin in drawer is gold) = 2/3.

☙ What is Random? -- The Subway Paradox.

The Red Line Subway in Boston runs from Harvard Square to Quincy Center via Park Street. Each day you arrive at the Park Street Station at a random time, go down to the central platform, and get on the first Red Line train to arrive. Nine days out of ten you end up at Harvard Square. How can this be?

Most people's intuition tells them that one should go to Quincy Center as often as one goes to Harvard Square. This is not necessarily the case. The error results from considering the wrong property as being random.

Insight: Notice that it is you, not the trains, which arrive at random. Imagine for example that trains from Harvard Square to Quincy Center run every ten minutes on a regular schedule. Also, to avoid having a build-up of trains at one end of the line or the other, trains also run from Quincy Center to Harvard Square every ten minutes.

Solution: To resolve the paradox, imagine that each train bound for Quincy Center arrives one minute after the train bound for Harvard Square.

Clearly, if your random arrival time falls anywhere between the time of a Quincy Center bound train and a Harvard Square bound train (9 minutes) you will end up at Harvard Square; while if your arrival falls between the time of a Harvard Square bound train and a Quincy Center bound train (1 minute), you will end up at Quincy Center.

ᨄ Intuitive Geometric Optimization: A Tale of Two Cities

Consider two cities on opposite sides of a river (with parallel lines for shores). It is desired to connect them with the shortest path that crosses a bridge (of finite length) that is perpendicular to the river. Where should the bridge be located?

The first idea is to connect the cities with a straight line, mark its intersection with the middle of the river, and build the bridge to pass through that point, then connect the cities to the bridge. The straight line was to assure a basis for the shortest distance. But in fact the total distance is longer than necessary.

Insight: The straight line idea is a good one but we note that when proceeding from either city, what is certain is that a bridge whose length is the width of the river is to be crossed, and then a shortest distance is needed.

Solution: As we just said, we start by eliminating the width of the river, and drawing a straight line for the rest of the distance. This is most easily accomplished by shifting the upper city downward by the width of the river, connecting it with a straight line to the lower city as if the river were not there. We put the river back, keep the portion of the line from the lower city to the edge of the river, put the bridge at that position and connect its upper point to the original position of the upper city. This line segment is parallel to the one resulting from the shifted position of the upper city and is equal to it in length.

ᨄ Too Little Information: The Early Commuter Problem

A man usually takes the 5:30 P.M. train, arriving at his station at 6:00, when his wife picks him up and drives him home. One day he took the 5:00 P.M. train, arriving at the station at 5:30 P.M. He began walking home. His wife, starting out from home to meet him at the usual time, met him on the way and brought him home 10 minutes before the usual time. How long did the man walk?

The first feeling about this problem is that there is not enough information to solve it. Nothing is said about how fast the man walked, or how fast the wife drove, or when she left home every day to meet him at the station. However, it is assumed that there is no ambiguity in the information so that an answer is possible.

Insight: Instead think about the man's walking time. After arriving a half-hour earlier than usual, he meets his wife driving to the station before 6:00 P.M. Suppose she were to go on to the station and then back to the point where she first met him. She then picks him

116

up and takes him home. Then they would arrive home at the usual time.

Solution: They arrived home 10 minutes earlier than usual, which represents twice the time it takes to drive the distance he has walked from the station. Thus the distance he walked would have taken five minutes to drive. So he walked 25 minutes, from 5:30 to 5:55, meeting his wife at a point where had she proceeded to the station she would have met the 6:00 P.M. train on time. Magic!

❧ A Stitch in Time: The Water Lily Problem

You are in charge of maintaining a pond in which water lilies grow. Each day the area of the plants doubles. You decide to do nothing until the pond is half covered. Only then will you cut the water lilies back. Given that the entire pond is just covered on the hundredth day, on what day do you start to cut?

The usual response to this problem is that you start to cut on the fiftieth day, which is wrong. The error results from assuming that the lilies grow at a fixed rate that is independent of their present number.

Insight: Not enough information is given to solve this problem "forward" in time. It is, however, possible to solve it "backward" in time.

Solution: The pond is just covered on the one-hundredth day. Each day the area covered doubles, thus going backwards in time, on the ninety-ninth day, the pond was half covered. According to the problem statement, this is the day you start to cut.

Philosophical Comment: That old adage "stitch in time saves nine" may be applied

here. It seems as if you could save yourself a lot of work if you cut the lilies back on the ninety-eighth day, when only a quarter of the pond is covered. Or perhaps the ninety-seventh day is even better, when an eighth of the pond must be cleared. We note that the animal population (including human) grows like the water lilies in proportion to the present population size.

❧ Quick and Dirty But Effective: The Gordian Knot

When traveling through Asia Minor during his conquests, Alexander was presented with the Gordian knot, which no one was able to untie. They probably thought this might cut him down to size. But he was not to be outdone; he pulled out his sword and slashed it open. He solved the problem.

Insight: To Alexander the Gordian knot was not a matter of finesse. It was a low priority problem for a conqueror to waste his time on, and he showed them how he would dismiss it from his mind.

We feel that the creative act, as Koestler wrote, "is the defeat of habit by originality." Those engaged in the art of modeling may find it useful to "fine tune" the mind of the student to subtleties of thought which may be large in number and which can perhaps be realized by examples akin to the foregoing. The hope is to improve intuition by alerting the student to principles that operate in a domain which requires closer reasoning than that encountered in daily discourse and in common thought.

117

Some Examples of Models

Modeling is a widely applied approach to problem solving. The following examples illustrate its versatility. Each was chosen with the hope that they would inspire you to incorporate modeling into your own problem solving endeavors.

✍ The Colored Cubes Problem: an example of a non-numerical model involving decomposition and invariance under transformation.

An illuminating illustration of the use of graph theory in problem-solving is Instant Insanity. We are given four cubes, the faces of which are colored with one of four colors. Since there are six faces, each cube would have more than one face colored with the same color. The coloring of the cubes is different so two cubes are not necessarily colored the same way. The problem is to stack the cubes vertically in such a way that we have a rectangular prism and each of the rectangles on the side has all four colors appearing in it, not necessarily in the same order.

The problem may not have a solution. For example, if all three faces meeting at a corner of each cube are colored with the same color for all four cubes, then that color appears in the stack at least eight times, not the required four and there is no solution. There are 3 possibilities for the first cube and 24 for each of the others in all $3 \times 24^3 = 41,472$ possible stacks of the cubes.

First we draw four points as corners of a square letting each corner represent a different color, and we label the cubes 1 to 4. Each cube has three pairs of opposite faces. We take the first cube and draw lines connecting the vertices associated with each pair

of opposite faces and label these three lines with number 1. We do the same for each of the other three cubes. In all, we have 12 lines with three labeled 1, three labeled 2, etc. A possible representation is shown in Figure 1, where the colors are labeled R, G, W and B. Now we have 81 possible stacks.

Next we decompose the problem into two parts. We solve the problem for one pair of opposite columns in the stack and then for the other pair. We note that in each pair each cube is used once and each color appears twice, once in each column. Thus, we draw the four points associated with the colors and choose four lines from the diagram that are labeled 1,2,3,4 (thus each cube is used once) but in such a way that each point is incident with two lines. When this is done, the same procedure is repeated for the remaining pair of opposite columns. Adjustment in the choice of lines for the first opposite pair of columns may be necessary to solve the problem for the second pair. The solutions for the two parts are independent. Given the solution of one partition, the other is obtained by a rotation around an axis passing through the centers of the two opposite faces of the cubes that appear in the first solution. Figures 2(a) and 2(b) portray these solutions taken from Figure 1. It is also easy stack the cubes to make the colors alternate from one column to the one on the opposite side. In this manner the problem is solved.

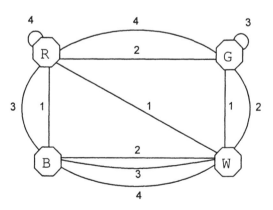

Figure 1

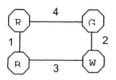   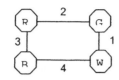

Figure 2 a   Figure 2 b

♣ The Cup of Coffee versus Cup of Milk Problem: an Example of a Leibnizian Analytic versus a Kantian Synthetic Solution.

Problem revisited: Suppose two cups, 1 and 2, have 5 teaspoons of milk (M) and coffee (C), respectively. One teaspoon of milk from cup 1 is transferred to cup 2. After having stirred cup 2 adequately, one teaspoonful from cup 2 is transferred back to cup 1. Does the coffee cup have more milk in it or does the milk cup have more coffee in it?

An analytic solution takes the following lines of argument. The coffee cup 2, after the first transfer, has 1/6 M and 5/6 C. If one teaspoonful is transferred to cup 1, it also contains the proportion 1/6 M and 5/6 C. Therefore, the composition of the two cups will be as follows:

Cup 1:   4 1/6 M and 5/6 C
Cup 2:   5/6 M and 4 1/6 C

Thus, there is as much milk in the coffee cup as there is coffee in the milk cup.

A synthetic solution may be argued as follows: the amount of milk missing at the end from the milk cup is in the coffee cup. Since the final quantities are equal, it must have been replaced by an equal amount of coffee. Therefore, they are equal.

♣ The Period of a Pendulum

In physics, physical variables originate largely in the operations symbolized in their dimensional formulas. Dimensional formulas and equations have a structure closely related to the operations of physical measurement. A small number of variables are selected and all other variables may then be expressed as a function of the basic set.

Usually mass m, length l, time T, and electric charge Q are used as the fundamental, or primary, variables. A theorem in dimensional analysis asserts that any physical variable f is proportional to a product of powers of primary variables

$$P_1, P_2, \ldots P_n$$

that is, if $a_1, a_2, \ldots, a_n$ are rational numbers, then

$$f = KP_1^{a_1} P_2^{a_2} \ldots P_n^{a_n}$$

where K is a proportionality constant. Frequently K is dropped and one writes

$$[f] = \left[P_1^{a_1} \ldots P_n^{a_n} \right]$$

where the brackets indicate dimensional equivalence.

For example, force may be expressed in terms of the primary variables given above as

$$F = K(MLT^{-2}).$$

As an illustration, suppose that it is required to calculate the period of a simple pendulum consisting of a rigid rod of length h supporting a mass m and having an angular displacement. The functional expression for the physical variables involved is

$$t = t(m,h,g).$$

or, dimensionally,

$$[T] = [M^a L^b (LT^{-2})^c].$$

The equations obtained by equating corresponding powers are

$$M : 0 = a,$$
$$L : 0 = b + c,$$
$$T : 1 = -2c.$$

Therefore a = 0, b = 1/2, c = -1/2, and

$$t = K(h^{1/2}/g^{1/2}).$$

Since we wish to take the angle into account, we include an unknown function $f(\theta)$ and write

$$t = K \sqrt{\frac{h}{g}} \, f(\theta).$$

Experimentally, one finds that, if the angle θ is small, $f(\theta)$ is almost constant and approximately 2π (assuming K = 1). Note that since the exponent of mass is zero the period is independent of the mass.

Thus,

$$t = 2\pi \sqrt{\frac{h}{g}}$$

By similar arguments the reader will have no difficulty in verifying the well-known elementary relations of physics,

$$s = 1/2 \; gt^2 \; and \; v^2 = 2as$$

where s is distance, v is velocity, a is acceleration, and g is the acceleration due to gravity.

Dimensional analysis plays an important role in forming "order of magnitude" estimates of certain properties of physical systems.

There are two aspects to any model. The first is to understand it well and the second is to apply it.

Spherical Efficiency Problem

It takes six pennies to surround a penny so that each one touches it. There are gaps between the pennies. Suppose that a large area is covered with pennies that are tightly packed like that, what is the fraction of the area covered with pennies to the total area that includes the part uncovered with pennies? A citrus fruit company in Israel was concerned about loading oranges in crates to load on a ship. What was desired was to pack the oranges tightly enough to occupy minimum space but not damage the oranges. Generalize the penny problem to equal size spherical oranges. What fraction of the total space is covered with oranges. Assume that the circle is large enough not to be concerned with its sides.

The Aquarium Problem

A fish aquarium contains n units of water. Each week one unit evaporates and must be replaced with fresh water. Because fresh water contains uniformly a certain amount of salt, there is a possibility that the concentration of salt in the aquarium will become dangerously high for the fish. To cut down this risk, at the end of the week, when n - 1 units are present, another unit is removed from the aquarium (leaving n - 2 behind) and then two units of fresh water are added. This will still lead to an increase in the concentration of salt, but not as much as if the additional unit was not removed. Prove that ultimately the concentration of salt per unit in the aquarium approaches twice that in fresh water.

Let c be the concentration of salt per unit of fresh water and let X_k be the total amount of salt in the aquarium at the end of the kth week with the level of water brought to normal. We have

$$X_k = X_{k-1} - \frac{X_{k-1}}{n-1} + 2c$$
$$= \frac{n-2}{n-1} X_{k-1} + 2c$$

with
$$X_0 = nc,$$

from which the concentration approaches 2c(n-1). To see this substitute successively into the equation to obtain a geometric progression, sum that progression and let k become very large.

The following is the general solution for any number of scoops taken out of the fish aquarium.

Let:

n = initial amount of water in aquarium (in scoops)

m = number of scoops added after evaporation of one scoop and taking (m-1) scoops out of aquarium, m < n

c = concentration of salt in fresh water per scoop

$X_0 = nc$ is the initial amount of salt in the aquarium.

In any k week, the amount of salt can be calculated as:

$$X_k = X_{k-1} - \frac{(n-1)X_{k-1}}{n-1} + mc$$
$$= \left(\frac{n-m}{n-1}\right) X_{k-1} + mc$$

$$X_k \rightarrow mc\left(\frac{n-1}{m-1}\right)$$

Operational Problems

1. On some distant planet, in another of the many possible solar systems about which astronomers tell us, live creatures whose state of knowledge is highly developed. We are able to communicate with them by radio. The signals are too diffuse to determine their direction. We wish to carry out an experiment with them in which our clockwise, counterclockwise sense plays an important role. We cannot be sure that our clockwise sense is not their counterclockwise sense. We wish to settle this point before proceeding with the experiment. How should we do it?

2. Suggest an experiment to measure the volume of blood of a living human being (without killing him).

3. With your acquaintance across a river and with a yardstick in your hand, you wish to estimate the width of the river. How?

4. The sense of smell adds to the pleasure of eating and of appreciating perfumes and flowers. Suggest three problems of the operational type in which smell plays an important role. For instance, used-car dealers spray the insides of used cars to give them a "new-car smell"; mercaptans are used in natural gas to aid leak detection. Differentiation between odors may depend on differences between the infrared spectrum of the substances involved. How might this theory be used in some operation where odor plays a significant role?

5. It was learned that much machinery sent by the United States to be used for agriculture in a technologically less developed country was abandoned because of lack of parts and know-how. Suggest a manner in which this type of waste might have been avoided and the farmers aided in utilizing the machines.

6. How might one study electronic equipment used in aircraft communication in order to discover facts about the reliability of its performance?

7. An industrial warehouse is needed for storing stock to control inventory. The total cost of stocking may be minimized by studying what factors regarding inventory?

8. Given four men and four tasks with a score indicating relative performance of each man at each task, how might one study the problem of assigning the men to the tasks?

9. Thirty per cent of the dollar volume of the gross sales of a mail-order company represented returned goods. There were two types of returns: unclaimed returns and actual customer returns. The mail-order business has great advantages despite this setback; however, it is desired to minimize these types of loss. How?

10. How would one analyze the profitability of keeping department stores open at night?

11. Advertising in newspapers is common for a department store. How may one test its profitability?

12. How may one organize the operation of traffic tollbooths to minimize waste and at the same time provide efficient service?

13. Describe some methods by means of which one may simulate a naval battle. What useful lessons can be learned about the real situation?

14. Point out some weaknesses of choosing the maximum output per man-hour as a measure of effective production of an industry.

15. A certain wine importer noticed that his sales of wine were not what they should be in comparison with other types of liquor. He hired you as a consultant to look into this problem with the intention of improving the wine business. What would you do?

16. Your college classmates have for you that particular type of contempt that is bred of familiarity, and you are their supervisor for a week in the testing department of a manufacturing plant. Your esprit de corps influences production, etc. They will, in turn, each supervise for one week. What plan of action would you follow to gain their respect?

17. What can you do to gain a sales interview with a purchasing agent who buys from your competitors and who has consistently refused to see you?

18. If your car were badly stuck in heavy mud in a wooded area, far from assistance, what are some methods you would use to free yourself? In addition to a jack and spare tire, you have a sizable length of stout rope and a few tools.

19. A large tractor-trailer, while traveling an unfamiliar route, became wedged beneath a low bridge over the road. The driver and several passing motorists were baffled by their attempts to free the trailer. A creative bystander then suggested a simple solution that enabled the driver to free the trailer within a few minutes. What was the suggestion?

20. A lively three-year-old boy was suffering from an infected arm that had to be treated at home by soaking the injured arm in a medicinal solution for a two-hour period each day. His mother, who had four other young children to care for without help, could not give the boy continuous or even close attention during the two-hour periods. Faced with this problem, the mother devised a gentle means of accomplishing the prescribed treatment. How?

21. You are in a rowboat; you have dropped anchor at a fairly deep spot in the lake, and the anchor is stuck in the mud. No amount of hauling has helped to bring the anchor into the boat. What can be done to save the anchor?

22. The captain of a sailing vessel wishes to leave a port. He has only a rowboat. There is no wind. It is desired to move the sailboat out of port, using the rowboat and without pulling. How?

Mathematical Problems

1. It is desired to divide a cube of side three units into 27 cubic pieces of side one unit. Give a lower bound on the number of cuts required; a cut consists of a single plane division of the piece, or pieces piled on top of each other, into two parts. Is this lower bound sufficient for solving the problem? Give proof.

2. Given n holes on a line beside each other and n identical marbles. It is desired to place the marbles in the holes in such a way that at no time does one place a marble in a hole without having previously placed a marble next to it (to its left or right). No gaps are left in placing the marbles. In how many ways can this be done?

3. A salesman wishes to travel the shortest total distance from his home to each of n - 1 specified cities and then return home. State the problem, using the matrix of the distances, and discuss the solution of the cases n = 3 and n = 4.

4. Given a 2 by 2 matrix with randomly selected integer coefficients, what is the probability of the determinant value being even?

5. A man has a map that gives the following instructions: "At the island go to the gallows and from there walk to the pine tree, measuring the distance. At the pine tree turn right and walk the same distance. Again, from the gallows, walk to the oak tree, measuring the distance; turn left and walk the same distance. Join these two

end points and you will find the treasure at the mid-point." When you go to the island, you find that the gallows is gone, but the trees are still there. How can you find the treasure?

6. A passenger train moves nine times as fast as a freight train. The schedule at a certain station calls for one passenger train per hour and one freight train per hour, not at the same time, but a fixed time for all hours. A man goes at random times to the station. He waits for the first train to arrive, and noting its arrival time and the type of train it is, he immediately leaves, observing that nine times out of ten the first train to enter is a passenger train. Explain.

7. If V denotes the number of vertices of a polyhedron, E the number of its edges, and F the number of its faces, by using samples of polyhedral and multiple-correlation methods, obtain the Euler formula which relates V, E, and F linearly.

8. Suggest a method of analysis with data collection, which provides a measure for the accuracy of a person shooting darts at a dart board. Use hypothetical numbers and carry out the analysis. Obtain the mean position of the fall of darts and the standard deviations. Determine the distribution of fall of darts (by actually carrying out an experiment) and the probability of scoring a hit. Give the expected number of throws needed to hit the bull's eye, which is a small circle of radius r.

9. There are thousands of persons engaged in economic forecasting. If all of them simply guessed, hundreds would be correct in their forecasts time and time

again. The record does not separate the sophisticated forecaster, who has used a scientific system, from the guesser and charlatan. Among 1000 coin-tossing forecasters, about how many forecasters, on an average, would be correct in nine consecutive forecasts. Discuss and compare with the above statement.

10. How would you estimate the number of board-feet (1 inch thick, 1 foot wide, and any length) in a stand, i.e., a forest, of timber of 10,000 acres?

11. Three runners, A, B, and C, participate in a 100-yard dash. Runner B was 10 yards behind A when the latter finished, and C was 10 yards behind B when B finished. How far was C behind A when A finished? Assume that they run at constant rates.

12. A sack of potatoes was observed to weigh 100 pounds when 99 per cent of the total weight was water. Later, dehydration reduced the moisture content to 98 per cent. What did the sack weigh?

13. A man rows at constant speed whether going upstream or downstream. He tosses his hat into the stream at some spot and rows up the stream for 15 minutes, after which he decides to retrieve his hat. He turns around with no loss of time and rows downstream and recovers his hat that had moved one mile down the stream. What is the speed of the stream?

14. A and B swim at the same speed V in a river of constant speed v. A swims a hundred yards up the stream and then swims back to the starting point. B swims a hundred yards across the stream and back at the starting point. If they start out at the same time from the same

point, which one arrives first at the starting point? Give proof.

15. How might one measure the radius of the earth, using only instruments that measure angular dip and distance? How would one measure the distance to the moon?

16. When a man and his wife approached a very long escalator in a London underground, she asked him how they might count the total steps on the escalator that would be necessary to walk up if the escalator were not moving. He provided a quick scheme whereby they could deduce the number of steps after having walked up the moving escalator once at different constant rates. How?

17. Four points can be arranged to form a square. Move only two of the four points to define a new square that has twice the area of the original square.

18. In attempting to assign an order of preference to several items, one may associate a different symbol with each item and obtain between every pair comparisons of the form $a > b$, $a > b$, or $a = b$, depending on whether a is more preferable than b or conversely, or whether they are equally preferred. These relations are used to obtain an ordering of preference among all the items. Obtain a set of pairwise preferences on five items for which your preference ordering is not immediately obvious. The symbols may now be assigned numerical values to indicate the relative magnitude of preference. If five seems too small, try six items.

19. Give an upper and a lower bound to the area of a unit circle by means of the circumscribed and inscribed squares. Gen-

eralize to three dimensions and then to n dimensions. Can you find better approximations? What are the errors incurred in each of these approximations?

20. The Pennsylvania Lottery sells tickets on which there are 7 numbers chosen from the numbers 1 to 80. In the lottery drawing, eleven numbers are chosen between 1 and 80. The winning ticket must have all seven numbers coinciding with seven of the eleven numbers chosen. What is the probability of a ticket winning?

21. RAINY DAY FUN PROBLEM

a. There are five (5) houses, each of a different color, and inhabited by men of different jobs with different cars, drinks, and different nationality wives.

b. The Librarian lives in the red house.

c. The Pilot owns the Mercedes.

d. Coffee is drunk in the green house.

e. The Detective drinks tea.

f. The green house is immediately to the right (your right) of the ivory house.

g. The man married to the Japanese wife owns a Ford.

h. The American wife lives in the yellow house.

i. Milk is drunk in the middle house.

j. The Actor lives in the first house on the left (your left).

k. The man who is married to the Chinese woman lives in the house next to the man with the Volvo.

l. The American wife lives in the house next to the house where the BMW is kept.

m. The man married to the French woman drinks orange juice.

n. The Fisherman is married to an Egyptian.

o. The actor lives next to the blue house.

Answer the Questions: Who Drinks Water? Who Owns the Honda?

22. What is the frequency of occurrence of Friday the 13th?

23. Show that for 23 people the probability that at least two people have a common birthday exceeds 1/2. In general given r people, the probability that all their birthdays are different is:

$$p = (1 - \frac{1}{365})(1 - \frac{2}{365})...(1 - \frac{r-1}{365})$$
$$\approx (1 - \frac{1 + 2 + ... + (r-1)}{365}) = 1 - \frac{r(r-1)}{365} .$$

Thus $(1 - p)$ is the probability that they are not all different i.e. that at least two are the same. Derive this approximation.

24. What is the minimum number of comparisons needed to find the largest of n numbers?

25. If seven men dig seven holes in seven days how many days does it take 1 1/2 men to dig 1 1/2 holes?

26. Suppose you're on a game show, and you're given the choice of three doors: Behind one door is a car; behind the others, goats. You pick a door, say No. 1, and the host, who knows what's behind the doors, opens another door, say No. 3, which has a goat. He then says to you, "Do you want to pick door No. 2?" Is it to your advantage to switch your choice?

Logic Problems

1. Is there another place on the earth, besides the North Pole, where one can travel 100 miles south, 100 east, and 100 north, and be back at the starting point?

2. The two hands of a clock cross at 12:00. At what time does the next crossing occur?

3. In his book "Patterns of Plausible Inference," Polya asks the question: To which language is English more closely related—Hungarian or Polish? He gives an interesting analysis of the problem. Find possible invariants and measures of effectiveness, that would enable a comparison.

4. A test on "Are you a good parent?" appeared in a Sunday newspaper. A high score was to indicate good parenthood, and conversely. Does one who theoretically knows the answers necessarily succeed in practicing good parenthood? How about the good parent; is he supposed to answer correctly? Derive some

conclusions on correspondence between thought and action.

5. Give an explanation of how one may go about learning to walk on hot coals, such as is done by some experts in India.

6. If A, B, C, and D each speak the truth once in three times (independently) and A affirms that B denies that C declares that D is a liar, what is the probability that D was telling the truth? Prove that the correct probability is 13/41, and that this is also the probability that A, B, and C each told the truth.

7. In a distant land dwelt the members of two political parties. The Mendacians were inveterate liars, while the Veracians were unfailingly truthful. Once a stranger visited the land, and on meeting a group of three inhabitants inquired as to which political party they belonged. The first murmured something that the stranger failed to hear. The second remarked, "He said he was a Mendacian." The third said to the second, "You're a liar!" To which political party did the third belong?

8. Three candidates for membership in a society were given the following test of logic. They were told that each would be blindfolded and a hat would be put on his head. The hat might be either black or white. Then the blindfolds would be removed, so that each might see the colors of the hats worn by the other two. Each man who saw a black hat was to raise a hand. The first to infer correctly the color of his own hat would be admitted to membership.

9. Discuss the "reality" in the operational sense of the following:

The sound when a tree falls in the forest with no ears within hearing distance.
Euclidean plane geometry
Genes (carriers of hereditary characteristics)
Distinguish as either valid or true and explain:
Light travels in vacuo at a speed of approximately 186,000 miles per second.
The sum of the length of any two sides of a triangle exceeds the length of the third side.
Nothing can travel faster than light.

10. In the defense of shipping from submarine attack, the value of various defensive tactics might be examined in the light of three different measures of effectiveness:
A. The number of enemy subs sunk per month at fixed cargo tonnage
B. The total cargo tonnage safely delivered per month
C. The ratio of cargo tonnage safely delivered to the total shipped
Comment on each of these with respect to their merits for long- and short-term war. Which would most likely be applicable to a war expected to last only three months?

11. Discuss the nature of the causal relation in the following statements:
The cause of ignorance is lack of school facilities.
Because you remained too long in the hot sun, you have an uncomfortable sunburn.
The spontaneous expansion of a gas is the result of the second law of thermodynamics.

12. Suggest how one might quantify the following:
The emotional stability of mice
The ability to write clear and readable prose
The musical talent of a violinist

The ability to distinguish odors

13. Point out the fallacies in the following statements:
This man has written inflammatory pamphlets against the United States government. He has demonstrably disturbed the tranquility of the nation . . . He should, therefore, be silenced.

14. If I am the devil, then the devil and I are one. I am not the devil; therefore we are two. Hence 2 = 1.

15. To allow every man an unbounded freedom of speech must always be, on the whole, advantageous to the State, for it is highly conductive to the interests of the community that each individual should enjoy a liberty, perfectly unlimited, of expressing his sentiments.

16. State explicitly and resolve the following paradoxes:
He shaves all those men of Seville and only those men of Seville who do not shave themselves. Does he shave himself?

17. Epimenides, the Cretan, said, "All Cretans always lie." How about Epimenides, himself?

Puzzles for the Virtuoso (and Virtuosa)

1. Three cannibals, only one of whom can row, and three missionaries, only one of whom can row, are faced with crossing a river in a boat which can take no more than two people. How is this done if at no place there are left more cannibals than missionaries, the former of which out of habit would naturally eat their mentors? The boat must always be considered to be either on one side or gone to the other side.

2. A cable running from London to New York is made up of one million independent wires. A single individual desires to identify the ends of these wires by means of three operations. Any number of short connecting cords is available, along with a strong battery and meter to test the flow of current. An operation consists of making any number of connections between wires, checking the flow of current and labeling as is necessary on one side. So the individual, starting in New York, connects, tests and labels; goes to London and does the same and finally returns to New York to do more such testing and labeling and then finishes by having each wire similarly labeled in both cities. How?

3. Can you cover a chess board in which the bottom left corner square and top right corner square are removed with dominos each of which covers two squares exactly, and so that there is no overlapping of dominos and no uncovered squares?

4. A man goes from A to B at the uniform rate of 30 miles per hour. How fast would he have to come back to average 60 miles an hour over the time taken in the whole trip?

5. You are in a bar and someone comes up to you and lays down six quarters on a line, three heads and three tails showing, but not in any specific order. He proposes the following game: You put a dollar down and he will expose one coin at a time. If it is a head he would give you $1.50 for the dollar and if it is tails, he would give you $.50. Then he pro-

ceeds to the next coin. If it is heads your $1.50 would become $2.25 or if it were $.50 it would become $.75 and so on, increasing the value respectively by one half again if the coin is a head or decreasing by one half if it is a tail. He arranges the coins randomly and wants to bet $1.00 that he can come closer to what the final amount would be than you can. Should you play the game and what is our guess about the final amount?

6. In a certain medieval city, the ruling Emir issued the following proclamation in the city's daily newspaper. "It has come to our ears that there is unfaithfulness in our city. As is usual in these cases, an unfaithful wife is known to be so to everyone except her husband. Any man who can prove that his wife is unfaithful has, by the law of the land, the right to put her to death." Forty days later, the newspaper carried the following announcement: "Forty women of the city have been found slain." Why?

7. How would you divide a cake fairly between two people so they are both happy with what they get? How would you divide a cake fairly between three people so each would be happy with his part?

8. The bank makes a mistake in cashing a check and gives dollars for pennies and pennies for dollars. After spending $3.50, a man finds that he has left twice the true amount of the check. What is this amount?

9. Hanging over a pulley there is a rope with a weight at one end; at the other end hangs a monkey of equal weight. The rope weighs 4 oz./ft. The combined ages of the monkey and its mother are 4 years and the weight of the monkey is as many pounds as its mother is years old. The mother is twice as old as the monkey was when the mother was half as old as the monkey will be when the monkey is three times as old as its mother was when she was 3 times as old as the monkey was. The weight of the rope is half as much again as the difference between the weight of the weight and the weight of the weight plus the weight of the monkey. What is the length of the rope?

10. A census-taker and a public opinion pollster both approach the house at 900 Main Street at the same time, each wanting to know the ages of its occupants. The owner gives his own age, and says three other people live there also, and that the product of their ages (three different whole numbers) is the same as the house number.

The owner says he will tell the census-taker the age of the middle person. He whispers this age to the census-taker, who then says he is unable to determine the other two ages.

Then the owner says he will tell the pollster the sum of the ages of the oldest and of one of the other two. He whispers this sum to the pollster, who says he too is unable to figure out the ages.

The owner asks each in turn and:
The census-taker says he can't determine the ages yet.
The pollster says he can't either.
The census-taker says he still can't.
The pollster says he can't yet.
The census-taker says he still doesn't know.
But the pollster says, "Now I know all three ages. What are the three ages?"

All the information needed to solve the problem is here.

11. Assign numbers to letters in the following division problem to get the final answer,

```
            AT
    WE │ SANG
        STY
        RAG
        RAG
        000
```

12. As an army 5 miles long began to march at constant speed, a bee left the rear flying to the front at constant speed. Upon reaching the front it immediately turned around and started for the rear and reached there after the army had traveled 5 miles.   How far did the bee travel? Suppose that the bee again goes to the front of the army and returns to the rear and keeps repeating this until the army travels five miles. What distance would he have traveled, if the army moves at three miles per hour and the bee moves at six miles per hour?

13. Given n identical cars whose gas tanks take identical amounts of gas and make the same mileage to the gallon. No other storage of gas is possible in any car. It is possible to take gas from the tank of one car and distribute it among any number of the cars. Starting out with full tanks, it is desired to advance one of the cars the maximum distance possible. Calculate this distance.

14. The Nazis imprisoned a Polish logician. One Saturday the guard came in and told him that he was going to be executed someday during the next week but he would never know the day. He reasoned that if he does not get executed on Friday

he would know that it would be Saturday, so it can't be Saturday. Similarly if he is not executed on Thursday he would know that it has to be on Friday because he knows it can't be on Saturday, and so on working backwards he was joyed to find that he can know the day. But the guard had said that he wouldn't, therefore he concluded that he would not be executed because he is so smart that he knows the day. Alas one morning during the week they took him out and shot him. Where did he go wrong even if the guard was honest?

15. Three men were brought before a judge. They are classified as honest or liar. The judge asked the first man what he was and he mumbled something, upon which the second man said that the first said he was a liar. The third man said that the second man is a liar and the first man is honest. Who is telling the truth?

16. A man comes to a fork in the road. Not knowing which branch to take he sees two men one a liar and the other honest. He knows the situation but does not know which is which. They know one another. He asks only one question from one man. The man answers yes, or no. The other man is there but says nothing. With this, he takes the right road. What does he ask, and how does he solve the problem?

17. Tom, Dick and Harry take several tests. On each test only one of them received the grade A, another B and the third C, where A, B and C are integers. After all the tests were completed three integer values were assigned to A, B and C. Tom's total score was 22, Dick's 9 and Harry's 9. The question is, "If Dick was first in spelling, who was second in arithmetic?"

18. There is more to a problem than meets the eye. The case of hidden assumptions. Mary is twice as old as Ann was when Mary was as old as Ann is. The sum of their ages is 28. What are their ages?

19. How would you find a counterfeit coin among eleven other good identical coins in three weighing on an equal arm balance, and also tell if it is heavier or lighter than a good coin?

20. There are n+1 mints in a country which, produce the same denomination coin. Only one mint is known to make a good coin. The others may or may not be counterfeiting, but all good coins have the same weight– and all false coins have the same weight. Given one good coin and any number of coins from each mint, and also given a scale for measuring weights in grams; determine which are the counterfeiter mints in three weightings.

21. A census taker knocked on the door of a house and got some information from a man who lived there. He asked him if anyone else lived there. The man said, "Yes, there are three other people who live here, their ages are all different. The sum of their ages is the number of this house (which the census taker knew), and the product of their ages is 1296". The census taker, after some calculations, asked a question to which he got a yes or no answer and left. What is the number of the house?

22. It has been snowing at a constant rate. A snowplough starts plowing snow sometime after it began snowing. It ploughed at the average rate of 2 miles per hour the first hour and one mile per hour the sec-

ond hour. How long before the snowplough started ploughing did it start snowing?

23. A man looking at a portrait says: "That person's father was my father's son. I have no brothers and no sons." What was the relationship of the person in the portrait to him? Don't jump to conclusions.

24. A thirty car and a twenty car train meet head on at a siding, which can only take ten cars. Using the siding it is desired to pass the trains without disturbing the order in which the cars were arranged.

25. If 12 oxen eat the grass (which is growing uniformly all the time) on 3 1/3 acres in 4 weeks, and if 21 oxen eat the grass on 10 acres in 9 weeks, how many oxen will it take to eat all the grass on 24 acres in 18 weeks?   – Isaac Newton, 1712

Solutions to Puzzles for the Virtuosi

1. First let the cannibal rower take the other two cannibals, one at a time returning empty each time. The second time he returns, the missionary rower takes another missionary and brings a cannibal. He then takes the rowing cannibal and brings the other cannibal back. Finally he takes the third missionary and lets the rowing cannibal take over completing the job.

2. Connect the wires in New York in pairs, leaving the last two wires unconnected if the number of wires n is even, and the last one unconnected if n is odd. In London, test to identify the pairs. Label them sequentially $(x_1, x_2), (x_3, x_4), ..., (x_{n-1}, x_n)$.

The last pair would not be connected if n is even. Connect x_{n-2} to x_{n-1}, x_{n-4} to x_{n-3}, and in general connect x_{n-2} to x_{n-2k+1}. In New York test one of the two free wires or the free one with all the rest until a current passes. If no current passes label it x_n and label the other free wire x_{n-1} and proceed to find x_{n-2}. Then it is connected to x_{n-3}. Label and proceed. Test the latter with all the wires to find x_{n-4} and label it. It is connected to x_{n-5}. Proceed similarly. If one wire is left free because n is odd the testing is simpler.

3. The two cut off squares are of the same color. A domino always covers two squares of opposite color. Since the board now has 30 squares of one color and 32 of the other, it is impossible to cover it as required.

4. Distance/time = velocity; time = distance/velocity; total distance traveled/total time = average velocity over entire trip. Thus 2d/(d/30 + d/x) = 2d/(2d/60); or d/30 + d/x = 2d/60; or 1/x= 0 and hence x = infinity.

5. Since three coins are heads and three are tails and one always multiplies to get the final result, it does not matter what the order is. The answer is always $.421875 obtained by multiplying ($1.00 x 3/2 x 3/2 x 3/2 x 1/2 x 1/2 x 1/2).

6. Assume that there is only one unfaithful wife. Every man knows it but her husband who does not know any unfaithful wife. But the trusted Emir had declared that there is at least one, and the husband as a good logician, reasons on the first day (or first unit of time) that it must be his wife that is unfaithful and he puts her to death on the first day. None of the other men can be sure about the unfaithfulness of their wives on that day, but seeing that one woman was put to death and knowing that her husband must have reasoned it out, they become sure that their own wives are in fact faithful. Note that the wife could not be unfaithful if she and her husband were the only members of the population. There has to be at least one other man to cause it if two wives are unfaithful, every man but their two husbands knows that there are at least two (there may be three if it turns out that his wife is also unfaithful). The two husbands each know of only one unfaithful wife, but still suspect their own. On the second day, either of them, and hence both, reason that had his wife been faithful the other husband would have concluded on the first day that his wife was unfaithful and put her to death. Since no death occurred on the first day, both husbands eliminate their wives on the second.

And so early in the morning of the fortieth day when each of the forty men (who knew that there are 39 unfaithful wives and suspecting his wife to be the fortieth) discovered that the 39 women he knew had not been slain on the 39th day, concluded that his own wife cannot be faithful. They all arrived at this conclusion, each and every one of them. Forty wives were then slain.

7. Cake division solution for two people: let one divide and the other choose; for three people: let the first divide into three parts and the second choose a piece which he keeps if the third does not object in which case the third can choose one of the other two pieces. If the third objects he can divide the piece chosen by the second into two parts of which the second chooses

132

one and the third takes the other. Of the remaining two parts either both the second and the third persons agree on one which they divide between them or if each of them thinks one of the two pieces is larger than the other he divides that piece with the first person each time using the fair division method between two people.

8. Solution to the Bank's Mistake: Let x denote dollars and y denote cents. Then $100y + x - 350 = 2(100x + y)$ or $98y - 2x$ $3x/98 - 3 - 56/98 = 0$. Now y, 2x, and 3 are integers. Therefore $(3x + 56)/98$ must be an integer k or $x = (98k - 56)/3$ is an integer which of course must also be positive for any k. Now 100 is greater than v cents which according to the problem is greater than x. As we start trying out different values, $k = 1,2,...,$ we find that k 1 is the only value which works, yielding $x = 14$, and $y = 32$.

9. Solution to the Monkey Problem: If q is the age of the mother and p is the age of the monkey then $q - p = c$ where c is some fixed number. The second long statement says algebraically $q = 2p_1, q_1 = p_2/2, p_2 = 3q_3, q_3 = 3p_3$. Obviously, $q_3-p_3=c$, so that $3p_3-p_3 = c$, or $p_3=c/2$ and hence $q_3=c+c/2=3c/2$. Now $2(9/2 p_3+c)=13/2c$, or $q_1=9/4c$, and $p_1=q_1-c=5/4c$. But $q-p=c$, and $q=2p_1=5/2c$, therefore $p=3/2c$. Since $q+p=4$, $c=1$, $q=5/2$, $p=3/2$. The weight of the monkey is 5/2 pounds and that of the rope is $1/2x5/2$ pounds or $16 x 5/4 = 20$ ounces, and its length is $20/4 = 5$ feet.

10. Solution to the Pollster and Census-taker Problem: Obtain all factorizations of 900 into 3 distinct factors. This gives Columns I below. Then take the sums of the largest number and each of the other two

numbers next to it in Columns I. This gives Columns II. The reasoning of the census-taker and the pollster go as follows:

a) The census-taker who knows the middle age cannot tell the ages because of the non-uniqueness of middle ages. And hence we must eliminate all rows of 5 numbers appearing in both Columns I and II which in Columns I have a unique middle age. The census-taker could not determine the answer.

b) The pollster knows the sum of the ages of the older and one of the two younger persons, but is unable to identify the row because the number he knows is not unique. Thus we eliminate all rows in which both numbers in Columns II are unique. The pollster still could not determine the answer.

c) Since the pollster couldn't tell the ages, the census-taker knows the pollster is in a non-unique situation, so he also does step 2. There are still non-unique middle ages and he says he cannot get the answer. Step 3 does not eliminate anything new.

d) The pollster concludes that the census-taker still has non-unique middle ages, so he eliminates all rows which have unique middle ages and still finds the sum of the ages which he knows occur in more than a single remaining row in Columns II. He still finds non-unique ones and says he does not know the answer.

e) The census-taker now eliminates all rows with unique pairs in the second columns and still finds non-unique middle ages in the first columns. He says he does not know the answer.

f) The pollster eliminates all rows in the first columns with unique middle ages but still finds a non-unique pair situation in

Columns II. He says he does not know the answer.

g) The census-taker eliminates all rows with unique pairs in Columns II and still finds non-unique middle ages in Columns I. He says he still does not know the answer.

h) The pollster eliminates the rows with unique middle ages and then says he knows the answer. After all the eliminations we are left with the two rows: 4 9 25 29 34 and 5 9 20 25 29

i) We reason as follows: The sum of the two ages the pollster knows is not 34 because this number is unique whereas 29 is repeated in these two rows and 25 appears in the last row which was eliminated earlier. Since he could actually determine the ages the sum must be 25, not 29 which occurs in both rows. Thus the ages are 5, 9, and 20.

Step in which rows are eliminated:

			I		II
1	1	2	450	451	452
2&3	1	3	300	301	303
2&3	1	4	225	226	229
2&3	1	5	180	181	185
2&3	1	6	150	151	156
2&3	1	9	100	101	109
2&3	1	10	90	91	100
2&3	1	12	75	76	87
2&3	1	15	60	61	75
1	1	18	50	51	68
1	1	20	45	46	65
1	1	25	36	37	61
2&3	2	3	150	152	153
2&3	2	5	90	92	95
2&3	2	6	75	77	81
2&3	2	9	50	52	59
2&3	2	10	45	47	55
2&3	2	15	30	32	45
4	2	18	25	27	43
2&3	3	4	75	78	79

2&3	3	5	60	63	65
2&3	3	6	50	53	56
2&3	3	10	30	33	40
6	3	12	25	28	37
4	3	15	20	23	35
2&3	4	5	45	49	50
Final	4	9	25	29	34
4	5	6	30	35	36
Final	5	9	20	25	20
7	5	10	18	23	28
5	5	12	15	20	27
8	6	10	15	21	25

11. Solution to the Division Problem: Note that A > T because there is no carryover. Begin the analysis assuming that G = 1 and let E = 1, then 2, then 3, etc. Each time running through the possibility for T, get:

```
                   63
         _____
     89 | 5607
         ——   534
         _____
              267
              267
              ———
              000
```

12. Solution to the army-bee problem. Since they travel with constant velocity, the ratio of the distance the bee travels to the distance the army travels is a constant. If x is the distance the bee travels, and y is the distance the army travels as the bee travels forward, then $x/5 = (5 + y)/y = y/(5 - y)$. From the two get $x = 5(1 + \sqrt{2})$.

Since it takes the army 5/3 hours to cover five miles, the bee travels a distance of 10 miles during this time. If you formed an infinite series, it should, converge to 10 as a limit.

13. Solution to the n car problem. The maximum distance is obtained if every other car is made to travel the minimum distance except the last one. Imagine that all the tanks are hooked together so that some of the car tanks are constantly drained into the others so that they are always full. Since the cars whose tanks are being emptied are traveling, the gas they burn may as well be burned by a single car going a farther distance. Let d be the distance any of them can travel on a tankful. All n cars will advance to a certain point where one car gives all its gas to the remaining n-1 and their tanks will then be full. Clearly they all advance to a distance d/n, since one tankful would have been expended by the n cars. Now the n-1 cars with tanks full will similarly advance to a point where one of them will give up the gas to n-2 of them and their tanks will be full. This distance is clearly d/(n-1) since again one tankful has been expended by n-1 cars. Repeating the process one has for the last car the distance d(1/n+1/(n-1)+...+1) = d/(1+1/2+...+1/n).

14. The Polish logician. We already know about the barber of Seville who only shaves men in Seville who do not shave themselves. Does he shave himself or doesn't he? If he does then by the statement of the problem he does not, and if he does not then the problem says that he does. This is a logical dilemma that was solved by Russell's theory of types. To avoid such a logical difficulty we must not use statements that refer to themselves. The logician was told that there was to be a day of execution, but it was to be on no day of the week that he could know. He concluded that it was on no

day of the week. This is a statement, which talks about itself, and no clear logical conclusion can be deduced from it.

15. The judge and the three men. Suppose that the third man was a liar. Then the second man was honest and the first a liar. But if the first was a liar, he would mumble that he is honest and the second, being honest would say so. This not being the case, the third man is honest, etc.

16. "Yes", or "no"? He points to one of the roads and asks one of the men, "If I were to ask him (pointing to the other man) if this is the right road would he say yes?"

The man had reasoned that if this question is asked of the liar he would say "no" (if the road is the right one) because he would lie about what the other man would say. If it is asked of the honest man he would also say "no" since the liar would naturally say no to it. So he expects a "no" answer from both if he is pointing to the right road. Similarly he expects a "yes" answer from both if he is pointing to the wrong road.

17. Solution to Tom, Dick and Harry: Let m be the number of tests, then we must have n(A+B+C) = 40; that is, 40 must be divisible by n. The problem says that n is greater than or equal to 2. Also n cannot be more than 6 because the minimum values for A, B, and C are 3, 2, and 1, and, for example, 7(3+2+1)=42. Since 40 must be divisible by n, n cannot be 6 or 3 and thus the number of tests is 5 or 4 or 2. Note that A is less than 9 - (# of tests - 1) because Dick can then score last on the remaining tests to be added to his first score on spelling. Now n cannot be 2 for then A+B+C = 20 and since the total

score for Dick and Harry is 9, A must be no more than 8 and hence C must be 1 to bring Dick's total to 9. But then B must be 11, which is impossible. Similarly, A = 7, C = 2, B = 11; A = 6, C = 3, B = 11; A = 5, C = 4, B = 11 are all impossible, hence n is either 4 or 5. If a = 4 then A, B, C can assume the values 6,3,1 or 5,4,1 or 5,3,2. The first is impossible because Harry would obtain a total score of more than 9 or Tom cannot score a total of 22. The second and third are impossible because Dick would score more than 9. Thus n = 5 and A, B, C are either 5,2,1 or 4,3,1. The second is impossible because Dick would obtain a score of more than 9. Thus since Dick is first at spelling his grades would be (5,1,1,1,1); Harry would get (1,2,2,2,2) and he would be second in arithmetic. Tom's score is (2,5,5,5,5).

18. Mary and Ann. A poor formulation. Let their ages now be a and b, and their ages before be x and y. Then, a=2y, x= b and a+b=28. We have three equations and four unknowns, and we need another equation to solve for the variables. The missing statement is that a-b = x-y. The solution is a=16, b=12, x=12, y=8.

Here is another good formulation that is simple. Let t be the time elapsed between their ages before and now. Then x=2(y-t), x-w = y, and x+y=28. We now only have three equations in three unknowns.

19. The counterfeit coin. Divide the coins into three groups of four, A, B, and C. In the first weighing, try A against B. if they balance, weigh three coins from C against three coins from A or B. If they balance, use the third weighing to determine whether the fourth coin in C is heavier or lighter than a good coin; if they do not balance, and if they are heavier, then the

counterfeit is heavier, or if they are lighter, then the counterfeit is lighter, and it can be found in the third weighing by putting one of the three in one pan of the balance and another in the other pan. If they balance, then the third is the counterfeit and we already know if it is heavier or lighter; and if they do not balance, then the heavier or lighter coin is accordingly the counterfeit.

If A and B do not balance, take out three coins from A and replace them with three coins from B and replace these with three coins from C which we know are good. If in the second weighing A and B balance, then the counterfeit is one of the three taken out and it can be determined in the remaining weighing as we just did for the three coins in C.

Note that we already know whether the counterfeit in C is heavier or lighter from the first weighing. If A and B do not balance, then if the balance maintains the same direction as in the first weighing, the counterfeit is the fourth coin of A or the fourth coin of B and we can determine which one it is in the remaining weighing. If the balance reverses direction, then the counterfeit is one of the three coins transferred from B to A and we know whether it is heavier or lighter and in one weighing by putting one coin against another we can determine which one of the three coins it is. In this manner we discover the counterfeit and whether it is heavier or lighter.

20. The Mints. First, weigh the good coin and let its weight be w grams. Next take one coin from each of the n possibly suspect mints and weigh these n coins as a collection. If their weight x is nw then there are no counterfeiters. Otherwise, take m,

where m>n, coins from the *ith* mint i =l, . . . ,n and weigh them. Denote this number of coins by s and its total weight by y. To find the counterfeiters, do the following calculations. First note that if there are j counterfeiters, then (x-nw)/j is the difference between the weights of a good coin and a counterfeit. If all n mints make a counterfeit, then (y-sw)/s=(x-nw)/n, or (y-sw)/(x-nw)=s/n. In general, the number of counterfeiters can be anything, and the number of coins taken from them would be different from s.

Thus we must try different ratios on the right side which relates to the counterfeiters. Since the number of counterfeiters and their identity must be known, the right side must be a unique ratio, otherwise it could be obtained for different subsets of mints, and it would be impossible to identify the counterfeiters. That is why we took b coins from the jth mint, so that the sum s is a finite sum of consecutive powers of b starting with zero and ending in n-1. Any other sum representing the number of coins from counterfeiters can be obtained from s by making the coefficients of the powers of b one or zero.

Let N(c) denote the number of ones in expressing c as a sum of powers of b. The number of mints being tested is equal to the number of ones. To see why the ratio for a number of mints not more than n is unique only if b is greater than n, consider two equal ratios, c/N(c) and d/N(d). We have N(c) d = N(d) c. When N(c) d is written as a sum of powers of b the coefficients would be either zero or N(c), having multiplied the expression for d in terms of powers of b by N(c). Similarly for N(d) c. Since the two numbers are the same, their expressions are the

same, and hence their coefficients are the same.

Thus N(c)=N(d), from which it follows that the original expressions must also be the same and hence c = d. Finally, N(c), which is the possible number of counterfeiters, can be as large as n, therefore the number b must be greater than n so that the coefficients in the expansion can be as large as N(c) so the preceding argument can be made, and uniqueness of the ratios for values of N(c) not more than n can be assured.

To see how non-uniqueness arises, let n=9, and let b=2. Then 69=2(power 6)+2(power 2)+2(power 0), and the first, third, and sixth mints are suspect, with a ratio of 69/3=23. However, 92=2(power 6)+2(power 4)+2(power 3) +2 (power 2), and ratio of also 92/4=23. Another ratio is 115/5=23. If N(23r)=r, then 23r >2 (power r- 1), and r < 9. The other possibilities, 1, 2, 6, 7, 8, do not give rise to the same ratio.

21. The census taker:

Ages	Ages	Sum	Sum
1	2	648	651
1	3	432	436
1	4	324	329
1	6	216	223
1	8	162	171
1	9	144	154
1	12	108	121
1	16	81	98
1	18	72	91
1	24	54	79
1	27	48	76
2	3	216	222
2	4	162	168
2	6	108	116

2	8	81	91
2	9	72	83
2	12	54	68
2	18	36	56
2	24	27	52
3	4	108	115
3	6	72	81
3	8	54	65
3	9	48	60
3	12	36	51
3	16	27	46
3	18	24	45
4	6	54	64
4	9	36	49
4	12	27	43
6	8	27	41
6	9	24	39
6	12	18	36
8	9	18	35

The only sum of the three ages, which is not unique and would give the census taker difficulty, is 91 and it is the number of the house. He asks a question to remove the ambiguity and determine the ages.

22. The snow plough problem. Let the snow plough start ploughing at time zero and let k be the length of time it started snowing before the snow plough began. Let c be the rate of snowfall. If the snow plough has ploughed for a time of length t, then the depth is $A=c(k+t)$. The rate of change in the distance s which the plough travels is inversely proportional to A, or $ds/dt=a/A$ where a is the constant of proportionality. Substituting for A we get $ds/dt=a/c(k+t)$. Integration yields $s=b \log (k+t)+\log C$, where $b-a/c$ and log C is the constant of integration. if we put $t=0$ at $s=0$, and solve for log C our equation becomes $s-b \log (k+t)/k$. If we now put $t=1$ and $s=2$ we get $b=2/\log (k+1)/k$. If we again put $t=2$ and $s=3$ we get $3=2[\log (k+2)/k]/\log (k+1)/k$ which simplifies to $k^2+k-1=0$ whose quadratic solution is $k=.618$ or about 37 minutes.

23. The person in the portrait was his daughter.

24. Disconnect 10 of the 20 car train, connect to back of 30 car train, pass the remaining 10 cars through the siding and back up the 30 car train to connect its last 10 cars to it.

25. 36 Oxen. Use x food ox/week, y grass at beginning on acre, z amount grass growing/week.

Our Heritage

Chapter Five

Introduction

We are a Manifestation of Consciousness: Awareness, Order and Control.

Our Destiny is More Consciousness and More Creativity.

Creativity requires putting forth an effort. That effort must be directed towards a goal: to create something new and original. We need to be creative to be effective problem solvers, so we can enhance our living and ensure our survival. We will study how to overcome obstacles and implement our best solutions. Is this challenge worth the effort? Consider the words of Neil Armstrong after landing on the moon, "One small step for a man, one giant step for mankind."

We can classify the large problems that challenge our survival and require our vigilance and creativity into three types:

1) How to prevent or overcome dangers from within the earth itself, such as earthquakes, volcanoes, gases, magnetic fields and the like;

2) How to deal with two kinds of problems we face on the surface of the earth. One is environmental, ranging from the greenhouse effect to radiation and the ozone layer, the ice age, air and water pollution and scarcity, drought, and plant and animal threats including insects, bacteria, and viruses. The second is threat from our own kind, ranging from over- or under-population to nuclear attack and other forms of violence, war, terrorism, crime, oppressive governments or groups, and other examples of man's inhumanity to man, to animals, to plants, and to the environment. There is also ignorance, bad decision making, waste of resources and inattentiveness to the problems around us, both real and potential.

3) How to anticipate and deal with problems from outer space. These problems include collisions with other bodies, increased radiation from the sun or from other sources, increased dust or gases and increased heat or cold, and finally falling into the sun or falling out into space and whether some form of humankind will eventually make it, and even

---

Creativity Is the Essence of Life

To Henri Bergson,(1859-1941) the French philosopher and Nobel Laureate, creativity — or the continuous birth of the new — is the essence of life. It is taking place in the real world every instant through creative evolution. Creativity is perfected in nature through birth, growth and maturation. In human consciousness it takes the form of continuous emergence of new images and experiences.

In place of Cartesian dualism of mind and matter, Bergson proposed a dualism of matter as (1) an aggregate of images surrounding the body, which is the center of action, and (2) pure memory, which is a source of images that present themselves in the abnormal states of fantasies, or in creative moments as insights unavailable to perception or conscious recall. This view of creativity is in contrast with the constructionist, instrumentalist and pragmatic idea that creativity is an invention that is a combination of concepts that leads to the solution of a problem. Another view of creativity is that of intellectualism or neorealism, in which creativity is regarded as intellectual contemplation, as the Platonists believed.

disassembling and reassembling the earth elsewhere before the sun engulfs it.

In this chapter we talk about five central influences on our creativity to deal with such gigantic problems of survival. We discuss how focusing on them can enhance our potential for creative application:

1. How to find inspiration which redirects the mind;
2. How evolution affects our ability to sense, perceive, understand, and create;
3. How linear cause–effect logical thinking limits our minds: there is a need to adopt and use nonlinear morphological analysis to help us synthesize diverse information and draw conclusions, formulate problems and apply creativity to deal with the complexity around us;
4. How we can use non-relativistic quantum theory to potentially validate predictions made by people whose insights are beyond the ordinary, but appear to us as absurd because of our single-world concept of reality. We need people who can look far ahead and help us anticipate problems that we might face in the future. We can then apply our talents long in advance to think about and to search for solutions to these problems or for ways to prevent them from materializing.
5. The role of aesthetics and order in the creative process.

Creativity and Inspiration

It is the complex layering of consciousness and unconsciousness that creates difficulty when we try to discuss art, ritual, mythology or religion. Gregory Bateson, in his book Steps to an Ecology of Mind (Ballantine Books, 1972), says that levels of the mind have been discussed from many points of view, including:

a) The better an organism "knows" something such as skill and art, the less conscious it becomes of its knowledge, because through habit and repetition, things sink to deeper and deeper levels of the mind ("The heart has its reasons which reason does not at all perceive").
b) We make conscious, three-dimensional images from what we see, using unconscious mathematical processes of perception we have no control over.
c) Dreams, art and religion are metaphors coded in the unconscious according to a primary process not accessible to the language or secondary process of the conscious, of which style, neatness and boldness of contrast are examples.
d) The unconscious is the cellar or cupboard to which fearful and painful memories are consigned by a process of repression. Many sorts of information are inaccessible to conscious inspection with its secondary process interpretations. Dreams, for example, are material unacceptable to conscious thought translated into the metaphoric idiom of primary process to avoid waking the dreamer.

The unconscious is the primary process of operation. In it, things or persons are not identified. Instead, what is highlighted are relationships between them. It communicates in metaphors in which patterns of relationship are preserved, but specific things or people can be replaced by other things or people between whom the same relationships hold. The primary process lacks negatives, temporal context (past, present, future) and linguistic mood (i.e., there is no identification of the indicative, subjunctive, etc. moods.) The secondary process is that of the conscious. It is coded by concrete thought and its rules are designed to serve specific purposes. It talks about things or persons, and attaches predicates to the specific things or persons that have been mentioned.

Although people once thought that the existence of the unconscious needed proof, nowadays we understand that unconscious components are continuously present in the multiple forms that we use in communication. Each skill we possess involves a large number of unconscious components. It is difficult to describe the efficient way these components work together. Things that we need to access often, such as control of behavior, must stay on the surface. Only those things that stay the same, even when the environment changes, sink to the unconscious.

Bateson says: " It is not conceivably possible for any system to be totally conscious. Suppose that on the screen of consciousness there are reports from many parts of the total mind, and consider the addition to consciousness of those reports necessary to cover what is, at a given stage of evolution, not already covered. This addition will involve a very great increase in the circuit structure of the brain but still will not achieve total coverage. The next step will be to cover the processes and events occurring in the circuit structure that we have just added. Clearly, the problem is insoluble, and every next step in the approach to total consciousness will involve a great increase in

> A sense of humor and willingness to have fun are essential to making creative contributions. The use of verbal humor in everyday encounters to charm and disarm others, even one's boss, is encouraged. It is said that life does not become less serious because it is more fun.

the circuitry required. It follows that all organisms must be content with little consciousness, and that economy in

consciousness will be of the first importance. No organism can afford to be conscious of matters with which it could deal at unconscious levels."

It is the conscious in which intelligence is manifest. Intuition and inspiration go with the subconscious. There is little relationship between natural intelligence and creativity. This may be a consequence of the fact that the conscious is not fully attuned and allied to the subconscious. Not too long ago, in our own time, creativity was regarded as a very special gift given only to some people but not to the rest of humanity. Creativity was thought to be something esoteric. Today we are told that one can be very intelligent but not creative at all, or one can be very creative but not very intelligent. One can teach people to be creative, but one cannot do much to improve people's level of natural intelligence.

Freud's view was that creativity originates in the individual, and that the creative process and neurosis (or psychosis), are closely identified. The creative artist uses the unconscious for personal gratification. Thus individual creativity originates in the tension between the conscious and unsatisfied unconscious biological drives. The creative process is indeed something of a mystery.

In the past, those who studied outstanding scientists were unable to identify the qualities that led them to make their significant contributions. More recently, observers have noted what they believe to be important factors in creativity. Solomon Snyder discusses the importance of mentorship in the December 1989 issue of the Johns Hopkins Magazine that, "IQ scores, schools attended, socioeconomic status, parental occupation, the warmth or coldness of the childhood environment do not seem to be particularly relevant." He says that most scientists are intelligent, but not remarkably brilliant, "The best way to predict who will make a discovery worthy of a Nobel Prize is simply to examine who trained them. "A good mentor needs both to train the intellect by emphasizing the analytical faculties and to strengthen the soul by nurturing self-confidence. Such encouragement leads to the transformation of a tentative student to a self-possessed, probing and innovative intellect.

If the idea of having a good mentor to become highly creative is valid, then in addition to reading books on creativity, such as this one, and doing stimulating exercises, one must find a mentor who interacts continuously to shape a disciple's attitude.

J. Aczél is a renowned mathematician of Hungarian origin responsible for significant developments in the field of functional equations. Citing some Hungarian and other mathematicians, Aczél has this to say about the practice of creativity: "Not only genius but most kinds of creativity are 90% perspiration, 10% inspiration. Inspiration can come anywhere, not only at your desk but also walking, on buses, in cars, planes, in the bathroom, during any part of the day, at night, even when you just wake up for a few moments. Recently mine have been coming quite often while swimming. Try to act on it or remember later. Of course, not every idea proves good but if you don't follow it up, you will never know. Work on it.

"This reminds me of an anecdote (rather authentic, which I heard from Fejer): Minkowski (a Russian) was fixing something in the house and his four year old son asked him questions and generally made a pest of himself. His mother warned him: 'Don't disturb your father while he is working'. The child looked up in amazement: 'What! Working? Does working not mean lying down on the sofa with your eyes closed?'

Evidently that was the way Minkowski got his mathematical ideas and in these situations the boy had also been told not to disturb his father because he was working."

"And here comes the perspiration part. First of all, if you don't work on something, it is very unlikely that you will get inspiration out of thin air. If you have a problem, don't just stare at it, do something with it: specialize, generalize, try to remember whether you have seen something similar (Polya's advice). Try to do some reading, writing, refereeing, reviewing, corresponding, every day of your life (Renyi's advice)."

"Develop regular work habits. Some people (surprisingly even artists and writers) work a fixed number of hours at the same time every day (I don't). Work in a way with which you are comfortable. But do not postpone it until you have an entire day or a half-day free: you won't have it and if you do, you will start to do trifles of other work and by the time you finish, you won't have your full (half) day anymore. You can also start working in the evening. Littlewood (an Englishman) counsels that you then stop in the middle of a proof or a paragraph and go to bed: this gives you incentive to continue right in the morning. Balance days of intensive work with rest or light work. Try to finish what you started but give up things that look hopeless."

Creativity begins with inspiration that is followed by hard work and perspiration. The work is frequently continued without much further inspiration. Hard work then carries the burden motivated by the need to complete the work.

Inspiration is opening the conscious mind to intuitions, feelings, and ideas that redirect the mind. How does one become inspired? Creativity depends both on our old and new experiences and memories, and on the structures of our individual brains arising from genetics that form our inclinations and talents. A musician's brain has connections that make possible the creation of melodies and form. It is a fact that many people have tried hard to be musicians but failed, so it seems likely that successful musicians have special talent. These two factors, nature and nurture, genetics and culture determine our potential range of creativity. But people with diverse genetics and environments are likely to possess wider dimensions of creativity. Thus creativity in a culture is served best by having many people with diverse backgrounds and genetics who have the potential of creating a richer culture because of their widespread talents.

In his book, The Celestine Prophecy (Warner Books, 1993), James Redfield mentions nine insights about how to bring inspiration and hence also creativity into our lives. They are, roughly speaking:

1. We need to take coincidences seriously – there is something operating underneath everything.
2. Have the awareness that the coincidences are something real; wake up to what is really going on.
3. The universe is pure energy that responds to how we think. Unlike other forms of life, we project our energy consciously.
4. Humans have the tendency to take energy from others by controlling them. We are inclined to do this when we forget to do our own reflection and feel depleted and cut off from our external source of energy. We must consciously remember not to get in that state of isolation that leads to depletion.
5. There is sufficient energy for all people if they learn to access it this way, and there

would be less conflict arising from control of others.
6. Everyone manipulates for energy either aggressively by forcing people to pay attention to them or passively by playing on their sympathy. Threatening people makes them pay attention and energy is taken from them.
7. We must consciously attempt to stay alert to every coincidence, and every answer provided for us. We have many more such thoughts than we realize. To recognize them we must take the position of observers who are open to sense and to receive.
8. Energy comes in two forms, and is polar. We are biologically made as males and females and are more open to receive one kind than the other, but we need both. We are likely to rely on the other sex to provide us with that part, than we are able to get on our own. If another person comes along and offers it to us, we may cut ourselves off from the true source. We need to learn to relate to others by recognizing that everyone needs fulfillment by tapping the energy source and heightening others' awareness about the need to meditate frequently in order to feel sufficient and complete.
9. We are part of a conscious evolution. With such inspiration, our vibrations increase. In this manner we become invisible to those with slower vibrations, and cross the barrier between this life and the other world from which we come and to which we go after death.

Geshe (master of Buddhism) Michael Roach with a degree from a Tibetan monastery after 22 years of study, is a fully ordained Buddhist monk, and a Princeton University graduate. He built the Diamond Division at Andin International, using principles culled from the ancient wisdom of Buddhism. In his book,

The Diamond Cutter (Doubleday, 2000), he provides an airtight logic that the world and people are not in themselves good or bad, but appear that way to us because of imprinting in our minds after years of conditioning. He suggests that with hard work one can change this conditioning. Imprinting implies that to do well and prosper in business one should maintain a generous state of mind; to see the world as a happy place, one should maintain a very ethical way of life; to see oneself as physically healthy and attractive, one should refuse to get angry; to see oneself as a leader, one should learn to take joy in constructive and helpful actions to others; to learn to focus, one should practice concentration and meditation; to free oneself from a world in which things don't work the way one wants them, one should learn principles of hidden potentials and mental imprints; and finally, to get all that one wishes for oneself and others, one should implant an attitude of compassion toward others. He solves 46 very real business problems.

> The Quakers believe that an inner light illuminates all people in the world. It is this light that Quakers attempt to experience through reflection and silent meditation in their meetinghouses of worship.

Creativity and Evolution

Speaking of the purpose of creativity in nature, we learn from evolution that the survival of a species ensures its proliferation and eventual spread throughout the earth and perhaps beyond. Plants, other animals and people are all creative. Some species of trees have been around for eons longer than the human race and some individual trees like the cedars live for thousands of years. Trees live synergistically with each other in forests.

They use nature to advantage. Plant spores may have traveled in outer space and settled on Mars. If that is so and the Martian spores can be traced back to life on earth, plants would have already achieved through their own kind of survival what mankind has tried to do using the most advanced forms of our kind of creativity in science and technology.

What is good for a monkey is what makes that monkey happy in the long run, without regrets. Who can decide what is good for a monkey better than the monkey itself, or what is better for a human being than the human being himself? There is a different set of criteria for each. A creature must be free to know what it is about and to experiment with its potentials by living, to know what makes it happy and fulfilled.

❧ Animals are Creative: Zandi's Squirrels

Professor Iraj Zandi, a friend of the author, has an apricot tree in his garden in Radnor, Pennsylvania. The squirrels started raiding the apricots as they ripened. So Professor Zandi made a cone of plastic and fitted it around the bottom of the tree to prevent them from climbing up the trunk. Then he noticed that one or two squirrels still got into the tree by climbing a nearby larger tree and leaping from its branches into the apricot tree. Soon, however, there were many, many squirrels in the tree and he wondered how they all got there. So he shooed the squirrels out of the tree and staked out a watch of several hours. Finally he saw one squirrel use the traditional route of leaping down from the bigger tree. Then he climbed on a small flexible branch of the apricot tree near the ground and walked out on it until it bent down to touch the ground. His squirrel friends climbed on one after another.

Who says animals are not intelligent and do not plan ahead?

Like all life forms, our picture of the universe is a product of our senses and our perception. There are forces of nature that we understand somewhat better than trees and squirrels because of the complexity that our brains have achieved through evolution. Still, most of the discoveries we have made that led to significant new knowledge and use were accidental.

For example, humans have no natural sense or means for detecting magnetism. Knowledge that there is magnetism can be obtained in the elementary form of holding two magnets near each other and seeing or feeling them attract or repel one another; our muscles struggle to prevent one magnet being attracted or repelled by the other magnet. Without eyes and muscles, we would have no concept of magnetism. We can also observe the rotation of a magnetic needle. In recent times we have discovered that magnetism can be used through movement to generate electricity. There could be myriad phenomena out there which we do not know about because we are not attuned to them with our minds and senses. Thus our knowledge of the world is never complete and depends on what we are made of. We owe much of our inclination to creative discovery to our complicated brains that are a product of evolution that produces change. We might learn much about creativity by watching how the evolutionary process does it with doggedness and diversity.

Evolution has been divided by some into three distinct and separate parts: cosmic, biological and human. The essence of biological evolution is the response of a biological species to the challenges of its environment. Natural selection is the method

by which species respond. The idea of evolution and man's part in it should not be viewed as degrading, as some have suggested. Rather, it should be seen as complementary because the potential to evolve is inherently a good thing. It means that we are not in a stagnant state but are involved in a process. Moreover, our long-term fulfillment depends on the success of this process.

The question then is, are the three evolutionary processes separate or do they form a single universal evolution? Certainly the phenomena of inorganic, organic and human evolution are subject to different laws. Yet what happens in one evolutionary domain (like the cosmic) can affect another domain (like the biological and the human). The converse effect is very local and of very limited significance at least for the present. We have ambitions.

For us, the ultimate purpose (and thus the ultimate fulfillment) is not the end of the journey but the journey itself. There is no magical point somewhere in the future when human evolution will be over and there would be no more room to go further. Sometimes we think that cosmic evolution produced life and biological evolution produced man and now we are waiting to see what human evolution will produce. But neither cosmic nor biological evolution stopped when they produced new forms of life. Human evolution is unlikely to stop at some new form of mankind or when we have invented some super-machine. All three will continue to develop and change, and together maybe eventually create a fourth, and that would produce a fifth 'form' of evolution and so on, just as cosmic evolution led to biological evolution which led to human evolution. The plants do it for their lineage by spreading pollen and seed. We do it by spreading ideas and knowledge.

But ideas, knowledge and understanding function in the present. Faith gives us hope for better understanding in the future. While faith itself does not reveal the mystery, it is a manifestion of our conviction that there is a mystery greater than we are. The mystery continually beckons us, and creativity impels us forward. We need it forever. If the time ever comes when we understand everything, we will stop growing, and meaning and purpose will no longer be important.

It is almost certain that by the time the sun burns out, we will have spread our kind throughout our own galaxy and others. We will build large ships that are self-contained ecologies; send them off to colonize worlds outside of our solar system. The speed of light according to our existing knowledge will limit our ability to span the universe. If we send some ship to the stars by any present system, it would take years to reach even the nearest star (Proxima Centauri), thousands of years to reach moderately distant stars, tens of thousands of years to span our galaxy, millions of years to reach even the nearer galaxies. As long as the speed of light limits us, we cannot expect to communicate between the stars in any way that we know about now. But it is almost certain that our sophisticated theories in physics will be surpassed by wider and more comprehensive theories. These theories will go beyond physics to incorporate thought and imagination. In a sense we are only as developed as the fastest speed we can move (25,000 miles per hour) is to the speed of light (186,000 miles per second), which now is about .00004.

In his book, The Blind Watchmaker (W.W. Norton and Company, 1987), Richard Dawkins says that evolution has no purpose. It operates on two principles: (1) mutation, which is very small random change in a ge-netic characteristic, and (2) natural selection. The latter serves as a sieve that filters more finely over time organisms that survive the conditions of the environment over radically different time scales than we experience over a lifetime. As the process of mutation and natural selection is slowly continued over a very, very long period of time, the resulting organisms will have come about from so many cumulative filterings. They are so complex and so fine, it is difficult to believe that they could have happened by chance. In the end the process of mutation and natural selection would appear to have creative intelligence with a purpose behind it to produce such complex, beautiful, and purposeful biological organisms as human beings. What is hard to fathom is that the only feasible way to beat the odds against obtaining such sophisticated complexity is a series of small steps, each one building on the accumulated success of the previous steps.

Here we have purposeless nature produce beings that are purposeful. Our survival is the incentive for us to reshape nature in our own image. What is amazing is that if this process goes on successfully, in the distant future random selection would be the means for turning a chaotic universe into an orderly one biologically, physically, mentally and spiritually.

There are scientists who think that no matter how limited the senses of a form of life are, they all more or less get the same idea of the universe from whatever perceptual means are available to them. In a fascinating and imaginative article in *Physics Today* (September 12, 1962), Jerome Rothstein used considerable imagination and understanding from physics to show how a lowly creature like a blind worm living at the bottom of the ocean can slowly develop inner "understanding" of what is going on out there that is not too dissimilar to our own understanding. Rothstein's wiggleworms are a race of worms that live in black, cold, sea bottom muck. A wiggleworm has senses it uses as the foundation for its unique definition of time, space, distance, social issues, and possibly communication. It possesses only the senses of touch, temperature, and a kind of taste. But it has no eyes, ears, or hands. It cannot use the sun or the stars to give it the notions of time as it is at the bottom of the ocean. It does not have rulers to measure length such as "foot" because it has no feet and its shape is elastic. Will the wiggleworm understand a ship passing many thousands of feet over its head? It would not be able to do that immediately. But the ship may create differences in current and how the local fish react. It is exposed to a sequence of sensations throughout its life. Some sensations recur with such frequency that the wiggleworm groups them. It is aware of the sequences of sensations, and can isolate them into subsets. It can tell when the information received is not part of a particular subset, i.e., it is random. Its memory is formed in states of subsets and in-between the subsets. Beginning with a structured view of the world, with information that is organized and information that is in-between, it forms an "understanding" of its own world. The wiggleworm begins to understand that an outside force is at work; not entirely conceptualized, but nevertheless realized. As the wiggleworm evolves, its perceptions change, and the description of the universe for wiggleworms also changes.

A kaleidoscope takes different forms each time it is turned. We need to find a way to connect the many different configurations taken on by the kaleidoscope. That is the essence of modern science: connecting movement and flow of matter and information into a consistent story. This is what Rothstein had in mind when he described the

wiggleworm's knowledge gathering mechanism.

Why is change important? Because it is a catalyst for expansion and redirection of meaning and purpose. It brings about growth and forces us to attach different interpretations and different meanings to happenings around us. To assimilate change, we need to absorb differences by integrating them with what we already know. Otherwise inconsistency can lead to confusion.

Change serves as a stimulus to imagination and lateral thinking. How fast must change happen before it ceases to be meaningful to us? We do not yet know the answer to this question, although we know that rapid change creates stress. We also know that no change leads to stagnation. Would very rapid change as in successive kaleidoscopic forms be meaningful to us? Can we ascribe purpose to relate the forms that appeal to our own existence and survival?

If change prompts us to assign new interpretation and meanings, fundamentally it is we who create the idea of purpose and meaning. If it is true that evolution began with the Big Bang, then we are legitimate contenders for defining purpose in the universe on our own terms. Without us there would be none. Purpose arises out of how we are made, so that we can relate things to our own lives and understanding. We cannot understand the ultimate purpose of everything that is out there because our evolution is not yet complete nor is it likely to be complete in the foreseeable future.

❧ Evolution and the Miraculous

The creative mind looks for plausible explanations and it is not easily surprised by what the logical mind thinks is miraculous.

Human beings are limited by their size, life span, and the laws of nature to which they may be sensitive. They learn to detect new stimuli through more sensitive instruments. They tend to imagine as plausible objects and time lengths for which their own size and life span are near averages. Things that fall outside these ranges are regarded as unthinkable, impossible, unbelievable and miraculous.

Dawkins writes, "Just as our eyes can see only a narrow band of electromagnetic frequencies that natural selection equipped our ancestors to see, so our brains are built to cope with narrow bands of sizes and time. There was no need to cope with things outside these bands, and our brains never evolved the capacity to imagine that". Here is a mathematical scale ladder of improbabilities that are calculable:

- Events that are all but certain like the sun rising tomorrow;
- The next rung is throwing a double six in dice (probability 1/36);
- Next is the probability of a perfect deal at bridge called the dealion, where each of the four players get all of the cards of one suit (probability $1/2.34 \times 10^{28}$);

Between the last two rungs are improbable events that sometimes happen, like being struck by lightning, scoring a hole-in-one in golf (considered a minor miracle) or dreaming of a person not seen for years only to learn later they died that night.

The next rung of the ladder is measured as one in a picodealion. The probability that a marble statue would wave its arm at us is so small that the age of the universe is much too small to allow enough time to write down all the zeros. Beyond this, there is a vast range of mathematically calculable improbabilities.

For example, the probability that we will be struck by a car when we cross the street is small—one in half a million. Yet because the media has brought the world closer, and informs us about people elsewhere in the world being struck by cars as they cross the street, we imagine that it can also easily happen to us. In other words, our idea of plausibility is a matter of what we are accustomed to, rather than what we know to be logical.

We conclude that the very, very slow and synergistic chemical processes of evolution which happen over the eons can appear to us, with our very limited life span, as inconceivable, impossible and miraculous. We tend to mystify occurrences by extrapolating far from what is familiar to us.

Early in the chapter we mentioned some problems that the human race may face in the remote future. We are often inclined to assume that there would be some continuity from us to biological people like us. But it is also likely that our survivable extensions into the future will be products not of our evolutionarily generated bodies, but of our minds, those creative problem solvers which no longer depend on natural mutation for durability and survival. In his book, The Physics of Immortality (Anchor Books, 1994), Frank J. Tipler says that if the human species is to continue to survive, it must eventually leave the earth and colonize space because the planet earth is doomed. The earth should be regarded as the womb of life - but one cannot remain in the womb forever. What we lack is computer technology to produce an intelligent machine that passes the Turing Test. The essential idea of the Turing Test is that what counts for personhood is behavior: if it behaves in all respects like a person, then it is a person. He argues that evidence is overwhelming that in about thirty-odd years we should be able to make a machine which is as intelligent as a human being, or more so. Analogous to the universal computer that can compute anything that can be computed, we also need a universal constructor that can construct anything that can be constructed, including making a copy of itself. He describes how to build an interstellar robot probe and how a space traveling species can ultimately engulf and control the whole universe.

Dependencies and Syntheses in Nature

How We Try to Understand the Forces that Influence our Lives

Nature is richer and more complicated than can be explained with linear cause-effect thinking. By evolving us as intelligent, thoughtful and feeling beings, nature affords us the opportunity to take over our own survivability. We can now purposefully explore the conditions that enhance or impede our biological and mental progress. The tools we use to explore the world are byproducts of our genetic makeup. These tools can themselves become dead-ended and need renewal. Our science is based on logical reasoning and hypothesis testing. When complexity sprouts many parts that need to be explored as a whole, our linear logic resists integrating the pieces into a whole that is as broad and general as complexity itself. The question then is what other way do we have to do the job of synthesis?

According to Edward de Bono (see Source Book for Creative Problem Solving, edited by Sidney J. Parnes, Creative Education Foundation Press, Buffalo, New York, 1992), vertical thinking, which is a sequential, step-by-step process, is concerned with digging

the same hole deeper. He says this about the leading approach to vertical thinking in which the next step depends on the preceding ones: "Logic and mathematics are highly developed algorithms for improving the natural behavior of the brain. As methods they have been extraordinarily successful. Their only limitation is that they are essentially non-creative." Logic and mathematics are concerned with finding the best alternative and are used after ideas are made available with the first stage process, lateral thinking. Lateral thinking, even when it is applied to pulling together the materials that go into a logical argument or a mathematical theory, does not have to be sequential and may involve jumping from one point to another in a haphazard manner looking for many alternatives. It is concerned with digging the hole somewhere else. It is the essential ingredient of creativity, as it is an attempt to improve the performance of the mind by compensating for its natural limitations that make it dependent on the senses to bring information from the outside.

De Bono describes four main categories of lateral thinking and says that education mainly teaches only vertical thinking. To him, the brain is not a physical information processing system, but a biological one. There is an essential difference between the two types. In physical information processing, the system works by selecting and rejecting information according to a fixed frame of reference. The processor is separate from what is being processed. In a biological system, the processor and what it processes are intimately linked. There is no active selection. The system functions as a self-organizing, self-maximizing memory and not as a computer. The material organizes itself and the processor and memory are the same. "It is the fixed defects of memory that give it a computing function. Biological systems are also iterative, adaptive systems and not formulated systems …Such a system has characteristic behavior definable in functional terms rather than in empirical word-descriptions. The natural behavior of this type of system is essentially non-creative. Creativity is then not some strange and magical faculty, but a defect in the functioning of the system, a temporary lapse of efficiency. "

Now we see how dependent we are on our lateral thinking and imagination. To the world around us, we apply a simple linear framework, mostly grounded in if-then logic, along with measurements of mass, distance, and time that arise from our own sensory perceptions. Our primitive idea of mass is that it is some kind of pull experienced with our bodies. Distance is something we traverse with our legs to go from A to B, or see with our eyes as space separating different shapes. Time is the span between occurrences reckoned by the rotation of the earth around the sun and the passing of stars. It is our invention to enable us to sequence events and arrange them in linear chains to make explanations possible. We understand speed as a relation between distance and time. Two primitive creations of our minds and bodies are used to create yet a third somewhat more complex one. We speak of distance, velocity, acceleration, momentum, the limiting speed of light, gravitational attraction, electric attraction and repulsion, and so on.

Creativity in a Non-Linear World

In the end, our thinking and the forces of nature that we can interpret will have to do with movement and flow of material and information. Is that our destiny? What is the creativity in combining the many shapes taken on by a fast changing kaleidoscope? What is the importance of change to the creative process? Change--physical, mental and spiritual--is the essence of evolution. The challenge for us is to direct it to our advantage.

We are victims of Aristotelian logic. Linear thinking makes it possible to assume causes and deduce their effects. Our minds are taught to think in linear terms of logic but our brains are made of feedback circuits. When we speak of cause and effect, we should not think of lines or curves that go from A to B, but of a field of mutual influences from A to B and back to A in numerous potential routes both direct and indirect. When we adopt a chain of thinking, we ignore influences along other chains. Even when we try different chains, the rules of logic do not tell us how to combine the outcomes of independent chains of reasoning to obtain a single best answer. Whenever we are led to a blind alley or an absurd conclusion with our customary if-then logic, we only need to look at our evidence in the context of a network and its synthesis to discover that the absurd can now fall in the realm of the possible.

Within the context of a nonlinear network with circuits and loops, one would not need to ask the question: who made this network, because what made it can also be made a part of its interactions and does not need to be left outside or placed at the top of the framework as one does with the overall goal of a hierarchy. It can include all the causes and all the effects. If the world around us is nonlinear in this general sense, and what we do is to linearize its events with our cause-effect thinking and with syllogistic logic, it is no wonder that it is an inadequate tool.

In their book, Einstein's Space and Van Gogh's Sky (MacMillan Publishing Co., Inc., 1982), psychologist Lawrence LeShan and physicist Henry Margenau say that the mind has numerous states or phases that transcend the processes and experiences upon which sensory or physical reality is built, but that we possess no universally accepted methodology, no single method of approach that gives these states a solid status. They compare and contrast four modes used by people to access reality: 1) Sensory (see, touch, and measure — the way of the scientist), 2) Clairvoyant, 3) Trans-psychic, and 4) Mythic. All these different kinds of influence are active in degrees that vary with time and occasion. In the first of the four modes, individuals construct reality as if they are detached observers of a larger whole; in the second, as if they are extensions of the whole without a sense of separation, as in dancing, music and meditation; in the third, as if they are reciprocals to the whole with their wishes and desires urging on the forces of nature, as people do in prayer; in the fourth, as if they are identical to the whole as happens in dreaming and play, keeping us fresh and alive, curious and creative.

A basic limiting principle of the sensory mode is the assumption that all phenomena are sequentially continuous in space and time and are related by linear cause and effect. Despite proof of this principle in quantum mechanics, "it has not been clearly understood that its abandonment means the complete collapse of the system of one rationality ruling the entire universe. A completely consistent cosmos cannot be inconsistent in one area. One exception collapses it all."

Causation, which is a basic tenet of science, works only for isolated systems such as we are able to bring about in the physical world, but not in the domain of consciousness where isolation such as sensory deprivation means damaging the mind and then breaking it down. Consciousness constantly reaches into the past and future, and to places and possi-

bilities. Only a non-causal perspective of numerous alternative realities allows us to understand this domain.

Clairvoyance is the supernatural ability to "see" objects or actions removed in space or time. It involves quick, intuitive and penetrating discernment about things and people. The artist shows clairvoyance in the way he or she sees the world. What the artist looks into is not the nature of the physical world, but the nature of our reactions to it. LeShan and Margenau say, "Art is a science of evocation of the psychology of the observer. The world outlook of the artist is of primary importance to him. He is the involved observer."

The trans-psychic mode is the domain of the parapsychologist who accesses the real world through extra-sensory perception in which specialized receptors in the brain and nervous system have the added psychic capacity that reciprocates and interacts with the intellect to receive and process information outside the scientific realm of the sensory. Most scientists believe that parapsychology contradicts the basic laws of science, but LeShan and Margenau found that it only contradicts the laws relating to observables in the see-touch realm which do not permit clairvoyance and telepathy. When occurrences that seem impossible to the scientist happen, the parapsychic redefines reality in such a way that the previously impossible now becomes possible. Reality as scientists define it is expected to be fixed and immutable, once and for all.

In the mythic mode we tend to assume that there are purposeful forces in nature that identify with our own purposes and dictate that we live and behave in a special way. According to Le Shan and Margenau, "in this way of organizing reality anything can be identical with anything else once they have been connected with each other spatially, temporally, or conceptually. The part is identical with the whole, the name with the thing, and the symbol with its object. Each can be treated as if it were the other."

Synthesizing

The Analytic Network Process (ANP) is the unifying thought, feelings and communication tool that allows us to combine and represent the four modes mentioned above within a framework that integrates consciousness for better overall understanding (see Chapter 7 and its references). They are a special case of networks briefly introduced there. The ANP makes possible the articulation of clusters of forces and things we believe exert influence on each other and eventually on us. The purpose of these influences can only be made explicit in terms of human goals and aspirations. In the end all reality is funneled and reinterpreted through the human experience. The broader our experience is and the more imagination we use to interpret it, the more seemingly objective our understanding becomes, thus extending our consciousness beyond its existing confines. That framework can be depicted as in the diagram on the next page.

If the only kind of logic we knew about were hierarchic, then we would not be able to see the world without a top goal for any hierarchy, and the concept of god would be mandatory. However, with network thinking where everything depends on everything, and nothing is independent of other things, a top goal is not necessary. That is a new kind of multicriteria logic to which we refer in this book (see my book The Analytic Network Process (ANP)). The ANP is both a powerful way to make decisions with dependence and feedback. All the elements depend on each other and there is no single overall goal.

People who pray must believe that God listens to people. If God listens, He must become aware of something he was unaware of before. Thus for God to become aware of certain things, He must listen to people. This means that God depends on people to catch His attention and supplicate Him. If we include everything in the universe that is drawing God's attention we must conclude that God depends on His creation. Thus the universe and God are more like a network than a hierarchy, better understood if we learned to use network thinking and synthesis.

154

Unity:
Provides a single, easily understood, flexible model for a wide range of unstructured ideas and problems

Process Repetition:
Enables people to refine their definition of a problem and improves their judgment and understanding through repetition

Complexity:
Integrates deductive and systems approaches in solving complex problems

Feedback:
Because it deals with interdependence, its synthesis uses feedback through a convergent sequence of iterations

Interdependence:
Deals with the interdependence of elements in a system and does not insist on linear cause-effect thinking

Judgment and Consensus:
Not insist on consensus but be capable of synthesizing a meaningful and realistic representative outcome from diverse judgments

The ANP Logic

Hierarchic and Network Structuring:
Reflects the natural tendency of the mind to sort elements of a system into clusters and to group like elements together

Tradeoffs:
Takes into consideration the relative priorities of factors in a system and enable groups of people to select the best outcomes in terms of their criteria and goals

Nonverbal:
Allows people not versed in logic and mathematics and even the latter in their personal lives to include their ideas feelings and emotions as an experienced artist might

Measurement:
Provides a scale for measuring intangibles side by side with tangibles with a way to establish priorities

Synthesis:
Combines and synthesizes information reliably leading to an overall estimate of the necessity and desirability of each outcome

Consistency:
Capable of tracking the logical consistency of the judgments used to determine priorities and use the information to improve the knowledge on which the judgments are based

Prediction and Quantum Theory

Those who apply their talents to probing the unknown are concerned with ways to deal with uncertainty and the problems of a remote and uncertain future. We now talk about people whose remarkable prophetic abilities are probably matched by their powerful creative imaginations and perhaps something deeper in context. Some people can discern possibilities and scenarios of future occurrences in ways that we do not understand, and therefore can neither do it ourselves nor teach it to others.

Quantum theory may provide insight into these mysteries, and help us accept that such things as clairvoyance and other strange phenomena can really happen.

Non-relativistic quantum theory has a very cogent concern with the problem of time, artificially introduced by us because of our need to deal with the world sequentially as causes and effects in order to understand it. The physical world has no time physically attached to it. We are the ones who impose the concept of time. The many-worlds interpretation of quantum mechanics can be understood by looking at Schrodinger's cat experiment, one of the most famous 'thought experiments' in physics. Let us imagine that we have a cat inside a steel chamber equipped with a radioactive device such that the cat has 0.50 probability to live and 0.50 probability to die by the end of the experiment. We know that at the end of such an experiment, the cat would be either alive or dead. Using the mathematics of non-relativistic quantum mechanics, however, neither would happen. At the end of the experiment, the wave function of the cat would be the sum of those of the dead cat and the live cat. In other words, the cat would be simultaneously dead and alive, or in the quantum state "dead cat plus live cat". Physicists universally agree that this sum is what standard quantum mechanics predicts, but they disagree on how to interpret it. The many-worlds interpretation resolves the obvious inconsistency between the theory and the observation by saying that radioactive decay of the atom has forced the cat to split into two different worlds. The cat is alive in one world and dead in the other. If we try to see whether the cat is alive or dead, then we also split into two different worlds: we see the cat dead in one and alive in the other. We are forced to accept the many-worlds interpretation. There is not one universe that passes through time, but there are many slightly different versions of ourselves that exist in a static universe that includes everything at once. There is no time, motion or change.

The controversial scientist, Rupert Sheldrake, says that telepathy can be accounted for in his theory of morphic resonance. He believes that invisible "morphic fields" direct and shape everything. In an interview on the program, *Thinking Allowed* (1998) he explains: "Morphic comes from the Greek word for form, morphe, and a morphic field is a field of form, or field of pattern or order or structure. Such fields organize not only the forms of living organisms, but also the forms of crystals, of molecules. Each kind of molecule, each protein, for example, has its own kind of morphic field – a hemoglobin field, an insulin field; each kind of crystal, each kind of organism, and each kind of instinct or pattern of behavior. So these fields are the organizing fields of nature. There are many kinds of them, because there are many kinds of things and patterns in nature. …Through this morphic field theory of organization in nature, we can come to have a new understanding of the nature of the mind – what would in the end be a field theory of the mind." Sheldrake says that dogs know when their masters are returning home because the bond they form through close association is a "social" morphic field.

In an article in *Discover* magazine (August 2000), science writer Brad Lemley synthesizes ideas of Sheldrake, the late theoretical physicist David Bohm, and physicist Hans-Peter Dürr of the Max Planck Institute in Munich. He says that Bohm "proposes that reality consists of two realms: a fundamental 'implicate order' that transcends time and space and an 'explicate order' comprising the familiar world of flowing time and discrete objects. Considering Sheldrake's theories in this context, Bohm proposed that 'for every moment that is projected out into the explicate there would be another movement in which that moment would be injected or 'introjected' back in the implicate order. If you have a fairly large number of repetitions of this process, past forms would tend to be repeated or replicated in the present, and that is very similar to what Sheldrake calls a morphogenetic field and morphic resonance.' Bohm also noted that since the implicate order, by its nature, is not located anywhere, attempts to isolate or identify it would be futile."

"Another physicist, Hans-Peter Dürr… has argued that Sheldrake's theories are among the first to reconcile 20th century breakthroughs in physics—which emphasize the primacy of fields and the indivisible nature of matter—with biology, which for the most part remains rotted in 19th century Newtonian physics."

There are other areas which science is hardput to explain. One of them is dreams and dreaming. Everybody dreams during sleep. Is there more to dreams than that they are accidental, sometimes inspiring, sometimes disturbing, outcomes of chemical and electrical flows in the brain? From Aristotle to Freud, many have written about dreams and dreaming. But beyond philosophical, psychological and scientific inquiry into dreams, there is another phenomenon: there are numerous accounts of people who dreamed in considerable detail about specific things that actually happened later, such as the sinking of the Titanic. One has to study the literature to believe that this is true and really happens. It is credible to believe that there is much more to these incidents than we know about or are willing to admit to.

It appears that science knows well how to go from energy to deal constructively with matter, but not how to go from matter to energy. We can talk about atoms and molecules and configurations of atoms and molecules. Once we annihilate matter through nuclear fission or fusion, we do not seem to be much bothered about the shape and form of the energy that is an outcome of this violent action. To us, energy is like gasoline in a car. It is thought of as an amorphous medium. It is not the end as matter is, since it takes on different forms that we can see or imagine. It is likely that the science of energy will depart from what we know about field theory, and reveal very elaborate interactions within and between fields that can be detected as sharply as the form of objects can be. One might say that any state of the mind of a human being is more easily described as a definite form of energy that we are not yet in a position to fully understand. It seems plausible that physics will some day expand into this domain to explain phenomena of spirits in the form of energy made concrete through information, of which information theory as understood today would be a special case.

A puzzling aspect of human nature that we need to look at as part of the creative process is our ability to synthesize and sometimes predict the future. Our proclivity to look ahead makes us more knowledgeable and at ease, less fearful and more hopeful and optimistic, at least in our imagination, about the future. By experimenting with an imaginary world of possibilities, even when its occurrence appears to be unpredictable and unmanageable, uncertain and random, we acquire greater mental familiarity, anticipation, and command of the unknown future. Gathering and synthesizing information leads to extrapolation and to prediction and finally to long term prediction that is often known as prophesying. We must allow that there are forces in the universe that we will only come to understand as we evolve. With this in mind, it is not so far-fetched that the prophets see things that most of the rest of us do not. One of the most puzzling prophets is Nostradamus (1503-1568).

In her book, The Prophecies of Nostradamus (Putnam, New York, 1974), Erika Cheetham says in the introduction: "I believe that mankind must have free will; but I also must admit the disturbing fact that although I can dismiss ninety-five percent of Nostradamus' predictions as historical coincidence, there remain a few quatrains which are hard to reconcile with this. What about the one describing Louis XVI's flight to Varennes, the ones mentioning Napoleon and Hitler? What about the verses giving the actual month and year of an occurrence, such as that which describes the obscure treaty between the Persians and the Turks in October 1727, or another which gives the day and month of the assassination of a Prince? (III. 96) I find this type of quatrain difficult to explain away completely. They appear to me to be more than coincidence."

It is difficult to explain how a person living more than four hundred years ago could mention names and places of events happening long after. Here are four of Nostradamus' quatrains that are noteworthy as they mention names and places that also occur in our history. Cheetham shows that events actually occurred that are very similar to what these quatrains predicted.

1. *Louis Pasteur*
The lost thing is discovered, hidden for many centuries. Pasteur will be celebrated almost as a god-like figure. This is when the moon completes her great cycle, but by other rumors he shall be dishonored.

2. *Adolf Hitler*
Beasts wild with hunger will cross the river, the greater part of the battle field will be against 'Hister'. He will drag the leader in a cage of iron', when the child of Germany observes no law.

3. *Francisco Franco and Primo de Rivera*
From Castille, Franco will bring out the assembly. The ambassadors will not agree and cause a schism. The people of Rivera will be in the crowd, and the great man will be denied entry to the gulf.

4. *1936 (The Civil war in Spain)*
One of the great men will flee to Spain which will bleed with a great wound thereafter. Troops will pass over the high mountains devastating everything, then he will reign in peace.

Associating Pasteur with discovery, "Hister" with Germany, Franco and Rivera with Spain are amazing.

Mother Shipton (born in 1488) was a clairvoyant who had a reputation as a witch and also apparently had telepathic powers including an ability to move things with her mind. She prophesied that towns in the South West of England "Watchet and Doniford both shall drown, and Williton become the seaport town." It is thought that this became true with the serious erosion of the coastline in that area in the 19th century."

A frontier psychic, Susanna Morgan foretold events 100 years before they happened: the two world wars, the jet plane, the atomic bomb, the assassination of president JFK, and the landing on the moon.

In 1898 a book by Morgan Robertson, called *Futility*, foretold in graphic detail how a ship which he called Titan (similar in dimensions and luxury to the Titanic) collides with an iceberg in the Atlantic, 14 years prior to the Titanic's maiden voyage. I have a copy of the original works of Nostradamus and of *Futility*, the first from Paris and the second from the Library of Congress and can testify that they contain the material that I have mentioned.

Uri Geller, a modern-day "magician", has demonstrated considerable telepathic power, clairvoyance, and psychokinetic abilities. Spoons bent under the forces of his will.

Zé Arigo - "Joe From-the-Sticks" – a Brazilian peasant from Congonhas do Campo, in the state of Minas Gerais, had a mystical talent that became more evident as he grew older. At first, his nights were tortured by a mysterious voice and strange visions of a man in a medical gown, wreathed in mist, consulting other doctors and carrying out interminable operations. Eventually, in 1955, the spirit announced itself as "Dr. Fritz," a German surgeon who died in the First World War. From that moment Zé was transformed into a great healer. Every day up to 1,500 people would flock to his office, a small

room with a rough table and chair. They came from all parts of Brazil looking for miraculous cures-and Zé provided them. The blind regained their sight; the lame threw away their crutches. Thousands were treated, and not one died or had his or her condition worsened because of Zé's ministrations. Doctors from Rio de Janeiro, Sao Paulo University, and Minas Gerais Medical Academy watched him at work. They were baffled by his methods, but all agreed that they were successful. He did not inquire about the symptoms people had, he stopped them if they started to elaborate on what was troubling them. "I know that already," he would say. He was invariably right. From, "Strange Stories, Amazing Facts," Readers Digest Books, 1976

Crossing the line from quack to visionary was Charles Darwin with his theory of evolution that was first thought to be fiction.

Unlike the foregoing, some predictions can be rationalized. Andrew Jackson Davis in 1856 foretold both the coming of the airplane and the car. His predictions, made in the mid-1800's, seem to be more consistent with the natural progression of technology and scientific advance. They are not the equivalent of cave drawings depicting modern man performing outrageous acts that had never been conceived before. Modes of transportation in Davis' time consisted of things such as steam engines and railroads. An equivalent prediction might be for us to say that within the next 50 to 100 years mankind will utilize energy derived from natural sources such as trees and plants to power transportation vehicles. It is also reasonable to think that man will also utilize the sky more and more as a transportation medium. Personal hovercrafts or airplanes may replace standard automobiles. It is even possible that people may be able to travel through time with a Star Trek type of transporter. The earlier unexplainable cases baffle us, and we gallantly dismiss them. We assume, as people have always done, that what we know is the truth, the whole truth and nothing but the truth. It is a great weakness in human perspective that we do not hold in abeyance things we cannot explain, but put them out of our minds so that we can continue to feel secure that we know everything we need to know.

By allowing into our thinking the thoughts and experiences of others, we open to our own selves the possibility of extending our senses and perceptions to include everything as part of the reality with which our minds deal. That way we do not shut out possible explanations and solutions that are beyond what the world accepts. When it is our turn to sense, feel, or experience something that may seem strange to others, we know that such resistance can be due to their own limitations than to our unrealistic thoughts and feelings. We will then dare to explore the unknown with greater confidence in our creativity guided by our instincts than to merely rely on what the rest of the world says. It usually tells us to ignore it until science can explain it, and that can take forever. But science is our own construction for finding the truth that we can understand. It is what we do with our minds to connect new experiences in a "palatable and rational" way to the old that we know, and we can only make these connections well by practicing the ways of creativity.

Do ideas have existence and power beyond matter and life, and where does creativity fit in this consideration?

Is the natural world the only real world of being and everything else fictional, or is the world of ideas also as real? What is the essence of the material world and are matter and energy and life qualities definable by ideas or do they have intrinsic substance not accessible to the domain of ideas so that ideas are really at the root of things that make minds that make ideas and forms? If ideas are the essence of things, then ideas are the only things that are accessible to minds that sense things around us and interpret them as sensations and forms used by the mind as the bases of ideas. Every feeling is a sensation of a property and of properties and collections of properties that are all there is in the material world.

❧ What the Philosophers Think (Reader Beware!)

Being is a reality which exists externally and independently of our consciousness, emotions and will. It pre-exists us. It is the source of all forms of human activity and imposes limits and conditions on us to make our acts commensurate with it. It is the object of our *creativity* as it defines the domain of possibilities for transforming reality. According to Immanuel Kant (1724-1804), being is not a concept that could be added to the concept of a thing, but an aspect of conscious judgment that deals with relations between known things posited for the purpose of understanding the relations to which judgment is applied. It adds nothing new to a thing by saying it exists. According to Friedrich Nietzsche (1844-1900), being is a generalization of the concept of life. Being can have sensory reality or is real.

According to Edmund Husserl (1859-1938), real being is external, factual and temporal, whereas ideal being represents the world of pure essences. The central point of Husserl's phenomenology is the study of the interrelationship between being and consciousness. To Jean Paul Sartre (1905-1980) and the existentialists, being is the horizon of possibilities within whose limits human freedom exists and develops. This sounds like saying that being is the many worlds of quantum theory.

Ideas are a form in which the phenomena of objective reality are understood by the mind. According to Plato (428-348 B.C.) and Platonism, ideas are incorporeal essences that constitute objective reality. They define a separate ideal world and exist apart from objects and phenomena. Matter is the reflection and outflow of an idea. Life is imitation of external ideas. The beauty and order in life are superior to and transcend beauty and order in art, which is an imitation of life, which itself is an imitation of the ideal world. According to Georg Wilhelm Friedrich Hegel (1770-1831), this world exists alongside the material world. The materialists regarded ideas as a function of matter organized in a special way. Karl Marx (1818-1883) thought it is the reflection of the material world through the mind that translates it to thoughts. But the brain itself is developing in a more or less ideal way to be a generator and synthesizer of ideas. It is not made independently from the conditions of the ideal world, but rather as an instrument that reaches and transforms ideas to human action and abstracts ideas from these actions.

It appears that creativity deals with profound matters that relate life to a transcendent world that shapes life. It is our way to reach out, or in, to bring about new ideas and forms that are not yet known to us. It is our bridge between the *ideal* and the *real* worlds.

❧ Exercises

Exercise: All creatures, including humans, are trapped in their skin and body and cannot access things or life-forms that may be out there according to those things' own goals of existence. If you had to communicate with an amoeba, what would you tell it so that it would know it is getting a message from an outside intelligence, and is could respond in a way to let you know that it got your message and understands its content? Do the same with a lion and then again to a starfish. What is the likelihood that "intelligent" life-forms somewhere else in the universe would develop precisely along our own lines of evolution with the same materials, having the same kind of senses and synthesizing apparatus as our brains are? Our own senses are one way for us to cope with the environment as an amoeba does with its senses. There may be more advanced forms of life, conditioned by their own limited senses, attempting to communicate with us to no avail as we would with an amoeba. Our inspiration may be the prodding we are receiving from them! Such creatures may themselves be like us, influenced by more advanced forms of life. How would we ever find out whether this is actually happening, and must we send radio signals to outer space to discover whether that is true?

Exercise: It is widely agreed that there are islands of order in the universe of which our own bodies and brains are examples. Order involves proportionality and harmony among the parts as they combine to form a whole. Proportionality is a concept that involves the idea of ratio, understood well in measurement theory and used widely in physics and other branches of science in the form of ratio scales of measurement. Thus in our effort to understand order, we need mathematics that endows our thinking with objectivity relating to our particular abilities to sense, observe and reason. In this way it is thought that we are able to relate and understand with mathematics the eternal truths from which order is derived. Still, in mathematics we always begin with assumptions that need not be true.

The theorems we prove always begin with a statement of something we already know and proceed to demonstrate its validity with the use of logic. Suggest a way to break from not knowing what is really true in the universe and what is simply valid with logic by relating logic to ratio and proportion to make everything we prove part of the order we perceive in the world in which we live. What is the difference between the factual *truth* of perception and the *validity* of logical reason? Which is a more reliable source of belief – seeing and sensing, or thinking and deducing, and why?

Exercise: Consider this: when you observe a fish in an aquarium, the fish comes forward to observe you as an equal. As long as you stay, it stays. After many hours and days, you notice that the fish is getting emaciated from starvation. What should an intelligent fish do? In addition, you get bored with staring and get to think that a fish should go about doing what a fish does and not stay there staring at you. We think a fish's greatest potential is to lead the life of a fish. How does this apply to us in seeking other forms of life in the universe? Our primary goal is to live out our potential as humans as fully as we can. That would create far greater curiosity about us, rather than spending our time wondering what superior beings are thinking about us. We should direct our energy much more to living and much less to speculating about what secrets the future may hold for us.

Beauty, Aesthetics and Order

It is difficult to associate chaos and ugliness with creativity and inventiveness. Beauty is listed as the last one of Abraham Maslow's seven needs for survival. It has been said that it is to sex, after all, that we owe most of the

things we consider aesthetically appealing in nature. A flower-filled meadow resounding with the dawn chorus of songbirds is a scene of frenzied sexual competition.

Everything extravagant about human life, from poetry to fast cars, is rooted in sexual triumphs. With poetry and painting we look for beauty through rhyme and symmetry and other characteristics that are elevating to the spirit and appealing to the imagination. Dance and sports activity have a style that excite the mind, pulling it to participate vicariously in the event. Our inventions, from the design of simple implements used around the house whether a spoon or a knife, a blender and a vacuum cleaner, to our more complicated monoliths like cars, airplanes and missiles, are all endowed with symmetries, smoothness, sleekness, efficiency and attractiveness that make them inviting and hospitable. They are not unlike agreeable and attractive friends who are willing to humor, oblige and share when called on to participate. Beauty enriches life, and often we pay much to obtain something that is endowed with a combination of qualities that give pleasure to the sight or the other senses. In mathematics, one often refers to the elegance of a proof in which one avoids proceeding, in the words of Leonardo da Vinci, " by a method of circumlocution and with great prolixity and confusion."

We learn about beauty best by experiencing it, in a rose, in an apple and a watermelon, in eating a meal at a three star French restaurant, in a Mozart symphony or a Bach cantata, in the face of a person and the subtle smile of the Mona Lisa, in the innocence of a child, in the architecture of a house, a bridge, a pyramid, or the design of a city, in the operation of a dam and a power generating plant, in the design of an accurate time piece, in the setting sun, in the flight of a bird, in the colors of a butterfly, in ballet dance, in the mystique of a poem, in the direct proof of a proposition, in the vast expanse of a piece of fertile land, in the climb of mount Everest, in the anatomy of a living thing, and on and on. Still, we do not express our appreciation for the beautiful in the same way. Appreciating beauty and order is a personal thing (beauty is in the eyes of the beholder) and needs to be constantly developed. Our creations need beauty and order to enhance our survival. The beautiful adds meaning to our existence.

Beauty has both spiritual and practical meaning for man and his society. To the Renaissance thinker L.B. Alberti, beauty is "strict proportionate harmony among all the parts, united by that to which they belong." F. von Schiller regarded beauty as a link between reason and feelings, between abstract duty and natural inclinations. Diderot believed that the perception of relationships is the basis of the beautiful. According to the American philosopher George Santayana (1863-1952), beauty is not an objective property of things. Rather, it is identical with the pleasure experienced when certain objects are perceived. He considered the physiological and psychological factors involved in experiencing beauty. Darwin attempted to explain the effect of colors in male birds to attract females. The result is that more brightly marked males perpetuate their progeny.

There are several evaluative theories in art: intuitionism, subjectivism, emotivism, and instrumentalism. There are also empirical methods for dealing with aesthetics: experimental psychology, introspective psychology, Gestalt psychology, and psychoanalysis. We believe that philosophical interpretation notwithstanding, so far as learning to appreciate and create beauty and order, passion for diversity and practice make perfect.

Confessions

Evolution leads to the survival of the fittest. Those who are genetically strong survive better. We have made sufficient advances in medicine to help the weak to also survive. Increased consciousness, with the helplessness and pain it causes us by making us aware of cruelty and injustice, also increases our self- awareness together with the ability to control nature and prolong life. Increased consciousness and pain go hand in hand with the progress we make to control our destiny. We also have conflicting interests because we are individualistic, not like ant colonies and beehives. We need to study and understand conflicts to make it possible for all of us to survive. The thing that we have not learned to control well is our proclivity to procreate. Increasing the number of people makes possible all sorts of human activity. However, it also creates pressures on the environment and leads to intolerable crowding and congestion that diminish the quality of life. The upshot is that life is not black and white, but comes in different shades of gray. We have learned from decision theory that best decisions are composites of many properties, which amounts to saying that they are compromises. According to Deepak Chopra, How to Know God (Harmony Books, 2000), there are seven distinct stages of god, that are a mirror of our own states of mind. There is the vengeful fight-or-flight god of fear and retribution ("I cope") who appeals to a primitive mind with its thrust to control and make sense out of chaos. This god's actions cannot be explained by people in a way compatible with their own nature. Second is the reactive god of competition and ambition ("I win"). He demands awe and obedience and suggests rules and commandments, which if adhered to lead to salvation. Third is the restful awareness god ("I stay centered") leading to reflection, meditation and peace, a guiding spirit rather than a demanding god. The fourth is the god of intuitive response, insight, and personal growth ("I understand"). Fifth is the god of creative and of inventive response (of the I intend). Sixth is the god of visionary response and enlightened awareness of prophets and wise people ("I love"). Seventh is the god of a transcendent world leading to sacred response ("I am"). He is source of self-awareness and sense of being.

There is a part of us that is loving, gentle and order seeking, seemingly more than the chaotic physical world in which we find ourselves. This tells us that as a whole, the universe is emergent because we are one of its products, and that it is incomplete, and that if order is its destiny then we each have an important small part to play in it. Since the task is formidable we must work together, doing our best to make things happen in ways that are compatible with our diverse points of view, again a mixed compromise. It is fortunate that we have courage and do not crumble as the going gets tough. Life is short but it is also a challenge and an opportunity. The future depends on those who have faith to try and the will to make things happen. One may conjecture that there is a spiritual dimension that we are creating which today, early in our progress, is weak and lacunary. If our race survives, and I have strong faith that it will, we would be the spiritual atoms or quanta that create this dimension. In a sense, then, religion provides a plausible insight by advocating love as our essence and our destiny, the compassion that we wish were here in perfect form. If our universe were perfect, we would have no challenges to face. Our lives would be more like cows in a pasture: eat, sleep, procreate and do what biology, not mind, dictates. In the final analysis we have a job to do and we must do it or it will take longer to happen. Besides, we would have let

our nature down by not following the inspiration that is built into our imperfect genetics. Stretch your nature to the limit and follow its calling. When you reflect, keep some humor in the background, remembering that nothing will ever be quite like you hope, but that you will try your best anyway.

In a very broad sense we can take comfort from what some microbiologists have carefully observed. If we do not make it due to a catastrophe or decline in mind and body, life can restart with far greater ease than it was once thought. We may not be the single greatest creative cosmic champions of order.

There are numerous animals on this earth that we know are able to communicate with each other. But we have not yet deciphered the language and full meaning of their communication that is better suited to their specific nervous system, environment and style of survival. Some of these animals are genetically very close to us. Yet some scientists naively believe that if life is abundant in the universe, there have to be creatures somewhere that are so much like us that they would be able to reason as we do, and notice electromagnetic signals we are sending out, and who would imitate us by responding meaningfully--soon after to become our mentors about their part of creation on request. One needs to combine the likelihood of life that is so close to us genetically, even closer than our simian relatives with whom we are told we share more than 95% of our genes and with whom we don't communicate very logically and precisely. We need to face the fact that our science is what our particular nervous system and senses construe about phenomena out there that we experience, conditioned by our own particular earthly environment. What is out there is not necessarily what we think it is, despite our ability to observe some causes and some effects. We

164

are just another form of existence and not the universal form. Let us first learn to understand the languages of animals living with us, like the elephants, the whales and the monkeys, the ants and the bees, and use them to communicate with them. Success depends on our own intelligence and not on chance and optimistic expectations.

In conclusion, we believe that with few exceptions, if people were shown prior to their existence all the trials and tribulations of their lives let alone some of the joys and ecstasies, and also shown how their biology turns dead chemicals to organic matter to bodies and brains so that they can perceive the difference between being — which is short and difficult and ends with senility, illness and death — as it is, and not being, the majority would opt for the experience of being with all its hazards and torments.

The challenge is to heighten the quality of being , and work to make it so for all life in this world. If we truly love one another, remembering how fragmentary and disconnected and fading our memories are, as our time comes to move on, we will courageously pass the torch of continuity with joy to the next generation. Through their lives and in turn they through their descendants and on and on for ever, we can hope that they will acquire the knowledge to perfect and prolong their own existence to whatever end they choose as they evolve over time. We concur with the definition of the true meaning of life as living fast, loving hard, dying young (I have no objection to dying old) and leaving a beautiful memory. Here is an inspiring essay on life, called "The Station", by Robert J. Hastings.

Tucked away in our subconscious minds is an idyllic vision. We see ourselves on a long, long trip that almost spans the continent. We're traveling by passenger train, and out the windows we drink in the passing scene of cars on nearby highways, of children waving at a crossing, of cattle grazing on a distant hillside, of smoke pouring from a power plant, of row upon row of corn and wheat, of flatlands and valleys, of mountains and rolling hillsides, or city skylines and villages, of biting winter and blazing summer and cavorting spring and docile fall.

But uppermost in our minds is the final destination. On a certain day at a certain hour we will pull into the station. There will be bands playing and flags waving. And once we get there, so many wonderful dreams will come true. So many wishes will be fulfilled and so many pieces of our lives finally will be neatly fit together like a completed jigsaw puzzle. How restlessly we pace the aisles, damning the minutes for loitering...waiting, waiting, waiting for the station.

However, sooner or later we must realize there is no one station, no one place to arrive at once and for all. The true joy of life is in the trip. The station is only a dream. It constantly outdistances us.

When we reach the station, that will be it! We cry. Translated it means, when I'm 18, that will be it! When I put the last kid through college, that will be it! When I have paid off the mortgage, that will be it! When I win a promotion, that will be it! When I reach the age of retirement, that will be it! I shall live happily ever after! Unfortunately, once we get "it" the 'it' disappears. The station somehow hides itself at the end of an endless track.

'Relish the moment' is a good motto. It isn't the burdens of today that drive mankind mad. Rather, it is regret over yesterday or fear of tomorrow. Regret and fear are twin thieves who would rob us of today.

So, stop pacing the aisles and counting the miles. Instead climb more mountains, eat more ice cream, go barefoot more often, swim more rivers, watch more sunsets, laugh more and cry less. Life must be lived as we go along. The station will come soon enough.

Estimation

Chapter Six

Introduction

This chapter provides the bridge between what de Bono calls non-creative mathematical thinking and its use in lateral thinking to expand horizons of imagination and understanding.

One of the most powerful elementary tools used to advance one's understanding of any problem is to practice estimating important measurements and parameters associated with that problem. Every student of creativity needs to be versed in making intelligent estimates of an otherwise complex, fuzzy and sometimes perhaps inscrutable problem.

When a piece of information is unknown, it is often necessary to estimate it. But when an important decision is to be based on the estimate, it is important to be able to defend your result by logical justification.

If you need to estimate how many widgets will be sold next month, then multiplying by 3 then adding 4 then subtracting a half and then squaring the result may be the "correct" method, but unless you can justify the 3, 4, half and the square, the reader has no way of knowing if your result is legitimate.

When conveying the results (and the process) of an estimate, it is common to take some information for granted, such as 50% of the population is male, 50% is female. Although this may be harmless, not all data should be taken for granted. When a slight deviation of the data causes very large changes in the

SOME HINTS FOR DOING SIMPLE ESTIMATION PROBLEMS

- Proceed from the abstract to the concrete. Do not go from the concrete to the concrete.

- Draw something from your experiences - try to interest your colleagues in your idea.

- Show your logic - assume your reader has no experience in what you are talking about. The next step is to find the actual answer and prove that you are right. If you cannot find the answer, try an alternative approach to again arrive at your conclusion. Do not find the answer before you begin your estimation!

- Always show in writing that you have learned something from the answer and how to revise your estimate. Do it and compute the discrepancy. Don't try to look perfect, no one believes it.

- Above all, **BE CREATIVE !!!**

overall estimate, then we can conclude that much of our error will be associated with the ratio. Therefore, all we need to do to improve the accuracy of our result is to do research on that ratio. Estimations must not be confused with derivations. Estimations usually have at least one unknown, while in derivations everything is known. For example, how many seconds are there in a century? This problem is merely one of converting units.

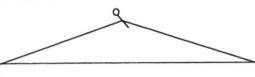

$$100\,\frac{years}{century} \times 365\,\frac{days}{year} \times 24\,\frac{hours}{day} \times 60\,\frac{minutes}{hour} \times 60\,\frac{seconds}{minute}$$

When one person says 12 inches and another says 1 foot, they are referring to the same length, therefore finding the number of inches in a foot is not an estimation problem, but one of derivation.

WHAT TO DO

State a problem for which it is useful to know an estimate of an answer by using common sense and readily available data and then carry out the estimation. Validate your result by looking up the answer and writing it down next to yours. Please do not alter your initial answer but rework the example if you can, changing your assumptions to come close to the answer.

There are some estimation problems of which derivations may be a part, but as a whole, estimation does not rely on unit conversions. For example, estimate the total number of coins in all currencies that are in current circulation. One approach may begin by "converting" all other currencies into Ameri-

can units, for example, yen into dollars, pounds into dollars, lira into dollars, etc. Now that we are working with one currency, the problem may be somewhat simplified. Once we have our answer, we would convert back the appropriate percentage into the original currency units.

Examples

Included in this section are both worked-out examples done by former students and proposed problems.

❧ Estimate milk consumption in the United States

How many gallons of milk are consumed each day in the U.S. in the form of liquid milk and cream, cheese, ice cream, condensed and evaporated milk, and milk solids?

When given to the class, only liquid milk drunk each day was estimated. The class thought they were typical people and estimated that they drank or ate with morning cereal about 10 ounces of milk per day. They realized that not everybody did, but they felt that some drank more and some less and gathered the number of glasses drunk by each and took the average. The 1990 population of nearly 250 million was multiplied by 10 ounces and divided by 128 ounces to the gallon, and then multiplied by 365 obtaining 7128×10^9 gallons per annum. Statistical Abstract of the United States gives a figure of 6975×10^9 per annum, or 10.4 ounces per day per person. The class estimate was not bad for a ten-minute exercise. Further, it was estimated that one third of the total production of milk goes into other products like butter, cheese, and cream. A milk cow gives about 2.5 gallons of milk twice a day. We have $(250{,}000000 \times 10 \times 3)/\ 128 \times 5 = 11.8$ million cows.

Statistical Abstract of the United States also shows 4.3 gallons of milk per day produced by each of 11×10^6 milk cows. Out of the total milk production of 17×10^9 gallons per annum, that which is not drunk in liquid form is used in other dairy products. There are 115×10^6 head of cattle altogether.

⇒ Estimate how many cars and how much mileage are driven daily on the Pennsylvania Turnpike.

The turnpike is around 350 miles long. Develop a theory to make the estimate and call the turnpike authority or look in the books to validate your answer. You might simulate your thinking on the computer to show the seasonal and holiday variability of the problem. Traffic may be more intense around the cities on the turnpike such as Philadelphia, Harrisburg and Pittsburgh. This project can be undertaken by a group of 3 to 4 people. The group with the 3 best approaches will present them in the class.

⇒ How much food does it take to feed the population of the United States each year?

I will estimated this under the following assumptions:

1. There are about 120 Million households in the United States.
2. On average, every household has two adults and two children and needs to eat 7 pounds of food per day (2 pounds × 2 + 1.5 pounds × 2 = 7 pounds day).
3. And each year every household needs to eat 2,555 pounds of food (7 pounds × 365 days = 2,555 pounds per year).

4. Therefore, it would take 2,555 pounds × 120 million households = 306 billion pounds or 153 million tons of food per year to feed the population of the United States.

⇒ Estimate the number of acres of cultivable land in the United States

Facts: 3.5 million sq. miles
1 sq. mile = 640 acres

$$3.5 \; mil \; sq \; mi \; \times 640 \; \frac{acres}{sq \; mi} = 2240 \; mil \; acres$$

I estimate that 15% of the acreage on the average is used for farming.

$2240 \; mil \; acres \times .15 = 336 \; million \; cultivable \; acres$

Assumptions: My estimate that 15% of US is available to be cultivated based on the fact that in my city of Butler, Pennsylvania approximately 70% of the land is housing and city utilization, and 30% is farming. This is about twice as much farming land as in most cities all over the country because farming is relatively popular in Pennsylvania.

Thus 15% is an average figure for the entire country. This includes both the extensive farming areas of the midwest and the northwest, as well as some of the non-mountainous areas of the north, east, and south. The West Coast would be too mountainous. Also, one should include potential farming acreage taken up by metropolises!

✍ Estimating the number of egg-producing hens in the United States

A population of 46 randomly surveyed people (on the streets of Oakland in Pittsburgh and by telephone to rural areas of SW Pennsylvania) indicated their total estimated weekly consumption of chicken eggs. They were instructed to consider their egg consumption over the entire year, averaging into weekly consumption eggs eaten in greater quantity than normal such as around the holidays (eg. Easter, Christmas - cookies, cakes, etc.) Accordingly, they were also instructed to figure in fractional eggs that are contained in regularly consumed foodstuff (eg. bread, pasta, mayonnaise, bagels, McMuffins, sauces, salads, etc.)

Average weekly egg consumption per person = 229 eggs/46 persons = 4.97826 eggs per person

Take the average per capita egg consumption and multiply by the approximate population of the U.S.: 4.97826 eggs/person/week × 250,000,000 persons = 1,244,565,000 eggs/week consumed in the U.S. according to my estimation.

Each chicken hen produces about 5-6 eggs every week, according to the poultry experts interviewed. Thus, if each hen produces 5.5 eggs per week on average we can determine how many hens are required to meet the demand for eggs each week:
1,245,000,000 eggs/week divided by 5.5 eggs/week/hen
(rounded up to allow for breakage)
= 226,363,636 hens

This result is very reasonable. According to the United Egg Producers Association, there are approximately 225,000,000 hens in the United States. Thus, my estimate has a margin of error of less than 1%.

✍ Estimation of the number of redwood trees in Redwood National Forest

For this estimation problem, I considered many different alternatives. I decided to follow my heart and estimate something that was truly important to me. The subject of my estimation problem was the Redwood National Forest. Its beauty and power speaks for itself (if you have ever been lucky enough to see it). To me, the Redwood National Forest demonstrates the magnificence and wonder of nature. I visited the park 3 times during various stages of my childhood. The images and facts that I can recall served as the basis for my estimation of the number of giant Redwood trees in the park.

As I remember, it took my family approximately one hour to drive through the park at an average speed of 20 mph. From this information I estimated the road to be approximately 20 miles long from the entrance of the park to its exit. I assumed that the acreage of the park was square in dimension and that the main visitor's road that we traveled cut diagonally through the park.

Using the Pythagorean theorem, I solved for the sides of the square which represented the boundaries of the park. These boundaries were approximately 14.14 miles long. Converting this number to feet resulted in a side

# eggs consumed/week	0	1	2	3	4	5	6	7	8	9	10	12	15
# responses for # eggs	1	3	6	11	6	5	2	2	2	1	3	3	1
Total weekly egg consumption	0	3	12	33	24	25	12	14	16	9	30	36	15

of the square, S, of 74,659 feet.

The total area of the square (the park) in feet is:

$74,659^2 = 5,573,996,145$ square feet.

I estimated the diameter of the trees by comparing them to the length of my parent's car, which I estimate to be 12 feet. Most of the trees that I remember seeing had a diameter about two times as wide as the length of the car. This gives:

2×12 feet $= 24$ feet in diameter

I estimated the height of the trees (on sight alone) at 275 feet. In addition, I remembered that the total branch span of a tree should be approximately equal to its height. To find the area that one average sized tree occupied in the park I used the formula for the area of a circle. I used the branch span of 275 feet as the diameter in the following formula.

Area of Circle $= \pi r^2$
Area of Circle $= 3.1416 \times (137.5)^2$
$\qquad\qquad\quad = 59,396$ square feet

From this I concluded that each giant Redwood in the park occupied approximately 59,395 square feet.

From my previous calculations:

Total Park Area = 5,573,996,145 sq. feet
Total Area/Tree = 59,396 sq. feet

Dividing these two numbers gave me approximately 93,845 trees in the Redwood National Forest, if the trees touched each other. I took this number 93,845 and multiplied it by .90 (density of circle packing) to get the actual density of trees in the forest, since most tree branches overlap and the

forest is not completely dense. This calculation gave me a total of 84,460 trees in the park.

To verify the number of trees I called the National Redwood Forest Service. They gave me a ballpark figure of 75,000 giant Redwood trees. The Forest Service was able to give me some additional information that helped me explain my difference of 9,460 trees. The main source of error I found was the fact that I did not account for the varying sizes of trees.

Additional information for estimating the number of redwood trees in Redwood National Forest to be added at the end of the exercise:

Redwood National Forest is 75,451 acres in size. An acre has 43,560 sq. ft., so the square footage of RNF is 3,286,645,560.

Of the total Redwood park system, which includes 3 California state parks, 5.4% of the acreage is submerged. Therefore, RNF has $3,286,645,560 \times .946 = 3,286,645,560$ arable sq. ft. Of that, only about half is old growth forest, i.e. redwoods. The remainder is younger trees from other families of fir. (Redwoods live an average of six centuries, and there was extensive logging in the century before the park was established). Hence, $3,286,645,560 / 2 = 1,643,322,780$.

Mature redwoods range from 100 to 300 ft. in height, so we can estimate the average to be 200 ft. Redwoods branches tend to be relatively close to the trunk, so I would estimate the branch span to be closer to .75 x (trees' height). Using the same process as above and a branch span of 150 ft as the diameter:

Area of a circle $= 3.1416 \times (75)^2 = 17,672$ sq. ft.

The total number of trees is equal to 1,643,322,780 / 17,672 = 92,990. Again using the .90 factor to adjust for the actual density of trees, we arrive at a total of 83,691 trees, very close to the original estimate of 84,460 and again somewhat more than the 75,000 estimate of the park service.

✍ Telephone survey estimate

A client wants a telephone survey done of large-sized middle market firms to determine the level of computing power, level of usage and particular application used. The client is only interested in the metropolitan Pittsburgh area and wants the calling completed in 5 working days.

Assumptions:
(1) Large-sized, middle market = revenue $50-125 million
(2) Survey questions = 10

Step I: Questionnaire Design
- Avg. 1 hr development time/question
- 10 questions

Step II: Determine Target Market Base
- Determine total middle market base - rev. $5-125 million
- Pittsburgh = large corporate base
  Therefore = 100 firms total middle market
-Shrinking large corporate base, therefore more small firms

Therefore assume 20% of total mid-market in $50-125 million target range. (20% ×1000 = 200 firms)
Therefore 200 firms = target market base

Step III: Determine # people needed to call
- 1 successful call takes about 15 min.
- Per 1 hr of time about 25% will be unsuccessful contacts

- 1 person can stand about 4-6 hours of continuous calling
  Therefore, assume 5 hours
- Calls/hour × total days =
- Number of days to contact all the target firms
      = 200 companies divided by 15 calls/day
      = 13.33 days to call Co's

- Add to this company-imposed constraint
      = 13.33 days divided by 5 days/calling = 2.667 callers = 3 people

Therefore, 3 people × 15 calls/day = 45 calls/day

200 Co's/45 calls/day = 4.44 days

Step IV: Determine Costs
- Assume $10/hr for calling
      = $10/hr × [4.44 days x 5 hrs/day x 3 people]
      = $666.00 total telephoning costs
- Collation of data
      200 calls - success rate of 60% - 80%, therefore 70%
      = 70% × 200 = 140 successful calls

Assume 1 hr of work (reading notes, data entry, simple statistics per 4 successful calls).

Therefore [140 divided by 4] × 1 = 35 hours.

Total costs estimated
Calling $666.00
Development   (10 hrs × $75/hr)*
      Collation   (35 hrs × $75/hr)
      Total $4,041.00

* Graduate student rate
Actual Figures
Over the weekend I had a friend at the Mellon Bank run a Dun & Bradstreet listing of

the Pittsburgh metro area middle market firms.

- Middle market firms (revenues between $5 and 125 MM) = <u>423</u>
- Firms within target range of ($50 - 125 MM) = <u>47</u>

$$47/423 = \underline{11\%}$$

Gross overestimation initially. I was probably thinking of the tri-state area when I did my original estimates.

Actual Figures

$$\frac{60 \min./15 \min}{15 \min./15 \min} \times 5 \; days = 15 \; \frac{calls}{day}$$

$$calls/hr \quad slack \; time$$

- 15 calls/day
- 47 Co's divided by 15 calls/day = 3.133 days to call Co's (under 5 day limit). I also should have included 1 extra day for callbacks. Therefore 3.133 days = 1 day (callback) = 44.133 days
- 1 person can do this. Therefore 4.133 days x 5 hrs/day x $10/hr = 206.67 = $207
- Collation of data: 70% of 47 = 32.9 = 33

(33 divided by 4) x 1 hr = <u>8.25 hrs</u>
8.25 hrs x $75/hr = $618.75

Therefore the new total costs are:

Calling	$207.00
Development	750.00
Collation	618.75
Total	$1,575.75

A difference of $2,465.25 from the original.

The client would be ecstatic and I need to further develop estimation skills.

Estimate the number of grains of sand on the coastlines of the United States

First one needs to look at the four coastlines in the United States - Atlantic, Arctic, Pacific and Gulf Coasts - and measure the length of each coastline in miles.

According to the Almanac, the Atlantic coast measures 2,069 miles, the Gulf coast measures 1,631 miles, the Pacific coast measures 7,623 miles and the Arctic coast (Alaska) measures 1,060. Therefore, the U.S. coastline totals 12,383 miles. For the purpose of this exercise, there is little benefit to be gained from measuring the depth of each coastline. The depth of a coastline is in constant flux, changing due to tides, storms and other environmental forces. Therefore, we will use a consistent measure of 6 inch depth for each of the coast lines. When you think of it, unless one is digging or building a sandcastle, you really only uncover at most 6 inches of sand by walking or strolling along the beach or coastline.

So now we have measurement for length and height. All we need is an estimate of the width of a coastline. Some coastlines measure only 20 feet to the water. Others will measure 100 feet or more. So let us take an average of say 50 feet. Now we have length in miles, height in inches and width in feet. Let us convert each to a common denominator of inches. Width, on the average is 600 inches. The length is 784,586,880 inches.

Now we need to estimate the number of grains of sand there are in a cubic inch. I estimate that one could fit about 25 grains of sand along the edge of a square inch. The estimate for a cubic inch is then 25x25x25 = 15,625 grains. The volume for this coastline would be:

175

6 (height) x 600 (width) x 784,586,880 (length) = 2,824,512,768,000 in^3
Multiplying by 15,625 grains/in^3 yields:

2,824,512,768,000 in^3 x 15,625 grains/in^3 = 4.4133x10^{16} grains

Therefore there are approximately 44 quadrillion grains of sand on U.S. coastlines, give or take a few.

☞ Estimate the number of blades of grass in the United States

There are 23 blades of grass per square inch in my backyard. There are 3,500,000 sq. miles. in the United States.

How the United States is broken down according to The Universal Almanac, 1993:

Not including Alaska: (In thousands of Acres)

Surface Area =	1,937,725
Water Area =	107,900
Federal Area =	404,063
Federal Parks =	258,683
State Parks =	8,007
Urban =	46,416
Rural Transport =	26,914
Cropland =	420,994
Pastureland =	132,356
Rangeland =	405,914
Forestland =	393,197

Estimate for each subregion:

Parks: After observing Ohiopyle State Park, I conclude that approximately 10% of state parks are covered by grass. Modifying for the Midwest and Eastern Marsh areas, I estimate 14%.

Urban: Observing Urban areas with parks and yards, I conclude that 30% is covered with grass. In rural urban areas, the typical plot is 1/3 acre with 50% covered in grass. In cities, yards are smaller and indicate a 20% estimation.

Cropland: If cropland is properly rotated, 1/3 of the land is allowed to "rest" yearly.

Pasture: Most of this area is grassland. Estimate 95% to be grassland.

Rangeland: Cover areas that are barren or covered with trees.

Forest: Forestland is not completely covered with trees. Estimate 10% to cover areas that are barren or covered with trees.

Rural: Road are typically 14 ft. a lane. Double lanes are 30 ft. a lane. Most have 15 ft. of right of way on both sides. Estimate that 50% of right-always are grass because of desert/barren lands. Estimate 25%.

Grassland = Parks + Urban + Cropland + Pasture/Range + Forest + Rural Transport

$$Grassland = \begin{array}{ll} (.14)(266,690) & + \\ (.40)(46,416) & + \\ (.33)(420,994) & + \\ (.95)(538,270) & + \\ (.10)(393,197) & + \\ (.25)(26,914) & \end{array}$$

Grassland = 742,953 thousand acres

Correction Factor: Not all grassland is covered with grass. Clover and weeds comprise 10%

Corrected Grassland: 668,657 thousand acres

1 Acre = 43,560 ft^2
43,560 ft^2 × (12 in/ft)^2 = 6,272,640 in^2/acre
Grassland = (668,657 thousand acres) × (6,272,640 in^2/acre) = 4.19 × 10^{15} in^2

Blades of Grass = (4.19 × 10^15 in^2)(23 blades/in^2)= 9.64 × 10^15 blades in the U.S.

Comments:

A. When undertaking this estimation, I did not realize how much estimation would be required between different segments (urban vs. cropland vs. pastureland). This can be beneficial because if an estimation is in error, it could have a small effect on the final number.

B. Not that the biggest contributors are Pasture/Range land and Cropland. This is where the estimation of grass in each sector is most crucial.

C. With confidence I can estimate there are 9.64×10^{15} blades in the United States (less Alaska). I have great confidence that this value is between 1.0×10^{15} blades and 1.0×10^{17} blades.

❧ Estimation of the number of horseshoes used by racehorses per year

Three types of racing horses run in the U.S. These are:
Thoroughbreds (flat-gallop), Standardbreds (harness-buggy) and Quarter Horses (short distance gallop).

As further refinement, let us consider only Standardbred or Harness Racing horses. This simplification is for convenience. The Meadow's Racetrack (harness racing) in nearby suburban Pittsburgh provided accessible data.

How many horseshoes does the Meadow's Racetrack use in one year? (Note: these are racing horseshoes)

Facts:
- The Meadows race 200 days per year
- Averaging 7 horses per race and 13 races per day

- Approximately 950 horses are stabled on the Meadow's grounds
- Racing horseshoes are lightweight - aluminum alloy metal which can bend rather easily
- Most horses are stabled at the Meadows on a year-round basis

Note that even though the horses race only

$$950 \ horses \times \frac{4 \ shoes/horse}{5 \ weeks} \times 52 \frac{weeks}{year} = 39,520 \frac{shoes}{year}$$

for 200 days they are trained (i.e. exercised at least 5 miles) on a <u>daily basis</u>. While talking to several trainers and harness drivers (jockeys) I discovered that on average horses change shoes approximately once per 4 to 6 weeks (assume 5 weeks). Thus,

$$950 \ horses \times \frac{0.80 \ pacers}{all \ horses} \times \frac{1.20 \ wear \ rate}{pacer} = 912 \ Pacer \ Rate$$

$$950 \ horses \times \frac{0.20 \ trotters}{all \ horses} \times \frac{1.00 \ wear \ rate}{trotter} = 190 \ Trotter \ Rate$$

However, later I talked to the Meadow's blacksmith who said that he went through 125,000 shoes in a year.

Obviously we are <u>underestimating</u> the process.

Obtaining more information from trainers and drivers I learned that:

(1) Horses with different "gaits" wear the shoes out at different rates:
Pacers ("sidewheelers") wear out shoes at a 20% faster rate than trotters. Approximately 80% of the Meadows horses are pacers. Trotters ("high steppers") make up 20% of the Meadows horses.

(2) During average training a horse will throw a shoe on the average of once per week.

177

(3) Horse's shoes are changed once per 4-6 weeks but they are re-set approximately every two weeks. At least one shoe needs to be replaced at that time.

(4) Horses can have accidents - i.e. tripping, stumbling, kicking the side of the stall, etc. and bending a shoe. These additional shoes constitute approximately 4% of the shoes a horse uses over the course of a year.

Let us now modify our previous calculations.

We have:

(1) Adjusted equivalent Horse Rate <u>1102</u>

(2) Extra shoes: throws

$$950 \text{ horses } \times 1 \frac{shoe}{week} \times 52 \frac{weeks}{year} = 49,400 \frac{shoes}{year}$$

(3) Extra: reset shoes

$$950 \text{ horses } x \frac{1 \text{ shoe}}{2 \text{ weeks}} \text{ x } 52 \frac{weeks}{year} = 24,700 \frac{shoes}{year}$$

(4) Extra 4% of total number of shoes

Now calculate the new adjusted horseshoe total:

(1) $$950 \text{ horses } \times \frac{0.80 \times 1.20}{pacers} \times \frac{0.20 \times 1.00}{trotters}$$

$$\times \frac{4 shoes/horse}{5 weeks} \times 52 \frac{weeks}{year} = 45,843 \frac{shoes}{year}$$

(2) Extra throws:

950 horses x 1 shoe/week x 52 weeks/year = 49,400

(3) Extra resets:

950 horses x 1 shoe/2 weeks x 52 weeks/year = 24,700
TOTAL: 119,943 shoes/year

(4) Now include the 4% accident figure (kicking stalls, etc.)

119,943 shoes/year x 1.04 = 124,741 shoes/year

This is much closer to the 125,000 shoes number given by the blacksmith.

❧ Estimate the number of times the house refrigerator is opened and shut

This estimation is based on the number of times a family's refrigerator door is opened during a one-week period. The estimate is based on the activities of a family of four (two adults and two children).

This estimate will be approached on the assumption that the weekdays are during the school year.

The week is broken down into weekdays and weekends and each day is divided into parts. An estimate will be made for each family member's opening of the door during each part of the day.

The total of all of these individual estimates will equal the number of times the refrigerator door is open in during a week's time.

WEEKDAY
Morning: everyone gets out juice and milk and makes lunches

MOM	4
DAD	3
KATE	4
SARAH	4

Late afternoon: snacks for the kids

MOM	0
DAD	0
KATE	3
SARAH	2

Dinnertime: getting dinner ready (everyone helps)

MOM	5
DAD	3
KATE	2
SARAH	2

Evening: snacks and drinks

MOM	2
DAD	3
KATE	3
SARAH	2

TOTAL WEEKDAY OPENINGS 42

WEEKEND
Morning: breakfast and coffee

MOM	3
DAD	2
KATE	3
SARAH	3

Lunch time: dad and kids cook

MOM	2
DAD	3
KATE	2
SARAH	2

Afternoon: drinks

MOM	2
DAD	3
KATE	2
SARAH	2

Dinnertime: cook a more complicated meal

MOM	5
DAD	2
KATE	3
SARAH	3

Evening: snacks and drinks

MOM	2
DAD	3
KATE	3
SARAH	3

TOTAL OPENINGS ON A WEEKEND DAY is 53.

TOTAL TIMES THE REFRIGERATOR DOOR IS OPENED DURING A WEEK:

$$42 \times 5 = 210$$
$$\underline{53 \times 2 = 106} \quad +$$
$$316$$

The estimated total for one week is 316 refrigerator openings and closings.

A tally sheet was posted on the refrigerator door on a Friday and Saturday. Each opening was marked on the sheet. The Friday total was 55 and the Saturday total was 70. When these results are applied to the entire week, the estimate was low by 99 openings (The total for the week would be 415). The time period that was most underestimated was dinnertime. The refrigerator was opened repeatedly while dinner was being prepared. A few times it was opened without anything being removed.

❧ Another student's estimate of refrigerator openings

I am going to estimate how many times my refrigerator is opened and closed per month. I live alone, however I usually have one guest in my house at least twice per week and I also have parties of approximately 20 people once per month. My guests always have the freedom to open and close my refrigerator. I have a "self service" rule in my house.

I will do the estimation by calculating the frequency of usage of the refrigerator by each group: me, the weekly guest, and the monthly guests. The estimations are shown in the table below.

Concept	Description	Total 4 weeks
Me (Elena)		
Buy food	Once a week I open the refrigerator 3 times to put the food bought in it. (3 x 4)	12
	Weekdays	
Breakfast	Open the refrigerator to see what is in there. (1 x 5 x 4)	20
	Open the refrigerator to get the food and shut it again. (1 x 5 x 4)	20
	Open the refrigerator to get the food I forgot and shut it. (1 x 5 x 4)	20
	Open the refrigerator to put the food I didn't eat. (1 x 5 x 4)	20
Food packet	Open the refrigerator to get the food I will take to the university. (1 x 5 x 4)	20
	Open the refrigerator to store the food. (1 x 5 x 4)	20
Lunch	I eat at school.	0
Dinner	Same routine as for breakfast.	80
Snack	Open the refrigerator to get some fruit or prepare a sandwich. (1 x 5 x 4)	20
	Open the refrigerator to put the food back again. (1 x 5 x 4)	20
Weekends		
Breakfast	Same routine (4 x 2 x 4)	32
Lunch	Same routine as for the breakfast, but only one day of the weekend.	16
Dinner	Same routine as for the breakfast, but only one day of the weekend.	16
Weekly Guests (2)		
Snack	Open the refrigerator to get some fruit or prepare a sandwich. (1 x 2 x 4)	8
	Open the refrigerator to put the food back again. (1 x 2 x 4)	8
Monthly Guests (20)		
	Open the refrigerator to put the snacks and drinks I buy for the party.	1
	Open the refrigerator to take out and prepare the snacks I bought for the party.	1
	Open the refrigerator to put the drinks in that the guests buy. Since the guests come usually in groups of 4 they open the refrigerator 5 times.	5
	Open the refrigerator to take out the drinks they brought to the party. Estimating that each guest on average drinks 3 beers and 2 mixed drinks. (5 x 20)	100
Total		729

❧ Still another student's estimate:

Morning 6:30 am:
1) Open to get some milk for breakfast
2) Open again to put back the milk in the refrigerator
3) Open again to get some fruit to eat after breakfast

Lunch time 11:30 am:
4) Open to check if there is enough food to cook

5) Get vegetables or eggs from the bottom part of the refrigerator to prepare to cook

6) Get some frozen food from the upper part of the refrigerator for cooking

7) Open again to get some more food to cook

8) Open to put the food not used back to its place in the refrigerator

9) Get some fruit to eat after lunch

10) Open again to get some drink to if thirsty

11) Open to put some food bought from Giant Eagle or Chinese supermarket in Penn Ave

12) Open to put the leftover of lunch in the refrigerator

13) Get some frozen food and let it thaw before dinner

14) Get some food from refrigerator to cook for dinner

15) Get some sources from the refrigerator to add the food when cooking

16) Get some fruit to eat after dinner

17) Get some snacks from refrigerator to eat when watching TV at night

18) Check the refrigerator if there is anything that should be eaten while it is fresh

19) Prepare lunch bag for the next day and put it in the refrigerator

20) Put the leftovers from dinner into the refrigerator

21) Check the refrigerator again before going to bed

Total: 20 times for a weekend day.

✌ Estimating the number of TV sets operational in United States households in 1980

The U.S. population in 1980 is estimated to be 225,000,000. What I call "family units" are groups either of individuals, couples, or families that live under one roof:

a) 50% are families -- consisting of 2 adults and 2.3 kids.

b) 25% are single

c) 25% are couples (no kids) -- 2 people.

I also estimate that the number of TV sets in each group is:

a) 2

b) 1

c) 1.5

Therefore, the estimated number of TV sets in the U.S. is:

a) (225,000,000 x 50% x 2)/4.3=
                    52,325,581

b) (225,000,000 x 25% x 1)/1=
                    56,250,000

c) (225,000,000 x 25% x 1.5)/2 =
42,187,500

TOTAL = 150,763,010

The actual number of TV's in the U.S. in 1980 was 108,900,000 (household). My estimate was off by 38%.

Actual statistics are as follows:

1980 population: 226,500,000 people in 84,000,000 households of which 73% are families - 61,320,000.

There are 2.71 people per family: 166,177,200 people in United States families.

    226,500,000 population
  -166,177,200 people in families
    60,322,800 single people

a) Families - 61,320,000
b) Singles   - 60,322,800
c) Couples - 22,680,000

(84,000,000 households - 61,320,000 families)

New estimates for number of TV's per:
a) Families: 1.25

b) Singles: 0.5
c) Couples: 0.75

New estimate of number of TV's in the U.S. is:

a) 61,320,000 x 1.25 = 76,650,000
b) 60,322,800 x .5 = 30,161,400
c) 22,680,000 x .75 = 17,010,000
TOTAL = 123,821,400 (only off by 13.7%)

ஐ Estimate the amount of money taken in annually from parking meters and parking lots in your city.

In the town of Dieburg, Germany, there are about 15.000 inhabitants.

The estimated number of parking meters is 40. One must pay between 8 am and 6 pm (10 hours), 5 days a week, though not on bank holidays. On the average 61% are in use (excluding in and out parking etc.). It is estimated that 1% do not pay or use it longer than it is being paid for. The price is about 2 DM / h 40 × 10 × (52-1) × (60% - 1%) × 2 = 24,480 DM

There is one parking lot. It has space for about 50 cars with payment required between 7 am and 8 pm (13 hours), 5 days a week, excluding bank holidays. On the average 40% of the spaces are in use (excluding in and out parking etc.) The price is about 2 DM/h on the average (long time parking is less expensive, short term more) 50 × 13 × (52-1) × 40% × 2 = 26,520 DM. The amount in dollars at the current exchange rate is: (24,480 + 26,520) / 1.8 = $28,333

ஐ How many identical spherically shaped cherries in a can? Remember the gaps.

Assumptions

- Cherry: Perfect sphere. Diameter=25 mm. Uniform size.
- Can: Cylindrical shape. Inner diameter=100 mm, Height=150 mm
- $\pi = 3.141592\ldots\ldots \approx 3.14$

Calculations

Total Volume of Can / Unit Volume of Cherry = 50 x 50 x π x 150/ (4/3π 12.5 x 12.5 x 12.5) = 144 cherries with no gaps considered.

Dense packing of spheres by considering the gaps to be about 74 percent of the total (justify this). Thus if we consider the gaps we get 144 × .74 $\cong$ 106 cherries.

What if the can is a rectangular box instead of being cylindrical?

ஐ How many bricks are there in a mile of residential brick road?

First, I measured the width of my street, and found it to be 30'.

Second, I measured the size of the pavers (bricks) used to make the alley behind my home. The pavers are 3" X 9". There appears to be .25" on each side of the pavers for spacing. This must be added to each brick for correct estimation. Therefore, for purposes of this exercise, pavers' dimensions are 3.25" X 9.25".

Third, the length in inches in a mile is 5280' X 12"=63,360".

The width of the street is 30' X 12"= 360" inches.

Next we divide the number of bricks into the inch dimensions:
63,360"/9.25"=19,495 pavers needed to pave one linear mile.

360"/3.25"= 39 pavers to pave the width of my street.

The rest is simple. We multiply width times length to arrive at

19,495 × 39 = 758,740 pavers needed to pave one mile of 30' wide residential street.

❧ How many adult runners (or joggers) are there in the United States?

This example was worked out as follows by a student who never came to grips with the estimate.

1) Let "adult" mean anyone over 18 years old. I found that there are 175,571,000 people in the U.S.A. About 75% of the population are over 18.
2) Let "runner" or "jogger" designate anyone who ran at least once in 1999.
3) I found that The Great Race (10-K run held in Pittsburgh in September) had 9,654 registered participants. Dividing 9,654 by 2,000,000 (pop. of Pittsburgh metro area) we get .48% of the Pittsburgh population ran at least once. However, this seems low. For one thing, a lot of people run in races without signing up (since they don't want to pay the fee). Also, many people who run one or more times per year did not run in this race.
4) I then found that over 12,000 people actually ran in the race; therefore, 12,000/2,000,000 = .6% which still seems low as it would mean there are only 1,053,426 runners in the U.S.
5) I decided to try something different. I found that there were 100 races run in the U.S. with not less than 2,400 participants in each. The average number of participants in each of these top 100 was 6,262.

That would mean 626,200 ran in these races.

For races under 2,400 participants, I estimate that there are at least 1,000 other races with an average number of participants of 500. That is another 500,000 for a total of 1,126,200. Since many runners never enter a race, I looked over the list of known runners in our class and discovered that only 1/3 to a 1/4 of those listed participated in races. Therefore, 1,126,200 x 4 = 4,504,800 estimated runners in America.

There are no right answers to this problem, because no one has been able to figure it out. However, it looks like I grossly under estimated my numbers since the two most recent estimates are as follows:

National Sporting Goods Association: 29.5 Million (based on 10 million pairs of running shoes sold in the US that year) Sporting Goods Dealer Magazine estimated the number at 40.83 Million

It is possible that I shouldn't have used students to get the number of runners who don't race since they are:
    1) young (usually 22-35 or so)
    2) overly competitive

A factor of 10 would result in about 11 million runners, still low, but wait - according to this same data, 3,000,000 to 4,000,000 ran at least one race, so I am way off there. Using my revised multiplier of 10 to denote non-racing runners, I would get between 30 and 40 million - fairly close to estimates.

❧ Estimation of total toothpaste consumption in the U.S.

I started on this problem by "data mining" toothpaste information on the Internet's World

Wide Web. My search yielded the following information:

- *Current Population* in 1997 was 265,000,000; so approx. 270,000,000 for 1998
- *Average times the population brush their teeth:* 2 times a day
- *Average # of tubes purchased a year:* 3
- *Average price of toothpaste*: $0.0182/ML
- *Average amount of time spent during each brushing*: 2.5 minutes
- *Range in trial tube size:* 75 ML to 130 ML1 (converted to 2.53575 to 4.3953 Oz).

Analysis of Size and Pricing of Toothpaste Tubes

Typical tubes of toothpaste range from trial size to 8 oz. Trial size tubes are used by companies to induce trial and/or are purchased by customers who travel. The average full size tube is either 6.4 or 7 ounces in size. I will assume that this has not changed. The average price of toothpaste as collected from the World Wide Web was $2.00.

The following formulas were used to convert milliliters and grams to ounces:

$$\text{\# mls.} \times .03381 = \text{\# ounces}$$

$$\text{\# gms.} \times .03257 = \text{\# ounces}$$

Usage Assumptions

I figure that individuals under 3 years of age do not brush their teeth on their own, and it is difficult to quantify how many parents brush the teeth of their toddlers. In my experience, children reaching pre-kindergarten brush their own teeth and fall into the average of 2 times a day category.

Removing the 3 year-old and less children from the total population count (approximately

1/2 of the 5 year-olds = 3.7%) we have an approximate total of (270,000,000-10,075,709) = 259,924,291 to work with. Approximately, 3 tubes of toothpaste are purchased by each individual in a year. Therefore, we have developed the following information:

Pricing and Revenue

6.4 oz average size/0.03381 = 189 ml.

189 ml. × $0.0182 average price per ml. = $3.45 per tube list price

Assume a 100% mark-up on a $1.72 tube to yield an overall profit of:

$1.72/tube × 3 tubes/yr × 259,924,291 = $1,341,200,000.

Unfortunately the answer was not found in the Statistical Abstract of the United States. Therefore, I used information from the June 13, 1988, Wall Street Journal article titled *Market Watch*. According to that analysis, there is a growth of 5% per year projected for the total toothpaste market. In 1988 this was $683,000,000, therefore in 1998 that should be $1,112,535,030. I am off by $228,674,311! I believe that this error is attributable to the price information and the fact that I left out the age 3 and under population in the equation. When I added this age group, my answer was much closer: $1,293,612,000, which is off only by $47,588,000.

Volume

When reviewing the volume of the average tube of 6.4 oz, I found the following results: (*Note: I did not take out the individuals age 3 and under*)

3 × 259,924,291 = 779,772,873 tubes sold per year

779,772,873 × 6.4 oz = 4,990,546,387 ounces sold per year

This converts to 311 million pounds per year. Incredibly this is 156,000 tons per year or 1.2 pounds per person consumed by the population. That is a lot of toothpaste!

❧ Estimate the percentage of the average magazine devoted to advertisements in the U.S.

Advertising has always played a large role in the financing of periodicals. What I will attempt to do is estimate what percentage of a particular magazine, e.g., Business Week, is

$$Actual\ Percentage = \frac{682}{1282} = .53\ or\ 53\%;$$

$$Error\ in\ Estimation = \frac{.56 - .53}{.53} = .06$$

attributed to sponsor advertisements.

My assumptions:

1. Average number of articles in Business Week...15

2. Average number of advertisements per article...3

3. Average number of brief news clips in Business Week.......................................30

4. Average number of advertisements per clip...4

5. Average number of pages per article...2

6. Average number of pages per clip...............2

7. Average number of pages per advertisement...1

8. Percentage of advertisements in Business Week:

Actual data using 10 magazines:

Magazine Date	Pages of Ads	Total Pages
Nov. 24, 1996	73	133
Dec. 1, 1996	98	155
Dec. 8, 1996	69	131
Dec. 15, 1996	66	123
Jan. 19, 1997	59	117
Jan. 26, 1997	66	119
Feb. 2, 1997	42	99
Feb. 9, 1997	53	111
Feb. 16, 1997	69	131
Feb. 23, 1997	87	163
Total	682	1282

❧ How many U.S. students (undergraduate) are currently enrolled in college?

There seem to be several different ways to attack this problem. Guessing the number of colleges in the U.S. and then attempting to determine the average number of students per institution is one way. Attacking the problem from a population standpoint seems more logical. First, I must estimate the number of people of college age. I consider college age to be 18-21. Then I must determine what percent of persons in this age group attend college.

Also, I must make allowance for foreign students enrolled in U.S. schools. The U.S. Population at the time of this exercise is about 240,000,000.

If the average person lives to be 70, then

$$Pages\ of\ Ads = \frac{(3)(15)(1\ ) + (.4)(30)(1\ )}{(3)(15)(1\ ) + (.4)(30)(1\ ) + (15)(2) + (.30)(.2)}$$
$$= .56\ or\ 56\%$$

240,000,000 / 70 = 3,500,000. I realize that at every age from 1 to 70 there are about 3,500,000 people. It seems like a good estimate.

3,500,000 × 4 = 14,000,000 from 18-21

I guess that 25% of them are enrolled in college = 3,500,000

Add 15% of 3,500,000 as a guess for foreign students and students of other ages.

$0.15 \times 3,500,000 + 3,500,000 = \underline{4,025,000}$
The Statistical Abstract of the U.S. for 1985 indicates that in 1982 there were 11,336,000 undergraduate students. This was an increase of .50% over 1981. If enrollment increases at .59% until 1986 there are currently 11,605,906 undergraduate students.

I have made a gross underestimate.

The Statistical Abstract of the United States shows that in 1982 there were 21,078,000 people ages 20-24. Thinking more logically now, I should have increased the 3,500,000 figure for the 18-21 age group. If I change this to 5,000,000 I am closer.

I missed the boat when I guessed there were 1.5 others for every student 18-21!
It turns out that other age groups and foreign students provide an equal amount of students. I never would have guessed this. Part-timers are a group that I did not consider and should have.

$5,000,000 + 5,000,000 = 10,000,000$

This revised estimate remains off by 1,500,000. I should have come up with a better way to estimate the 18-21 population from the beginning.

➢ Estimate the average gross yearly earnings of U.S. psychiatrists.

Assumptions:
1) Average psychiatrist spends 8 hours per day seeing patients.

2) Psychiatrists spend 4 hours seeing patients in a hospital and another 4 hours in an office.
3) In an hour in the hospital, the psychiatrist can see 3 patients and earn $30/patient.
4) In an hour in an office the psychiatrist can see one patient and earn $80.
5) Psychiatrists on average work 48 weeks/year and 5 days/week.

Earnings/day = $4 \times \$90 + 4 \times \$80 = \$680$
Earnings/week = $5 \times \$680 = \$3400$
48 weeks $\times \$3400 = \$163,200$/year

According to a 1982 survey, the actual average gross income is $82,180 - approximately 50% under my estimate.

My major incorrect assumption was in the number of patients seen. I estimated 32 different patients/week (12 in the hospital and 20 in the office). In reality, only 22 different patients are seen (and thus billed for) per week. Also, I overestimated the hourly office charge (it is $70, rather than $80/hour). Finally, only slightly over half of the survey psychiatrists are in private practice (which I used as my model). The others are in salaried positions (where they presumably have lower gross incomes).

➢ Estimate the duration of survival in an airtight sealed room

A room with measurements of:
   Length = 10 ft. = 300 cm
   Width = 10 ft. = 300 cm
   Height = 8 ft. = 240 cm

contains approximately = $10 \times 10 \times 8 = 800$ cubic feet of air, or $300 \times 300 \times 240 = 21,600,000$ cm^3 (cc) of air.

From medical data (Medical Dictionary from Health Science Library) one finds that:

186

a) The frequency of respiration of an adult per minute is approximately 14 to 20 breaths with an average of 17.
   Question and modification situation: *A person's frequency of respiration changes with exercise or when nervous.*

b) In normal breathing, each breath inhaled contains 500 cc of air.
   Question and modification: *An old man or a fat lady each breath different volumes of air than 500 cc.*

c) Atmospheric air inhaled contains 21% oxygen and 0.03% carbon dioxide which in a single breath is 21% × 500 cc = 105 cc of oxygen and 0.03% × 500 cc = 15 cc of carbon dioxide.

d) The air exhaled contains 14% oxygen and 5.6% carbon dioxide or 70 cc of oxygen and 28cc of carbon dioxide. Hence the oxygen consumed with each breath is 105cc – 70cc = 35 cc. Each minute an average adult will consume 35 × 17 = 595 cc of oxygen. As a result, the approximate time will be: 21,600,000 cc/ 595 cc = 36302.52 minutes or 25.21 days.

The student who did this estimation failed to consider the poisonous effect of the increasing concentration of inhaled carbon dioxide. A more sophisticated model is needed.

﹖ Another analysis by a different student

Basic assumption about the cc's of air consumed per minute:

One person will inhale 520 cc/min x 18 times/min = 9,360 cc/min of air

The inhalations per minute per person contain:

9,360 x 21% = 1,965.6 cc of Oxygen
9,360 x 0.03% = 2.808 cc of Carbon Dioxide

The exhalations per minute per person contain:

9,360 x 14% = 1,310.4 cc of Oxygen
9,360 x 5.6% = 524.16 cc of Carbon Dioxide

Therefore,

Oxygen loss per minute = 1,965.6 cc – 1,310.4 cc = 655.2 cc
Oxygen contained in the room = 21,600,000 x 21% = 4,536,000 cc
4,536,000 cc / 655.2 cc = 6923.08 minutes = 115.38 hours = 4.8 days

Again, this student did not take into consideration the cumulative effect of the carbon dioxide.

﹖ What is the least area of paddy field needed to grow enough rice for people in Taiwan.

What is the smallest area of paddy fields needed to grow enough rice for the people of Taiwan? Factors taken into consideration are:

a. Average rice consumption per person per day = 340 grams

b. Population of Taiwan = 18 million

c. Average loss from natural causes = 10%

d. Efficient area = 90%

e. Harvest is twice a year, but the first harvest is larger than the second.

   i)   Each plant grows an average of 125 grains

   ii) Each bunch has 5 rice plants

iii) The space between each bunch of plants is approximately 20 centimeters

iv) One gram of medium rice contains 50 grains

Given the above, calculations show that the paddy field area required is 4,412.4 square kilometers.

Validation: The area of the existing paddy fields in Taiwan is about 5000 to 5500 square kilometers.

The deficiency in my estimate may be due to the fact that:

a. Some of the rice is consumed for other purposes.

b. There is more rice produced than is necessary for the Taiwanese.

≈ Estimation of the number of PAT buses in Pittsburgh

As a disgruntled Port Authority Transit patron, I have often wondered how many Port Authority Buses there are in the City of Pittsburgh. (I especially wonder when wind chill factors are below zero and the bus is late or over crowded).

To estimate the number of buses I first needed to estimate the number of routes the Port Authority runs. To do this, I visited a Port Authority schedule display rack and counted the number of different schedules.

A rack contained 16 rows and 15 columns. Therefore there are:

$$16 \times 15 = 240 \text{ routes}$$

I then categorized each route into subcategories, with the following estimates:

I. Short Route
    Average Route
    Time - 40 min.

II. Medium Route
     Average Route
     Time - 60 min.

III. Long Route
      Average Route
      Time - 180 min.

Estimated numbers of different types of routes:

% of Short Routes: 10% of 240 = 24
% of Medium Routes: 60% = 144
% of Long Routes: 30% = 72
2.6 buses/short route x 24 short routes = 62.4 buses for short routes

2.6 buses/medium route x 144 medium routes= 374.4 buses for medium routes

3.5 buses/long route x 72 long routes = 252 long routes

Sum of buses required is:

$$62.4 + 374 + 252 = 688.8$$

I also estimated that there were additional buses needed for chartered bus service (for trips, school buses, etc.)

This amount I estimated to be:

$$688.8 \times .2 = 137.76$$

My total estimate is:

688.2 + 137.6 = 825.8 buses owned by PAT

The actual number of buses owned by PAT is 912.

	Short routes	Medium routes	Long routes
Average # of buses/hr	3	2	1
Est. # of buses/route	2	2	3
Est. # of replacement buses needed for preventive maintenance, breakdowns, etc.	30% down time due to inner city travel 0.6	30% down time due to inner city travel 0.6	16% down time 0.5
Total est.buses/route	**2.6**	**2.6**	**3.5**

Maybe I should have taken 30% down time for long routes also. In that case the total number of buses needed would be:

Long Routes   = 72 x 3.9 = 280.8
Increased Total = 62.4 + 374.4 + 280.8
= 717.6
Total Number of Buses Needed = 717.6 x 1.2 = 861.2, which would come closer to the actual number.

➳ Estimate the number of hours Americans spend watching television commercials in a year

Estimation steps

I. a. Average portion of a television show devoted to commercials.
    b. Average number of television viewing hours per day per person.

II. a. Population of the U. S.
    b. Portion of U.S. population that is television viewers.

Combine results of Part I and II above to obtain average commercial viewing time per year.

Estimation

I. a. Viewed approximately 30 minutes of television with the following time sequence results:

2 minutes commercials

5 minutes 35 seconds program
2 minutes commercials
1 minute 30 seconds   program
30 seconds commercials
11 minutes 40 seconds program - news
2 minutes commercials
6 minutes 55 seconds program - news

Total viewing time = 1930 seconds
Total commercial time = 390 seconds
Commercial time as a % of total time = 20%

    b. As a rough guess, I would estimate that an average person watches 2 hours of television per day.

II. a. Estimate of the population of the U.S.: 240 million.
    b. Estimate of the portion of U.S. population that are television viewers: 90%

Calculation:

240 million x .90 = 216 million viewers
2 hours x .20 = 0.4 hour commercials per person per day

0.4 x 365 = 146 hours commercials per person per year

146 hours x 216 million = 31,536 million hours spent yearly watching TV commercials.

Approximately 51,430 lifetimes.

Actual Data

II. a. Population of the U.S. (1983)= 235 million, (Statistical Abstract of the U.S.)
     b. Portion of the U.S. population that are television viewers, (Simmons Target Market - 1982)= approximately 161.656 M/235 M = 69%
     c. Average number of television viewing hours per person per day, (Simmons Target Market - 1982)= approximately 3.4 hours/day.

Actual Calculation

235 million x .69 = 162.15 M

3.4 x .20 = 0.68

0.68 x 365 = 248.2

248.2 x 162.15 million = 40,245.63 Million hours (yearly) spent watching TV commercials.

Difference Between Estimate & Actual

40,245.63 M - 31,536 M = 8709.63 M
actual   estimate

≈ Another student's estimate of time spent viewing commercials

Estimation steps

I. Average number of television viewing hours per week per person.

II. Portion of television viewing hours in different programs.

III. Average portion of a television program devoted to commercials.

Combine results of Part I, II and III above to obtain average commercial viewing time per year.
Estimation

I. As a rough guess, I would estimate that

Commercial time	# of commercials	Programs
2 minutes	2	News
2 minutes and 30 sec.	3	Entertainment
3 minutes	3	Series
2 minutes and 30 sec.	2	Movies
5 minutes	1	Sports

the average individual watches 20 hours of television per week.

Average hours for each program per week:
5 hours - News
2 hours and 30 minutes – Entertainment
4 hours – Series
4 hours and 30 minutes– Movies
4 hours - Sports

II. Viewed approximately 30 minutes of television programs with the following time sequence results:

III. News:
(2 minutes and 30 seconds × 3 commercials) × 2 × 5 hrs = 75 minutes

Entertainment:
(2 minutes × 4 commercials) × 2 × 2.5 hrs = 40 minutes

Series:
(2 minutes × 4 commercials) × 2 × 4 hrs = 64 minutes

Movies:

(3 minutes × 2 commercials) × 2 × 4.5hrs = 54 minutes

Sports:
(4 minutes × 1 commercials) × 2 × 4hrs = 32 minutes

Total viewing commercial time per week = 265 minutes

Total commercial viewing time per person per year = 265 minutes × 52 weeks = 13780 minutes = 230 hrs = 9.6 days

❧ Another estimate from the same student using a slightly different method

Estimation steps

1. Average number of television viewing hours per week per person.

2. Portion of television viewing hours in different programs.

3. Average portion of a television program devoted to commercials.

Combine results of Part I, II and III above to obtain average commercial viewing time per year.

Estimation

1. As a rough guess, I would estimate that the average individual watches 18 hours of television per week.

2. Viewed approximately 30 minutes of television programs with the following time sequence results:

Average hours for each program per week
4.5 hours -- News
3 hours   -- Entertainment

4 hours   -- Series
4 hours   -- Movies
2.5 hours -- Sports

3. Calculation:

News:
(2 minutes × 2 commercials) × 2 × 4.5 hrs = 36minutes

Entertainment:
(2 minutes and 30 seconds × 3 commercials) × 2 × 3hrs = 45 minutes

Series:
(3 minutes × 3 commercials) × 2 × 4 hrs = 72minutes

Movies:
(2 minutes and 30 seconds × 2 commercials) × 2 × 4hrs = 40 minutes

Sports:
(5 minutes × 1 commercials) × 2 × 2.5hrs = 25minutes

Total viewing commercial time per week = 218 minutes

Total commercial viewing time per person per year = 218 minutes × 52 weeks = 11336 minutes = 189 hrs = 7.9 days.

❧ Estimate Peoples Gas Co.'s additional residential revenues for a one degree drop in temperature

1. The mailer in my bill states that Peoples Gas serves approximately 310,000 residential customers.

2. Assume that I am representative of an average customer. I know that I use about $75 worth of gas each month throughout the year.

3. Some of that gas is used on non-furnace items (i.e. the dryer, and water heater.) Assume that 75% of the gas I use fuels my furnace.

4. It would follow, then, that I spend about $56.25 each month to fuel my furnace. (.75 x $75)

5. I turn my heat on when it gets below 65 outside -- this is usually between October and the first of April.

6. The colder it is outside, the more gas I must use to maintain my temperature inside.

7. I am considering 7 months of about 30 days each or a total of 210 "heating" days. Cumulative temperature difference from my base (no heat required) of 65 would be :

Month	# days	Δ temp from 65	day de-grees
October	30	10	300
November	30	20	600
December	30	30	900
January	30	40	1200
February	30	30	900
March	30	20	600
April	30	10	300
TOTAL	210		4800

8. The total I spend on heat for the season is:

$56.25/month × 7 mo. = $394

9. $394/4800 = .08 per day degree under 65.

10. (.08) × 310,000 households) = $24,800 change in revenue each time the temperature changes one degree in a day.
Solution Check

I called a customer representative at Peoples Gas Co. and discussed my assumptions and solutions.

- They do serve 310,000 residential customers (confirmed)

- The average customer uses 90,000 cubic feet of gas each year for space heating. Their average residential retail rate is $5.75 per 1,000 cubic feet. So, the average customer spends $517.50 a year on heating ($517.50/394 ==> 31% error)

- The average degree days for the Pittsburgh Area is 5950.

(5950/4800 ==> 24% error)

(517.50/5950)(310,000) = $26,962

(26,962/24,800 ==> 8.7 % error)

- While talking with the customer representative, I asked if anyone uses gas for air-conditioning in the summer. He said that this was rare.

✍ Estimate the total number of Americans who ever lived on the North American Continent

Assume that a generation = 20 years
Assume that the number of children in a generation per family is:
    1990 ⇒ 2.5
    1970 ⇒ 3
    1950 ⇒ 5
    1930 ⇒ 5
    1910 ⇒ 6
    1790 to 1890 ⇒ 6

Population base -- assume there were "x" people before 1780.

Up to 1790:	Σ = 11,037,302	= 11,037,302
1910:	(.7) × (17.1) × (11,037,302)	= 132,116,505
1950:	(.6) × (21.85) × (11,037,302)	= 144,699,029
1970:	(.6) × (23.275) × (11,037,302)	= 154,135,922
1990:	(.6) × (24.463) × (11,037,302)	= 162,000,000
	Total:	= 603,988,758

Assume the male/female ratio is 50/50.

Assume only 95% of women have children; therefore, only 47.5% of the population gives birth.

Current population = 270 million.

Pop. Base + (# of females bearing children) × (# of children born to each female) × (# of generations) = new population base

$x + (x \times 0.475) \times (6) \times (6) = 17.1x$ = population in 1910

$17.1x + (x \times 0.475) \times (5) \times (2) = 21.85x$ = population in 1950

$21.85x + (x \times 0.475) \times (3) \times (1) = 23.275x$ = population in 1970

$23.275x + (x \times 0.475) \times (2.5) \times (1) = 24.4625x$ = population in 1990

$24.4625 \, x = 270$ million

Therefore, $x = 11,037,302$
To avoid double counting, a sliding factor is used to adjust for the percentage of the population that has already been counted.

  1990 ⇒ .6 (assume we have already counted 40% of the population)
  1970 ⇒ .6
  1950 ⇒ .6
  1930 ⇒ .6
  1790 to 1910 ⇒ .7

🐚 Estimate the amount of water used in the U.S. by people taking showers each day

Assumptions :

1) Population of the U.S.A. is approximately 280 million people.

2) On average, each person in the U.S.A. takes a shower once a day. This assumption is OK because some persons will bathe more than once a day, but others will not bathe every day, and some will simply fill the bathtub and take a bath (using more water than the average shower)

3) The average time spent showering is approximately 8 minutes (My showers are about 5-7 minutes, but I realize many people take considerably longer.)

4) The average water use per time in a shower is approximately 5 gallons per minute. I base this on my own test which yielded 5 gal./min. and a phone call to a hardware store which stated that normal showers (with approx. 40 psi water pressure) use 8 gal/min. and a water saver head would use 3 gal./min. (which many homes now use.) I think this assumption is reasonable. We have:
Shower water consumed/day = # of people showering x length of shower x
Water used / unit time

= (280 x 10^6 people)(8 min/person)(5 gal./min) = <u>11.2 billion gallons</u>

There are about 0.134 cubic feet to a gallon; 11.2 x 0.134 = 1.5 cubic feet or 1.5 / 147.2 = .012 cubic mile.

❧ Estimate the number of baseballs lost by major league teams in one season

Each team plays 162 games. Being a former pitcher and currently a pitching coach, I re-estimated the average number of pitches to be 18 per inning. Over a nine-inning game, a pitching staff would throw 162 pitches (18x9).

Of these 162 pitches, I would estimate that 3/5 of them are strikes and 2/5 are balls. That would leave us with 97 strikes and 65 balls that is a good ratio. I kept the same distribution of 21 balls in play for outs, 8 hits and 1 error. That leaves us with 67 remaining strikes to account for.

Of these 67 remaining strikes, I would estimate that 35% would be swung at and missed, 35% would be called strikes and 30% would be foul balls. This would mean that roughly 23 pitches would be swung at and missed, 24 would be called a strike, and 20 would be foul balls. Of these 20, I would estimate that 3/5 would be in play while 2/5 would be out of play. So, 12 foul balls would be in play while 8 would be lost.

162 (games/year/team) x 8 (foul balls lost/game) =1296 foul balls lost /team

1296 (foul balls lost/team) x 30 (teams) = 38,880 foul balls lost in a season

Note: 4 additional teams have been added through expansion.

But we also have to figure in the number of home runs per team because they are also balls that are lost. So, I figured one home run per team/game. Over a 162 game season this would be 162 home runs. Some teams like the Pirates and Mets hit less home runs than that but teams like the Cardinals with Mark McGwire or the Mariners with Ken Griffey tend to hit a little more.

162 (home runs /year/team) x 30 (teams) = 4860 total home runs

From this figure, 81 home runs have to be subtracted out because the fans at Wrigley field always throw the opposing team's home run balls back onto the field of play. You can basically estimate that there are 162 home runs hit in each ballpark. So, in Wrigley field, half of the home runs will be throw back and that half is equivalent to 81. So, here is our final total of balls lost:

38,880 + 4860 – 81 = 43,659 total balls lost per season through home runs and foul balls

❧ Second Estimate

At Three Rivers Stadium at last night's play-off game while watching Andy Van Slyke foul off pitch after pitch, I wondered how many baseballs were lost to the team by being caught by fans during the entire season throughout major league baseball.

Facts:

There are 26 major league baseball teams.

Each baseball team plays 162 games in a season.

Foul balls that leave the playing field are assumed to be claimed by fans and not returned.

194

An average baseball game, determined through years of personal study, consists of approximately 180 pitches for each team. While shutouts consist of less pitches and high scoring games have more, on the average 20 pitches per inning occur.

Of the total number of pitches thrown, approximately 2/3 are strikes. A strike also includes pitches that may be foul balls when the batter has 2 strikes on him and any ball put into play is assumed to have been a strike.

Of these 180 pitches, 120 strikes are thrown/team/game, an average of 21 are put in play for outs, 8 are put in play and 1 is put in play for an error. Deducting these 30 strikes from the 120 total leaves 90 strikes/team/game that are either called strikes, swung at and missed or hit foul. Assuming an equal amount of each type of strike, this leaves us with 30 foul balls/team/game. However, not all foul balls are lost, as some do not leave the playing field. Based on last night's game, 2/3 of the foul balls remained in play and 1/3 went out of the field of play so we have 10 foul balls lost/team/game, or 20 baseballs lost every game.

Extending this to all of major league baseball for one season we would have 26 teams multiplied by 162 games multiplied by 20 baseballs lost per gamed divided by 2 teams playing in the game. One must not forget to divide by 2, because we estimated 10 balls lost/team/game and multiplied by 2 teams playing 1 game. Also, the home team must furnish baseballs for both teams for the 81 home games it holds.

Doing the math, our estimate is 42,120 baseballs lost in a season by major league baseball through foul balls leaving play, or 1620 baseballs lost by each team in baseball.

While some clubs may lose less because of generous amounts of foul territory in play (for example, Atlanta's Fulton County Stadium), some will lose more because of less room (for example, Chicago's Wrigley Field).

I have attended major league baseball games at 9 different stadiums but Three Rivers Stadium was used in this observation, so as it may have more or less foul territory than the average ballpark, possibly affecting the accuracy of the totals.

Also not taken into account in this estimation are baseballs lost due to home runs or batting practice or the amount used in preseason. While I was unsuccessful in obtaining from the Pittsburgh Pirates the number of baseballs purchased by the organization for this season, the number would have reflected the variables listed above and would not have been relevant to the estimation attempted here. As the Pirates, and many other professional baseball teams, now chart each pitch thrown in every game and compile the information on a database, it may be possible to ascertain how many baseballs are lost, but only if the data differentiates between foul balls hit out of play and those remaining on the field.

❧ Third Estimate

There are 26 baseball teams, and each plays 162 games for a total of 2106 games per year (at two teams per game). Each game has 9 innings and each inning sees an average of 5.2 batters per half inning, for a total of 197121.6 batters coming to the plate per year. Each batter fouls approximately 1.5 balls into the stands for a total of 295682.4 balls lost through foul balls. Add that to the approximately 1,200 home runs hit per year and the 6,318 (at 1 ball per 3 innings thrown by a player to an admiring fan) balls given away per year, and you have a total of 303,200 or so balls lost per year during major league baseball games.

☙ Estimate the number of electrons in the universe

Using an example from the book "Thinking with Models" (pg. 21) by Saaty, first we are concerned with estimating the size of the observable universe. Hubble's law states that the velocity of recession of a galaxy varies directly with its distance from the earth. Thus, we may "reach" a point where a galaxy is receding from us at the speed of light and in consequence nothing from that galaxy or points beyond can be observed by us. The first part of the problem is to estimate this distance and hence the diameter of the observable universe.

By Hubble's law: $V = kD$,

where V is the velocity of recession in km/sec, D is the distance from the earth in millions of light years, and k is Hubble's constant.

To find k, we use the following information. The Virgo cluster is receding from us at 1145 km/sec, as shown by the red shift of its components. The brightness of the Virgo cluster when compared with the brightness of the Andromeda galaxy shows that it is 16.5 times as far away as the Andromeda galaxy, which is 2,300,000 light years away.

Thus for Virgo, we have:

$$D = \frac{16.5 \times 2,300,000}{1,000,000} = 38$$

Therefore k = 1145/38 = 30.1. Some recent calculations suggest that this is somewhat large. We assume that k = 25. Using V = 300,000 km/sec (speed of light) yields:

$$D = \frac{300,000}{25} = 12,000 \text{ million light years}$$

The volume of a sphere is $4/3\ \pi r^3$ where r is the radius.

The volume of the observable universe is $4/3\ \pi (12,000 \times 10^6)^3 = 7.24 \times 10^{30} / \text{yr}^3$
Converting this to cubic meters yields:
$7.24 \times 10^{30} \text{ lyr}^3 \times (3 \times 10^8 \text{ meter/sec} \times 3600 \text{ sec/hr} \times 24 \text{ hr/day} \times 365 \text{ day/yr})^3$
$= 6.13 \times 10^{78}$ cubic meters in the observable universe.

If the average is 1 particle (hydrogen) per cubic meter in space and we disregard the relatively small inaccuracies in computing how much space there is where there is a much greater concentration in stars and planets, etc., we get 6.13×10^{78} electrons in the observable universe. From James Jeans' "The Universe Around Us" we get 1×10^{-29} g/cc of matter on the average which is equivalent to about 60 H atoms/m^3 which brings us to 3.678×10^{80} hydrogen atoms in the entire universe.

☙ Estimate the number of miles traveled in the rain by full-time MBA students during the academic year

We obtained the number of full-time MBA students during the 1997-1998 academic year by using the Full-time MBA picture book. There are 308 students.

Next we estimate the number of miles traveled daily by each student. A random sample of full time students (a sample size of 30 students, 9.74%) was asked to estimate their daily mileage. They were instructed to include their travel to and from school, errands, etc. and to consider all modes of transportation in their calculations.

Estimated Miles Traveled Daily	# of Students
0-4.99	14
5-9.99	8
10-14.99	1
15-19.99	2
20-24.99	1
25-29.99	0
30-34.99	2
35-39.99	0
40-44.99	0
45-49.99	0
50-54.99	1
55-59.99	1

From the above survey results, we obtained the following frequency distribution:

Sample #	Miles Traveled	Sample #	Miles Traveled	Sample #	Miles Traveled
1	2.5	11	3.5	21	5
2	5	12	6	22	2
3	4.2	13	2	23	30
4	2	14	6	24	1
5	.75	15	5.5	25	5
6	2	16	10	26	24
7	17.5	17	55	27	1
8	8	18	7	28	2.5
9	2.5	19	30	29	1
10	2.5	20	15	30	50

The average miles traveled per day are 10.28, with a standard deviation of 14.05 miles. The range was from 0 miles to 24.33 miles. Estimate the total precipitation during the 1997-1998 academic year.

According to the US Weather Services (http://www.cas.psu.edu/docs/CASDEP/NMP ennState/raindata/allegheny.htm), the average number of days of rainfall are:

Month	Average days of rain
September	9
October	10
November	12
December	14
January	16
February	14
March	15
April	13
May	13
June	12
July	12
August	12

The total precipitation days from the above table during the academic calendar are 140.

Calculate the estimated miles traveled in the rain by full-time MBA students during the school year as follows: 308 students x 10.28 miles x 140 days = 443,273.6 miles/year.

The total number of miles traveled in the rain by MBA students is estimated to be: 443,273.6 miles per year.

> ## Estimation of the number of minutes that a general dentist actually has his/her fingers in patients' mouths each week

I wanted to determine how long the average general dentist actually has his/her fingers in someone else's mouth each week. My estimations are based on conversations with my father-in-law, a cousin, my brother-in-law, and several of their co-workers, all of whom are dentists.

First, *how many* patients does a dentist see each day, on average?

We'll assume a dentist is in the office from 8:00 A.M. till 5:00 P.M., with one hour for lunch; thus, 8 hours each day are allotted for treating patients.

Not all patients spend the same amount of time in the dental chair. For example, some patients may only require a basic cleaning, while other patients may require more extensive dental work.

We will classify patients into one of three groups:

Those who need only basic cleaning (40 minutes total "chair" time, on average). Those who need a basic cleaning and need a cavity(s) filled (55 minutes total chair time).

Those who need more extensive, restorative dental work (e.g. crowns, bridges, dentures, bonding, etc.) This group may also need cavities filled (80 minutes total chair time).

Because of improvements in toothpaste formulas, the fluorination of water systems, and a generally heightened awareness of oral hygiene, we would expect fewer cases of cavities today than 20 years ago. Thus, I estimate that 35% of all dental patients simply require a routine check-up and cleaning (this includes a visual inspection of the mouth, x-rays, etc.).

I estimate that 30% of all dental patients are treated for cavities (cavities are phenomena that will always be with us, at least in the foreseeable future).

Because of the aging of the population and because of the relatively increasing national prosperity over the years, we would expect to see an increasing number of people requiring crowns, bridges, dentures, etc. than 2 decades ago. Hence, I estimate that 35% of all dental patients require such services.

There are 480 minutes in a working day (8hrs. × 60mins/hr.)

35% of 480 minutes = 168 minutes
$\Rightarrow$ 30% of 480 minutes = 144 minutes.

(168 minutes allotted for cleaning patients/day) / (40 min./cleaning patient) = 4.2 basic cleaning patients

(144 minutes allotted for cavity patients/day) / (55 min./cavity patient) = 2.62 cavity patients/day

(168 min. allotted for restorative patients/day) / (80 minutes/restorative patient) = 2.1 restorative patients/day

This is roughly 9 patients/day (a quick phone-call to my father-in-law confirmed that this is a pretty good estimate).

Next, we need to determine how many minutes on the average the dentist's hands are actually in a particular patient's mouth. First, we need to recognize that only a fraction of a patient's total chair time is spent with the fingers of a dentist in his/her mouth (there is often a time-lag between getting settled in the chair with the help of the dental assistant and actually seeing the dentist, there is often introductory small-talk, taking fingers out of a mouth to re-adjust standing position and/or receive instruments from the assistant, waiting for x-rays to develop, a brief discussion of a recommended oral-hygiene routine, etc.).

Because a regular check-up is one of the simplest of dental treatments, I estimate that 30% of the time will be spent with fingers in the mouth of a patient:

30% × 40 min. = 12 min/cleaning patient

For a cavity patient (because of injections and more drooling), I'll estimate 45% of the time is spent with fingers in mouth:

45% × 55 min. = 24.8 min/patient

For restorative work (being more involving), I'll estimate 60%:

60% × 80 minutes = 48 min/restorative patient

Hence, putting this all together, the total is estimated to be:

[(4.2 basic patients × 12 min.) + (2.62 cavity patients × 24.8 min.) + (2.1 restorative patients × 48 min.)] = 218.4 min/day

Or, per week:

218.4 min/day × 5 working days/week = *1,092 min/week (18.2 hours)* spent each week with fingers in patients' mouths.

❧ Estimate the number of disposable diapers used in the U.S. in one year and the amount of waste generated for landfill disposal

The first step is to determine the number of babies in the US.

There are 270m people residing in the US (data from 1998).

The average life expectancy in the US is about 72 years.

Therefore (270million people/72 years) = 3.75million per year.   (This assumes equal distribution in ages)

By polling mothers we determined the average number of years they remembered a child to be in diapers was 2.5 years. Again by polling mothers we found that the vast majority, 90%, use disposable diapers. Some mothers try cloth and then switch; others cannot afford disposable diapers. On the one hand the number of people not using disposable diapers may be increasing for reasons such as protecting the environment, whereas on the other hand very simple versions of disposable diapers are becoming available at lower prices, resulting in more people being able to buy them.

Again by polling mothers, the average number of diapers used was found to be 6 per day. New technologies allow the use of one diaper for the whole night resulting in a decrease of diapers used, and on the other hand, diapers are also available at a lower price, thereby resulting in mothers changing the "simpler versions" more frequently.

The number of disposable diapers used in the US is calculated as:

3.75million/year x 2.5 years x 6 diapers/day x 365 days/year x .90 disposable use = 18.5 billion diapers/year in the U.S.

The average weight of dirty disposable diapers was found to be, by polling mothers, 2lbs/diaper. Even though the material used for diapers is becoming lighter, more features for closing them etc. probably keep the average weight at 2 lbs./diaper.

The amount of waste generated from disposable diapers in one year is:

18.5/year x 2lbs/diaper = 37 billion lbs.

The actual statistical information as obtained from the Internet is that the average number of diapers used in the US is 18 billion/year compared to the 18.5 billion estimated.

Revising the estimate

Using a different birthrate the number would be 3.85million instead of 3.75million, and the estimate would be revised downward so that the result would be 18 billion diapers/year used in the US.

➥ Estimate the number of flowers used in funeral arrangements in 1990

My brother is a florist and based upon his expert opinion, he stated that the average funeral arrangement costs $35 and has about 20 flowers in it. A friend of mine who is a funeral director estimated the average number of funeral arrangements per funeral to be 15 arrangements. Thus the number of flowers per funeral is estimated as follows:

15 arrangements × 20 flowers = 300 flowers/funeral

There is a growing trend in this business where the family of the decedent will ask attendees at funeral services to donate to a local charity in lieu of flowers. Since this is still a minority of the total business, my brother estimates that roughly 90% of the funerals for the industry still include flowers.

The total number of deaths in the U.S. in 1990 was 2,162,000 people according to the Statistical Abstract of the U.S. Thus we can calculate as follows:

2,162,000 funerals × 90% × 300 flowers per funeral = 583,740,000 flowers used in funerals in 1990.

➥ A certain wine importer noticed that his sales of wine were not what they should be in comparison with other types of liquor. He hired you as a consultant to look into this problem with the intention of improving the wine business. What would you do?

First of all, I would rejoice that I got a job as a consultant. Then I would get down to work.

Reflecting on my joyous experience at The Katz School (particularly in CGE & MSP), I would consider conducting an industry analysis, complete with a "Porter Five Forces" model and a bunch of charts & graphs. I'm sure I could throw in a few fancy looking matrixes too. But that would take a lot of time, and I'll assume that the wine importer does not want me to spend hundreds of hours (billable at $250 per hour) analyzing the booze biz. I would then consider an in-depth strategic analysis of the company using a resource-based view of the firm. But again, the wine importer doesn't want me to spend my time working on bulls.

At that point, I would reflect upon the experience I gained with my Management Learning Organization (MLO) at The Katz School. The MLO (pronounced M-Hell-O) taught me very little. But it did provide one important lesson that I will carry with me for the rest of my life...
...fire people.

The sum of the parts in most organizations is actually less than the whole, or something like that. I'm not sure who the wine importer should fire, but I'm sure that there are some people in the organization who should be kicked in the ass and given their walking papers. Particularly those in the IS department.

For example, at my MLO at The Katz School, there were eight of us. We fired one person. Our MLO improved, but it still was not good enough. At least four or five more of us should have been fired for various reasons.

The firings serve two purposes. First, it gets rid of people and helps reduce costs. Second, it sends a message that the others need to work harder in order to keep their jobs. In fact, I would have the wine importer fire people on a regular basis, say every quarter or so. By the way, I would recommend that the company use euphemisms. For example, rather than "firing" people, the company would "undertake creative restructuring policies regarding human resource deployment."

Finally, if all else failed, I would ask for some wine in order to get sloppy drunk and come up with some new ideas.

❧ Estimate the number of adult American females under 5'3" that are less than 35 years old

1. Survey of 10 females in age group to get height.

	Age	Height
1	26	5'2"
2	27	5'3"
3	33	5'5"
4	25	5'8"
5	28	5'4"
6	22	5'0"
7	31	5'4"
8	28	5'3"
9	23	5'1"
10	29	5'3"

Results $\Rightarrow$ 3 out of 10 < 5'3"

2. Total # of Adult Females < 35 years old.
   Total Population = 269,239,000
   % Female = 51.02%
   Total Females = 137,386,000
   Est. between 20-35 yr. Old (15 yr. Span) w/68 year life expectancy and even distribution of all ages 15/68 = 22% $\Rightarrow$ 30,224,609

3. Estimated # of Females < 5'3", 20-35 years old.

   Total Females = 30,224,609
   Estimated rate from sample = 30%
   Estimate # of Females < 5'3" = 9,067,383 in age range 20-35 yr.

4. Actual results / FACTS

	20 –24 yr.	25 – 34 yr.
% of Females in age group < 5'3"	29.06%	32.964%
Female population in age group	8,580,000	19,515,000
Total of Females in age group < 5'3"	2,493,348	6,432,923

Total = 8,926,271

5. Conclusion

Estimate off by (9,067,383 − 8,485,606) = 581,777 or 6.41 %

Estimate off due to small sample size and bad assumption of distribution of Females' ages.

Increase sample size

Use results from first sample where 3 out of 10 in that age group were under 5'3".

The next samples were taken randomly from a list of females in the MBA program:

	Age	*Under 5'3"*
11.	22	Yes
12.	28	No
13.	27	No
14.	24	No
15.	27	Yes
16.	28	No
17.	23	Yes
18.	25	Yes
19.	22	No
20.	30	No

So, now we estimate that 7 out of 20, or 35% fit into this group.

2. Total Population = 270,000,000
    % Female = 55%
    Total Females = 148,500,000

We assume that the average life expectancy is 70 years, and the 15- year life span is 21.4% of the average life.

*148,000,000 (total females) * .27 (% 20 –34) = 39,600,000 total females between 20-34*

3. 39,6000,000 (total females between 20 – 34) * .35 (% under 5'3") = 13,860,000

Total estimate 13,860,000 females between 20 – 34, under 5'3"

Other Proposed Estimation Problems

1. How many hairs on your head? Give a number and how you actually got it.

2. Estimate the height of a building.

3. Estimate how much gasoline is used in the U.S. each day and then check it out. (Improve on 280 x 10^6 (people) x (.6 drivers) x 30 miles per day at 20 mpg.)

4. How much does the U.S. collect in taxes each year? Validate the answer.

5. Estimate the bi-weekly payroll in dollars for a particular Corporation including merit, turnover, new hires, etc.

6. How much money does an average restaurant take in per day? How much is profit?

7. Estimate the number of cars parked in your local area on a working day.

8. Estimate the amount of food and liquid needed to fill the stomachs of the 6 billion people in the world. Distinguish between: very young, older and very old.

9. Estimate the amount of airconditioning and heating needed for an average house.

10. There are about 5.8 billion people on earth. If we assign each person a number we would be using 10 digit numbers for some people. Find a way to assign numbers or letters to people uniquely so there would never be more than nine characters needed. If you succeed, try it for eight.

11. How many tons of cow manure is generated in the U.S. per day from the total of 115 million cows? Where does it all go?

12. What is the total cubic mile volume of the nearly six billion people on earth. How much space would they fill in familiar imagery, e.g. box cars or World Trade Center buildings?

13. How much do Americans spend on electricity on Christmas Eve? There are $280/4 \times 10^6 \times 70\% = 49 \times 10^6$ Christmas Eve lit houses. A monthly electric bill of $60 implies $2 per day. We assume it is doubled for Christmas Eve. Of this $98 $\times 10^6$ assume 60% profit and the utilities make $ 58.8×10^6 profit on that day. Do this for your city using its population and call your electric company to validate.

14. Estimate the space the Library of Congress needs to store 120 million titles. A single title can include an encyclopedia with many volumes. How much shelf space, how many buildings, and how much total space in cubic feet does it take to store these titles and allow for paths to access the books, desks and tables for readers and space for other administrative activities. In addition to the Jefferson, Adams and Madison buildings in Washington, DC, the library has 100 acres of storage space for old titles in nearby Virginia that can be accessed by sending a driver to get the requested order.

15. Estimate in three distinctly different ways how many people fly in the United States every day. For example,1) By estimating the number of airlines and airplanes and airhops per plane per day and passengers on a plane; 2) By estimating the number of people in the population who fly and how often they fly, etc.; 3) By estimating the average number of passengers on each trip of the train from the main terminal of a given city to the gates terminal and how often the train leaves each hour, the population of the city as a fraction of the population of the country, etc. Note that in 2008 the population of the US has increased to nearly 302,000,000 people and that of the world to 6.8 billion.

16. What fraction of the energy of the sun is received by the earth?

17. How many people can you feed from an acre? The U.S. has 343 million acres (divide by 2.47 to get hectares) of arable land. How many people can it sustain?

18. Estimate the number of people that can comfortably survive on this earth.

19. How high would the seas rise if the Antarctic polar ice cap of 3 million square miles area by two miles high melts?

20. Estimate the number of people in the U.S who are between the ages of 20 and 40.

21. Estimate how long you are going to live using heredity, exercise and diet and how hard you strain yourself.

22. How many people die in the world each day? In your city?

23. How many squares of toilet paper does the average American use in a year?

24. How long will the current brand of terrorism last? How would you go about habilitating terrorists and terrorism, for example by giving them representatives in world bodies?

26. Chicxulub is a 110 mile diameter crater in Yucatan, Mexico, made by a 6 mile diameter asteroid 65 million years ago whose collision sent a heat wave north that killed all the dinosaurs in North America. Estimate the time and method for humans or autonomous computers to be built that can carry the essence of human civilization out of the earth before such a disaster strikes again. Where can they settle in this universe: the Moon, Mars, or somewhere else?

How to Strengthen your Memory *

- Imagine things happening in a sequence and repeat them one by one.
- Put things you use often in the same place so you can find them without thinking.
- Put a strange object to shock you like a shoe on the table with a note to remind you what must be done.
- Read things aloud to remember them.
- Look at a list, try to remember it and close the page and see how much you can remember.
- Read, type and listen to a recording to memorize a speech.
- Abbreviate a sequence of words by their first letters.
- Make a song of a sequence of things you have to do.
- Associate your feelings with a name, word or idea like eating an apple and it is very sour or imagine a basket of apples falling on you.
- Make emotional associations with words and ideas, enlarge them as if you are interacting with them, and make images on familiar wall spaces in a sequence.
- Make a map of a familiar place and put a word on each street.
- Make a story of words that rhyme with numbers to remember the numbers.
- Make a song of a sequence of things you have to do and repeat the song.

- Go through the alphabet aloud to remember a word or name you have forgotten. Remember an unpleasant situation to experience carefully its details.
- Associate things with your body parts in a sequence and led them hang out for you to feel. Use color for headings to remember them better.
- Pay attention to names when meeting people and repeat them before the people and make association between the sound and the image that rhymes with the sound of the name.
- Make a written note of a name, word or idea.

---

* See also the article "Your Brain" by Patricia Curtis in Readers Digest 03/08.

Decision Making

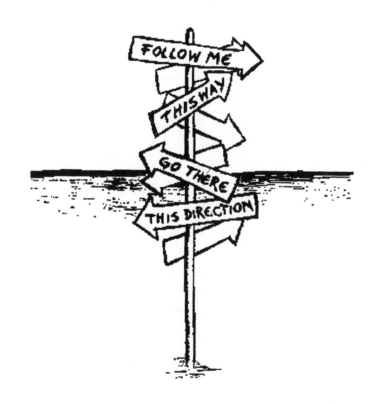

Chapter Seven

A Fact of Life

We are all decision makers first, problem solvers second, and creative thinkers third. We are born with the talent of automatic decision making, close to our instincts, in order to survive. Next we have to solve problems we face during survival. Creative thinking is a talent whose degree of practice distinguishes human beings from all other forms of life.

Morphological Analysis

Arranging ideas and their connections in a hierarchic framework and establishing priorities: Decision-making

Morphological Analysis was introduced by Fritz Zwicky as a step in creativity. The different possible forms of the solution, the physical materials from which an alternative solution can be made, the ways in which it can be constructed, the different uses that can be made of it, and so on, each category takes on the form of an independent variable.

Then one forms combinations (a vector), each of whose components is taken from one of the variables. Such combinations can be examined to determine which ones are best suited to solve the problem. This approach enriches brainstorming by bringing together many properties, forms and uses, but it stops short of relating them in a logical and systematic way as we have learned to do in the framework of hierarchic and network decision making.

In this chapter we will show the reader how to deal with decision problems creatively, and conversely how to deal with creative problems systematically and decisively. We use judgment and measurements in the process of deriving priorities for all the elements, including the alternatives that provide the solution to a decision problem. Such priorities can be used to allocate resources in the form of money, materials, attention, and other commitments one has to make.

Policy makers at all levels of decision making in organizations use multiple criteria to analyze their complex problems. Decision making, along with creative thinking and problem solving, are three areas with which the unconscious mind is partly active. Decision making is certainly one of the best examples of morphological analysis. It involves generating ideas, connecting them in an appropriate framework, and applying understanding and judgment to prioritize them. Every aspect of creativity can be seen in decision making:

- *brainstorming* for criteria and alternatives of choice,
- *synectics* for connecting them as part of a structure,
- *morphological analysis* to arrange the ideas and the connections in a decision hierarchy or a decision network,
- and finally, by viewing decision making as a process, subject to revision, *lateral thinking* is used to expand the framework or revise it to improve the decision.

By making tradeoffs, multicriteria decision making clarifies the advantages and disadvantages of policy options under circumstances of risk and uncertainty. It is also a tool vital in forming corporate strategies needed for effective competition.

Nearly all of us, in one way or another, have been brought up to believe that clear-headed logical thinking is our only sure way to face and solve problems. We also believe that our feelings and our judgments must be subjected to the acid test of deductive thinking. But experience suggests that deductive thinking is not natural. Indeed, we have to practice, and for a long time, before we can do it well. Since complex problems usually have many related factors, traditional logical thinking leads to sequences of ideas that are so tangled that their interconnections are not readily discerned.

The lack of a coherent procedure to make decisions is especially troublesome when our intuition alone cannot help us to determine which of several options is the most desirable, or the least objectionable, and neither logic nor intuition are of help. Therefore, we need a way to determine which objective outweighs another, both in the near and long terms. Since we are concerned with real-life problems, we must recognize the necessity for tradeoffs to best serve the common interest. Therefore, this process should also allow for consensus building and compromise.

Individual knowledge and experience are inadequate in making decisions concerning the welfare and quality of life for a group. Participation and debate are needed both among individuals and among the groups affected. Here two aspects of group decision making have to be considered. The first is a rather minor complication, namely, the discussion and exchange within the group to reach some kind of consensus on the given problem. The second is of much greater difficulty. The holistic nature of the given problem necessitates that it be divided into smaller subject-matter areas within which different groups of experts determine how each area affects the total problem. A large and complex problem can rarely be deconstructed simply into a number of smaller problems whose solutions can be combined into an overall answer. If this proc-

ess is successful, one can then reconstruct the initial question and review the proposed solutions. A last and often crucial disadvantage of many traditional decision-making methods is that they require specialized expertise to design the appropriate structure and then to embed the decision-making process in it.

A decision-making approach should have the following characteristics:

- be simple in structure,
- be adaptable to both groups and individuals,
- be natural to our intuition and general thinking,
- encourage compromise and consensus building, and
- not require inordinate specialization to master and communicate.

In addition, the details of the processes leading up to the decision-making process should be easy to review.

At the core of the problems that our approach addresses is the need to assess the benefits, the costs, and the risks and opportunities of the proposed solutions. We must answer such questions as the following: Which consequences weigh more heavily than others? Which aims are more important than others? What is likely to take place? What should we plan for and how do we bring it about? These and other questions demand a multicriteria logic. Practitioners who use the theory discussed in this chapter have repeatedly demonstrated that multicriteria logic gives different and often better answers to these questions than ordinary logic, and does it efficiently.

To make a decision, one needs various kinds of knowledge, information, and technical data. These concern:

- details about the problem for which a decision is needed,
- the people or actors involved,
- their objectives and policies,
- the influences affecting the outcomes, and,
- the time horizons, scenarios, and constraints.

The set of potential outcomes and the alternatives from which to choose are the essence of decision making. In laying out the framework for making a decision, one needs to sort the elements into groupings or clusters that have similar influences or effects. One must also arrange them in some rational order to trace the outcome of these influences. Briefly, we see decision making as a process that involves the following steps:

(1) Structure a problem with a model that shows the problem's key elements and their relationships.
(2) Elicit judgments that reflect knowledge, feelings, or emotions.
(3) Represent those judgments with meaningful numbers.
(4) Use these numbers to calculate the priorities of the elements of the hierarchy.
(5) Synthesize these results to determine an overall outcome.
(6) Analyze sensitivity to changes in judgment.

The decision-making process here meets these criteria. I call it the analytic hierarchy process (AHP). The AHP is about breaking a problem down and then aggregating the solutions of all the sub-problems into a conclusion. It facilitates decision making by organizing perceptions, feelings, judgments, and memories into a framework that exhibits the forces that influence a decision. In the simple and most common case, the forces are arranged from the more general and less controllable to the more specific and controllable. The AHP is based on the innate human ability to make sound judgments about small problems. It has been applied in a variety of decisions and planning projects in many countries with its widely known computer program, Expert Choice.

In the analytic hierarchy process, _rationality_ is
- Focusing on the goal of solving the problem;
- Knowing enough about a problem to develop a complete structure of relations and influences;
- Having enough knowledge and experience and access to the knowledge and experience of others to assess the priority of influence and dominance (importance, preference, or likelihood to the goal as appropriate) among the relations in the structure;
- Allowing for differences in opinion with an ability to develop a best compromise.

How to Structure a Hierarchy

Perhaps the most creative part of decision making that has a significant effect on the outcome is modeling the problem. In the AHP, a problem is structured as a hierarchy. A process of prioritization, which we describe in detail below, then follows. Prioritization involves eliciting judgments in response to questions about the dominance of one element over another when compared with respect to a property. The basic principle in creating this structure is always to see if one can answer the following question: Can I compare the elements on a lower level using some or all of the elements on the next higher level as criteria or attributes of the lower level elements?

A useful way to proceed in structuring a decision is to come down from the goal as far as one can by breaking it up into the most general and most easily controlled factors. One can then go up from the alternatives beginning with the simplest subcriteria that they must satisfy and aggregating the subcriteria into generic higher level criteria, until the levels of the two processes are linked in a way that makes comparison possible.

Here are some suggestions for an elaborate design of a hierarchy:

(1) Identify the overall goal. What are you trying to accomplish? What is the main question?

(2) Identify the subgoals of the overall goal. If relevant, identify time horizons that affect the decision.

(3) Identify criteria that must be satisfied to fulfill the subgoals of the overall goal.

(4) Identify subcriteria under each criterion. Note that criteria or subcriteria may be specified in terms of ranges of values of parameters or in terms of verbal intensities such as high, medium, low.

(5) Identify the actors involved.

(6) Identify the actors' goals.

(7) Identify the actors' policies.

(8) Identify options or outcomes.

(9) For yes-no decisions, take the most preferred outcome and compare the benefits and costs of making the decision with those of not making it.

(10) Do a benefit/cost analysis using marginal values. Because we are dealing with dominance hierarchies, ask which alternative yields the greatest benefit; for costs, which alternative costs the most, and for risks, which alternative is more risky, and for opportunities, which alternative has the most chance to create opportunities.

❧ The Hospice Problem

Westmoreland County Hospital in Western Pennsylvania, like hospitals in many other counties around the nation, has been concerned with the costs of the facilities and manpower involved in taking care of terminally ill pa-

tients. Normally these patients do not need as much medical attention as do other patients. Those who best utilize the limited resources in a hospital are patients who require the medical attention of its specialists and advanced technology equipment, whose utilization depends on the demand of patients admitted into the hospital. The terminally ill need medical attention only episodically. Most of the time such patients need psychological support. Such support is best given by the patient's family, whose members are able to supply the love and care the patients most need. For the mental health of the patient, home therapy is a benefit. From the medical standpoint, especially during a crisis, the hospital provides a greater benefit. Most patients need the help of medical professionals only during a crisis. Some will also need equipment and surgery.

The planning association of the hospital wanted to develop alternatives and to choose the best one, considering various criteria from the standpoint of the patient, the hospital, the community, and society at large.

In this problem, we need to consider the costs and benefits of the decision. Cost includes economic costs and all sorts of intangibles, such as inconvenience and pain. Such disbenefits are not directly related to benefits as their mathematical inverses, because patients infinitely prefer the benefits of good health to these intangible disbenefits. To study the problem, one needs to deal with benefits and with costs separately.

❧ Approaching the Problem

I met with representatives of the planning association for several hours to decide on the best alternative. To make a decision by considering benefits and costs, one must first answer the question: In this problem, do the benefits justify the costs? If they do, then

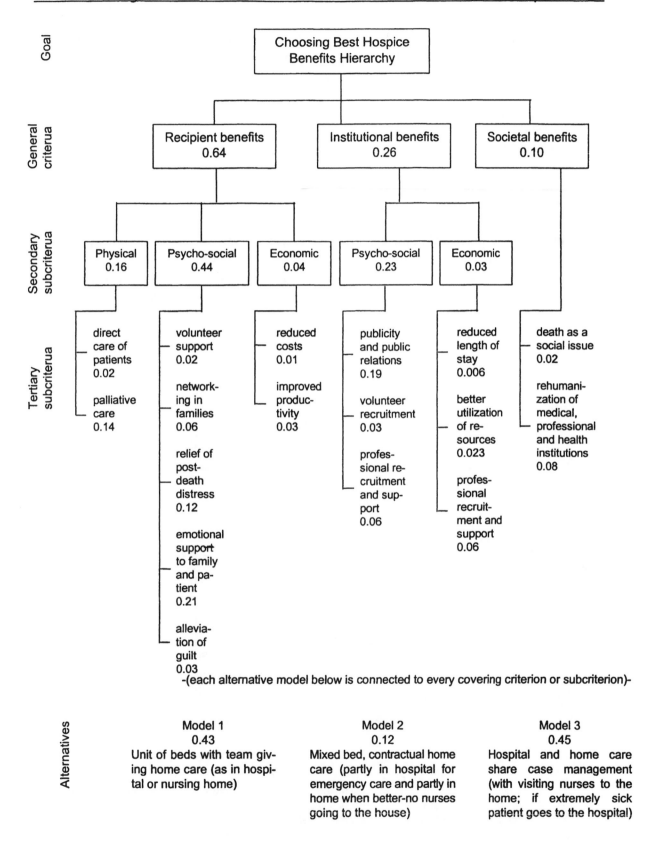

Figure 1: The benefits hierarchy for choosing the best hospice plan.

either the benefits are so much more important than the costs that the decision is based simply on benefits, or the two are so close in value that both the benefits and the costs should be considered. One constructs a hierarchy modeling the benefits, shown in Figure 1, and a hierarchy modeling the costs, shown in Figure 2, to the patient, to the institution, and to society. We make the choice by forming the ratio from them of the (benefits priority/cost priority) for each alternative. One asks which is most beneficial in the benefits hierarchy (Figure 1) and which is most costly in the costs hierarchy (Figure 2).

If the benefits do not justify the costs, the costs alone determine the best alternative, that which is the least costly. Here we decided to consider the benefits and costs in separate hierarchies. In a risk problem, a third hierarchy for risks is used. We have a way to prioritize benefits, costs opportunities and risks and combine the outcomes not shown here because of space limitation.

For some decisions one uses only a single hierarchy, but here we construct two hierarchies, 1) benefits or gains (which model of hospice care yields the greater benefit) and 2) costs or pains (which model costs more).

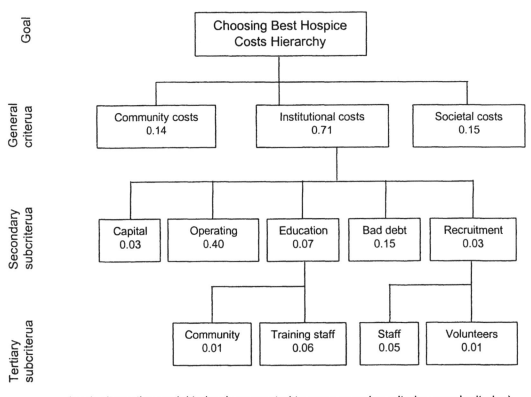

Figure 2: The costs hierarchy for choosing the best hospice plan.

The planning association thought the concepts of benefits and costs were too general to enable it to make a decision. Thus, the planners and I further subdivided each (benefits and costs) into detailed subcriteria to enable the group to develop alternatives and to evaluate the finer distinctions the members perceived between the three alternatives. The alternatives were to care for terminally ill patients at the hospital, at home, or partly at the hospital and partly at home.

For each of the two hierarchies, benefits and costs, the goal clearly had to be choosing the best hospice. We placed this goal at the top of each hierarchy. Then the group discussed and identified overall criteria for each hierarchy; these criteria need not be the same for the benefits as for the costs.

The two hierarchies are fairly clear and straightforward in their description. They descend from the more general criteria in the second level to secondary subcriteria in the third level and then to tertiary subcriteria in the fourth level on to the alternatives at the bottom or fifth level.

At the general criteria level, each of the hierarchies, benefits or costs, involved three major interests. The decision should benefit the recipient, the institution, and society as a whole, and their relative importance is the prime determinant as to which outcome is more likely to be preferred. We located these three elements on the second level of the benefits hierarchy. As the decision would benefit each party differently and the importance of the benefits to each recipient affects the outcome, the group thought that it was important to specify the types of benefit for the recipient and the institution. Recipients want physical, psycho-social and economic benefits, while the institution wants only psychosocial and

economic benefits. We located these benefits in the third level of the hierarchy.

Each of these in turn needed further decomposition into specific items in terms of which one can evaluate the decision alternatives. For example, while the recipient measures economic benefits in terms of reduced costs and improved productivity, the institution needed the more specific measurements of reduced length of stay, better utilization of resources, and increased financial support from the community. There was no reason to decompose the societal benefits into a third level subcriteria, hence societal benefits connects directly to the fourth level. The group considered three models for the decision alternatives, and they are at the bottom (or fifth level in this case) of the hierarchy: in Model 1, the hospital provided full care to the patients; in Model 2, the family cares for the patient at home, and the hospital provides only emergency treatment (no nurses go to the house); and in Model 3, the hospital and the home share patient care (with visiting nurses going to the home). The alternatives are evaluated in terms of a criterion or subcriterion if it has no further subcriteria, or in terms of the lowest level subcriteria. We call the criteria without subcriteria and the lowest level of subcriteria when there are some *covering criteria*. The level to which they belong does not matter. They are the elements used to evaluate the alternatives.

In the costs hierarchy there were also three major interests in the second level that would incur costs or pains: community, institution, and society. In this decision the costs incurred by the patient were not included as a separate factor. Patient and family could be thought of as part of the community. We thought decomposition was necessary only for institutional costs. We included five such costs in the third level: capital costs, operating costs, education costs, bad debt costs, and recruitment costs. Educational costs apply to educating the community and training the staff. Recruitment costs apply to staff and volunteers. Since both the costs hierarchy and the benefits hierarchy concern the same decision, they both have the same alternatives in their bottom levels, even though the costs hierarchy has fewer levels.

Judgments and Comparisons

A judgment or comparison is the numerical representation of a relationship between two elements that share a common parent. The set of all such judgments can be represented in a square matrix in which the set of elements is compared with itself. Each judgment represents the dominance of an element in the column on the left over an element in the row on top. It reflects the answers to two questions: which of the two elements is more important with respect to a higher level criterion, and how strongly, using the 1-9 scale shown in Table 1 for the element on the left over the element at the top of the matrix. In this scale absolute numbers are used to assign numerical values to judgments made by comparing two elements with the smaller element used as the unit and the larger one assigned a value from the scale that is a multiple of that unit.

If the element on the left is less important than that on the top of the matrix, we enter the reciprocal value in the corresponding position in the matrix. It is important to note that the lesser element is always used as the unit and the greater one is estimated as a multiple of that unit. From all the paired comparisons we calculate the priorities and exhibit them on the right of the matrix. For a set of n elements in a matrix one needs $n(n-1)/2$ comparisons because there are n 1's on the diagonal for comparing elements with themselves and of the remaining judgments, half are reciprocals.

Thus we have $(n^2-n)/2$ judgments. In some problems one may elicit only the minimum of n-1 judgments.

As usual with the AHP, in both the cost and the benefits models, we compared the criteria and subcriteria according to their relative importance with respect to the parent element in the adjacent upper level. For example, in the first matrix of comparisons of the three benefits criteria with respect to the goal of choosing the best hospice alternative shown in Table 2, recipient benefits are moderately more important than institutional benefits and are assigned the absolute number 3 in the (1, 2) or first-row second-column position. Three signifies three times more. The reciprocal value is automatically entered in the (2,1) position, where institutional benefits on the left are compared with recipient benefits at the top. Similarly a 5, corresponding to strong dominance or importance, is assigned to recipient benefits over social benefits in the (1,3) position, and a 3, corresponding to moderate dominance, is assigned to institutional benefits over social benefits in the (2,3) position with corresponding reciprocals in the transpose positions of the matrix.

Judgments in a matrix may not be consistent. In eliciting judgments, one makes redundant comparisons to improve the validity of the answer, given that respondents may be uncertain or may make poor comparisons of some of the elements. Redundancy gives rise to multiple comparisons of an element with other elements and hence to numerical inconsistencies. For example, where we compare recipient benefits with institutional benefits and with societal benefits, we have the respective judgments 3 and 5. Now if $x = 3y$ and $x = 5z$ then $3y = 5z$ or $y = 5/3\ z$. If the judges were consistent, institutional benefits would be assigned the value 5/3 instead of the 3 given in the matrix. Thus the judgments are inconsistent.

In fact, we are not sure which judgments are the accurate ones and which are the cause of the inconsistency. Inconsistency is inherent in the judgment process. Inconsistency may be considered a tolerable error in measurement only when it is of a lower order of magnitude (10 percent) than the actual measurement itself; otherwise the inconsistency would bias the result by a sizable error comparable to or exceeding the actual measurement itself.

When the judgments are inconsistent, the decision-maker may not know where the greatest inconsistency is. The AHP can show one by one in sequential order which judgments are the most inconsistent, and that suggests the value that best improves consistency. However, this recommendation may not necessarily lead to a more accurate set of priorities that correspond to some underlying preference of the decision-makers.

Greater consistency does not imply greater accuracy and one should go about improving consistency (if one can, given the available knowledge) by making slight changes compatible with one's understanding. If one cannot reach an acceptable level of consistency, one should gather more information or reexamine the framework of the hierarchy.

Under each matrix I have indicated a consistency ratio (CR) comparing the inconsistency of the set of judgments in that matrix with what it would be if the judgments and the corresponding reciprocals were taken at random from the scale. For a 3-by-3 matrix this ratio should be about five percent, for a 4-by-4 about eight percent, and for larger matrices, about 10 percent.

Table 1: The Fundamental Scale.

Intensity of Importance	Definition	Explanation
1	Equal Importance	Two activities contribute equally to the objective
3	Moderate importance	Experience and judgment slightly favor one activity over another
5	Strong importance	Experience and judgment strongly favor one activity over another
7	Very strong or demonstrated importance	An activity is favored very strongly over another; its dominance demonstrated in practice
9	Extreme importance	The evidence favoring one activity over another is of the highest possible order of affirmation
2,4,6,8	For compromise between the above values	Sometimes one needs to interpolate a compromise judgment numerically because there is no good word to describe it.
Reciprocals of above	If activity i has one of the above nonzero numbers assigned to it when compared with activity j, then j has the reciprocal value when compared with i	A comparison mandated by choosing the smaller element as the unit to estimate the larger one as a multiple of that unit.
Rationals	Ratios arising from the scale	If consistency were to be forced by obtaining n numerical values to span the matrix
1.1-1.9	For tied activities	When elements are close and nearly indistinguishable; moderate is 1.3 and extreme is 1.9.

Priorities are numerical ranks measured on a ratio scale. A ratio scale is a set of positive numbers whose ratios remain the same if all the numbers are multiplied by an arbitrary positive number. An example is the scale used to measure weight. The ratio of these weights is the same in pounds and in kilograms. Here one scale is just a constant multiple of the other. The object of evaluation is to elicit judgments concerning relative importance of the elements of the hierarchy to create scales of priority of influence.

Because the priorities of the alternatives in the benefits hierarchy belong to a ratio scale and the priorities of the alternatives in the costs hierarchy also belong to a ratio scale, then their product or quotient (but not the sum or the difference) is also a ratio scale. To derive the answer we divide the benefits priority of each alternative by its costs priority. We then choose the alternative with the largest of these ratios. It is also possible to allocate a resource proportionately among the alternatives (see below).

I will explain how priorities are developed from judgments and how they are synthesized down the hierarchy by a process of weighting and adding. Judgments are used to derive local priorities for a set of nodes (alternatives, say) with respect to a single criterion. Global priorities are obtained by multiplying these local priorities by the priority of the criterion. The overall priority of an element (an alternative) is obtained by adding its global priorities throughout the model. The local priorities are listed on the right of each matrix. If the judgments are perfectly consistent, that is, the inconsistency ratio equals zero, we can obtain the local priorities by adding the values in each row and dividing by the sum of all the judgments in the entire matrix, or by normalizing the judgments in any column by dividing each entry by the sum of the entries in that column.

If the judgments are inconsistent but have a tolerable level of inconsistency, we obtain the priorities by raising the matrix to large powers, which is known to take into consideration all intransitivities between the elements, such as those I showed above between x, y, and z. Again, we obtain the priorities from this matrix by adding the judgment values in each row and dividing by the sum of all the judgments. To summarize, the global priorities at the level immediately under the goal are equal to the local priorities because the priority of the goal is equal to one. The global priorities at the next level are obtained by weighting the local priorities of this level by the global priority at the level immediately above and so on. The overall priorities of the alternatives are obtained by weighting the local priorities by the global priorities of all the parent criteria or subcriteria in terms of which they are compared and then adding. (If an element in a set is comparable with the others on some property and should be left out, the local priorities can be augmented by adding a zero in the appropriate position.)

The process is repeated in all the matrices by asking the appropriate dominance or importance question. For example, for the matrix shown comparing the subcriteria of the parent criterion institutional benefits (Table 3), psycho-social benefits are regarded as very strongly more important than economic benefits, and 7 is entered in the (1,2) position and 1/7 in the (2,1) position.

In comparing the three models for patient care, we asked members of the planning association which model they preferred with respect to each of the covering or parent secondary criterion in level 3 or with respect to the tertiary criteria in level 4. For example, for the subcriterion direct care (located on the left-most branch in the benefits hierarchy), we obtained a matrix of paired comparisons

Table 2: The entries in this matrix respond to the question, Which criterion is more important with respect to choosing the best hospice alternative and how strongly?

Choosing best hospice	Recipient benefits	Institutional benefits	Social benefits	Priorities
Recipient benefits	1	3	5	.64
Institutional benefits	1/3	1	3	.26
Social benefits	1/5	1/3	1	.11
				C.R. = .033

Table 3: The entries in this matrix respond to the question: Which subcriterion yields the greater benefit with respect to institutional benefits and how strongly?

Institutional benefits	Psycho-social	Economic	Priorities
Psycho-social	1	7	.875
Economic	1/7	1	.125
			C.R. = .000

Table 4: The entries in this matrix respond to the question, which model yields the greater benefit with respect to direct care of patient and how strongly?

Benefits – Direct care of patient	Model I	Model II	Model III	Priorities
Model I unit team	1	5	3	.64
Model II mixed/home care	1/5	1	1/3	.10
Model III case management	1/3	3	1	.26

Table 5: The entries in this matrix respond to the question, which criterion is a greater determinant of cost with respect to the care method and how strongly?

Choosing best hospice (costs)	Community	Institutional	Societal	Priorities
Community costs	1	1/5	1	.14
Institutional costs	5	1	5	.71
Societal costs	1	1/5	1	.14

Table 6: The entries in this matrix respond to the question, which criterion incurs greater institutional costs and how strongly?

Institutional costs	Capital	Operating	Education	Bad debt	Recruitment	Priorities
Capital	1	1/7	1/4	1/7	1	.05
Operating	7	1	9	4	5	.57
Education	4	1/9	1	1/2	1	.01
Bad debt	7	1/4	2	1	3	.21
Recruitment	1	1/5	1	1/3	1	.07

Table 7: The entries in this matrix respond to the question, Which model incurs greater cost with respect to institutional costs for recruiting staff and how strongly?

Institutional costs for recruiting staff	Model I	Model II	Model III	Priorities
Model I unit team	1	5	3	.64
Model II mixed/home care	1/5	1	1/3	.10
Model III case management	1/3	3	1	.26

Table 8: The benefit/cost ratios of the three models (bottom row of table) for distributive and ideal modes.

Benefits	Priorities	Distributive Mode			Ideal Mode		
		Model 1	Model 2	Model 3	Model	Model 2	Model 3
Direct Care of Patient	.02	0.64	0.10	0.26	1.000	0.156	0.406
Palliative Care	.14	0.64	0.10	0.26	1.000	0.156	0.406
Volunteer Support	.02	0.09	0.17	0.74	0.122	0.230	1.000
Networking in Families	.06	0.46	0.22	0.32	1.000	0.478	0.696
Relief of Post Death Stress	.12	0.30	0.08	0.62	0.484	0.129	1.000
Emotional Support of Family and Patient	.21	0.30	0.08	0.62	0.484	0.129	1.000
Alleviation of Guilt	.03	0.30	0.08	0.62	0.484	0.129	1.000
Reduced Economic Costs for Patient	.01	0.12	0.65	0.23	0.185	1.000	0.354
Improved Productivity	.03	0.12	0.27	0.61	0.197	0.443	1.000
Publicity and Public Relations	.19	0.63	0.08	0.29	1.000	0.127	0.460
Volunteer Recruitment	.03	0.64	0.10	0.26	1.000	0.156	0.406
Professional Recruitment and Support	.06	0.65	0.23	0.12	1.000	0.354	0.185
Reduced Length of Stay	.006	0.26	0.10	0.64	0.406	0.406	1.000
Better Utilization of Resources	.023	0.09	0.22	0.69	0.130	0.130	1.000
Increased Monetary Support	.001	0.73	0.08	0.19	1.000	1.000	0.260
Death as a Social Issue	.02	0.20	0.20	0.60	0.333	0.333	1.000
Rehumanization of Institutions	.08	0.24	0.14	0.62	0.387	0.226	1.000
Synthesis		0.428	0.121	0.451	0.424	0.123	0.453
Costs							
Community Costs	.14	0.33	0.33	0.33	1.000	1.000	1.000
Institutional Capital Costs	.03	0.76	0.09	0.15	1.000	0.118	0.197
Institutional Operating Costs	.40	0.73	0.08	0.19	1.000	0.110	0.260
Institutional Costs for Educating the Community	.01	0.65	0.24	0.11	1.000	0.369	0.169
	.06	0.56	0.32	0.12	1.000	0.571	0.214
Institutional Costs for Training Staff	.15	0.60	0.20	0.20	1.000	0.333	0.333
Institutional Bad Debt	.05	0.66	0.17	0.17	1.000	0.258	0.258
Institutional Costs of Recruiting Staff	.01	0.60	0.20	0.20	1.000	0.333	0.333
Institutional Costs of Recruiting Volunteers Societal Costs	.15	0.33	0.33	0.33	1.000	1.000	1.000
Synthesis		0.583	0.192	0.224	0.523	0.229	0.249
Benefit/Cost Ratio		0.734	0.630	2.013	0.811	0.537	1.819

(Table 4) in which Model 1 is preferred over Models 2 and 3 by 5 and 3 respectively and Model 3 is preferred by 3 over Model 2. The group first made all the comparisons using semantic terms for the fundamental scale and then translated them to the corresponding numbers.

For the costs hierarchy, I again illustrate with three matrices. First the group compared the three major cost criteria and provided judgments in response to the question: which criterion is a more important determinant of the cost of a hospice model? Table 5 shows the judgments obtained.

The group then compared the subcriteria under institutional costs and obtained the importance matrix shown in Table 6. Finally we compared the three models to find out which incurs the highest cost for each criterion or subcriterion. Table 7 shows the results of comparing them with respect to the costs of recruiting staff.

As shown in Table 8, we divided the benefits priorities by the costs priorities for each alternative to obtain the best alternative, model 3, the one with the largest value for the ratio.

Table 8 shows two ways or modes of synthesizing the local priorities of the alternatives using the global priorities of their parent criteria: The distributive mode and the ideal mode. Here one multiplies each of the six columns of priorities of a model by the column of criteria weights on the left and adds to obtain the synthesis of overall priorities, once for the benefits (top half of table) and once for the costs (bottom half of table) and forms the ratios of corresponding synthesis numbers to arrive at the benefit/cost ratio (bottom row of table).

In the distributive mode, the weights of the alternatives sum to one. It is used when one wants the best alternative in the group. The ideal mode is used to obtain the best alternative when performance with respect to an ideal is desired. In the ideal mode, the local priorities of the alternatives are divided by the largest value among them.

This is done for each criterion; for each criterion one alternative becomes an ideal with value one. In both modes, the local priorities are weighted by the global priorities of the parent criteria and synthesized and the benefit-to-cost ratios formed. In this case, both modes lead to the same outcome for hospice, which is model 3. As we shall see below, we need these two modes to deal with the effect of adding (or deleting) alternatives on an already ranked set.

Model 3 has the largest ratio scale values of benefits to costs in both the distributive and ideal modes, and the hospital selected it for treating terminal patients.

This need not always be the case. In this case, there is dependence of the personnel resources allocated to the three models because some of these resources would be shifted based on the decision. Therefore the distributive mode is the appropriate method of synthesis. If the alternatives were sufficiently distinct with no dependence in their definition, the ideal mode would be the way to synthesize.

I also performed marginal analysis to determine where the hospital should allocate additional resources for the greatest marginal return. To perform marginal analysis, I first ordered the alternatives by increasing cost priorities and then formed the benefit-to-cost ratios corresponding to the smallest cost, followed by the ratios of the differences of successive benefits to costs. If this difference in benefits is negative, the new alternative is dropped from consideration and the process continued. The alternative with the largest marginal ratio is then chosen. For the costs and corresponding benefits from the synthesis rows in Table 8 we have:

Costs: .20   .21   .59

Benefits: .12   .45   .43

Marginal Ratios:

$$\frac{.12}{.20} = 0.60 \qquad \frac{.45 - .12}{.21 - .20} = 33 \qquad \frac{.43 - .45}{.59 - .21} = -0.051$$

The third alternative is not a contender for resources because its marginal return is negative. The second alternative is best. In fact, in addition to adopting the third model, the hospital management chose the second model of hospice care for further development.

Nowadays, we have a better way. We use absolute measurement discussed below. With it we can identify hospice-oriented criteria such as economy, humaneness, convenience, etc., for the planning association, prioritize them, and use intensities under each to *rate* the benefits and the costs separately, and then normalize the resulting priorities and use them to weight the priorities of the alternatives for the benefits and for the reciprocal of their values under costs, add, and then choose the best outcome.
For brevity, we do not do that here.

✍ A Sustainable Metropolitan Growth Problem

In the following illustration there are nine alternatives evaluated in terms of benefit, cost and risk impacts to sustain metropolitan growth. Here again one asks which is more risky (or hazardous) and in the end one divides the benefit to cost ratios by the overall risk priorities of each alternative.

The alternatives are: build infrastructure (of roads, telecommunication, banking, etc.), improve quality of life, reduce taxes, status quo (or do nothing), provide land for expan -sion, foster increased tourism, expand port, support industries and improve regional con-nections. The criteria in each of the three hierarchies are different and will not be de-scribed in the text because they are laid out in the diagrams. The distributive mode was used to synthesize the priorities of the alter-natives. The hierarchies for the benefits, costs, and risks are shown in Figures 3a-3c.

The ranking of the alternatives descends from reduce taxes, improve quality of life, provide land, maintain status quo, build infrastructure and so on. One could allocate resources proportionately to these ratio scale outcomes.

In making the paired comparisons one has to answer questions like the following: Which criterion is a more important benefit? In comparing the alternatives with respect to each criterion in a separate matrix one asks: Which alternative yields greater benefit with respect to that criterion? Which criterion is a more important cost? Which alternative incurs greater cost with respect to that sub-criterion? Which subcriterion is a more im-portant social cost? Which Criterion is a more important risk? Which alternative incurs greater risk with respect to that subcriterion?

The synthesized outcome for the alternatives is shown in Table 9.

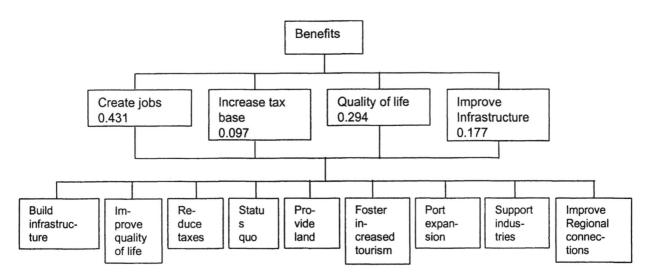

Figure 3a. The Benefits Hierarchy for Sustainable Metropolitan Growth.

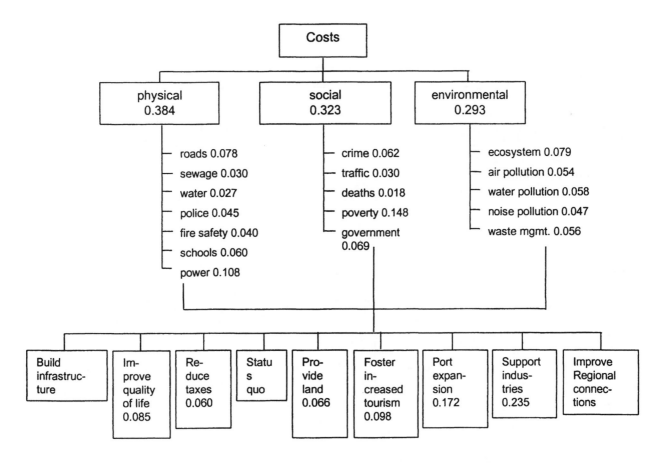

Figure 3b. The Costs Hierarchy for Sustainable Metropolitan Growth

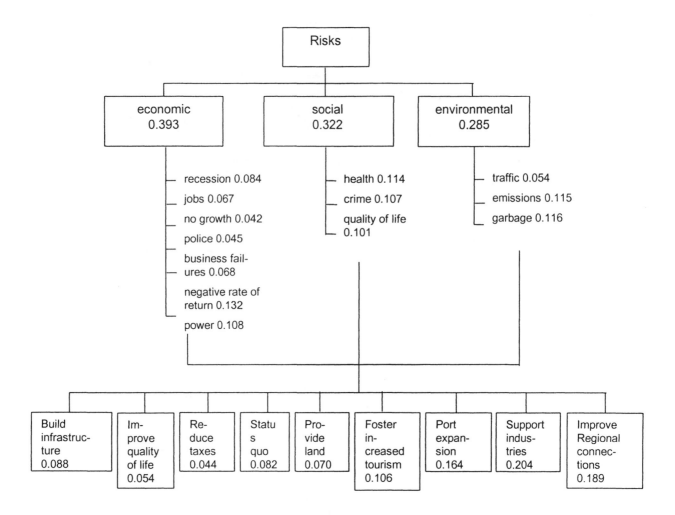

Figure 3C. The Risks Hierarchy for Sustainable Metropolitan Growth

Table 9. Summary of the Benefits, Costs, and Risks and the Final B/CR Ratio for the Alternatives.

	Infra	Life	Tax	Status	Land	Tourism	Port	Industry	Region
Benefit	0.125	0.104	0.103	0.052	0.091	0.092	0.128	0.191	0.113
Cost	0.104	0.085	0.060	0.044	0.066	0.098	0.172	0.235	0.135
B/C	1.202	1.224	1.717	1.182	1.379	0.939	0.744	0.813	0.985
Risk	0.088	0.054	0.044	0.082	0.070	0.106	0.164	0.204	0.189
B/CR	13.659	22.66	39.02	14.415	19.70	8.858	4.537	3.984	5.212

Absolute Measurement

Cognitive psychologists have recognized for some time that people are able to make two kinds of comparisons - absolute and relative. In absolute comparisons, people compare alternatives with a standard in their memory that they have developed through experience. In relative comparisons, they compare alternatives in pairs according to a common attribute, as we did throughout the hospice example.

to be ranked is performance in mathematics, the mathematics ratings might be: excellent, good, average, below average, poor; or, using the usual school terminology, A, B, C, D, and F. Relative comparisons are first used to set priorities on the ratings themselves. If desired, one can fit a continuous curve through the derived intensities. This concept may go against our socialization. However, it is perfectly reasonable to ask how much an A is preferred to a B or to a C. The judgment of how much an A is preferred to a B might be

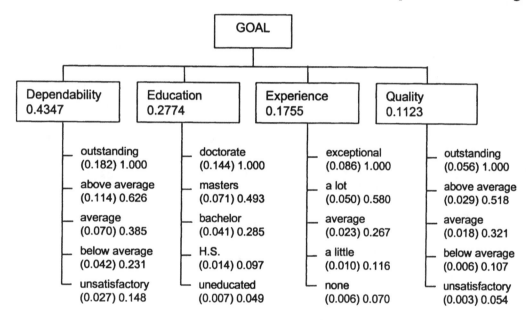

Figure 4. An evaluation hierarchy for rating employees.

People use absolute measurement (sometimes also called rating) to rank independent alternatives one at a time in terms of rating intensities for each of the criteria. An intensity is a range of variation of a criterion that enables one to distinguish the quality of an alternative for that criterion. An intensity may be expressed as a numerical range of values if the criterion is measurable or in qualitative terms.

For example, if ranking students is the objective and one of the criteria on which they are

different under different criteria. Perhaps for mathematics an A is very strongly preferred to a B, while for physical education an A is only moderately preferred to a B. So the end result might be that the ratings are scaled differently. For example one could have scale values for the ratings as shown in Table 10 below.

Table 10. Scale Values for the Ratings

	Math	Physical Education
A	0.50	0.30
B	0.30	0.30
C	0.15	0.20
D	0.04	0.10
E	0.01	0.10

The alternatives are then rated or ticked off one at a time on the intensities.

Let us illustrate absolute measurement with an example. A firm evaluates its employees for raises. The criteria are dependability, education, experience, and quality. Each criterion is subdivided into intensities, standards, or subcriteria (Figure 4). The managers set priorities for the criteria by comparing them in pairs. They then pairwise compare the intensities according to priority with respect to their parent criterion (as in Table 11) or with respect to a subcriterion if they are using a deeper hierarchy. The priorities of the intensities are divided by the largest intensity for each criterion (second column of priorities in Figure 4).

Table 11 shows a paired comparison matrix of intensities with respect to dependability. The managers answer the question: which intensity is more important and by how much with respect to dependability. Finally, the managers rate each individual (Table 12) by assigning the intensity rating that applies to him or her under each criterion. The scores of these intensities are each weighted by the priority of its criterion and summed to derive a total ratio scale score for the individual (shown on the right of Table 12). These numbers belong to a ratio scale, and the managers can give salary increases precisely in proportion to the ratios of these numbers. Adams gets the highest score and Kesselman

Table 11: Ranking intensities: Which intensity is preferred most with respect to dependability and how strongly?

	Outstanding	Above Average	Average	Below Average	Unsatisfactory	Priorities
Outstanding	1.0	2.0	3.0	4.0	5.0	0.419
Above Average	1/2	1.0	2.0	3.0	4.0	0.263
Average	1/3	1/2	1.0	2.0	3.0	0.160
Below Average	1/4	1/3	1/2	1.0	2.0	0.097
Unsatisfactory	1/5	1/4	1/3	1/2	1.0	0.062

C.R. = 0.015

Table 12: Ranking alternatives. The priorities of the intensities for each criterion are divided by the largest one and multiplied by the priority of the criterion. Each alternative is rated on each criterion by assigning the appropriate intensity. The weighted intensities are added to yield the total on the right.

	Dependability .4347	Education .2774	Experience .1775	Quality .1123	Total
1. Adams, V	Outstanding	Bachelor	A Little	Outstanding	0.646
2. Becker, L	Average	Bachelor	A Little	Outstanding	0.379
3. Hayat, F	Average	Masters	A Lot	Below Average	0.418
4. Kesselman, S	Above Average	H.S.	None	Above Average	0.369
5. O'Shea, K	Average	Doctorate	A Lot	Above Average	0.605
6. Peters, T	Average	Doctorate	A Lot	Average	0.583
7. Tobias, K	Above Average	Bachelor	Average	Above Average	0.456

the lowest. This approach can be used whenever it is possible to set priorities for intensities of criteria; people can usually do this when they have sufficient experience with a given operation. This mode requires that alternatives be rated one by one without regard to how many there may be and how high or low any of them rates on prior standards. Still, when there is wide agreement on standards, the absolute mode saves time in rating a large number of alternatives.

Homogeneity and Clustering

Think of the following situation: we need to determine the relative size of a blueberry and a watermelon. Here, we need a range greater than 1-9. Human beings have difficulty establishing appropriate relationships when the ratios get beyond 9. To resolve this human difficulty, we can use a method in which we cluster different elements so we can rate them within a cluster and then rate them across the clusters. We need to add other fruits to make the comparison possible and then form groups of comparable fruits. In the first group we include the blueberry, a grape, and a plum. In the second group we include the same plum, an apple, and a grapefruit. In the third group we include the same grapefruit, a melon, and the watermelon. The AHP requires reciprocal comparisons of homogeneous elements whose ratios do not differ by much on a property, hence the absolute scale ranges from one to nine. When the ratios are larger, one must cluster the elements in different groups and use a common element (pivot) that is the largest in one cluster and the smallest element in the next cluster of the next higher order of magnitude. The weights of the elements in the second group are divided by the priority of the pivot in that group and then multiplied by the priority of the same pivot element (whose value is generally

different) from the first group, making them comparable with the first group. The process is then continued. The AHP software program Expert Choice performs these functions for the user. The reason for using clusters of a few elements is to ensure greater stability of the priorities in face of inconsistent judgments. Comparing more than two elements allows for redundancy and hence also for greater validity of real-world information. The AHP often uses seven elements and puts them in clusters if there are more. (Elaborate mathematical derivations are given in the AHP to show that the number of elements compared should not be too large in order to obtain priorities with admissible consistency.)

Problems with Analytic Decision Making

At this point you may wonder why we have three different modes for establishing priorities, the absolute measurement mode and the distributive and ideal modes of relative measurement. Isn't one enough? Let me explain why we need more than one mode.

A major reason for having more than one mode is concerned with this question. What happens to the synthesized ranks of alternatives when new ones are added or old ones deleted? With consistent judgments, the original relative rank order cannot change under any single criterion, but it can under several criteria.

Assume that an individual has expressed preference among a set of alternatives, and that as a result, he or she has developed a ranking for them. Can and should that individual's preferences and the resulting rank order of the alternatives be affected if alternatives are added to the set or deleted from it, and if no criteria are added or deleted, which would affect the weights of the old criteria? What if the added alternatives are copies or near copies of one or of several of the original alternatives and their number is large? Rank reversal is an unpleasant property if it is caused by the addition of truly irrelevant alternatives. However, the addition of alternatives may just reflect human nature: the straw that broke the camel's back was considered irrelevant along with all those that went before it. Mathematically, the number and quality of newly added alternatives are known to affect preference among the original alternatives.

Most people, unaided by theory and computation, make each decision separately, and they are not very concerned with rank reversal unless they are forced for some reason to refer to their earlier conclusions. I think it is essential to understand and deal with this phenomenon.

❧ An Example of Rank Reversal

Two products A and B are evaluated according to two equally important attributes P and Q as in the following matrices:

P	A	B	Priorities
A	1	5	.83
B	1/5	1	.17

Q	A	B	Priorities
A	1	1/3	.25
B	3	1	.75

We obtain the following priorities: W_A = .542, W_B = .458, and A is preferred to B.

A third product C is then introduced and compared with A and B as follows:

P	A	B	C	Priorities
A	1	5	1	.455
B	1/5	1	1/5	.090
C	1	5	1	.455

Q	A	B	C	Priorities
A	1	1/3	2	.222
B	3	1	6	.666
C	1/2	1/6	1	.111

Synthesis yields W_A = .338, W_B = .379, and W_C = .283. Here B is preferred to A and there is rank reversal.

For a decision theory to have a lasting value, it must consider how people make decisions naturally and assist them in organizing their thinking to improve their decisions in that natural direction. Its assumptions should be tied to evolution and not to present day determinism. This is the fundamental concept on which the AHP is based. It was developed as a result of a decade of unsuccessful attempts to use normative theories, with the assistance of some of the world's best minds, to deal with negotiation and trade-off in the strategic political and diplomatic arena at the Arms Control and Disarmament Agency in the Department of State. In the early 1970s, I asked the question, how do ordinary people process information in their minds in attempting to make a decision and how do they express the strength of their judgments? The answer to this question led me to consider hierarchies and networks, paired comparisons, ratio scales, homogenity and consistency, priorities, ranking, and the AHP.

The Benefits of Analytic Decision Making

Many excellent decision-makers do not rely on a theory to make their decisions. Are their good decisions accidental, or are there implicit logical principles that guide the mind in the process of making a decision, and are these principles complete and consistent? I believe that there are such principles, and that in thoughtful people, they work as formalized and described in the analytic hierarchy process. Still academics differ about how people should and should not make decisions. Experiments with people have shown that what people do differs from the theoretical and normative considerations the experts consider important. This may lead one to believe that analytical decision making is of little value. But our experience and that of many others indicate the opposite.

Analytic decision making is of tremendous value, but it must be simple and accessible to the lay user, and must have scientific justification of the highest order. Here are a few ideas about the benefits of the descriptive analytical approach. First is the morphological way of thoroughly modeling the decision, inducing people to make explicit their tacit knowledge. This leads people to organize and harmonize their different feelings and understanding. An agreed upon structure provides ground for a complete multisided debate. Second, particularly in the framework of hierarchies and feedback systems, the process permits decision makers to use judgments and observations to surmise relations and strengths of relations in the flow of interacting forces moving from the general to the particular and to make predictions of most likely outcomes. Third, people are able to incorporate and trade off values and influences with greater accuracy of understanding than they can using language alone. Fourth, people are able to include judgments that result from intuition and emotion as well those that result from logic. Reasoning takes a long time to learn, and it is not a skill common to all people. By representing the strength of judgments numerically and agreeing on a value, decision-making groups do not need to participate in prolonged argument. Finally, a formal approach allows people to make gradual and more thorough revisions and to combine the conclusions of different people studying the same problem in different places. One can also use such an approach to piece together partial analyses of the components of a bigger problem, or to decompose a larger problem into its constituent parts. This is an exhaustive list of the uses of the AHP. However, to deal with complexity we need rationality, and that is best manifested in the analytical approach.

The Analytic Network Process (ANP)

Many decision problems cannot be structured hierarchically because they involve the interaction and dependence of higher-level elements on lower-level elements. Not only does the importance of the criteria determine the importance of the alternatives as in a hierarchy, but also the importance of the alternatives themselves determines the importance of the criteria. Two bridges, both strong, but the stronger is also uglier, would lead one to choose the strong but ugly one unless the criteria themselves are evaluated in terms of the bridges, and strength receives a smaller value and appearance a larger value because both bridges are strong. Feedback enables us to factor the future into the present to determine what we have to do to attain a desired future.

The feedback structure does not have the linear top-to-bottom form of a hierarchy but looks more like a network, with cycles connecting its clusters of elements, which we can no longer call levels, and with loops that connect a cluster to itself. A decision problem involving feedback arises often in practice. It typically has many interactions, which in the limit converge toward the goal. Our minds need a tool to manage this complexity.

At present, in their effort to simplify and deal with complexity, people who work in decision making use mostly very simple hierarchic structures consisting of a goal, criteria, and alternatives. Yet, not only are decisions obtained from a simple hierarchy of three levels different from those obtained from a multilevel hierarchy, but also decisions obtained from a network can be significantly different from those obtained from a more complex hierarchy. We cannot collapse complexity artificially into a simplistic structure of two levels, criteria and alternatives, and hope to capture the outcome of interactions in the form of highly condensed judgments that correctly reflect all that goes on in the world. We must learn to decompose these judgments through more elaborate structures and organize our reasoning and calculations in sophisticated but simple ways to serve our understanding of the complexity around us. Experience indicates that it is not very difficult to do this although it takes more time and effort. Indeed, we must use feedback networks to arrive at the kind of decisions needed to cope with the future.

The data provided in the ANP is very similar to that given in the AHP. But the calculations are somewhat more complicated. To learn more about this subject that would take us too far afield to discuss and illustrate, see "Decisions with Dependent Feedback: The Ana-

lytic Network Process", by this author, RWS publications, 1996.

A Mathematical Explanation

The AHP has four axioms, (1) reciprocal judgments, (2) homogeneous elements, (3) hierarchic or feedback dependent structure, and (4) rank order expectations.

Assume that one is given n stones, $A_1, ..., A_n$, with known weights $w_1, ..., w_n$, respectively, and suppose that a matrix of pairwise ratios is formed whose rows give the ratios of the weights of each stone with respect to all others. Thus one has the equation:

$$
Aw = \begin{array}{c} \\ A_1 \\ \vdots \\ \vdots \\ A_n \end{array}
\begin{array}{c} A_1 \quad \cdots \quad A_n \end{array}
\begin{bmatrix} \dfrac{w_1}{w_1} & \cdots & \dfrac{w_1}{w_n} \\ \vdots & & \vdots \\ \dfrac{w_n}{w_1} & \cdots & \dfrac{w_n}{w_n} \end{bmatrix}
\begin{bmatrix} w_1 \\ \vdots \\ \vdots \\ w_n \end{bmatrix}
= n \begin{bmatrix} w_1 \\ \vdots \\ \vdots \\ w_n \end{bmatrix} = nw
$$

where $\mathbf{A}$ has been multiplied on the right by the vector of weights w. The result of this multiplication is nw. Thus, to recover the scale from the matrix of ratios, one must solve the problem $\mathbf{A}w = nw$ or $(\mathbf{A} - n\mathbf{I})w = 0$. This is a system of homogeneous linear equations. It has a nontrivial solution if and only if the determinant of $\mathbf{A}\text{-}n\mathbf{I}$ vanishes, that is, n is an eigenvalue of $\mathbf{A}$. Now $\mathbf{A}$ has unit rank since every row is a constant multiple of the first row. Thus all its eigenvalues except one are zero. The sum of the eigenvalues of a matrix is equal to its trace, the sum of its diagonal elements, and in this case the trace of $\mathbf{A}$ is equal to n. Thus n is an eigenvalue of $\mathbf{A}$, and one has a nontrivial solution. The

228

solution consists of positive entries and is unique to within a multiplicative constant.

To make w unique, one can normalize its entries by dividing by their sum. Thus, given the comparison matrix, one can recover the scale. In this case, the solution is any column of A normalized. Notice that in A the reciprocal property $a_{ji} = 1/a_{ij}$ holds; thus, also $a_{ii} = 1$. Another property of A is that it is consistent: its entries satisfy the condition $a_{jk} = a_{ik}/a_{ij}$. Thus the entire matrix can be constructed from a set of n elements which form a chain across the rows and columns.

In the general case, the precise value of w_i/w_j cannot be given, but instead only an estimate of it as a judgment. For the moment, consider an estimate of these values by an expert who is assumed to make small perturbations of the coefficients. This implies small perturbations of the eigenvalues. The problem now becomes $A'w' = \lambda_{max}w'$ where λ_{max} is the largest eigenvalue of A'. To simplify the notation, we shall continue to write $Aw = \lambda_{max}w$, where A is the matrix of pairwise comparisons. The problem now is how good is the estimate of w. Notice that if w is obtained by solving this problem, the matrix whose entries are w_i/w_j is a consistent matrix. It is a consistent estimate of the matrix A. A itself need not be consistent. In fact, the entries of A need not even be transitive; that is, A_1 may be preferred to A_2 and A_2 to A_3 but A_3 may be preferred to A_1. What we would like is a measure of the error due to inconsistency. It turns out that A is consistent if and only if $\lambda_{max} = n$ and that we always have $\lambda_{max} \geq n$.

Since small changes in a_{ij} imply a small change in λ_{max}, the deviation of the latter from n is a deviation from consistency and can be represented by $(\lambda_{max} - n)/(n-1)$, which is called the *consistency ratio (C.I.)*. When the consistency has been calculated, the result is compared with those of the average value of the same index computed for many randomly generated reciprocal matrices from the scale 1 to 9, with reciprocals forced. This index is called the *random index (R.I.)*. Table 13 gives the order of the matrix (first column) and the R.I. (second column) as computed by generating the R.I. for tens of thousands of matrices of the given order and averaging: The ratio of C.I. to the average R.I. for the same order matrix is called the *consistency ratio (C.R.)*. A consistency ratio of 0.10 or less is positive evidence for informed judgment.

Table 13. Average Random Index Values

n	Average Random Index (R.I.)
1	0
2	0
3	.52
4	.89
5	1.11
6	1.25
7	1.35
8	1.40
9	1.45
10	1.49

The relations $a_{ji} = 1/a_{ij}$ and $a_{ii} = 1$ are preserved in these matrices to improve consistency. The reason for this is that if stone #1 is estimated to be k times heavier than stone #2, one should require that stone #2 be estimated to be $1/k$ times the weight of the first. If the consistency ratio is significantly small, the estimates are accepted; otherwise, an attempt is made to improve consistency by obtaining additional information. The things that contribute to the consistency of a judgment are: (1) the homogeneity of the elements in a group, that is, not comparing a grain of sand with a mountain; (2) the sparseness of elements in the group, because an individual cannot hold in mind simultaneously the relations of many more than a few objects; and (3) the knowledge and care of the decision maker about the problem under study.

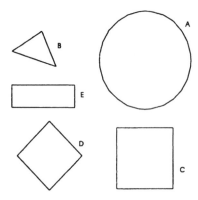

Figure 5. Five Areas to Pairwise Compare

Figure 5 shows five areas to which we can apply to the paired comparison process in a matrix and use the 1-9 scale to test the validity of the procedure. We can approximate the priorities in the matrix by assuming that it is consistent. We normalize each column and then take the average of the corresponding entries in the columns.

Five figures drawn with appropriate size of area. The object is to compare them in pairs to reproduce their relative weights.

The actual relative values of these areas are A=0.47, B=0.05, C=0.24, D=0.14, and E=0.09 with which the answer may be compared. By comparing more than two alternatives in a decision problem, one is able to obtain better values for the derived scale because of redundancy in the comparisons, which helps improve the overall accuracy of the judgments.

The Mousetrap Example

≈ **Designing a Mousetrap (by Arthur Dobias).**

To design a new mousetrap, initial thinking centered around how today's mousetraps function and what makes them effective.

Brainstorming revealed various methods of exterminating a rodent's life (Figure 6).

To evaluate the various methods of execution, criteria had to be identified for judging the effectiveness of the trap and the neatness of the kill to distinguish one method from another. Other criteria included were low cost, reusability and ease of use. The alternative methods to kill a mouse were electric shock, gas, poison, hanging, smashing and

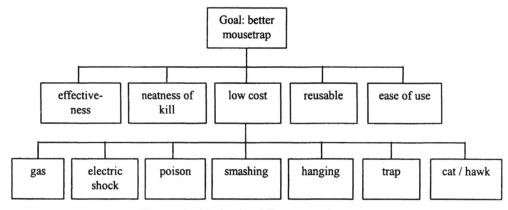

Figure 6. Methods of Extermination

Table 14. Priorities of Alternative Methods of Extermination

	Effectiveness	Neatness of kill	Low cost	Reusable	Ease of use	Composite priorities
	(0.564)	(0.220)	(0.137)	(0.039)	(0.039)	
Gas	0.208	0.228	0.040	0.216	0.161	0.188
Electric Shock	0.208	0.403	0.090	0.210	0.161	0.223
Poison	0.208	0.091	0.052	0.032	0.161	0.152
Smashing	0.208	0.164	0.141	0.210	0.161	0.187
Hanging	0.093	0.057	0.247	0.045	0.161	0.107
Trap	0.055	0.037	0.405	0.210	0.161	0.109
Cat/Hawk	0.022	0.021	0.025	0.077	0.032	0.025

Goal = Better mousetrap, Criteria

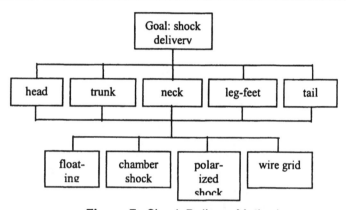

Figure 7. Shock Delivery Methods

Table 15. Judgments and Priorities for where to deliver shock (from Figure 7)

	HEAD	TRUNK	NECK	LEG-FEET	TAIL	COMPOSITE PRIORITIES
HEAD		3.0	2.0	1/4	5.0	.216
TRUNK			1/2	1/5	4.0	.099
NECK				1/4	4.0	.142
LEG-FEET					5.0	.497
TAIL						.047

Table 16. Alternative Methods for Delivering the Shock (from Figure 7)

	Head (0.216)	Trunk (0.099)	Neck (0.120)	Leg/Feet (0.497)	Tail (0.047)	Composite priorities
Floating wire	0.130	0.095	0.077	0.550	0.005	0.090
Chamber Shock	0.377	0.594	0.294	0.148	0.408	0.274
Polarized Shock	0.377	0.26	0.572	0.135	0.424	0.273
Pattern Wire Grid	0.073	0.064	0.056	0.662	0.063	0.362

Goal = Shock delivery, Criteria

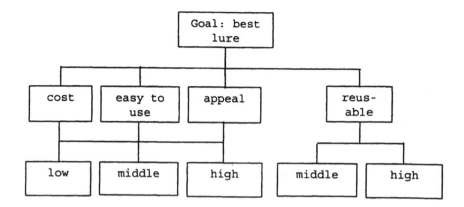

Figure 8. Ratings for Alternative Lures

Table 17. Alternative Shapes Composite Priorities

| | Criteria | | | | |
	Design appeal (0.226)	Natural appeal (0.590)	Materials needed (0.092)	Manufact. Needs (0.092)	Composite priorities
Box	0.158	0.156	0.166	0.230	0.164
Dome	0.205	0.143	0.084	0.107	0.148
Tube	0.465	0.534	0.425	0.215	0.479
Platform	0.075	0.067	0.259	0.364	0.114
Sphere	0.097	0.100	0.066	0.083	0.095

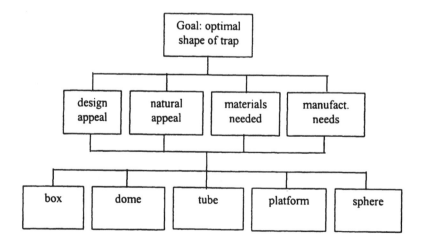

Figure 9. Optimal Shape of Trap

232

Table 18. Ratings for Alternative Lures

	Goal = best lure			
	Criteria			
	Cost	Easy to use	Appeal	Reusable
Alternatives	0.062	0.126	0.594	0.218
Low	0.673	0.075	0.073	N/A
Middle	0.258	0.229	0.226	N/A
High	0.105	0.696	0.700	N/A
Yes	N/A	N/A	N/A	0.615
No	N/A	N/A	N/A	0.662

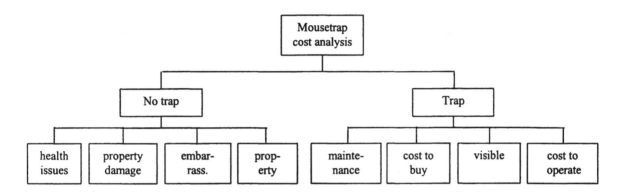

Figure 10. Mousetrap Cost Analysis

Table 19. Mousetrap Cost Analysis

No trap		Trap	
0.385		0.615	
Health Issues	0.606	Maintenance needs	0.495
Property Damage	0.166	Cost to buy	0.128
Embarrassment	0.063	Visible	0.290
Property Value	0.166	Cost to Operate	0.088

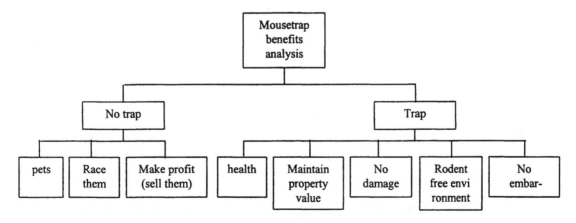

Figure 11. Mousetrap Benefits Analysis

Table 20. Mousetrap benefits analysis

	No trap 0.417		Trap 0.583
Pets	0.504	Health	0.483
Race them	0.279	Maintain property value	0.228
Make profit (sell them)	0.217	No damage	0.131
		Rodent free environment	0.106
		No embarrassment	0.053

trapping. Based on the evaluation of the six criteria, it was determined that electric shock was the most desirable method (Table 14).

The next step was to determine where to aim the shock (Level 2 in Figure 7). The results of the hierarchy (Table 15) led to the legs and feet being evaluated at .497, the head of the mouse coming in second at .216 and an inconsistency ratio of .077.

The findings from the second model led to the development of a third model (Level 3 in Figure 7). In it the alternatives of the second model were used to evaluate various methods for delivering the electric shock. This third model, the optimal shock delivery system had, as its alternatives, a floating wire system, a wire griding system, a full chamber shock system using a side-to-side delivery wave of electricity and a polarized shock pattern which would run from end to end on the trap (Table 16).

Once the synthesis was completed it was clear that given the weights assigned to the criteria, a wire grid design would provide the best means of delivering the shock to the mouse's legs and feet (and even any other body parts). As can be seen from the first three models, the decisions made in each model drive those made in the subsequent model. With that in mind it was clear how to kill the rodent, what area should receive the shock and the optimal means to do it.

Attracting the Mouse

The next issue was how to attract the mouse to the trap. For this a fourth model was developed whose goal was to identify the best luring device (Figure 8). Criteria included cost, with a set of sub-criteria; ease of use, also with sub-criteria; appeal (attracting power), with its own sub-criteria; and reusability. The alternative means of attracting a mouse were developed and evaluated under each set of criteria and sub-criteria.

The alternative lures were rated using Table 18. Among the alternatives that were rated were food and sex scent and real food and dim lighting. The alternatives of food scent and sex scent were found to be within .001 of each other. For this reason it was decided to include both lures in the mousetrap by combining food and sex scent.

The Trap Shape

The fifth model was used to decide on the optimal shape of the trap given that the trap was to perform electrically (Figure 9). The alternatives generated included a sphere, a tube, a platform, a box and a dome. Each alternative was evaluated for its design appeal based on the presumed human need for an attractive trap. From the rodent's perspective, the trap needed natural appeal that would focus on the mouse's curious nature. Other criteria were materials needed in construction and the various considerations about ease of manufacture (Table 17).

The Costs and Benefits of the Trap

Once the synthesis was completed, with an inconsistency ratio of .05, the obvious clear shape of choice was a tube design with a composite priority of 0.479. Up to this point it has been clear how each previous model drove the subsequent model's creation. Now, with all the elements in place, an idea born of the AHP could begin to take form. Before entering the actual design phase, however, it was important to evaluate the costs and benefits of actual mousetraps. Two models were developed; one for the costs (Figure 10) of the trap and the other for the benefits (Figure 11). The mousetrap costs model looked at both using a trap and not using it. Under not using a trap further considerations included health issues, property damage, lower property value and the potential embarrassment of having rodents in the house. Sub-criteria under using a trap were the purchasing cost, the operating cost, trap maintenance time, and the visibility of the trap in the house. Under the sub-criteria of not using the trap (i.e., health issue and property damage) were food damage, mouse's excrement in the house, the bite factor and damage considerations to clothes and furniture.

With the synthesis completed it became clear that the costs of having the trap outweighed those of not having the trap (Table 19). Attention now focused on the benefits of using the trap given the findings of the last model (Table 20).

The benefits model, similar to the costs model, looked at both using and not using the mousetrap. Under using the trap, the issues included a clean home environment, maintaining current property value, no damage to food/clothes or property, a rodent free environment and no embarrassment due to the lack of a mouse. Considered under not using the trap were the opportunity to earn money by breeding and selling them, development of mouse races and the chance to obtain low cost pets. The mousetrap benefits model showed that the benefits of using a trap outweighed those of not using one and a subjective judgment followed that we would pursue the idea of making a trap.

A Marketing Model

At this point it seemed that only the trap design itself was left to be developed, but a question arose as to whether this trap, once developed, could prosper monetarily. Our concern now focused on profits and on the development of a model (Figures 12 and 13) that would assist in deciding which markets should be entered once the trap took physical form. Criteria included the trap's profit potential, customer need and geographic location. Both profit potential and customer need used sub-criteria of high, medium and low with greatest weight going to high. Geographic location had sub-criteria of sections of the country (i.e., Eastern, Midwest, Central, Mountain and Western). Under these were the alternatives of metro cities, metro suburbs and rural areas. Once the synthesis was completed the first choice of a market to enter was found to be metro suburbs at 0.549, followed by metro cities at 0.266 and rural at 0.185 (Tables 21 and 22).

Table 21: Priorities of Alternative Regional Markets

Criteria:	Goal = Market to Enter		
	Profit Potential	Customer Need	Geographic Location
Alternatives	0.660	0.211	0.129
High	0.938	0.738	N/A
Medium	0.196	0.196	N/A
Low	0.065	0.065	N/A
Eastern	N/A	N/A	0.362
Midwest	N/A	N/A	0.251
Central	N/A	N/A	0.148
Mountain	N/A	N/A	0.100
Western	N/A	N/A	0.134

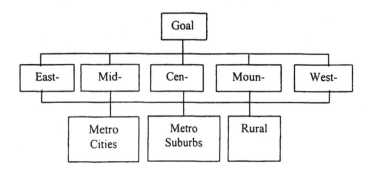

Figure 12. Alternative Marketing Locations

Table 22. Priorities of Alternative Marketing Locations

	Eastern	Midwest	Central	Mountain	Western
Alternatives	0.302	0.251	0.148	0.100	0.138
Metro Cities	0.249	0.249	0.249	0.249	0.249
Metro Suburbs	0.594	0.594	0.594	0.594	0.594
Rural	0.157	0.157	0.157	0.157	0.157

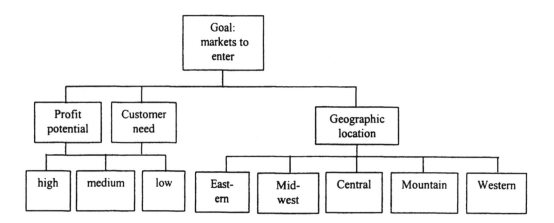

Figure 13. Markets to Enter

❧ The Design

With regard to the actual trap, some of the design questions included the shape of the entrance to the trap, how long should the trap be, where to place wire griding, how to make it reusable and a number of other questions.

Figure 14 contains the preliminary drawings of the front and back of the trap and one complete sideview. Also, a picture of the front and back with the wire grid floor is included to aid in understanding the design.

Figures 15 through 17 contain the formal design plans. Figure 15 gives an overview of the trap. The 3 1/4" section outlines the inner chamber while the 4 1/4" section shows the outlays of the chamber. All solid lines depict the outer layer of steel and the inner dashed line depicts the thickness of the materials used. This convention is adhered to for all the following exhibits.

Figure 15. Overview

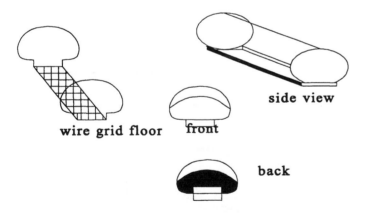

Figure 14. Preliminary Drawing of the Trap

Figure 16 contains views of the front and rear ends. If the trap was "electrified" at all times, it was unlikely that a mouse would enter. A means of detecting entry was needed to send a signal to the delay mechanism housing assembly. At 1.2 seconds after the beam is broken, the four corners of the wire griding receive an electrical charge of one hundred

Figure 17 is the rear elevation, the view of the trap from its magnetic closure side.

Figure 18 contains two views, a front elevation and Section A-A.

The front elevation is the hinge side. The overall length of the complete trap is 9" long

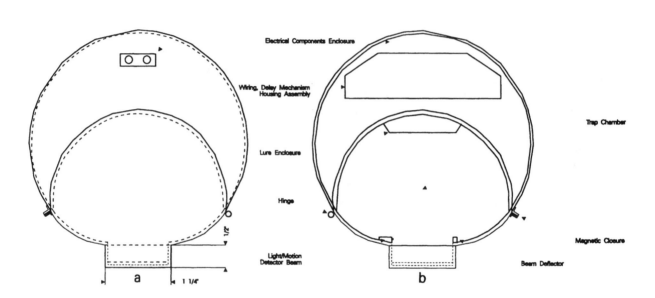

Figure 16. End Views

and ten volts. The trap chamber is the section that the mouse enters while the electrical components enclosure opens to dispose of the dead rodent with a twist of the wrist.

This is why a seven inch piano hinge, and the magnetic closure are included. Remember the first hierarchy. Reusability and ease of use were indeed among the initial criteria. The lure was located on the top section of the trap chamber to make replacement easy and to force the mouse's weight downward on the wire grid as it pushed up to get toward the lure.

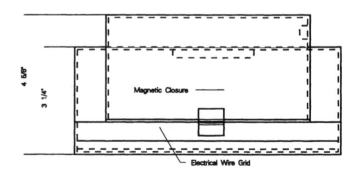

Figure 17. Rear Elevation

while the section that opens is 7" long. While

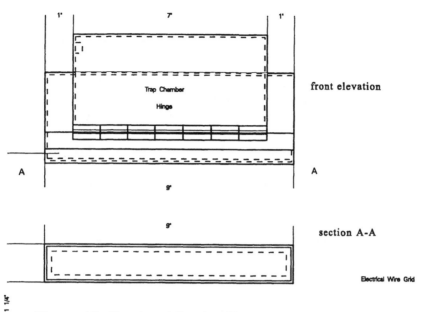

Figure 18. Front and Section Elevations

observing the front elevation, note the two downward pointing arrows labeled "A". This represents a cross-section of this area and a top down view can be seen in section A-A. This is the complete 9" electrical wire grid that is located in the channel of the trap chamber.

It is important to note that this type of thinking and design can come only when you ask not only how it has been done, but how you might do it differently.

ᴢᴡ Conclusions

The AHP was used to model the stages of designing a new mousetrap. The model helps elucidate the thinking process. Without the beginning models as stepping stones, the later models would be meaningless separate entities with no tie to the overall goal of building a better mouse trap.

Table 23 contains an overall view of the reconstituted master hierarchy. Note that this exhibit displays only the first three levels of

the total picture. To understand the complete model, it is useful to examine the previous tables and visualize where each component part fits.

This exercise (the overall model) demonstrates how decisions in one model lead to the creation of another model and affect choices made for each model thereafter. The cost/benefit analysis and the decision about what markets to enter were driven by the preceding models but not to the same extent that the first five models were.

Although the master hierarchy model was created after the completion of the project, it serves to demonstrate the sequence of events followed and the relative importance of each with respect to those models they affected.

Table 23 Master Hierarchy

TYPE	SHK-AREA	SHK-DEL	OPT-LURE	OPT-SHAP	CTS-BENE	MARKETS
0.430	0.223	0.123	0.073	0.060	0.050	0.041
-L-COST	-HEAD	-FLT-WIRE	-COST	-DSGN-APP	-COST	PROFPOT
0.092	0.198	0.056	0.062	0.280	0.500	0.640
-EFFECTI	-TRUNK	-WIREGRID	-EASY USE	-NTL APPL	-BENEFITS	CUST-ND
0.426	0.067	0.612	0.151	0.614	0.500	0.288
-NEAT	-NECK	-CHMB-SHK	-APPEAL	-MAT-NEED		GEO-LOC
0.315	0.132	0.160	0.635	0.053		0.073
-REUSABLE	-LEG-FEET	-POLZ-SHK	-REUSABLE	-MFG-NEED		
0.095	0.552	0.173	0.151	0.053		
-EASY USE	-TAIL					
0.072	0.051					

ADDENDUM

Creativity Test by Eugene Raudsepp

We live in an age when tests are taken in order to indicate how well we qualify in a certain field. To me, the most important aspect of a test is the kind of questions and concerns that are brought to a person's attention. This excellent test is found in Eugene Raudsepp's book, "Games for the Creative Manager", a Perigee book, 1987 (now out of print – he died in 1995 and expressed the wish that his writings live on into the next century). He was a highly original person who was an expert in the field of creative management. His book has many similar interesting tests.

❧ Test Your Creativity Quotient

For each statement write the appropriate letter in the blank:
A_____Agree
B_____Undecided or don't know
C_____Disagree.

Be as frank as possible. Try not to guess how you feel a creative manager might respond.

* PLEASE SEE ANSWERS AT THE END OF THE CHAPTER *

1. I always work with a great deal of certainty that I am following the correct procedure for solving a particular problem.
2. It would be a waste of time for me to ask questions if I have no hope of obtaining answers.
3. I concentrate harder on whatever interests me than most people do.
4. I feel that a logical step-by-step method is best for solving problems.
5. I occasionally voice opinions that seem to turn some people off.
6. I spend a great deal of time thinking about what others think of me.
7. It is more important for me to do what I believe to be right than to try to win the approval of others.
8. People who seem uncertain about things lose my respect.
9. More than other people, I need to have things that are interesting and exciting to work.
10. I know how to keep my inner impulses in check.
11. I am able to stick with different problems over extended periods of time.
12. On occasion I get overly enthusiastic.
13. I often get my best ideas when doing nothing in particular.
14. I rely on intuitive hunches and the feeling of "rightness" or "wrongness" when moving toward the solution of a problem.
15. I work faster when analyzing a problem and slower when synthesizing the information I have gathered.
16. I sometimes get a kick out of breaking the rules and doing things I am not supposed to do.
17. I like hobbies that involve collecting things.
18. Daydreaming has provided the impetus for many of my more important projects.
19. I like people who are objective and rational.
20. If I had to choose, I would rather be a physician than an explorer.
21. I can get along more easily with people if they belong to about the same social class and business level as myself.
22. I have a high degree of aesthetic sensitivity.

23. Status and power are important to me.
24. I like people who are confident in their conclusions.
25. Inspiration has nothing to do with the successful solution of problems.
26. When I am in an argument, I want the person who disagrees with me to like me, even at the price of sacrificing my point of view.
27. I am much more interested in coming up with new ideas than in trying to sell them to others.
28. I would enjoy spending an entire day alone, just thinking.
29. I tend to avoid situations in which I might feel inferior.
30. In evaluating information, the source is more important to me than the content.
31. I resent things being uncertain and unpredictable.
32. I like people who follow the rule, "business before pleasure.
33. Self-respect is much more important than the respect of others.
34. I feel that it is unwise to strive for perfection.
35. I prefer to work with others in a team effort rather than alone.
36. I like work in which I must influence others.
37. Many problems that I encounter cannot be resolved in terms of right or wrong solutions.
38. It is important for me to have a place for everything and everything in its place.
39. Writers who use strange and unusual words merely want to show off.
40. Below is a list of terms that describe people. Choose 10 words that best characterize you.

energetic	factual	courageous
persuasive	open-minded	efficient
observant	tactful	helpful
fashionable	inhibited	perceptive
self-confident	enthusiastic	quick
persevering	innovative	good-natured
original	poised	thorough
cautious	acquisitive	impulsive
habit-bound	practical	determined
resourceful	alert	realistic
egotistical	curious	modest
independent	organized	involved
stern	unemotional	absent-mind
predictable	clear-thinking	flexible
formal	understanding	sociable
informal	dynamic	well-liked
dedicated	self-demanding	restless
forward-looking	polished	retiring

Answers, Possibilities, and Analyses

❧ Scoring

To compute your score, circle and add up the values assigned to each item.

	A	B	C			A	B	C
1.	0	1	2		20.	0	1	2
2.	0	1	2		21.	0	1	2
3.	4	1	0		22.	3	0	-1
4.	-2	0	3		23.	0	1	2
5.	2	1	0		24.	-1	0	2
6.	1	0	3		25.	0	1	3
7.	3	0	1		26.	-1	0	2
8.	0	1	2		27.	2	1	0
9.	3	0	1		28.	2	0	-1
10.	1	0	3		29.	0	1	2
11.	4	1	0		30.	-2	0	3
12.	3	0	-1		31.	0	1	2
13.	2	1	0		32.	0	1	2
14.	4	0	-2		33.	3	0	-1
15.	-1	0	2		34.	-1	0	2
16.	2	1	0		35.	0	1	2
17.	0	1	2		36.	1	2	3
18.	3	0	-1		37.	2	1	0
19.	0	1	2		38.	0	1	2
					39.	-1	0	2

40. The following have values of 2:

energetic	dynamic	perceptive	dedicated
resourceful	flexible	innovative	courageous
original	observant	self-demanding	curious
enthusiastic	independent	persevering	involved

The following have values of 1:

self-confident determined informal forward-looking
thorough restless alert open-minded

The rest have values of 0.

❧ What Your Score Means

95-116	Exceptionally Creative
65-94	Very Creative
40-64	Above Average
20-39	Average
10-19	Below Average
Below 10	Noncreative

If you scored below your expectations, don't despair. By conscientiously doing the exercises and games in this book you can enhance your creative powers. Keep track of your ideas at all times. Carry a notebook wherever you go, and keep it at your bedside. Ideas come at strange times, frequently when we least expect them, and they may never come again. Listen to your hunches and intuitions, particularly during moments of relaxation, before going to sleep, or upon awakening.

Pose new questions every day. An inquiring mind is a creatively active mind. It is also a mind that constantly enlarges the area of its awareness.

Learn about things outside of your specialty. Seemingly unrelated pieces of knowledge can often be brought together to solve problems or create new products and services.

Avoid rigid, set patterns of doing things. Overcome fixed ideas and look for new viewpoints; try new ways. Attempt to find several solutions to each problem and develop the ability to drop one idea in favor of another.

Be open and receptive to ideas, others' as well as yours. New ideas are fragile-listen positively to them. Seize on tentative, half-formed concepts and possibilities: A new idea seldom arrives as a complete ready-made package. Freely entertain apparently wild, farfetched, or even silly ideas.

Be alert in observation. Look for similarities, differences, and unique and distinguishing features in objects, situations, processes, and ideas. The more new associations you can form, greater are your chances of coming up with really original combinations and solutions.

Engage in hobbies. Try ones that allow you to construct something with your hands. This allows you to relax and enhances the creative problem-solving abilities so useful in your work. Also, keep

your brain trim by playing games and doing puzzles and exercises.

Improve your sense of humor and laugh easily. This helps you to put yourself and your problems into proper perspective. Humor relieves tension, and you are more creative when you are relaxed.

Adopt a risk-taking attitude. Nothing is more fatal to creativity than fear of failure.

Observations, Comments and Assignments Developed in Teaching about Creativity

Come to this class expecting to give and not expecting to receive. Open up in whatever ways you always wanted to know your real self. Do it soon. This is a class in creativity, not in psychiatry. We don't have much time and want to be made happy by learning or experiencing something new and different from you. Be positive and willing to try new approaches and new ideas. Leave your hang-ups and inhibitions outside when you join us.

Do not wait to be shown the way, try to create your own way. Let go of your inhibitions and rigid attitudes and allow your feelings, emotions, and introspection to lead you. Think, imagine and feel as you go along. Be happy or sad, peaceful or angry. Be expressive and use a medium to communicate your expression. Initially, anything you do is OK, for final product, when perfection is needed, you must revise, revise and revise.

Feel secure and loved and know that this one time you will be appreciated without conditions. Use your aesthetics to bring beauty and style into your creation.

To demonstrate that your own creativity has been stimulated by the class, and that it has become an ongoing process, you need to do a project whose ideas germinate and hatch during the period of the course. By doing this, it is hoped that you will develop the confidence to repeat the performance at other times in your life when there may be no one to encourage and applaud you. You may be compelled at that time to be especially creative and self motivated. Please do not bring an old project that you did sometime ago no matter how proud of it

you may be. Your work should be imaginative, different, loose but inspiring, colorful and far out but in good taste, ingenious but not too clever to be appreciated by others, attracts attention, short but not trivial. Submit a paragraph describing what it is.

Weekly Project

The first step in using ones creativity is getting started. Try something different, maybe you will discover a talent or skill you never knew existed. Creativity does not just happen, it takes effort and some exercising of the mind to make it into a subconscious habit. Each week, students are required to open their safe of creative ideas and impress the instructor. Keep a notebook to show your creative contributions from among the following subjects, preferably a different one each week. The notebook will be collected in the final class.

Examples of Subjects

1. A short essay on what this book is about, how it compares with other books and what ideas need more emphasis and what other ideas are missing and should be included.

2. How to update the design of compact city (see my book with this title) so that global warming due to transportation, production and heating is no longer a major problem and a large part of humanity is preserved if there were many such cities around the globe and an asteroid of a large size were to create havoc with the seas and atmosphere for a year or two. Electric generation has to be close and protected; food must be grown within and waste appropriately disposed of; the air purified in case of atmospheric contamination and oxygen depletion; what sort of materials to use and what kind of repairs and how to make the protective structure of the city; what kinds of raw materials would

be needed and where to store them; anti terrorism and large scale harmful agents and explosives and how to monitor and prevent large scale damage to the city and loss of life; how to communicate with other cities before and after a disaster; methods of transportation to the outside; living in a closed up compact city would be like living in a submarine: how to overcome claustrophobia and boredom; can the city be built inside a mountain, or in the sea?

3. Art
- Sketch - landscape, portrait, objects, abstract drawing, etc.
- Sculpture: stone, clay, wood, construction paper, etc.
- Mosaic or collage of clippings/pictures on various subjects
- Drawing
- Painting: water, oil, acrylic, etc.
- Building / furniture construction/ restoring furniture, etc.
- Photography and computer animation; videos.

4. Invention
- Design plans or sketches for an invention, house, building, landscape, machine, etc.
- Rearrangement of something to make more efficient (example: closet, town layout, roads, office, kitchen, handicapped bathroom, manufacturing facility, etc.)
- A talking device to thank a person appropriately for a thing done, and also to scold him/her silently in your mind to vent your emotions and frustration. Use any conceivable vocabulary, both delicate and harsh as needed.

5. Business
- Solution to a problem, new way of looking at existing problem

- Small business plan or ideas for new business venture or product; advertising
- Planning of an event, (example: birthday party, wedding, awards banquet, decorations, etc.)

6. Literature
- Poetry
- Short Story or newspaper article
- Greeting card
- Magazine advertisement for a product
- Children's book or illustration
- Humor and jokes

7. Miscellaneous
- Movie critique
- Song
- Music composition
- Kids game
- Special diet
- Food recipe
- Philosophy or explanation of how something works or why something happened (e.g. evolution, religion, industry)

Learning About Creativity (an outline)

What is Creativity?
Personal and Historical Creativity

Product of invention or imagination. The ability to generate novel and useful ideas and solutions to everyday problems and challenges.

Motivation Preparation Incubation Illumination Verification Evaluation Action

Five Kinds of Creative Activity

1. Solution of a well-defined problem (Watson and Crick's double helix)
2. Devising of an encompassing theory (Einstein's relativity)
3. The creation of a frozen work (Picasso's Guernica)
4. The performance of a ritualized work (Martha Graham's dance)
5. A high stakes performance which cannot be worked out in advance (Gandhi's political passive resistance)

Six Distinctions in Creativity and Novelty

1. Individual versus social definitions of creativity (daily innovation)
2. Deliberate versus non-intentional creation (special construction)
3. Goal-defined creativity (the kind of solution that fits the end state of the problem)
4. Subjective sense and awareness of novelty
5. Degrees of novelty (distinguish old from the new)
6. Continuous versus discontinuous problem-solving (interrupting search for an interval)

Forces Working

1. Dreams are a creative, highly structured activity. They are not novel, but are reconstruction of what we have experienced and are unconstrained by reality.
2. Incubation combined with periodic conscious work.
3. Consciousness restricts possible solution and prevents fantasy, at least in science, so internalize and then consciously examine.
4. Mind-popping revelations are sudden solutions that come to mind

Support and Commitment

1. Cognitive support with affection from people close to him or her are needed by the creative person.
2. Faustian bargains are made by the creative person who trades off sacrifice for the promise of creative success.

Creativity and Intelligence.

There is no relation between creativity and intelligence past an IQ of 120. There are eight kinds of intelligence:

1. Linguistic
2. Logical-mathematical
3. Spatial
4. Musical
5. Bodily/kinesthetic
6. Interpersonal
7. Intrapersonal
8. Naturalistic

These are purposeful, focused and goal-oriented approaches to creativity:

1. Finding the problem and getting a feel for it
2. Brainstorming the problem and its solution
3. Synectics
4. Morphological analysis
5. Lateral thinking

These are the symptoms of purposeless creativity: distraction, daydreaming, emotions, bursts of excitement and mania, humor, eloquence, etc. with sporadic original contributions.

Three Aspects of Creativity
To the snob creativity is limited to the following triangle:

Humor

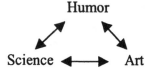

Science ⟷ Art

To the non-snob creativity is everywhere. According to Koestler, humor is the only domain of creative activity where a stimulus on a high level of complexity produces a massive and sharply defined response on the level of physiological reflexes.

Personality Traits and Practices of Creativity
Creativity is introspection through and through which gives rise to inspiration, spontaneity, persistence to the point of obsession, humor, association in sequence,

The creative person also needs memory to link ideas, reason to develop them, and education to learn to order thinking.

Creativity also requires practice, remembering cases and examples, knowing how to ask questions, learning about hierarchies and systems and prioritization to organize thinking and action.

It helps to have a childlike attitude, dedication, humility, eclectic interests and to be discriminating in the face of variety.

A world class creative contribution involves much study, thinking and doing, setting goals, receptiveness and reaching out to new ideas and experiences, development of an attitude for possibilities. It often means involving others in the grand

pursuit and being political to achieve one's aims.

"To develop creativeness, the mind needs not only to be exercised, but to be filled with material out of which ideas can best be formed."

–Alex F. Osborn

Overcoming Barriers and Inhibitions to Creativity
Interact with people and with the environment using observation, knowledge, humor, thinking, talking, listening, doing (making, writing, composing, painting, sculpting, acting).

Learn about the lives of creative people and how they overcame difficulties to meet the challenges they faced. Try to understand the central character of these creative people one by one.

How to Activate and Practice Personal and Group Creativity
"I wish that" (if you want it badly enough, you are motivated to make it happen).
"Wouldn't it be nice?" (another way to wish).
"What can't be done today, but if it could, would revolutionize my business."

How to Let the World Know— You need to Market your Work

You have to be your own best salesperson and advocate: there are no two ways about it. It is sheer fantasy to assume that the world is made of honest, intelligent people who have an astute talent for sniffing out creativity at long range and who would then rush and humble themselves to acclaim you and take it to the world, and furthermore enrich you instead of themselves. This fantasy is only a fantasy. It has rarely if ever happened that way in the real world. All one has to do is think of the conflicts of Newton, and Einstein, and even of Galileo, who had to pretend that he was taking back his discovery to save his neck, and think of the hard work and salesmanship and many failures along with the successes of Edison, and of Colonel Sanders of Kentucky Fried Chicken fame. Also think of the abuses Moses received on bringing down the commandments, and those Jesus Christ received on bringing his message of love. Creativity does not work that easily in this world and is usually resisted and rebuffed with energy by people who acclaim themselves as protectors of the system from the wrong and evil that might ensue from your ideas. You have to overcome them with patience and persistence.

Exercise: Extend, refine and consolidate works to improve this outline. Write a little about each of the above topics.

Exercise: Work with two or more colleagues to develop a creative theory, invention, masquerade, essay, poem, painting, story, work of hand, idea that reaches far beyond the prosaic and mundane chore. It should bear the marks of elegance and beauty, imagination and originality that you can be proud of.

Creativity Class Schedule

Seven 3-hour classes, one a week, with a final exhibit of the best that a student can show in the 7th class attended by invited guests and a several thousand dollar prize to distribute to the best performers in creativity as judged by the guests.

Class 1.

What is creativity?
Cover the ten points on how to be creative from the slides.

A request from the class: for the duration of this course try to be positive all the time and avoid being judgmental and critical. Be open minded and receptive to new ideas. If you get bored, invent an object or a process, write a poem or an essay, paint or draw a picture, try to pontificate about how to be creative and ask for the opportunity to show or demonstrate to the rest of us. You are free to try anything innovative of your own making. That is the spirit of the class. The requirement is that you must do something.

I am convinced that it is by far better to get people to be creative by doing things than to philosophize about creativity. The latter not only gets boring, tiring and mundane, but also can damage the listener's interest in ever again being accessible to learn about creativity. If one must philosophize, one must be enthusiastic and inspirational in discussing the subject. Of all things, learning about creativity should not be boring.

Are you a collector of anything? If not, start by collecting something you have wanted to have and to care for. Caring is an important aspect of creativity and may even be an incentive for nurturing it. One does not have to collect objects. It can be ideas, jokes, poems, or mathematical formulas.

Assign exercises on variations on the 10 points about how to be creative.

Do four aspects of creativity with examples:
- Brainstorming
- Synectics
- Morphological Analysis
- Lateral Thinking

Tell jokes
Assign 2 problems from the end of Chapter 1 to each student.

Assign project for final day; they may choose anything and must present their project at the final class. They can work in a group of 2 or 3.

Show student Matt Duddy's computer-generated video about manhole covers in Pittsburgh; 96 kinds around which he built his prize-winning story using powerful sounds. He spent 60 hours on this class project.

Tell about books and wide interest in creativity.

Go through the Power Point slides of the short 50 minute creativity presentation

Estimate on a scale 1-9 (with 9 being the highest), how creative you think you are.

Take the creativity test.

How well do you match your estimate with how you did on the test.

Engage class in a discussion of creativity

Show the 9-dot video
Puzzles
• Gold bar puzzle: bar to be cut twice to pay a man for each day of the week.
• The hats puzzle
• Game show puzzle: the two donkeys and car.

Describe the method of Loci for remembering

Class 2.
Talk about habits of creativity.
What relationship is there between creativity and morality? Can a crook be creative? Can a religious zealot be creative?
Can an animal be creative? Give examples.
Can a plant be creative? Give examples.

Can rocks and dirt and water be creative? Would you say that the earth, having given forth all sorts of life-forms is creative?
Ask class to do Kirkegaard Puzzle.
Ask class to do A, B, C, D grid puzzle
Democracy is associated with freedom and laissez faire needed for most kinds of creativity. Democracy is characterized by a complicated processes that include electing officials; free, fair and frequent elections; freedom of expression; alternative sources of information; "associational autonomy"; and inclusive citizenship. It is also related to market capitalism, may hinder it by saving it from its own excesses and in undermining its ability to serve the general good. Capitalism itself both favors and hinders democracy. How is freedom related to creativity, and do they always go hand in hand? Can freedom hinder and stultify creativity? Can there be creativity in an oppressive atmosphere? On the whole which is better for creativity, freedom or supervision? A little of each, illustrated with examples.

Write a two-page report on some book on creativity of your own choosing.
Bring an invention of your own making to class. Making it is much preferred to talking about making it. It can be simple but tickles the imagination and has the element of originality and novelty in it.

Class 3.
Problem solving
Identify with the class some shared problem. Ask, "Why is it a problem and from whose standpoint? What are some reasons why it is a problem? What are all possible solutions? Which appears to be the best solution? How is it the best? How best can one implement this solution?"

A) Cube problem
B) Do the wire around the earth problem

250

C) Students do a puzzle together: the 12 coiner problem

D) Give class 20 minutes to construct the 5 regular polyhedra with whatever they can find around them. They can go outside to do it.

E) Assign students to write a poem or draw or paint something.

Ask students to bring a painting, drawing, poem, essay, joke, musical composition, a dance, a riddle of their own to class next time.

Class 4.
- Students show their art works.
- Do common exercise to brainstorm, such as how many uses can one make of a cantaloupe. Write them down on the board as fast as they say them.
- Estimation example
- Estimate how many books are in the Library of Congress. Validate your result by getting the real answer
- Estimate the population of the world
- Estimate the number of students getting MBAs this year in the U. S.
- Estimate the total amount and average height of ice in Antarctica.
- What percentage of the water on Earth is locked up in Antarctic ice?
- Develop an estimation method so that any person could use it to determine how many calories are consumed in different levels of intensity of exercise, including thinking and sitting in front of a computer.

Class 5.
Trees are known to add one additional ring to their bark each year. How is a ring added, from the middle or from the outside. Explain.

Humans do not have a way to sense magnetism. It is the pull of a magnet or its rotation and the attraction or repulsion of magnets that they can feel or see. Mention five other discoveries we have made that have great value and which our bodies are not equipped to detect directly. Now mention five other basically different fantasies of your own which could be a boon to have in our arsenal of increased sensing and expanded understanding. Can the human dimension be extended this way ad infinitum and is it attributable to our ability to synthesize information from our basic senses or to some other latent talent that we have? Can other forms of life extend their sensing and synthesizing in this way and how? Invent a way for a tree to extend its basic biology and enhance its own survival through human technology in a manner that trees cannot do on their own.

Class 6.
Create a hierarchy of your own goals and criteria and use it to establish priorities for deciding on the best place to live or the best job to choose.

Class 7 (Final).
Bring your own project whatever it may be to show to the class and to invited guests. Be your own best advocate.

The Grand Finale

Felix the Flying Frog: A Parable about Schedules, Cycle Times, and Shaping New Behaviors (Anonymous)

Once upon a time, there lived a man named Clarence who had a pet frog named Felix. Clarence lived a modestly comfortable existence on what he earned working at the Wal-Mart, but he always dreamed of being rich.

"Felix!" he exclaimed one day, "We're going to be rich! I'm going to teach you how to fly!"

Felix, of course, was terrified at the prospect: "I can't fly, you idiot. I'm a frog, not a canary!"

Clarence, disappointed at the initial reaction, told Felix: "That negative attitude of yours could be a real problem. I'm sending you to class."

So Felix went to a three-day class and learned about problem solving, time management, and effective communication.... but nothing about flying.

On the first day of "flying lessons", Clarence could barely control his excitement (and Felix could barely control his bladder). Clarence explained that their apartment had 15 floors, and each day Felix would jump out of a window starting with the first floor eventually getting to the top floor.

After each jump, Felix would analyze how well he flew, isolate on the most effective flying techniques, and implement the improved process for the next flight. By the time they reached the top floor, Felix would surely be able to fly.

Felix pleaded for his life, but it fell on deaf ears. "He just doesn't understand how important this is..." thought Clarence, "but I won't let nay-sawyers get in my way."

So, with that, Clarence opened the window and threw Felix out (who landed with a thud).

Next day (poised for his second flying lesson) Felix again begged not to be thrown out of the window. With that, Clarence opened his pocket guide to Managing More Effectively and showed Felix the part about how one must always expect resistance when implementing new programs.
And with that, he threw Felix out the window. (THUD)

On the third day (at the third floor) Felix tried a different ploy: stalling, he asked for a delay in the "project" until better weather would make flying conditions more favorable.

But Clarence was ready for him: he produced a timeline and pointed to the third milestone and asked, "You don't want to slip the schedule do you?"

From his training, Felix knew that not jumping today would mean that he would have to jump TWICE tomorrow.... so he just said: "OK. Let's go." And out the window he went.

Now this is not to say that Felix wasn't trying his best. On the fifth day he flapped his feet madly in a vain attempt to fly. On the sixth day he tied a small red cape around his neck and tried to think "Superman" thoughts. But try as he might, he couldn't fly.

By the seventh day, Felix (accepting his fate) no longer begged for mercy. He simply looked at Clarence and said: "You know you're killing me, don't you?"

Clarence pointed out that Felix's performance so far had been less than exemplary, failing to meet any of the milestone goals he had set for him.

With that, Felix said quietly: "Shut up and open the window," and he leaped out, taking careful aim on the large jagged rock by the corner of the building.

And Felix went to that great lily pad in the sky.

Clarence was extremely upset, as his project had failed to meet a single goal that he set out to accomplish. Felix had not only failed to fly, he didn't even learn how to steer his flight as he fell like a sack of cement.... nor did he improve his productivity when Clarence had told him to "Fall smarter, not harder."

The only thing left for Clarence to do was to analyze the process and try to determine where it had gone wrong. After much thought, Clarence smiled and said: "Next time I'm getting a smarter frog!"

Final Words

Creativity is the actualizing of our potential. It involves: Originality, Novelty, Significance, Elegance, and Grandeur and Magnificence. "Everyone is born a genius but the process of living de-geniuses them" wrote Buckminster Fuller.

Challenge, so essential for creativity, is stimulation in the presence of difficulties and obstacles. If one wants to be creative, one must look for and take up challenge as an opportunity. Surmounting challenges is a great gift for making progress. A chal-

lenge is a motivator of ideas. When a challenge is strong but manageable, the likelihood of successful accomplishment is high. The question is not whether we are smart enough to be creative. Rather, it is whether we can make the time and find the determination to be creative at something no matter how small. For most things I believe that it is perseverance rather than intelligence that contributes the most to creativity. How to persevere needs practice to the far end and even beyond boredom to death. If you can do that, you have great hope to be creative and to create something new.

Scientific research has demonstrated that children become vulnerable to failure and fearful of challenges by repeatedly telling them that they are especially smart or talented. They develop the belief that intelligence is fixed, and working hard to learn is not as important as seeming smart. They are threatened by challenges, mistakes, and effort rather than opportunities to improve. Instead, children need to have a "growth mind-set," which encourages effort and hard work rather than intelligence or talent. It involves descriptions of great scientists and mathematicians with malleable intelligence, who developed amazing skills and achievements over time and were "mastery oriented" not afraid to make mistakes. It is in contrast to developing a "fixed mind set" with stories about math geniuses who were born with great intelligence.

Creativity is an intrinsic attribute of our mind that we need to recognize and cultivate. It is not an alien entity that we have to import into our practices. We are all creative to the extent that we are passionate, persistent and successful until we are identified with our own creativity. We are riddled with myriad suggestions about how to develop our creativity. They are all more or less useful if we learn to prioritize and internalize them. William James wrote that "The greatest discovery of any generation is that a human being can alter his life by altering his attitude". So we need to change our attitude to look at life in a positive way. According to Henri Bergson, "To exist is to change, to change is to mature, to mature is to go on creating oneself endlessly."

The foremost attitude of a human being is to care about everybody and everything. To care is to love and nurture even when it is oneself and even more when it is one's enemies. To care is to stick one's neck out when others are running away. To care is to love to the breaking point. Creativity is a gift to those who care. One cannot create if one does not care, and care with great passion.

George Constable and Bob Somerville include 20 chapters in their book about the creative accomplishments of the 20the century: Electrification, Automobile, Airplane, Water Supply and Distribution, Electronics, Radio and Television, Agricultural Mechanization, Computers, Telephony, Air Conditioning and Refrigeration, Highways, Spacecraft, Internet, Imaging, Household Appliances, Health Technology, Petroleum and Petrochemical Technologies, Lasers and Fiber Optics, Nuclear Technologies, High Performance Materials.

There are many creative solutions to the nine-dot problem of Chapter 1. They depend on the size of the points, the kind of lines allowed to connect them, whether lines can be retraced or not, and on the shape of the paper.

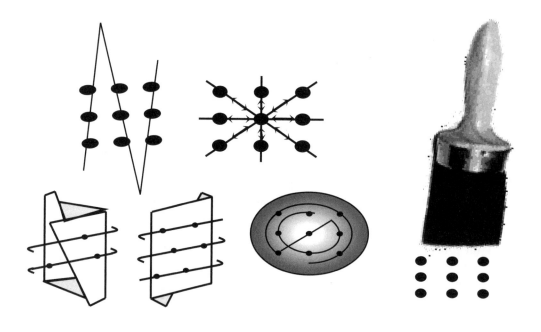

Bibliography

Ackoff, R.L., *Art of Problem Solving*, New York: Wiley, and Sons, 1978.

Adair, J., *Creative Thinking*, Surrey, England: Talbot Adair Press, 1990.

Adair, J., *Effective Innovation*, Surrey, England: Talbot Adair Press, 1996.

Adams, J.L., *Conceptual Blockbusting*, Reading, MA: Addison-Wesley Publishing Co., 1986.

Adams, J.L., *The Care and Feeding of Ideas*, Reading, MA: Addison-Wesley Publishing Co., 1986.

Albrecht, K. & S. Albrecht, *The Creative Corporation*, Homewood, IL: D.Jones-Irwin, 1987.

Amabile, Teresa M., (1988) A Model of Creativity and Innovation in Organizations, Research in Organizational Behavior 10, 123-167.

Amabile, Teresa M., (1982) Children's artistic creativity : Detrimental effects of competition in a field setting, Personality and Social Psychology Bulletin, 8, 573-578.

Amabile, Teresa M., The Social Psychology of Creativity Springer-Verlag, New York, 1983.

Arieti, S. *Creativity: the magic synthesis*, New York: Basic Books, 1976.

Arnold, J.E., "Useful Creativity Techniques," in Parnes (ed.), *Sourcebook for CreativeThinking*, New York: Charles Scribner's Sons, 1962.

Ayan, J., *Aha!* New York: Crown Trade Paperbacks, 1997.

Baker, Samm S., *Your Key to Creative Thinking*, New York: Bantam, 1962.

Barker, J.A., *Future Edge,* New York: William Morrow and Co., 1992.

Barron, F. Creative person and creative process. New York: Holt, Rinehart & Winston, 1969.

Barron, F. Artists in the making. San Francisco: Freeman, 1972.

Barron, F. (1955) The disposition toward originality, Journal o Abnormal and Social Psychology, 51, 478-485.

Barron, F., *Creativity and Personal Freedom*, New York: Van Nostrand, 1968.

Basadur, M., *Creative Problem Solving,* Ancaster, Ontario, Canada: Center for Research in Applied Creativity, 1989

Beardsley, M.C., *Thinking Straight,* Englewood Cliffs, NJ: Prentice- Hall, Inc., 1966.

Berlyne, D., *Conflict, Arousal and Curiosity,* New York: McGraw-Hill, 1960.

Bloom, B.S. and L.J. Broder, *Problem-Solving Processes of College Students: An Exploratory Investigation*, Chicago: University of Chicago Press, 1950.

Boden, M., *The Creative Mind*, New York: Basic books, 1990.

Bowra, J., *Inspiration and Poetry,* Cambridge: Cambridge University Press, 1955.

Bransford, J.D., and B.S. Stein, *The Ideal Problem Solver*, New York: W.H. Freeman and Company, 1984.

255

Brightman, H.J., *Group Problem* Solving: An Business Publishing Division, Georgia State University, 1988.

Brogden, H.E. and T.B. Sprecher, "Criteria of Creativity," in Taylor, E.W. (ed.), *Creativity, Progress and Potential,* New York: McGraw Hill, 1964.

Brown, K.A., *Inventors at Work,* Redmond, WA: Tempus, 1988.

Capacchione, L., *The Creative Journal: The Art of Finding,* North Hollywood: *Yourself* Newcastle Publishing, 1989.

Clark, C.C., *Idea Management: How to Motivate Creativity and Innovation,* New York: Amacom, 1990.

Couger, J. Daniel, *Creative Problem Solving and Opportunity Finding,* New York: boyd & fraser publishing company, 1995.

Crosby, Andrew C., *Creativity and Performance in Industrial Organization,* New York: Tavistock Publications, 1968.

Cummings, L. (1965) Organizational climates for creativity, Journal of the Academy of Management, 8, 220-227.

Dacey, J.S., *Fundamentals of Creative Thinking,* New York: Lexington Books, 1989.

Davis, G.A., *Creativity Is Forever,* Dubuque, IA:Kendall/Hunt Publishing Co., 1986.

de Bono, E., *Lateral Thinking. Creativity Step by Step,* New York: Harper and Row, 1970.

de Bono, E., *Teaching Thinking,* New York: Penguin Books, 1976.

de Bono, E., *Serious Creativity,* New York: Harper Business, 1992.

Improved Managerial Approach, Atlanta:

de Bono, E., *Six Thinking Hats,* Des Moines, IA: Perfection Learning, 1985.

de Bono, E., *de Bono's Thinking Course* Facts on File Publications, Oxford, England, 1982.
Dewey, J., *How We Think,* Lexington, MA: D.C. Heath, 1933.

Drucker, P.F., *Innovation and Entrepreneurship: Practice and Principles*, Heinemann, London, 1985.

Duncker, K., On *Problem-Solving,* Westport, CT: Greenwood, 1945.

Edwards, M.O., *Idea Power*, Buffalo, NY:Bearly Limited, 1986.

Eggers, T., Will you help me create the future today? *Buffalo, NY: D.O.K. Publishers, 1981.*

Evans, J.R., *Creative Thinking.- In the Decision and Management Sciences,* Cincinnati: SouthWestern Publishing Co., 1991.

Fabian, *J., Creative Thinking and Problem Solving,* Chelsea, MI: Lewis Publishers, Inc., 1990.

Fehrman, C., *Poetic Creation: Inspiration or* Craft, Minneapolis: University of Minnesota Press, 1980.

Frauenthal, J.C. and T. Saaty, "Foresight-Insight-Hindsight",*TCMJ Journal.* Vol. 10, No 4, 1979.

Freud, S., Creativity and the unconscious. *New York: Harper, 1925.*

Gallagher, J., *Teaching the gifted child., Boston, MA: Allyn & Bacon, 1975.*

Gardner, H. *Frames of Mind*, New York: Basic Books, Inc., 1983.

Geis, G.T., "Making Companies Creative: An Organizational Psychology of Creativity," *Handbook for Creative and Innovative Managers,* Kuhn, R.L., Ced.), New York, 1988.

Geschka, H., G.R. Schaude, and H. Schlick-supp, "Modern Techniques Solving Problems," *Chemical Engineering,* August 1973.

Getzels, J., K.C.,, Jackson,. *Creativity and intelligence.* New York: John Wiley, 1962.

Ghiselin, B. *The creative process. Berkeley, CA: University of California, 1954.*

Gibb, J., "Managing Creativity in the Organization," in Taylor, C. W., (ed.), *Climate for Creativity,* New York: Pergamon Press, 1972.

Gleick, J., *Genius: The Life and science of Richard Feynman,* New York: Vintage Books, 1992.

Hofstadter, D. R., *Godel, Escher, Bach: An Eternal Golden Braid,* New York:Vintage Books,1979.

Goleman, D., *Emotional Intelligence: Why It Can Matter More Than IQ,* New York:Bantam Books; 1995.

Goodman, N., and C.Z. Elgin, *Reconceptions in Philosophy and Other Arts and Sciences,* London: Routledge, 1988.

Gordon, W.J.J., and T. Poze, *The New Art of the Impossible,* Cambridge, MA: Porpoise Books, 1980.

Gordon, W.J.J., *Synectics: The Development of Creative Capacity,* New York: Harper & Row, 1961.

Gowan, J.C. *The development of the creative individual,* San Diego, CA: Knapp, 1972.

Grant, C.E., *Teaching Critical Thinking,* New York: Praeger, 1988.

Gutman, H. *Biological roots of creativity.* Genetic Psychology Monographs, 1961.

Hadamard, *J., The Psychology of Invention in the Mathematical Field,* New York: Dover, 1954.

Hall, A.R., and H.A.F. Smith, "Invention," *The Encyclopedia Americana,* Danbury, CT: Grolier, Inc., 1987.

Hanks, K. and J. Parry, *Wake Up Your Creative Genius,* Los Altos, CA: William Kaufmann, Inc., 1983.

Harrison, G.R., "How the Brain Works", The Atlantic Monthly, September 1956.

Havelock, R.G., *Planning for Innovation,* Center for Research on Utilization of Scientific Knowledge, University of Michigan, Ann Arbor, 1970.

Hayes, J.R., *The Complete Problem Solver,* Hillsdale, NJ: Lawrence Erlbaum Associates, Publishers, 1989.

Herrmann, *N., The Creative Brain,* Lake Lure, NC: Brain Books, 1990.

Holsinger, R., Jordan, C. & Levenson, *L. The creative encounter,* Glenview, IL: Scott, Foresman, 1971.

Hunt, M.M., "How to Overcome Mental Blocks", Reader's Digest, January 1957.

Huxley, J. *Man in the Modern World,* New York: Mentor Books, 1953.

Isaksen, S.G., and D.J. Treffinger, *Creative Problem Solving,* Buffalo, NY: Bearley, Ltd., 1985.

Jay, D., *Creativity,* New York: CEA, 1991.

John-Steiner, V., *Notebooks of the* Mind: *Explorations of* Thinking, Albuquerque, NM: University of New Mexico Press, 1985.

Jones, E., "Nature of Genius", The Scientific Monthly, February 1957.

Kabie, L.S. *Neurotic distortion of the creative process.* Lawrence, KS: University of Kansas, 1958.

Kao, *J.J., Managing Creativity,* Englewood Cliffs, NJ: Prentice-Hall, 1991.

Kawakami, K., *Unuseless Japanese Inventions,* New York: W.W. Norton & Company, 1995.

Keil, John M., *The Creative Mystique: How to Manage It, Nurture It, and Make It Pay* New York: Wiley, 1985.

Kidder, T., *The Soul of a New Machine,* Boston: Little Brown, 1981.

Kimberley, J.R., Managerial Innovation", Handbook of Organizational Design, Oxford University Press, Oxford, 1981.

Kiplinger, K., "Beyond 1987," Changing Times, 1987.

Klatzky,R.L., and H.Wernory, *Structures* and *Processes,* San Francisco: W.H. Freeman, 1975.

Kneller, G. F., *The Art and Science of Creativity,* New York: Holt, Rinehart and Winston, 1967.

Koestler, *The Act of Creation,* New York: Macmillan, 1964.

Kubie, L.S., *Neurotic Distortion of the Creative Process,* New York: Farrar, Straus and Giroux,1966.

Kuhn, T.A., *The Structure of Scientific Revolutions,* Chicago: University of Chicago Press, 1970.

Kuhn, R. L., editor in chief, Handbook for Creative and Innovative Managers McGraw-Hill, New York, 1988.

Kuratko, D.F., and R.M. Hodgetts, *Entrepreneurship: A Contemporary Approach,* (1965) Chicago:The Dryden Press, 1989.

Lamb, D., *Discovery, Creativity and Problem Solving,* Brookfield, VT: Gower Publishing Co., 1991.

Land, G., *Grow or Die,* New York: Random House, 1973.

Langer, E.J., *Mindfulness,* Reading, MA: Addison-Wesley, 1989.

Lawrence, J. Alpha brainwaves, New York: Avon, 1972.

Leatherdale, W.H., *The Role of Analogy Model and Metaphor in Science,* Amsterdam: North Holland Publishing Co., 1974.

LeBoeuf M., *Imagineering,* New York: Berkeley Books, 1980.

Lehman, H.C., *Age of Achievement,* , Princeton, NJ: Princeton University Press 1953.

MacCormac, E. *A Cognitive Theory of Metaphor.* MIT Press, 1985.

MacKinnon, D.W., In search of human effectiveness. Buffalo, NY: Creative Education Foundation, 1978.

MacKinnon, D.W., "The nature and nurture of creative talent", American Psychologist, 17, 484-495, 1962.

MacKinnon, D.W., "Personality and the re-alization of creative potential", American Psychologist, 20, 273-281, 1965.

Maltzman, I., On the training of originality. Psychological Review, 67,229-242, 1960.

Maslow, A., "A Holistic Approach to Creativity," in Taylor, C.W., (ed.), Climate for Creativity, New York: Pergamon Press, 1972.

Maslow, A.N., Toward a Psychology of Being, Princeton, NJ: Van Nostrand, 1968.

Maslow, A.H. Creativity in self-actualizing people. In Anderson, H.H.. (ed.), Creativity and its cultivation. New York: Harper & Row, 1959.

Mears, H., Creative Power: The Education of Youth in the Creative Arts, New York: Dover Publications, revised 1958, originally published in 1929.

Mayer, R.E., Thinking, Problem Solving, Cognition, New York: W.H. Freeman and Co., 1992.

Medniclc, S.A., "The associative basis of the creative process", Psychological Review, 69, 220-232, 1962.

Michalko, M., Thinkertoys, Berkeley, CA: Ten Speed Press, 1991.

Miller, W.C., The Creative Edge, Reading, MA: Addison-Wesley Publishing Co., 1987.

Miller, W., Creativity: The Eight Master Keys to Discover, Unlock and Fulfill Your Creative Potential, Pleasanton, CA: SyberVision Systems, Inc., 1989.

Miller, William C., The Creative Edge: Fostering Innovation Where You Work, Reading, MASS: Addison-Wesley, 1987.

Moore, L.B., "Creative Action - The Evaluation, Development and Use of Ideas," in Nadel, L., Sixth Sense, New York: Prentice Hall Press, 1990.

Nayak, P.R. and J.M. Ketteringham, Breakthroughs, New York: Rawson Associates, 1986.

Newell, A., J.C. Shaw, and H.A. Simon, "The process of creative thinking," in Gruber, H.E., C. Terrell, and M. Wertheimer, Contemporary Approaches to Creative Thinking, New York: Atherton Press, 1962.

Nicholson, S., "Group Creative Thinking", Management Record, 18, 7, 234-237, July 1956.

Nystrom, H. Creativity and Innovation, Wiley, London, 1979.

Ornstein, R., The Psychology of Consciousness, New York: Harcourt Brace Jovanovich, 1977.

Osborn, A., Applied Imagination, New York: Scribner's, 1957.

Osborn, Alex, Your Creative Power: How to Use Imagination, New York: Charles Scribner's Sons, 1948.

Osborn, Alex, "Brainstorming", Time Magazine, Feb 18, 1957.

Pames, S.J., The Magic of Your Mind, Buffalo, NY: CEA and Bearley Ltd., 1981.

Pames, J. J., Sourcebook for Creative Problem Solving, Buffalo, New York: 1992.

Parnes, S., The Magic of Your Mind, Buffalo, NY: CEA and Bearley Ltd., 1981.

Parnes, S.J., "The Creative Studies Project," in S.G. Isaksen, (ed.), Frontiers of Creative Research, Buffalo, NY: Bearley Ltd., 1987.

Parnes, S.J., *Creative Behavior Guidebook,* New York: Charles Scribner's Sons, 1967.

Parnes, S.J., *Visionizing,* East Aurora, NY: D.O.K. Publishers, 1988.

Parnes, S.J., *Creativity: Unlocking Human Potential*, Buffalo, NY: D.O.K. Publishers, 1972.

Parnes, S.J. (ed), *Source Book for Creative Problem Solving*, Buffalo, New York: Creative Education Foundation Press, 1992.

Parnes, S.J., and H.F. Harding, (eds.), A *Sourcebook for Creative* Thinking, New York: Scribner, 1962.

Parnes, S.J., *The Magic of Your Mind*, Creative Education Foundation, Buffalo, NY, 1981.

Parnes, S.J., R.B. Noller, & A.M. Biondi, *Guide to Creative Action*, Scribner's, New York, 1977.

Peters, L. and B. Dana, *The Laughter Prescription,* New York: Ballantine Books, 1987.

Polya, G., *Mathematics and Plausible Reasoning, Vols. I & II,* Princeton, NJ: Princeton University Press, 1954.

Polya, G., *How to Solve it* New York: Doubleday Anchor Books, 1957

Porterfield, A., *Creative Factors in Scientiic Research*, Durham, NC: Duke University Sociological Series, Duke University Press, 1941.

Prince, G.M., *The Practice of Creativity*, Collier Books, New York, 1970.

Raudseep, E., *How Creative Are You?* New York: Perigee Books, 1987.

Ray, M., and R. Myers, *Creativity in Business,* Garden City, NY: Doubleday & Co., Inc., 1986.

Roberts, R., and A. Weiss, *The Innovation Formula*, Cambridge, MA: Ballinger Publishing Co., 1988.

Rogers, C.R., "Toward a Theory for Creativity," in Parnes, S.J., and H.F. Harding, (eds.),

Rosner, S., and L.E. Abt, *Essays in Creativity,* Croton-On-Hudson, NY: North River Press, 1974.

Rosner, S. & Abi, L. The creative experience. New York: Grossman, 1970.

Rothenberg, A., and C.R. Hausman, The *Creativity Question,* Durham, NC: Duke University Press, 1976.

Rowelon, W., Creativity: a review of theory and research, Buffalo, NY: Creative Education Foundation, 1972.

Ruggiero, V.R., *The Art of Thinking,* New York: Harper Collins Publishers, 1991.

Ruggiero, V.R., *Beyond Feelings,* Mountain View, CA: Mayfield Publishing Co., 1990.

Saaty, T.L., *The Analytic Hierarchy Process.* New York: McGraw-Hill, 1980.

Saaty, T.L., and J. Alexander. *Thinking with Models*. Pergamon Press, 1981.

Saaty, T.L., and J. Alexander. *Thinking with Models*. Pergamon Press, 1981.

Saaty, T.L., "A scaling method for priorities in hierarchical structures," Journal of Mathematical Psychology, Vol. 15, No. 3, pp. 234-281, 1977

Saaty, T.L., *Decision Making for Leaders*, RWS Publications, 4922 Ellsworth Ave., Pittsburgh, Pennsylvania, 2000.

Saaty, T.L., "Axiomatic foundations of the analytic hierarchy process," Management Science, Vol.32, No. 7.,pp. 841-855, 1986.

Saaty, T.L. and L.W. Boone, *Embracing the Future*, Praeger, New York, 1990.

Saaty, T.L., *Fundamentals of the Analytic Hierarchy Process*, RWS Publications, 4922 Ellsworth Ave., Pittsburgh, Pennsylvania, 1994.

Saaty, T.L. and Alexander, J., *Conflict Resolution: The Analytic Hierarchy Process*, Praeger, New York, 1989.

Saaty, T.L. and Vargas, L.G., *Prediction, Projection and Forecasting*, Kluwer Academic Publishers, Boston, Massachusetts, 1991.

Saaty, T.L., *The Analytic Network Process*, Pittsburgh, PA: RWS Publications, 1996.

Saaty, T.L., *The Brain: Unraveling the Mystery of How it Works*, Pittsburgh, PA: RWS Publications, 2000.

Schneider, E., *Coleridge, Opium, and Kubla Khan*, Chicago: University of Chicago Press, 1953.

Shallcross, D.J., *Teaching Creative Behavior*, Buffalo, NY: Bearley, Ltd., 1985.

Shekerjian, D., *Uncommon Genius: How Great Ideas Are Born*, New York: Viking, 1990.

Simon, H.A., "Understanding Creativity and Creative Management," *Handbook for Creative and Innovative Managers*, Kuhn, R.L. (ed.), New York, 1988.

Sinnott, E., *The creativeness of life*, In Anderson, H.H. (ed.), Creativity and its cultivation. New York: Harper & Row, 1959.

Skinner, B.F. *The technology of teaching*, New York: Appleton, 1968.

Stein, M.I., *Stimulating Creativity, Vol. 1*, Academic Press, New York, 1974.

Stein, M.I., *Stimulating Creativity, Vol. 2*, Academic Press, New York, 1975.

Sternberg, R.J., "Intelligence, Wisdom and Creativity: Their Natures and Interrelationships," Chapter 4 in Intelligence: Measurement, Theory, and Public Policy, Edited by R.L.Linn, University of Illinois Press, Urbana and Chicago, 1989.

Sulloway, F.J., *Born to Rebel: Birth Order, Family Dynamics, and Creative Lives*; New York: Pantheon Books; 1996.

Tart, C.T. (ed.), Altered states of consciousness, New York: John Wiley, 1969.

Tatsuno, S.M., *Created in* Japan, New York: Harper Business, 1990.

Thurstone, L.L., *The Nature of Intelligence*, Patterson, NJ: Littlefield, Adams, 1960.

Torrance, E.P., "Teaching for Creativity," in Isaksen, S.C. *(ed.), Frontiers of Creative Research,* Buffalo, NY: Bearley Ltd., 1987.

Torrance, E.P., *Torrance Tests of Creative Thinking,* Chicago: University of Chicago Press, 1984.

Torrance, E.P. Rewarding creative behavior. *Englewood Ckffs, NJ: Prentice-Hal4 1965.*

Treffinger, D., Isaksen, S. & Firestien, R. Handbook of creative learning. *Williamsville, NY: Cenierfor Creative Learning, 1982.*

Van de Ven, A.H., Central problems in the management of innovation, Management Science, 32, 590-607, 1986.

VanGundy, A.B., Jr., *Techniques of Structured Problem Solving,* 2nd ed., New York: Van Nostrand Reinhold Co., 1988.

VanGundy, Arthur B., *Creative Problem Solving: A Guide for Trainers and Management*, New York: Quorum Books, 1987.

von Oech, R., A *Kick in the Seat of the Pants,* New York: Warner Books, 1983.

Von Oech, Roger, Ph. D. *A Whack on the Side of the Head, How to Unlock Your Mind for Innovation,* 1983.

Wallach, M. and N. Kogan, *Modes of Thinking in Young Children.* New York:Holt, Rinehart & Winston, 1965.

Wallas, G., The Art of Thought, New York: Harcourt, Brace, 1926.

Weil, A.,*The Natural Mind,* Boston, MA: Houghton-Miflin, 1972.

Weisberg, R., *Creativity: Genius and Other Myths,* New York: W.H. Freeman and Co., 1986.

Wertheimer, M. Productive thinking, New York: Harper & Row, 1945.

Westwood, A.R.C., and Y. Sekine, "Fostering Creativity and Innovation in an Industrial R&D Laboratory," *Research-Technology Management,* July-August, 1988.

Whiting, C.S., *Creative Thinking,* New York: Van Nostrand Reinhold, 1958.

Wickelgren, W., *How to Solve Problems: Elements of a Theory of Problems and Problem Solving.* San Francisco: W.H. Freeman and Company, 1974.

Yukawa, H., *Creativity and Intuition,* Tokyo: Kodansha International Ltd., 1973.

Zaleznick, A., "Making Managers Creative: The Psychodynamics of Creativity and Innovation," in *Handbook for Creative and Innovative -Managers,* New York: McGraw-Hill, 1988.

Zaltman, G, R. Duncan & J. Holbeck, *Innovations and Organizations*, Wiley, London, 1973.

Index

A

abracadabra, 103
absolute measurement, 223
abstraction, 6
    mathematical, 6
acres cultivable in US, 171
Aczél, 144
addendum, 241
age, productivity, 7
Alexander, 117
amateur, 7
amount of food to feed US, 171
Analytic Network Process (ANP), 154, 227
animals, 3, 146
aquarium, 120
Archimedes, 11
aristocrat, 110
assignments, 245
astronomy, age of productivity, 7
attitude, 103
awareness, 14

B

Bach, 11
Bateson, 142
Beethoven, 9
Bergson, 141
bibliography, 255
big bang, 90
brains, 150
brainstorming, 16
Bransford, 108
budgeting, 105
buses in Pittsburgh, 188
business practice, 8

C

Celestine Prophecy, 145
cherries in a can, 181

child, guidance of, 6
clairvoyant, 153
collective mind, 3
collective unconscious, 101
colored cubes, 117
communication, 9
comparisons, 214
comprehension, 13
computers, 3
conflict resolution, 3, 106
consciousness, 3, 19
    universal, 23
corpsman, 18
costs and benefits, 234
    in hospice problem, 211, 212
creation, 3
creative, 104
    mind, 149
    subconscious, 104
creative ideas, 4
creative thinking, 3
creativity, 3, 8, 141
    and non-linear world, 152
    assignments, 245
    being a collector, 21
    constraints, 18
    evolution, 146
    exercises, 28
    group process, 16
    imagery, 14
    in animals, 146
    individuality, 20
    inspiration, 142, 144
    judgment, 13
    limits to, 5
    measurement of, 8
    memory, 13
    methods, 10
    motivation, 9
    neurosis, 143
    practicing of, 21
    psychosis, 143
    solutions to exercises, 29
    teaching it, 19
culture
    American, 6

The End

Something like the following story was related by the humorist genius, Mark Twain:

He once attended a prayer meeting where a missionary spoke about the misery and suffering of the native people. He spoke so passionately and eloquently and the appeal so stirred him he could hardly wait for the hat or plate to come his way. Twain mentally doubled the fifty cents he had intended to contribute when the collection plate was passed through the congregation. As the preacher continued to vividly describe in detail the plight of his people, Twain gradually raised his intended contribution to five dollars, to ten dollars, and eventually to a huge check.

"Then he went on," recounted Twain, "and on and on and on about the dreadful state of the natives, and I abandoned the idea of the check. And he went on, and the fever-heat of beneficence was going down lower and lower. My impulse then was to give ten dollars; I repented of that and reduced it to five dollars; repented of that and reduced it to one dollar; then reduced it to fifty cents: and still he went on. When the collection plate came around, I took ten cents out of it!"

Creativity Crossword Answers

Down

1. Leonardo da Vinci
2. Persistence
3. Caring
4. Frances
5. Creation
6. Apple
7. Whitney
8. Conviction
9. Heisenberg
10. Perception
11. Anderson
12. Independence
13. Lateral Thinking
14. Gauss
15. Richter
16. Intuition
17. Intelligence
18. Art
19. Risk Taking
20. Ford
21. Different
22. Creativity
23. Improvement
24. Novelty
25. Purpose
26. Playfulness
27. Evolution
28. Sigmund
29. Imperfection
30. Attitude
31. Chaos
32. Satisfaction
33. Lying
34. Flexibility
35. Talent
36. Play
37. Kant

Across

4. Fichte
5. Darwin
6. Impulsive
7. Courage
8. Gabe
9. Persevere
10. Marion Donovan
11. Duke
12. Love
13. Laughter
14. Spontaneity
15. Expression
16. Inspiration
17. Banneker
18. Tie
20. Freedom
21. Passion
22. Challenge
23. Rodeo
24. Paint
25. Plant
26. Pasteur
27. Originality
28. Bach
29. Incentive
30. Openness
32. Theory
33. Necessity
34. Fantasy
38. Potential
39. Observation
40. Values
41. Self Expression
42. Hypotheses
43. Invention
45. Man
46. Excitement
47. Judgment
48. Imagination
49. Rap
51. Mozart
52. Accidental
53. Einstein
54. Edison
55. Share
56. Bi-association
57. Uncertainty
58. Impossible
59. Washington
60. Wilson
61. Pain
62. Idealism
63. Michelangelo
64. Goal

38. Perspiration
39. Benjamin Franklin
40. Alternative
41. Volta
42. Humor
43. Pen
44. Skepticism
45. Re-Creation
46. Curiosity
47. Tile
48. Poetry
49. Failure
50. Problem
51. Mona Lisa
52. Disney
53. Memory
54. Obsess
55. Tattoo

Creativity Crossword Puzzle Answers

Creativity Crossword Clues

Down

1. Renowned primarily as a painter but was also an Italian polymath, scientist, mathematician, engineer, inventor, anatomist, sculptor, architect, botanist, musician and writer. Many of his designs were not feasible to manufacture in his day.
2. One of the two handmaidens of creativity. (Perseverance is the other one.)
3. To be this, one must love and nurture even when it is oneself and even more when it is one's enemies.
4. First name of the woman who invented equipment to make her home self-cleaning. See 8 Across for her last name.
5. This with processing and sharing of information are the major themes of creativity and progress in our time.
6. Object that hit Sir Isaac Newton in the head that led to discovering the Universal Laws of Gravitation.
7. Credited with successfully building and patenting the cotton gin. Also created machines to make standardized musket parts and implementing assembly line-like production techniques in the firearms industry.
8. We must have this to achieve most goals; otherwise we fall to the mercy of chance and circumstance.
9. German physicist. Applied a mathematical system to atomic physics so he could work out problems with experimental data instead of visual models.
10. Our sensory experience of the world around us.
11. Invented the windshield wiper.
12. Having this characteristic means one is not overly influenced by the opinions of others and not afraid to maturely express viewpoints, even if others disagree strongly
13. An attitude and a way for expanding thought and imagination. The attitude is to look at things in different ways.
14. A child prodigy and one of the most influential mathematicians. Arrived at a proof of theorem not through painful effort, but like a sudden streak of lightning.
15. Developed a more accurate scale used to measure California earthquakes.
16. Ability to sense or know immediately without reasoning
17. The mental ability to learn and understand.
18. Example of this are: sketch, sculpture, mosaic or collage of pictures on various subjects, drawings, painting.
19. One will never produce anything creative without this
20. Invented the assembly line for the manufacturing of the automobile. Now the name of one of the 3 big car companies.
21. To do something this way is to disrupt your habitual patterns.
22. The ability to break through constraints imposed by habit and tradition to find "new" solutions to problems.
23. To make something more efficient.
24. Something new, unusual or original
25. An end to be obtained. The reason you do something.
26. Kind of atmosphere that helps people look at problems from every possible perspective
27. Leads to the survival of the fittest. Has been divided by some into three distinct and separate parts: cosmic, biological and human.
28. Freud. Laid the groundwork for what would become known as "psychoanalysis".
29. When something is not perfect it has one of these
30. "The greatest discovery of any generation is that a human being can alter his life by altering his _____." – William James
31. Unpredictability in the behavior of a complex natural system
32. In order to have this an individual must be able to achieve a modicum of success in resolving a problem with a given technical discipline. In the end this is our goal in life.
33. A form of creativity.
34. Ability to adapt to different circumstances.
35. _____ + Training + Persistence + Passion ⇔ Creativity
36. Do this to free your mind and get your creative juices flowing.
37. Developed the philosophy that logic alone cannot reach the ultimate truth.
38. "Genius is 1 percent inspiration and 99 percent _____." – Thomas Edison
39. A prolific inventor. Invented bifocals, which he made for himself at age 83.
40. In decision making and problem solving this can be another way to solve a problem that will provide the solution or it can be another solution to the problem.
41. Credited with inventing the modern electric battery. The force that moves electric current is named for him.
42. The only domain of creative activity where a highly complex stimulus produces a massive and specific physiological reflex - laughter.
43. Writing Instrument
44. An attitude of doubt
45. A way to achieve creative results. Viewing a familiar object, or idea from several points of view at once by cutting the whole into pieces and putting those pieces back together again in an unconventional way.
46. One must exhibit this trait to learn about our environment and learn how to deal with its problems. It killed the cat.
47. Used more imaginatively and consistently as an art form in Portugal than in any other nation.
48. Writing that creates a specific emotional response through meaning, sound and rhythm.
49. One of life's greatest creativity drivers.
50. An unacceptable local condition that can be altered. Use creativity to solve this.
51. Leonardo da Vinci's most famous painting. On display at the Louvre in Paris, France.
52. The creative genius behind Disneyland.
53. Conscious recall of past events and the recognition and retention of knowledge and skill.
54. To excessively preoccupy the mind.
55. Permanent means of self expression on one's skin - spelled wrong...

Across

4. Constructed a philosophy of pure idealism
5. Developed the theories of evolution and natural selection.
6. To be this, a person must not hold back. He must not repress new ideas or thoughts.
7. Success breeds this and in turn this spawns enterprise.
8. Last name of the women who invented equipment to make her home self-cleaning. See 4 Down for her first name.
9. To keep working on an idea
10. Invented disposable diapers.
11. Highest ranking peer of the king; wife is a duchess.
12. "I _____ you.": What Prof. Saaty suggests we say to someone who is not our girlfriend or boyfriend in order to loosen us up.
13. The safety valve for an overflow of emotional energy. A unique possession of humankind. Creativity begins with this and is followed by hard work and perspiration.
14. Doing something just because you feel like it at the moment.
15. The way in which we manifest talent.
16. Opening the conscious mind to intuitions, feelings and ideas that redirect the mind.
17. Known as a mechanical genius.
18. A piece of clothing Prof. Saaty wears with his suit to be creative.
20. The absence of necessity, coercion, or constraint in choice or action.
21. The obsessive striving to attain a higher awareness of the world.
22. Is often the fuel that powers creativity; the motivator of ideas.
23. A public performance featuring bronco riding, calf roping, steer wrestling and bull riding.
24. "If you hear a voice within you saying 'You are not a painter,' then by all means _____ ... and that voice will be silenced" –Vincent Van Gogh
25. Lead man for Led Zeppelin. Said to have improvised most of the lyrics to "Stairway to Heaven".
26. Theorized that microscopic organisms called germs caused fermentation and expanded his theory to include diseases. Applied his theories about preventing spoilage of perishable foods to beverages.
27. One test of creative thinking. Convention is a great discourager of this.
28. Composed more than 200 church cantatas, oratorios, masses, preludes and hymns. Often reprimanded by church authorities for the daring improvisations he created.
29. A factor that motivates a particular course of action.
30. Accepting of different points of views and/or ideas.
32. A brief, policy, or procedure proposed or followed as the basis of action.
33. _____ is the mother of invention"
34. An essential element in education. (Other essential elements are stimulation of creativity and imagination.)
38. Capable of developing into actuality.
39. Creative people have a keen power of this.
40. Beliefs and attitudes about the way things should be. They involve what is important to us.
41. The expression of one's own personality.
42. Usually based on previous observations; these are tentative assumptions that state what the experimenter thinks will occur.
43. A purposeful, new, largely original or novel way of making or doing something trivial or serious. Usually done to solve a problem.
45. The measure of all things according to Protagoras
46. An emotion of arousal.
47. Interpretation aided by previously acquired ideas or concepts, can help guide us in our creative process.
48. _____ is more important than knowledge" – Einstein
49. Some can argue this is a musical form of creativity.
51. Is known for receiving inspiration in dreams and during his waking state, and for his ability to conceive of an entire concerto at one time and hurry to write it down before it disappeared from his mind. Composed more than 600 pieces of music.
52. Occurring unexpectedly or by chance. Happening without intent.
53. Discovered the theory of relativity.
54. Has the record for the most patents: 1,000. Invented the light bulb.
55. To talk about one's thoughts, feelings or experiences with others.
56. Finding connections or analogies between two or more objects or ideas not previously known to have any bearing on each other.
57. In a competition, the person who deals with this the best will be the winner.
58. "The difficult we do immediately, the _____ takes a little longer."
59. George _____ Carver. Born a slave but went on to earn a Master's degree in agriculture and developed more than 300 uses for the peanut and 100 uses for the sweet potato.
60. 28th President of the United States. Pushed his progressive views after the U.S. entered World War I.
61. Increased consciousness go hand in hand with the progress we make to control our destiny.
62. Across constructed a philosophy of this.
63. Renaissance painter. Painted the ceiling of the Sistine Chapel.
64. Necessary for creativity even when not immediately apparent.